7

A Passion for Wings

The natural function of the wing is
to soar upwards and carry that which
is heavy up to the place where
dwells the race of gods. More than
any other thing that pertains to the
body it partakes of the nature of the
divine.

Plato, *Phaedrus*

A PASSION FOR WINGS

Aviation and the Western Imagination

1908–1918

ROBERT WOHL

YALE UNIVERSITY PRESS
NEW HAVEN AND LONDON
1994

FOR MARISOL

Who taught me how to soar

Designed by John Nicoll

Set in Bembo by Best-set Typesetter Ltd, Hong Kong
Printed in Singapore by C. S. Graphics Ltd

Library of Congress Cataloging-in-Publication Data
Wohl, Robert.
A passion for wings: aviation and the western imagination,
1908–1918/Robert Wohl.
p. cm.
Includes bibliographical references and index.
ISBN 0–300–05778–4
1. Aeronautics—Europe—History. 2. Aeronautics—United States—
History. 3. Aeronautics—Social aspects—Europe. 4. Aeronautics—
Social aspects—United States. 5. Civilization, Western.
I. Title. TL526.E85W65 1994 94–17559 CIP

A catalogue record for this book is available from the British Library.

Contents

Acknowledgements

THE DEBTS that I incurred while writing this book are so many and varied that I cannot hope to acknowledge all of them; the list would be too long and would try the patience of the most indulgent reader. Yet there are people who made contributions so vital to the present shape and argument – indeed, to the very existence – of the book that they cannot go unmentioned. I had the leisure to begin thinking and reading about aviation during my tenure as a Guggenheim Fellow in 1981–2. The idea of this book was born during that year. I drafted the first chapters of the present volume at the Woodrow Wilson Center in Washington, D.C., a paradise for scholars in need of time and congenial circumstances in which to write. The Center's staff did everything in their power to facilitate my work and make my stay a memorable one. It was in the beautiful, relaxed, and intellectually stimulating setting of the Rockefeller Foundation's Villa Serbelloni at Bellagio that I realized that I wanted to write a book quite different than the one I had originally envisaged. I was fortunate to have an editor, John Nicoll, whose interest in the pages I was shipping to London *par la voie des airs* overcame the trauma of discovering that he was being asked to publish three volumes rather than the one he had contracted. He has since responded to my queries and swings of mood with alacrity and unfailing good humor. His contributions to the present work defy summary.

My university, the University of California at Los Angeles, provided me with the on-going assistance necessary to complete this project once I had begun it. I am especially grateful to the former Provost of the UCLA College of Letters and Science, Raymond Orbach, whose support for my work went far beyond what anyone has a right to expect of a university administrator. And let me also thank the reference librarians and staff of UCLA's interlibrary loan service who located and obtained for me a steady stream of rare books and periodicals. Without their support, this book would have looked very different than it does.

"Why do you write?" a famous French writer was once asked. *Pour chercher des amis*, he replied. Though not its original motivation, the cultivation of friendships – both new and old – was one of this book's most deeply satisfying results. In France, Patrick Fridenson was an unending source of helpful suggestions and research materials. The series of seminars that he arranged for me to give at the Ecole des Hautes Etudes in Paris (and that Christophe Prochasson and Marc Ferro so amicably facilitated) was an inspiring example of what that often abused term "the community of scholars" can actually mean under the most ideal of circumstances. Emmanuel Chadeau generously shared with me his remarkable knowledge of French aviation history, spicing doses of hard fact with characteristic verve and wit. Henri de Montmarin opened to me the collections of the Aéro-Club de France and sponsored my membership in that historic organization. Maria Fede Caproni mobilized her impressive network of contacts to smooth my path in Italy. Lucia Re led me through the labyrinth of Gabriele D'Annunzio studies. Claudio Segre was prompt to answer my questions and put me on the track of Italian aviation writings that might otherwise have evaded me. Samuel Hynes and James Joll responded on the shortest of notice to my plea for a reading of an earlier version of the book and reminded me of the high standards to which they have always held themselves – and others. T. J. Clark and Robert Lubar made penetrating critiques of Chapter 6. Joanne Gernstein, Louise McReynolds, and Christine White provided me with photographs that I had despaired of finding through other means. Jan Castro saved me precious time by supplying information about the Delaunay papers and the present location of Robert Delaunay's paintings. Von Hardesty of the National Air and Space Museum was a sure guide in Russian matters and representative of the Aeronautical Department's readiness to help outside researchers. Jean-Jacques Fouché kindly oriented me in the photographic archive of the Musée de l'Air et de l'Espace at Le Bourget. General Charles Christienne was a gracious host at the Service Historique de l'Armée de l'Air at the Chateau de Vincennes. Claude Carlier arranged for me to attend the conference he organized on military aviation in Paris in September 1984 and thus introduced to me a topic that would take on greater importance for me than I had originally thought. My fellow Serbellonian Halina Parafionowicz helped me to trace the Polish itinerary of Vasily Kamensky. Robert Rosenstone and Eugen Weber were always there to help when help was needed; both shaped this work in ways they might not suspect through the example of their own distinctive ways of writing history.

I have also benefited greatly from the assistance of my students. At an early point in my research, Robert Sumser put into my hands what would turn out to be the most precious resource for getting an overview of my theme. Hermann Beck, Giuseppe Casale, David Dennis, Michele Fine, Claudio Fogu, Peter Pozefsky, and Kevin Thomas took time out from their own work in order to pursue some of my more quixotic leads. Chris Gatner performed miracles of photographic wizadry with hundreds of old pictures under stringent deadlines. Emine and Levant Turan taught me what Turkish hospitality means and intervened at critical moments to provide me with the most precious of commodities – time. Nor will I forget the patience of Isidre Jacas and Leonor Santoll who let themselves be enlisted in the assembling of the typescript and made available to me a charming Catalan setting in which I could work undisturbed. To all these people – and the many others I have not mentioned by name – I express my thanks.

But my main debt is to my wife, Marisol Jacas-Santoll, who shared and participated in every twist and turn of the book's development, who gathered its illustrations and helped to design it, and who became its most demanding critic. Neither Washington insects and snow storms nor Los Angeles fires and earthquakes could dampen her spirits. What follows is hers as much as it is mine.

Introduction

For I dipt into the future,
    far as human eye could see,
Saw the Vision of the world,
    and all the wonder that would be;
Saw the heavens filled with commerce,
    argosies of magic sails,
Pilots of the purple twilight,
    dropping down with costly bales,
Heard the heavens filled with shouting,
    and there rain'd a ghastly dew
From the nation's airy navies grappling
    in the central blue.

Alfred Tennyson, *Locksley Hall*, 1842

THIS is the history of a complex of emotions – the passion for wings – and the impact that it had on Western culture during the decade between 1908 and 1918. Strange as it may seem to us today, weary veterans of crowded commercial airliners and depressing airports, the invention of the airplane was at first perceived by many as an *aesthetic* event with far-reaching implications for the new century's artistic and moral sensibility. Long dreamt about, enshrined in fable and myth, the miracle of flight, once achieved, opened vistas of further conquests over Nature that excited people's imagination and appeared to guarantee the coming of a New Age. The irony is that in comparison with other technologies, such as electricity, the telephone, the automobile, the cinema, or radio, the airplane had little or no immediate or direct impact on the way that most people lived their lives; yet its invention nonetheless inspired an extraordinary outpouring of feeling and gave rise to utopian hopes and gnawing fears. An aviator in the sky – what did it mean during the early years of flight? To seek to answer this question, to relive in *our* imagination some of these emotions, is to be reminded that the twentieth century has been a voracious consumer of ideals and a relentless shatterer of dreams.[1]

The circuitous path that led toward the composition of this book began over a decade ago. While writing the history of the generation of 1914, I was puzzled by T. E. Lawrence's decision to abandon the life of intellectual and political celebrity he had won in the Arabian Desert in order to enlist as a humble private in the Royal Air Force. The air, he told a friend, was "the only first-class thing that our generation has to do. So everyone should either take to the air themselves or help it forward." I dutifully recorded the comment in my book, but I had no idea what Lawrence meant by it.[2]

Later, in response to a criticism of *The Generation of 1914*,[3] I began to examine the role that Lawrence's coevals had played in the development of commercial aviation. What I discovered both fascinated and dismayed me. Fascinated me because the stories I read equalled or surpassed in high drama anything I had encountered in adventure fiction or mythology. Dismayed me because, though I had been practicing the historian's craft for more than two decades, I now had to acknowledge a major territory of ignorance in my understanding of the recent past. Aviation history, I came to realize, lived in a well-

1. Awed spectators observing French aviators during the army maneuvers of 1910. By Louis Sabattier. That same year, describing the emotions experienced by the people who saw the first plane fly above the city of Chicago, Mary M. Parker wrote: "We bowed our heads before the mystery of it and then lifted our eyes with a new feeling in our souls that seemed to link us all, and hope sprang eternal for the great new future of the world." (Quoted by Joseph Corn in *The Winged Gospel* (New York: Oxford University Press, 1983), p. 30).

furnished but essentially walled-off compartment that most historians (like myself) had felt no need to visit. To integrate that history into the main narrative of the twentieth-century West was the ambition that led to the writing of this book.[4]

As a cultural historian, what intrigued me above all in this story was the compulsion that people felt to transform, through the play of their imagination, the most mechanical of events – the invention and development of the flying machine – into a form of spiritual creation. It is this process of spiritualization – the encounter between the Western imagination and the airplane – that I reconstruct and analyze in the pages that follow. An encounter that gave rise to a culture that did not exist in the West before 1908 and whose horizons extend to the present day. What needs to be emphasized, however, is that the achievements of aeronautical technology, as dramatic as they were, acted as mere catalysts for an explosion of cultural creativity whose essential elements were already in place. Indeed, impatient for the arrival of aerial navigation, the Western imagination had already invented the airplane and the aviator long before the Wrights succeeded in making their first machines leave the ground.[5]

The results of this flight of the imagination could take many forms, ranging from newspaper articles, illustrated magazines, books, photographs, postcards, and newsreels that reached a mass public to poems, novels, short stories, drawings, and paintings that were directed towards small coteries who identified themselves with the modernist avant-garde. From my perspective, all these cultural artifacts are potentially precious records of experience, and I have refused to assign priority to one over the other, though I emphasize the different publics toward which they were aimed.

Indeed, the close relationship between aviation and the modernist avant-garde constitutes one of the leit-motifs of this book. F. T. Marinetti's first Futurist manifesto was published in the direct aftermath of Wilbur Wright's triumphant flights in France. His 1909 play, *Poupées électriques* (Electric Puppets), was dedicated to Wright "who knew how to raise our migrating hearts higher than the captivating mouths of women."[6] Pablo Picasso, Georges Braque, and Robert and Sonia Delaunay were among the many artists, poets, and intellectuals who made their way to Issy-les-Moulineaux, a field on the outskirts of Paris, to watch with astonished and admiring eyes the early airplanes fly. As Le Corbusier, a student in Paris at this time, was later to put it, modernists believed that the airplane was "the vanguard of the conquering armies of the New Age."[7] Though one may argue over what was cause, what was effect, and what was pure coincidence in the relationship between the two, it is indisputable that aviation culture coexisted with and was nourished in a myriad of ways by the culture of modernism; whereas aeronautical achievements (in Le Corbusier's phrase) aroused the "energies" and "faith" of modernists.[8] To explain why this was so is one of the objectives of this book.

Some American and British readers may be surprised that Paris and the French play such an important role in my story. After all, it was two Americans from Dayton, Ohio, who first achieved controlled powered flight. Do not the Americans still dominate aviation today? True, but during the years before 1914 the French identified themselves and were identified by others as the "winged nation" par excellence. It was a French-man, Louis Blériot, who was the first to fly the English Channel; and it was the French who organized the first successful aviation competition, staged the first exhibition of aircraft, opened the first flight training schools, and led the world before 1914 in the manufacture of airplanes. Much of this activity was concentrated in or around Paris. Paris, as one Russian poet-aviator remembered it, "the capital of Europe, the capital of art, the capital of aviation."[9] In emphasizing the centrality of France in pre-1918 aviation culture, then, my book reflects widespread perceptions and realities of the period.

The cultural history of aviation takes us deeply into the human psyche and the sensibility of the twentieth-century West. It provides an exemplary illustration of the West's dynamism and idealism – but also, alas, of its alarming tendencies toward conquest, violence, and self-destruction. One of my more disturbing realizations was the extent to which flight was identified with an attraction toward death – the death of aviators themselves, to be sure, but also increasingly after 1911 the death of people on the ground, an outcome that Friederich Nietzsche had already anticipated in *Also sprach Zarathustra* when he asked: "And if man were to learn to fly – woe, to *what heights* would his rapaciousness fly?"[10] The ace and bombardier of the First World War would not have caught him by surprise.

From an early point, I realized that the visual imagery of aviation would have to occupy a central place in this history. Flight lent itself to visual representation. The airplanes of the early period were perceived as aesthetic objects and displayed as such in heavily attended exhibitions. As the illustrations in this book will show, photographers were present in force at aviation's most important moments. Even the Wright brothers, who went to extremes to shun publicity, left behind a precious photographic record of their most important flights. When one thinks about it, what is more beautiful than an airplane silhouetted against blue sky and pink cloud? The images I have chosen to illustrate this book tell us much about the emotions with which the peoples of the West greeted the advent of the flying machine; I consider them an intregal part of this history, to be read as carefully as the text.

I did not set out to write a book for aviators and there is little in these pages about the technical details of flight, but I will be pleased if some pilots are tempted to accompany me on this archaeological dig into the ruins of aviation's past. Learning how to fly was an unexpected bonus that came with the undertaking of this project. Had I not become a pilot, I would have written a very different book. I think I now understand, even if dimly, what early aviators used to call the "intoxication of flight." It cannot be learned in books.

I had originally intended to cover the entire century in a single volume; what I discovered was that many, if not most, of aviation culture's most enduring themes had appeared during the airplane's first decade. The French identification of the aviator as a poet and an artist, a theme that would run throughout French literature in the interwar period, was foreshadowed in their reaction to the taciturn American Wilbur Wright in 1908. The emotion unleashed by Lindbergh's transatlantic flight of 1927 had been prefigured in the delirious reception given to Blériot in London and Paris after he succeeded in crossing the Channel in 1909. The bombing of Europe's cities that took place during the Second World War had been anticipated in graphic detail by H. G. Wells and Rudolf Martin as early as 1907. The misogynism of Hollywood's aviation films of the 1930s was fully present in Gabriele D'Annunzio's 1910 novel, *Forse che sì forse che no*, as was Antoine de Saint-Exupéry's later vision of aviators as a heroic brotherhood. The transformation of the airman into an avenging angel strafing defenseless civilians on the ground, a stock image of Western newsreels and films between 1937 and 1945, had been imagined by Marinetti in a poem of 1912. The idea of the airplane as a metaphor for modernity and an inspiration for modern design that Le Corbusier and others would later champion during the interwar years was already a favored theme of the Russian painter Kazimir Malevich before 1918. The figure of the chivalrous and happy-go-lucky ace, omnipresent in the films and pulp fiction of the 1930s, was the creation of a brief period of aerial warfare between 1915 and 1917.

All reasons why I decided to limit this volume to the decade between 1908 and 1918. It will be followed by two more that will carry the story up to the present day.

I

The Fanatic of Flight

There was something strange about the tall, gaunt figure. The face was remarkable, the head suggested that of a bird, and the features, dominated by a long, prominent nose that heightened the birdlike effect were long and bony . . . From behind the greyish blue depths of his eyes there seemed to shine something of the light of the sun. From the first moments of my conversation with him I judged Wilbur Wright to be a fanatic of flight, and I had no longer any doubt that he had accomplished all he claimed to have done. He seemed born to fly.

Daily Mail, 17 August 1908

LATE on a Saturday afternoon, on 8 August 1908, in the melancholy twilight of western France, a gaunt and deeply tanned American, with piercing blue-grey eyes, a beak-like nose, and a forward-jutting jaw, insinuated himself into the narrow seat of his flying machine. Through his tightly clenched teeth he whistled an unrecognizable tune. In sharp contrast to the stark white wings of his biplane, he wore the somber urban uniform of his class and time: a dark grey suit, a starched white wing collar, and a nondescript tie designed to help him melt, unnoticed, into the middle-class mass. His one sartorial concession to the novelty of what he was about to accomplish was to reverse the bill of his green cap to prevent it from being blown away by the wind.

Unperturbed by the evident impatience of the handful of onlookers, who had made their way to the race track at Hanaudières, eight kilometers from Le Mans, he set about his final preparations. After what seemed like an interminable delay, he at last announced tersely: "Gentlemen, I'm going to fly." On a signal from him, the twin propellers to the rear of his right and left shoulders were simultaneously put into motion by two of his assistants, creating a whistling sound accompanied by the muted clattering of bicycle chains revolving around enclosed pulleys.[1] Having methodically checked his controls and listening intently to the turning over of his engine, the American fixed his gnarled hands around the two wooden levers to his right and left, rested his carefully shined shoes on the transverse bar in front and slightly beneath the level of the lower wing on which he was seated, measured with his glance the half-mile that separated him from the clump of pine trees at the end of the field, then released a small lever. Behind him six large discs of iron dropped from a derrick twenty-five feet high and catapulted his machine along a metal rail. In less than four seconds he was airborne, heading toward the end of the field at a height of thirty feet and already beginning a graceful banking turn toward the left that would bring him back along the side of the track toward the spectators who were watching from the stands. One more turn around the track, then

2. Wilbur Wright flying at Auvours in the twilight on 21 September 1908.

3. Wilbur Wright at the controls of the Flyer.

4. The Wright Flyer poised on its track with the pylon to the left.

5. A group of spectators from different social classes hoist the weight that will catapult the Flyer into the air.

6. The Flyer leaving the rail and beginning its ascent.

7. Wilbur Wright flies past the grandstand at the Hanaudières race track in August 1908.

the pilot brought his machine back to earth, "like a partridge returning to its nest," gently sliding to a stop on its two skids before the sixty-odd stunned and cheering persons who had leapt spontaneously to their feet and, extending their arms toward him, burst forth into an "immense acclamation."[2]

The flight had lasted only one minute and forty-five seconds; but this was more than sufficient to persuade those who had watched it that the man at the controls, the American Wilbur Wright, had solved the problem that had eluded humanity throughout its history and stymied the most brilliant inventors and scientists in late nineteenth-century Europe and America. Wright was capable of sustained and controlled flight in a machine moved through the air by means of its own power; and those members of the Aéro-Club de France present that day at Hanaudières, who had themselves attempted to fly or studied the problem of flight, had no doubts about the importance and the implications of what they had just witnessed. As one of them exclaimed in admiration, "We are as children compared to the Wrights."[3]

Two days later, before a crowd of two thousand people, Wright flew again, making a figure eight and landing "with unbelievable precision" between the derrick and the grandstand, as the spectators looked on with horror and then amazement. The correspondent of the Parisian daily *Le Figaro*, Frantz Reichel, described these feats with awe, concluding that "Nothing can give an idea of the emotion experienced and the impression felt, at this last flight, a flight of masterly assurance and incomparable elegance." To Reichel, even the Wrights' flying machine was a triumph of art. Looking at its graceful and harmonious lines, people exclaimed: "How simple it is!" And to this, the correspondent of *Le Figaro* added: "How beautiful it is!" For like the real artists they

7

were, Reichel continued, the Wright brothers had insisted on giving their machine a harmonious shape, and they had obtained it in the graceful curve of the skids, "on which the bird is received when it returns to earth."[4] Wilbur Wright, the impassive American from Dayton, Ohio, had revealed to his French audience, as no other aviator had before, the aesthetics of flight.

A French journalist who witnessed Wilbur Wright's flight on 8 August later claimed that, on landing, Wright's usually phlegmatic face "paled with emotion."[5] If so, it was understandable; for the road that led from Dayton to Le Mans, where Wilbur achieved fame and cleared the way to fortune, had been long and dotted with setbacks and frustration.[6] The son of a bishop of the United Brethren Church, a relatively small Protestant sect founded by evangelical preachers in 1800, Wilbur was an excellent high-school student and thought he might be suited for a career in teaching. His father had other plans: convinced that of his three sons, Wilbur was the most likely to carry on his work in the Church, Bishop Wright hoped to send him to divinity school at Yale. In 1885, however, at the age of eighteen, Wilbur suffered an injury while skating on an artificial lake and soon afterwards displayed symptoms that were interpreted as signs of a weak and irregular heart. The period that follows this obscure incident is like a black hole in Wilbur's biography. All we know for certain is that instead of attending university, as he had hoped to do, he spent the next three years cloistered at home with his fatally ill mother, caring for her and administering to her needs, reading his way through his often-absent father's well-stocked library, and undergoing a long and apparently deep depression from which he did not emerge until 1889.

During the next ten years Wilbur Wright searched for an outlet for his talents that would enable him to earn a living. In this, he was not different from many young Americans who were faced by a dislocated economy created by the depression of 1893. The characteristics which single Wright out, in a period when Americans were restlessly on the move and rugged individualism was so much admired, were first, his decision to settle permanently in his father's household; and second, the close working relationship he developed with his brother Orville, four years younger than himself, but, though distinctly different in temperament and appearance, remarkably attuned to Wilbur's patterns of thought and similar to him in his unusual combination of imagination and mechanical skills.

The Wright brothers' activities during the 1890s reflect the technologies and enthusiasms that were sweeping through and transforming the fin-de-siècle West. After launching a small printing press with modest success, they briefly published a local newspaper, the *West Side News*, which they then transformed into the *Evening Item*, promising their readers grandiosely "all the news of the world that most people care to read, and in such shape that people will have time to read it."[7] Their lurid headlines and the racy style of their stories echoed, in a minor key, the sensationalistic journalism of the Pulitzers and the Hearsts who were building newsprint empires and entertaining mass audiences with a mixture of fantasy and fact. The trend in journalism, however, as in many other industries, was towards combination and concentration. Unable to compete with newspapers able to afford the new high-speed presses, thick editions, and dramatic illustrations that readers were coming to expect, the Wrights saw a business opportunity in their favorite sport and opened a shop in which they repaired, rented, and sold bicycles.

Their timing could not have been better. The craze for cycling reached its peak in the mid-1890s. Moreover, unlike newspapers, bicycles were a business in which the small

8. Orville Wright (in shirt
sleeves) and assistant working
in the Wright Brothers bicycle
shop in 1897.

entrepreneur could flourish. The capital required to launch a successful enterprise was
minimal. Taking advantage of the ready availability of parts, the Wrights decided to
construct their own bicycles. Their efforts were crowned with success. By 1896 their
bicycle business was earning them between $2,000 and $3,000 a year, a respectable if by
no means large income that, together with the revenues from their printing press,
permitted them to envisage other, more stimulating and ambitious projects.

The last decades of the nineteenth century in the United States and elsewhere in
the West had been a period of extraordinary invention. The railway, the telegraph, the
electric light, the telephone, the bicycle, the electrified trolley, the automobile, the
wireless, photography, and the cinema were transforming the way people lived and
the way they perceived the world. It was not only the steady succession of these
inventions, but their rapid clustering at the end of the century, that captured the
imagination of Americans born, like the Wrights, around 1870.[8] Yet the most extraordinary invention of all, a vehicle that would allow people to fly, to move at will through
the air like birds, remained to be designed. It was this project that engaged Wilbur
Wright's attention in 1899, in the aftermath of a series of aeronautical experiments and
accidents that had been reported prominently in the American press. Believing that
human flight was possible and that the moment was close when someone would achieve
it, Wilbur Wright set out to survey what had been done and written on the subject and
to dedicate his energies and talents to the resolution of the problem of flight. His
younger brother soon joined him in this quest and the closeness of their collaboration
was such that after 1900 it is difficult, perhaps impossible, to distinguish which technical
breakthroughs or innovations should be ascribed to Wilbur or to Orville. The two had
become an indissoluble partnership. And both seemed to have understood, implicitly,
that the only marriage they would have would be with one another.

Reading the story of the Wright brothers between the moment in 1899 when Wilbur
took up aeronautics and the triumph at Le Mans in 1908, what impresses is the
unswerving confidence the Wrights brought to their aeronautical experiments, the
rapidity with which they solved the technical problems that had defied earlier inventors

9, 10. Otto Lilienthal gliding in 1895.

and theoreticians, and the demoralizing difficulties they subsequently encountered in selling their discovery to a doubting world. Why, one wonders, did two bicycle manufacturers, with no higher education in science or technology and nothing but a smattering of mathematics, think that they could solve the riddle of flight?

One answer to this question is that Wilbur Wright had grasped intuitively that the bicycle and automobile technology developed during the 1890s, along with the well publicized aeronautical experiments of Otto Lilienthal, Samuel Langley, and Octave Chanute, had brought the solution within reach. Indeed, although it might seem paradoxical to us today, it was precisely as designers and riders of bicycles that the Wrights were well equipped technically to understand and solve certain of the problems posed by flight. What, after all, was a flying machine except a powered bicycle that moved through the air by means of wings?[9]

In any case, it never seems to have occurred to Wilbur that he lacked the technical education necessary to make a contribution to the science of aeronautics. Take, for example, the letter he wrote to his father in September 1900. It must not have been easy to explain to a man as austere and inflexible as Bishop Wright why his favorite son intended to dedicate his time, talents, and income to an enterprise that was commonly associated in the public mind with cranks and madmen. Describing his intentions, Wilbur manages to be both sober and supremely self-confident:

> I am intending to start in a few days for a trip to the coast of North Carolina in the vicinity of Roanoke Island, for the purpose of making some experiments with a flying machine. It is my belief that flight is possible and while I am taking up the investigation for pleasure rather than profit, I think there is a slight possibility of achieving fame and fortune from it. It is almost the only great problem which has not been pursued by a multitude of investigators, and therefore carried to a point where further progress is very difficult. I am certain I can reach a point much in advance of any previous workers in this field even if complete success is not attained at present.[10]

Wilbur Wright, of course, was not alone in thinking that men would soon fly. But no one approached the problem so methodically or pursued it with such patience and dogged determination as he and his brother. Indeed, even granting the Wrights' undisputed "genius," it seems impossible to understand their success without having recourse to the old-fashioned concept of character – and beyond character, nationality. Everyone who met Wilbur Wright was struck by his forthright bearing, his determined

11. "The ideal airplane: a bicycle with wings that would cost 1.75 francs and would permit its rider to fly one hundred centimeters above the ground."

L'AÉROPLANE IDÉAL

glance, his absolute self-reliance, and his insistence on doing things his way regardless of what those around him thought. The French aviator Léon Delagrange, who went to Hanaudières in August 1908 to see Wright fly and waited impatiently with the others there until the American was satisfied that the conditions were right, believed that he was "the most beautiful example of strong character that I have ever seen. In spite of the sarcastic remarks and the jokes, in spite of the traps laid for him from every side, in spite of the offers and the challenges people made to him, over a period of years this man never faltered; sure of himself and his genius, he kept his secret."[11]

Wilbur Wright's personality combined confidence in self with suspicion of others, imagination in conception with stubbornness in execution. He depended upon and heeded the commands of no organization, whether governmental or private. The only authority he respected emanated from his father. The only persons in whom he put his total trust were his brother and his sister. He acknowledged no God, no master, and no mentors. He believed in his rights and was determined to assert them. He thought that nature could be tamed by men willing to invest their time, money, and labor and that wealth was the just reward for persistence and success. He knew that the experiments he planned to make were hazardous – the German Lilienthal had recently died in a gliding accident – but he was equally convinced that "carelessness and overconfidence are usually more dangerous than deliberately accepted risks."[12]

In no Western country in 1900 were these characteristics so likely to be found as in the United States. And nowhere else would they have been given such free rein to develop themselves. There was something of the solitary frontiersman in Wilbur Wright, a streak of taciturn individualism so deep that it defied the comprehension of his European contemporaries. Even today, retracing Wilbur's path to Kitty Hawk, gazing back toward the mainland across the Albemarle Sound that no bridge then spanned, one is amazed by the tenacity of spirit that led this son of Ohio to make his way to a lonely beach on a remote island off the North Carolina coast and to live there with his brother for months at a stretch over a period of years. Standing on Kill Devil Hill, feeling the December winds sweep in from the North Atlantic, one cannot help but feel that the Wrights' success was somehow born out of this spartan and self-imposed exile.

Wilbur Wright himself did not see things this way. When explaining the success of his brother and himself, he was inclined to emphasize the role of chance. "If the wheels of time could be turned back," he wrote a friend in 1906, "it is not at all probable that we would do again what we have done . . . It was due to a peculiar combination of circumstances which might never occur again."[13] In retrospect, however, the technical breakthroughs the Wrights achieved between 1899 and 1903 appear anything but fortuitous.[14] After carefully surveying the existing literature on flight, Wilbur became convinced that the critical problem to be solved was not how to lift a flying machine into the air, or how to propel it once it had left the ground, but how to control its movements and maintain its balance in the midst of unpredictable currents of air. Where other well-known inventors, like Hiram Maxim and Samuel Langley, applied themselves to the development of an aeronautical engine, the Wrights built gliders and experimented with airfoils and control surfaces. Their objective was not to formulate a theory of flight but to learn how to fly. To do this, Wilbur reasoned, it would be necessary to accumulate more hours in the air than anyone else had ever done. It was to gain this vital experience that Wilbur chose to go to Kitty Hawk, where winds could be counted upon to be consistent and strong enough to lift their gliders.

Wilbur and Orville spent the late summer and fall of the next four years in the vicinity

12–14. "This man's face is already well known; but what neither the caricatures nor the portraits of him convey are his eyes and a look that at the same time has something indomitable and candid about it." (Paul Painlevé, *Le Matin*, 11 October 1908).

15. The Wrights' camp seen from Kill Devil Hill.

16. Albemarle Sound viewed across the bridge from the Outer Banks where the Wright's camp was located; this bridge did not exist when the Wrights came to Kitty Hawk, and communication with the mainland was by boat only.

of Kitty Hawk, eventually setting up their camp at the foot of a barren sandhill a little over a hundred feet high called (somewhat ominously) Big Kill Devil Hill. Though the brothers referred to their stays there as "vacations" and insisted that it was good for their health, getting across the Sound from Elizabeth City in the local sailboats was an unpredictable and sometimes perilous adventure, and life in the camp was a constant battle with voracious mosquitoes, gusty northeast winds, heavy rain, bone-chilling cold, and the omnipresent sand that blinded them and buried their glider. There was little decent food to be had in Kitty Hawk — least of all fish, since the local fishermen shipped their substantial catch off to Baltimore and other northern cities. Supplies from the outside world took at least three weeks to arrive. Yet the sunsets were the most beautiful that Orville had ever seen: they lighted up the deep-blue clouds with streaks of gold, and the moonlight was so intense that night was as bright as midday. When not soaring or working on the gliders, Wilbur spent his time studying the flight of vultures, eagles, ospreys, and hawks, trying to discover the secret of their ability to maneuver with their wings in unstable air.[15] To those who later asked him how he learned to fly, he loved to reply through his scarcely opened lips: "Like a bird."[16]

To the Wrights, their progress seemed snail-like and agonizing. At one despondent moment, in 1901, Wilbur confessed that he did not expect to live to see men fly.[17] Human flight would be achieved, he said, but not in less than fifty years. To us today, however, the Wrights' advance toward a solution to a problem that had baffled the West's most talented inventors can only appear extraordinarily swift. By 1900 the brothers had discovered that a glider could be controlled in flight if the outer portion of the trailing edge of the wings was twisted in inverse directions. This system of "wing warping," which makes possible smooth and controllable turns, is used, in modified form, by every airplane that flies today. By the end of the following year, the Wrights had determined empirically that the coefficients of lift and drag determining a wing's ability to fly — which they had taken from the authoritative tables published by Lilienthal and Chanute — were seriously in error. They then calculated new figures, using instruments and a wind tunnel of their own design. By October 1902 they had incorporated these discoveries into a redesigned glider and understood that to counter-act the aerodynamic effects of wing warping, it was necessary to attach a controllable rudder to the rear of the fuselage. By March 1903 they had made yet one more imaginative leap and had grasped that a propeller could be conceived as "an aeroplane [wing] travelling in a spiral course."[18]

This theory of aerial propulsion was an essential prerequisite for further progress, since the Wrights had decided that they were now ready to equip their glider with a motor — a twelve horsepower engine, which they designed and built themselves, using

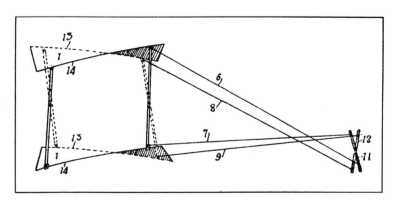

17. A side view of the wings of the 1899 kite-model, showing how wing warping was achieved by means of cords attached to the wingtips.

18. The instrument the Wrights devised for measuring lift and drag coefficient.

bicycle chains to turn two pusher propellers that they counterrotated in order to avoid excessive torque. The objective of powered heavier-than-air flight was now finally within reach. On 17 December 1903 both Orville and Wilbur succeeded in flying their airplane into the air. Their confidence in themselves, their awareness that they were performing an act of immense historical importance, their understanding that the act must be visually recorded, is suggested by the carefully composed photograph that they conceived and arranged to be taken by one of their assistants. Whether by chance or by design, they managed to convey through this image the lonely and collaborative nature of their enterprise, as Orville lying tensely stretched across the lower wing and Wilbur running alongside are united photographically with their machine.

It would take several years and countless flights and crashes before the Wrights would produce an airplane that could "fly" in the sense that we use the term today. Their longest flight on 17 December had been more like a long leap and had lasted only 59 seconds and covered a distance of less than three football fields laid end to end. It would not be until September 1905, when Wilbur remained in the air for almost forty minutes over a course of $24\frac{1}{5}$ miles, that the Wrights could claim to possess an airplane capable of any practical use. But in December 1903, practicality seemed unimportant. What mattered was that the essential breakthrough had been made. The Wrights had no doubts – nor would they ever – that they had "invented" the airplane, just as Thomas Edison had invented the electric light and Alexander Graham Bell the telephone. The new problem thus became what to do with it. And this was when things began to go less smoothly for the brothers.

The Wrights always insisted that they had taken up their flying experiments for pleasure and recreation – just for "the fun of it," as Amelia Earhart later entitled a book she wrote about her love for aviation.[19] Their autumn trips to Kitty Hawk were extended vacations in the open air, made possible by the seasonal nature of their cycling business. Later – and with good reason – the Wrights were careful to distinguish themselves from "sportsmen" and claimed that as "inventors" they were primarily interested in advancing the "science" of aeronautics. They became especially sensitive to accusations, often

19. Wilbur Wright making a right turn during a glide in October 1902: note the vertical rudder in the rear, which was connected by wires to the wingwarping mechanism so that they moved in unison on a single command from the pilot.

20. The Wrights' first powered flight on 17 December 1903.

made in Europe, that they were nothing but talented "mechanics" and unusually gifted "acrobats" who, by dint of years of practice, had learned to control the movements of their flying machine. But the evidence is clear that by January of 1905 the Wrights had also begun to think of themselves as entrepreneurs who had a precious article to sell; and they were keenly aware that, in the increasingly militarized and conflict-ridden atmosphere of that year when France and Germany came to the brink of war, the most likely clients for their invention were governments that could ill afford to risk falling behind technologically in the race to develop ever more sophisticated and destructive engines of war.[20]

As patriotic Americans, the Wrights first offered to sell their Flyer to their own government. But when the U.S. Army Board of Ordinance and Fortification, to which their letter had been forwarded, replied that they had no intention of financing "devices for mechanical flight" that had not been "brought to the stage of practical operation," the Wrights felt free to enter into negotiations with foreign powers. From their letters, it is hard to tell whether the affront of not being taken seriously by their own government was compensated by the awareness that they could now offer their machine to the highest bidder, playing off one customer against the other. What they make clear is that, having been given "a flat turn down" by the American War Department, their conscience was clean. "It has for years been our business practice," Wilbur wrote to a

21. "There is no sport in all the world quite equal to that which aviators enjoy while being carried through the air on great white wings. Compared with the motion of a jolting automobile is not flying real poetry?" (Wilbur Wright in a letter to Aldo Corazza, 15 December 1905. Reproduced by Mario Cobianchi in *Pioneri dell' aviazione in Italia* (Rome: Editoriale Aeronautica, 1943), table lxxxviii).

friend on 1 June 1905, "to sell to those who wished to buy, instead of trying to force goods upon people who did not want them."[21]

They first offered the Flyer to the British government, suggesting a price of £500 for each mile covered with a load of two men. When these negotiations broke down – in part because of the large sum being demanded by the Wrights, even more so because the British aeronautical specialists were convinced that they could produce a flying machine of their own within short order – the Wrights turned to France, which seemed a more likely customer in view of the increasing probability of war with Germany, a country whose manpower and military potential far exceeded those of France.

The French aeronautical establishment had been aware of the Wrights' gliding experiments ever since April 1903, when their friend and advisor, Octave Chanute, had delivered an address to the Aéro-Club de France, in which he had managed to give the impression that the brothers from Dayton were his "dedicated collaborators," a phrase which the French immediately interpreted as meaning his disciples.[22] When news of the first powered flights of 17 December 1903 reached France, the reaction of the Aéro-Club's leaders was dismay at the thought that aviation, "born in France," might only become practical as a result of the intervention of the Americans. "The first flying machine journey," exclaimed the highly respected aeronautical experimenter Victor Tatin, "must be made in France. We only need the determination. So let us get to work."[23]

One member of the Aéro-Club who needed no convincing was Ferdinand Ferber, a captain in the French artillery and a dedicated aeronaut. Mercurial by nature and inclined to take the world by storm rather than by strategem, Ferber had been aware of the Wrights' experiments ever since November 1901, when he first entered into correspondence with the omnipresent Chanute. Hesitant at first to adopt Chanute's biplane configuration for what he later termed "aesthetic" reasons – "an all too French scrupule that made Monsieur Chanute laugh a lot when he found out about it" – he quickly yielded to the American's arguments and built a glider based on what Chanute had told him about the Wrights' design. To Ferber's delight, it escaped from the hands of his assistants and was lifted by rising air currents "like a sheet of paper," before the captain lost lateral control of the machine and came crashing down to earth.[24]

Supplied by Chanute with details about the Wrights' 1901 experiments, Ferber understood that it was only a matter of time before they would achieve powered flight. He still saw reason to hope, however, that the French would be able to catch up with their American competitors. Unlike most of his colleagues in the Aéro-Club de France, though, he believed that the fastest way of doing this was to learn from the Wrights. In early 1903 Ferber wrote repeatedly to Chanute, indicating his desire to purchase the Wrights' machine and trying to wangle an invitation to Kitty Hawk. The Wrights, increasingly suspicious of outsiders, demurred. Wilbur's laconic letter to Chanute, though polite, postponed Ferber's visit to some indeterminate moment in the future. Playing the role of go-between, which he clearly relished, Chanute explained to Ferber that the Wrights would have been delighted to receive him, had they possessed the necessary conveniences "in their desert" and if their "vacation" had not been so brief.[25]

Captain Ferber was never invited to enjoy the fall delights of Kitty Hawk and Kill Devil Hill. Nonetheless he was, naturally enough, the person towards whom the Wrights turned when, spurned by the American and British governments, they began to explore the possibility of negotiations with the French. In October 1905 Wilbur wrote Ferber giving him the details of their most recent flights and informing him that they now possessed a practical flying machine that could be used for military purposes.

24. Ferber gliding in 1902.

Knowing what he did about the Wrights, Ferber did not doubt for an instant the veracity of their account. Passing the information on through official army channels, he urged the French War Ministry to buy the Wright Flyer, despite what he considered to be the excessively high price the Wrights were demanding: one million francs or $200,000. Moreover, publicly he insisted that the Wrights' machine was worth every franc they were asking for it. To the Parisian newspaper *Le Matin*, he declared that had he one million francs at his disposal, he would have left for Dayton two weeks ago.[26] No one who knew this singleminded and impetuous man doubted that he meant it.

But Ferber was a voice crying in the wilderness. Inspired by leading French aeronautical personalities like Ernest Archdeacon, the Parisian press continued to express doubts about the Wrights' achievements and cried bluff. With every week, however, the case against the Wrights became shakier. In December 1905 a reporter for the sports newspaper *L'Auto* made his way to Dayton. After interviewing the Wrights and several witnesses of their flights, Robert Coquelle cabled Paris, confirming the Wrights' claims.[27] The Wright story, however, was too tempting to leave on the level of cold, uncommented fact. Liberally using his imagination whenever he lacked more precise information, Coquelle then went on to file an amusing series of articles, designed to play on existing French conceptions of Americans, from which the Wrights emerged as provincial and eccentric but wily businessmen who were determined to keep the details of their Flyer secret until it had been sold at a handsome price.[28]

Two years after their first powered flights, the Wrights were finally becoming a news item – but a news item with potentially powerful political implications in France. French "aeronauts" believed themselves to be in the forefront of aeronautical progress. French newspaper readers worried about Germany and nervously followed the development of new technologies of war, looking for an arm that might allow the French to overcome their lack of manpower. One French entrepreneur who grasped the potential of the Wright story was Henri Letellier, son of the proprietor of *Le Journal*, a widely read Parisian daily. Urged on by Ferber, who was seeking to bring pressure to bear on his government, Letellier dispatched his secretary to Dayton. Once there, Arnold Fordyce presented himself as the agent of a syndicate of patriotic French investors and signed a preliminary agreement with the Wrights that gave his group two months in which to raise the $200,000 purchase price the Wrights were demanding for their invention.

To be sure, no syndicate existed; and Letellier had no intention of producing such a princely sum himself. His plan was to prod the French government into action; to share the glory of having brought the Wright's invention to France; and, in the process, to get exclusive rights to what had the makings of a smash story.[29] The Wrights, for their part, appear to have believed that Fordyce was acting in good faith as an intermediary for the French government. Had they known that Fordyce was committing funds he did not possess, their deepest suspicions about the deviousness of human nature would only have been confirmed.

The French government responded, as Letellier hoped, by sending an official delegation to Dayton. The delegation was suitably impressed and urged the government to do what had to be done to get possession of the Flyer. But Dayton was very far away, the amount of money being asked for a yet unproven and even unseen machine seemed excessive, and enthusiasm for the Wrights' invention in Paris waned, as war with Germany appeared less imminent. Eventually negotiations between the Wrights and the French broke down over the term during which the French would have exclusive rights to the brothers' invention and French insistence that the Wrights fly to a height of three hundred meters before 1 August 1906.[30] This initial encounter between the Wrights and the French, rife with misunderstandings, journalistic exaggeration, and deliberate deception, would be nothing but the overture to what turned out to be a complex and highly emotional relationship in which alternating and conflicting feelings ran high on both sides.

Throughout 1906, the brothers had operated on the assumption that, if they sat tight and guarded their secrets, governments would eventually be forced to come to them and accept their terms. They knew that they were far in advance of their American and European competitors. Wilbur believed that there was not one chance in a hundred that anyone would produce a machine "of the least practical usefulness" within the next five years. If this was true, it made sense to proceed on the assumption that "all good things come to him who waits."[31] Thus the Wrights stubbornly refused all requests to demonstrate in public the performance characteristics of their airplane and zealously censored the information released by their friends.

However, when news arrived (by way of an increasingly critical Chanute) of a spectacular flight by the Brazilian Santos-Dumont in Paris, the Wrights began to reconsider their tactics.[32] It was not that the brothers were inclined to assign any aeronautical significance to the uncontrolled hop of Santos-Dumont. If anything, the details of the Brazilian's feat confirmed them in their belief that they held an overwhelming technological advantage over their European rivals. But they were concerned, and rightly so, that Santos's exploit would create a perception that controlled flight was within easy reach and thus diminish the value of their machine in the eyes of potential customers. From a business point of view, what people thought was more important than the technological realities.

Determined to go his own way as usual, Wilbur resisted Chanute's suggestions that the Wrights might now have reason to show themselves less demanding in negotiation with European governments. But he was more susceptible to advice that came from a new and unexpected source. In December 1906 the Wrights entered into negotiations with the firm of the powerful and well-connected financier and arms dealer Charles

Flint. Flint was not the sort of man likely to appeal to the "spartan and fastidious" Wilbur Wright. "He [Flint] sold guns, warships, and submarines to anyone who could pay for them. On one occasion he purchased, equipped, and manned an entire fleet for a South American country."[33] A "merchant of death," then, if there ever was one, who made fortunes from the anxieties generated by a constantly escalating arms race among the world's great and would-be great powers.

Wilbur was by no means taken in by Flint; he realized that Flint was an unscrupulous "hustler" who would hawk the Flyer on the international arms market to the highest bidders. If Flint was allowed to have his way, the Wright Flyer would be sold first to imperial Russia. This might mean a new and bloody war between Russia and Japan.[34] But whatever Wilbur's reservations about Flint's ethics, he and his brother were confident that they could use him for their own ends without losing control of their invention. Thus, after a series of negotiations, they agreed to engage Flint as their agent outside the United States in return for a commission. And when in May 1907 Flint telegraphed the Wrights, requesting that one of the brothers should come to Europe to help sell the Flyer, Wilbur threw together a few pieces of clothing and left Dayton for New York that very evening. Clearly, the Wrights were keen to make a deal.

Wilbur's trip to France led to more frustrations. The leading aeronautical figures he met in Paris were in general cool and skeptical of his claims. He developed a deep dislike of Captain Ferber, whom he suspected of maneuvering behind his back to undermine the deal that he and Flint's European representative, Hart O. Berg, were trying to put together with the French government. He found himself in the midst of power plays between the movers and shakers of Parisian political and economic life, shadowy figures whose motives and intentions he could only guess at and denounce in letters to his brother. And his rigorous sense of honesty was offended by a far from subtle suggestion that negotiations would proceed more smoothly if an additional 225,000 francs were added to his price, for the purpose of rewarding highly-placed collaborators. Eager as he was to strike a deal, bribery was not his style.

Wright's disillusionment with the French even spilled over into his perception of Paris, its monuments, and its museums. Visiting the Louvre, he found many famous paintings there no more impressive than the reproductions he had earlier seen in black and white. Notre Dame seemed dark and its nave not much "wider than a store room." Houses were built so that only their owners could appreciate their inner courts, and roads were so highly walled along their sides that they resembled alleys. This, he commented in a letter to his father, was not "the American way." Even the "magnificence" of the French capital – which he grudgingly acknowledged – he thought was due not so much to its buildings and monuments as to its public spaces. "If the fine public and business buildings of New York could be arranged in the same way it would equal or surpass Paris . . ." In September, after Orville had joined him, Wilbur departed for Berlin in search of business associates the brothers "could trust further" than the undependable French.[35]

In the end, though, the Germans were just as reluctant to commit hard cash as the British and the French had been. Why pay for a machine that no one had yet seen? Frustrated at every turn, certain that he and his brother would make no sale before the end of the year, Wilbur returned to America in November 1907, just in time to spend Thanksgiving with his family. Orville followed in December. Both had ample reasons for discouragement. Relations with Berg had become strained because of the Wrights' determination to maintain control of their patents. Authoritative figures within the French aeronautical establishment, like Ernest Archdeacon, were ridiculing them and explaining why the French government would be "throwing out the window" any money it paid for a machine that would soon be duplicated and superseded by French aviators.[36] Even friends, like Chanute, were urging the brothers to compromise before they lost their advantage. "My feeling would be to sell, even though you do not get your original price, which I always thought too high."[37]

The Wrights were unimpressed, insisting to their correspondents that they were years ahead of their European competitors. And as in their technical experiments between 1899 and 1905, persistence paid off. In December 1908, after more negotiations with the Wrights, the U.S. Signal Corps issued an advertisement for a "heavier-than-air flying machine" that corresponded exactly to the specifications of the Flyer and met the Wrights' rock-bottom demand for a price of $25,000, to be paid after a series of demonstration flights. Typically, the Wrights then set immediately to work to renegotiate the terms of the Signal Corps' competition. Soon afterwards Hart Berg reached an agreement with the French. It was not the deal the Wrights had wanted. Instead of dealing directly with the Ministry of War, they agreed to sell their patents and the right to manufacture and sell Wright airplanes in France to a syndicate headed by the financier Lazare Weiller and Henry Deutsch de la Meurthe, a powerful industrialist and long-time supporter of aviation within the Aéro-Club de France. The Wrights were pleased, however, that the shady Letellier, whom they had come increasingly to mistrust, had at last been eliminated from any participation in their French operations. By contrast, Weiller and Deutsch de la Meurthe commanded respect in the markets that the Wrights were determined to penetrate. Leaving Orville in the United States to satisfy the terms of the Signal Corps' competition, Wilbur returned to France in May 1908. The moment had at last come to show the French what the Flyer could do in the hands of its designer and constructor.

Wilbur arrived in Paris in late May to find their business "flat on its back" and the atmosphere chilly.[38] The skeptics were out in force, with the nationalistic Georges Prade leading the attack in *Les Sports*. Nor was *Les Sports* alone. Just a few days after his arrival the widely read weekly *L'Illustration* published a heavily touched up photograph taken of the Flyer at Kitty Hawk, commenting that "its appearance is quite dubious and one finds in it every element of a 'fabrication,' not especially well done moreover."[39] In addition, Wilbur had other, more immediate problems to cope with. The Flyer Orville had shipped arrived in dreadful condition; and in the process of rebuilding it, Wilbur burned himself badly, thus delaying even further the beginning of his demonstration flights. Then came the triumphs of 8 and 10 August.

Though Wilbur was inclined to underplay the significance of these "little flights," the truth is that he was flying a greatly modified machine in which he had accumulated a total of fifteen minutes of experience, after not having flown at all for two and a half years.[40] Moreover, the Wright Flyer of 1908 was a highly unstable aircraft that required sharply refined pilot skills and constant vigilance to control. The so-called canard – or elevators – in the front had a tendency to produce sudden climbs or dives unless perfectly operated. By any standard, then, the "little flights" that Wilbur executed at Hanaudières in August 1908 were highly dangerous feats performed in front of a skeptical and potentially hostile crowd. Small wonder that Wilbur took a malicious satisfaction in reporting to Orville the reactions of the French aviators. "Blériot & Delagrange were so excited they could scarcely speak, and [Henry] Kapperer could only gasp, and could not talk at all. You would have almost died of laughter if you could have seen them."[41]

25, 26. Above, a heavily touched up photograph of the Wrights flying at Kill Devil Hill in May 1908, just before Wilbur left for France; compare with the untouched up photograph of the same flight below.

27. A sketch of the flying machine that Wilbur Wright assembled after arriving in France in June 1908.

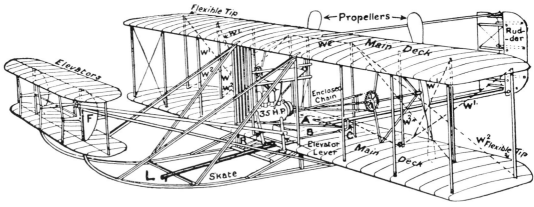

During the next five months, Wilbur flew continuously, first at Hanaudières, where he remained until the end of August, then at Auvours, an army artillery range on the outskirts of Le Mans where the crowds were so large that tickets of admission had to be sold. Wright had come to France a *marchand de bicyclettes* whom many suspected of being a charlatan and a fraud. After 8 August, he became a hero lavished with praise, feted at ceremonial dinners by those who had earlier denounced him, and the recipient of numerous medals, prizes, and distinctions, including the Legion of Honor.

To be sure, some French aeronautical experts expressed guarded reservations about the construction of Wright's machine, proclaiming it to be "rustic," "rudimentary," and dangerously unstable. They criticized its dependence on a catapult for taking off and offered suggestions for how the Flyer's design might be improved. When Orville crashed at Fort Myers, Virginia, on 17 September and his passenger Lieutenant Thomas Selfridge died, becoming the first victim of heavier-than-air flight, the Wrights' French critics said it was inevitable because catastrophe awaited these "prodigious acrobats" and their "rebellious instrument" at every turn.[42]

The fact remained, however, that Wilbur Wright could fly and his French critics could not; and this was what mattered to the public who read about his exploits and flocked by the thousands to see his flights.[43] They bought postcard images of his profile, rendered appropriately bird-like, and replicas of his green cap – now popularly known as a "Vilbour." They sang songs about or inspired by him. They consumed an unending stream of newspapers and magazines that bore his portrait and recounted anecdotes about his eccentricities, such as his refusal to use French string. They quoted with delight his outrageously un-Gallic statement made when asked to give a speech before a banquet of aviation enthusiasts: "The only birds who speak are parrots; they can't fly very high."[44] And they even tried to get a peek at him while bathing.[45]

Yet as much as the French admired Wilbur Wright, they confessed that they could not understand him. He seemed like a being from another planet. The aviator Delagrange marvelled at Wright's ability to postpone his flights for ten hours while the crowd waited, "restless and impatient." Had there been a hundred thousand people in the grandstands, Delagrange insisted with evident amazement, Wright would not have

28. One of the many postcards bearing Wilbur Wright's image produced in France during his flights at Le Mans. This one, sent by Wilbur to Orville in September 1908, refers to his brother's record-breaking flights at Fort Myers, Virginia.

29. A postcard of Wilbur Wright showing him repairing the Flyer; Wright became famous in France for his insistence on making all his own repairs with parts he had fashioned himself.

30. Wilbur Wright portrayed as a hard-living *apache* (Wright neither smoked nor drank and was seldom seen in the company of women other than his sister.)

31. Wilbur Wright addressing the banquet given in his honor at the Aéro-Club de France in November 1908.

taken off a minute earlier. Delagrange wondered what went on beneath that bronze-like mask that was Wilbur's face. "Even if this man sometimes deigns to smile, one can say with certainty that he has never known the *douceur* of tears. Has he a heart? Has he loved? Has he suffered? An enigma, a mystery."[46]

François Peyrey, the most respected aeronautical journalist in France and a great admirer of Wilbur Wright, could not pretend to answer these questions about the American aviator's emotional life. But he nonetheless tried, on the basis of his observation of Wright at Hanaudières and Auvours, to give his readers some insight into Wright's character. The portrait he sketched in August 1908 is extraordinary, an indissoluble mixture of straightforward description and poetic fantasy, reflecting not only what Wright was but even to a greater degree what Peyrey wanted him to be.

Contrary to the impression the newspapers gave, Peyrey said, Wright was a reserved and simple man – *un timide* – who had astounded the employees at the Bollée automobile factory (where he had assembled the Flyer) by his meticulous craftmanship and his punctuality. At the sound of the factory's whistle, he resumed or abandoned his work like any other salaried employee. He worked alone, counting on no one but himself. He made his own parts, going so far as to fabricate a needle when the one he

32. A group of spectators at Hanaudières on 10 August 1908; note the sparseness of the crowd, the presence of several elegantly dressed ladies, and the prominence of military officers.

33. The mysterious Wilbur Wright captured by the camera of Jacques Lartigue when Wright was flying at Pau in February 1909.

had brought from America broke. He cooked his own meals. He never lost his plane from sight. And at the end of his long days of work, "he wraps himself up in a blanket and goes to sleep, while dreaming of the loneliness of Kitty Hawk or Kill Devil Hill under the wings of his mechanical bird."[47]

34. The photograph chosen by François Peyrey to illustrate Wilbur Wright's intelligence and eyes.

Wright's high forehead revealed his admirable intelligence; his large clear eyes were "the crystal-clear mirror of his beautiful, pure soul." All one had to do was to speak to this gentle, serious, and dignified man in order to know that he had never lied. Astonishingly phlegmatic and silent, the American airman was capable of maintaining his isolation even in the midst of a crowd. "The impatience of a hundred thousand persons would not accelerate the rhythm of his stride."[48] He was deeply cultured and, in his rare moments of relaxation, discussed literature, science, music, and painting with authority and insight. Wright knew all the paintings in the Louvre. A natural artist, when asked by Peyrey about Kitty Hawk, he had produced "in a second" a sketch in which he had indicated all the essential points of reference. Seeking to articulate for his readers the ascetic and spiritual qualities he sensed in Wright, Peyrey could only propose a religious metaphor. "One day when he was daydreaming for a moment, his eyes lost in the woods that surround his bird-like house, he made me think of those monks of Asia Minor who lived perched on the tops of inaccessible mountain peaks. The soul of Wilbur Wright is just as high and faraway."[49]

This, to my knowledge, is the first full-blown portrait of a real, as opposed to an imaginary, aviator. Though brief, it ascribes to Wilbur Wright many of the characteristics and qualities that would later become identified with countless other famous fliers: the unusual eyes;[50] self-reliance; determination; attention to detail; extraordinary patience; an artisan-like dedication to work; loneliness; genius; indifference to the superficial emotions of the masses; trustworthiness; imperturbability; purity; aesthetic sensitivity; spirituality; loyalty; simplicity; and above all, height and distance from the ordinary run of human beings.[51]

A year later, Peyrey repeated almost word for word what he had written about Wilbur Wright in 1908, but added one passage, introducing a theme that would run through French aviation literature over the decades to come. While at Auvours, nothing – neither the cold nor the rains that often flooded his hangar – could persuade Wright to leave the spartan quarters where he slept next to his plane. "A poet, he despises hotels and human agglomerations. But he adores mornings deliciously veiled with bluish fog and melancholy twilights."[52] The American inventor who came to France to sell his airplane had now, through the miracle of French sensibility, been magically transported away from the urban and industrial civilization that had spawned him to the lonely pastoral heights of Parnassus. Henceforth few French writers who took up the aviation theme would be able to avoid the equation between the aviator and the poet.[53]

Yet if Wilbur Wright was a poet, he was a new breed of poet: one who wrote his verses in the sky. Frustrated at trying to convey in words an experience that could only truly be captured in images, Peyrey reproduced a photograph taken of Wright while flying at Auvours during one of those "marvelous sunsets whose magic intensifies when it merges with the mist that floats above the cool land of the Sarthe." In the sky the clouds were still streaked with red from the setting sun, but "the vast polygon of Auvours, surrounded by its pine forest, had taken on its mysterious and tragic appearance." Seized by emotion, Peyrey observed Wright for more than an hour, as he circled the field, suspended between the "dead earth" and an "overwhelming, resplendent sky." For Peyrey, the spectacle had a "religious grandeur" that set him to musing on the meaning of Wright's achievement.

35. The sketch of Kitty Hawk Wilbur Wright made for Peyrey.

36. Wilbur Wright flying at
sunset at Auvours on 21
September 1908.

The day we had longed for had finally come! In the mechanical body of the great
bird dwells a man, the man who had the admirable idea for it, the man whose
powerful brain created its architecture which is so ingenious and at the same time
so simple! And as my mind roamed through the future, I had a vision of the times
to come and imagined a friend, for whom I was waiting, flying towards my
threshold.[54]

Though one can only speculate about what Wright would have thought about these
words if he had been able to read them, there is no doubt that they contrast in important
ways with what we know about him and with what he thought of himself. Keenly
aware of his strengths and his weaknesses, Wright warned others about ascribing to him
qualities he did not possess. "Very often what you take for some special quality of
mind," he wrote to one of his collaborators in 1903, "is merely facility arising from
constant practice. It is a characteristic of our family to be able to see the weak points of
anything, but this is not always a desirable quality as it makes us too conservative for
successful businessmen and limits our friendships to a very limited circle."[55]

As so often happened in his judgment of others, Wright in this letter was being too
harsh. One of the most fascinating and complex figures in the history of flight, Wilbur
did indeed have a special quality of mind. A surprisingly fluent writer, imaginative,
meticulous, self-reliant and patient to an extraordinary degree, tough both physically
and mentally, shrewd, suspicious, secretive but careful to document his every move,
self-righteous and legalistic yet often very funny, he evaded every category within
which the European press endeavored to ensnare him. Perhaps the metaphor of the
"birdman," which Peyrey made fashionable, is appropriate after all. Wilbur took flight
before the Europeans could get close to him. "*Il vole . . . il vole.*"[56]

28

Moreover, it was this very elusiveness that made it easier for Wright's French observers to invest this intensely practical and down-to-earth man with an air of mystery, poetic sensibility, and heroism. Reading what was written about Wilbur in 1908, looking at the countless images of him that were produced, it is hard not to believe that many, if not all, of the elements of the figure of the aviator had already been forged when he arrived in France. They were waiting impatiently for the first person capable of bringing them to life through the achievement of controlled flight. The twentieth century was born yearning for a new type of hero: someone able to master the cold, inhuman machines that the nineteenth century had bequeathed and at the same time capable of transforming them into resplendent art and myth. Unknown to themselves, the Western peoples secretly desired an epic poetry of technological deeds.

Wilbur Wright was the unlikely candidate chosen by fate to play this role. As one of his European admirers lyrically put it, he was the first to realize the "elusive dream that man had cherished from far distant days." His was "the victory o'er the realms of the air." He was the "father of flight," a hero larger than life whose aeronautical inventions would "cleave the air to trumpet forth his fame to all the distant corners of the earth."[57]

Yet what added a discordant note to Wright's image, especially for the French, was his unmistakable Americanness. He lacked *tenue*, *élégance*, and *esprit* and seemed more interested in profit than in *gloire*. The French found this difficult to understand and

37. A highly idealized drawing of Wilbur Wright, which gives him an uncharacteristic happy-go-lucky look.

could never forgive him for his lack of sophistication and generosity. There was something deeply middle–class and unheroic about Wright and his approach to flight. He never talked about his contributions to mankind and guarded his patents with his life. How could one admire, unreservedly, a *mécanicien* who insisted on eating out of cans and lubricating his own engine, a self-proclaimed businessman who never allowed the word "humanity" to pass his tightly puckered lips, a "birdman" who so often refused to fly?

Wilbur Wright's story illustrates a paradox that will run throughout my history: the qualities required for success in aviation often had little to do with the characteristics that the public has wanted to ascribe to aviators. Dubbed "the fanatic of flight" by a journalist writing in the *Daily Mail* in August 1908 and described as a man "born to fly," Wright was an extraordinarily prudent pilot who did not believe in taking chances and who, unlike Orville, happily gave up flying once he had achieved fame and fortune in 1910.[58] The letters he wrote from Le Mans to his brother in August 1908, when Orville was preparing to go to Fort Myers, Virginia, to demonstrate the Flyer to the American government, are full of admonitions to be cautious and to avoid all risks. "*Do not let yourself be forced into doing anything before your are ready.*"[59] Usually extremely terse and matter-of-fact in his description of flights that marked turning points in aviation and broke records, he wrote most eloquently about the aesthetic pleasures of flight after a leisurely ascent in a balloon in 1907.[60] And when he died prematurely in 1912, it was not as the result of an aviation accident – as had happened by that date to many other pilots of the Wright Flyer – but from typhoid fever after his health and morale had been weakened by his attempt to defend the Wrights' patents in endless litigation with other aviators and airplane builders. By this time, sadly, the dogged legal battles of the inventor, the entrepreneur, and the capitalist had swept away in many minds memories of the "poet" and "artist," the "fanatic" who was "born to fly."[61]

38. Wilbur Wright at Pau in 1909. Rather than the "fanatic of flight," Wright deserves to be known as the "fanatic of *pre*flight" because of the care with which he examined his airplane before undertaking an ascent. "Whistling in a way which was said to be particularly irritating to those on the tiptoe of expectation, the airman would walk negligently round and round his machine for many minutes, touching a wire here and a strut there. Then he would test the control mechanism time after time. After another interval, he would direct the engine to be started. Then sitting in the pilot's seat, he would listen to the way in which the engine ran for another long period." Claude Grahame-White, *The Story of the Aeroplane* (Boston: Small, Maynard and Co., 1911), p. 33.

2

French wings over Dover

Vive la France! . . . It was necessary
and natural . . . that the invention of
aviation should take place on French
soil, for it's a soil that brings
happiness to the human spirit.

Charles Fontaine, 25 July 1909[1]

WILBUR WRIGHT'S triumphant season at Le Mans was a terrible
blow to the French aeronautical establishment. Henceforth it could
no longer be denied that powered flight had first been achieved in
the United States; two obscure Americans had wrested from the
French the right to be called "the fathers of aviation." "*Nous
sommes battus*" (we are beaten), the French record holder Léon Delagrange exclaimed
disconsolately in the aftermath of Wilbur's flight on 8 August 1908.[2]

Furthermore, Wright was not satisfied to demonstrate the brothers' earlier claims but
went on to exceed them, breaking record after record. On the last day of the year, with
glistening snow covering the grounds at Auvours and a numbing wind sweeping across
the field, Wright was catapulted down the Flyer's rail, rose gracefully into the air, and
remained aloft for two hours and twenty minutes during which he traversed almost 125
kilometers, breaking his own and Orville's records for distance and duration and thereby
winning the Coupe Michelin and 20,000 francs ($4,000). That night, as François Peyrey
dutifully recorded, the "simple hero" attended a reception given in his honor in Le
Mans, then returned to his hangar where amidst "the warlike sounds of his camp, the
muffled roll of drums, and the light songs of trumpets," he peacefully fell asleep "with
an admirable simplicity, beside his mechanical bird, on a folding bed."[3]

Formulating and executing his plan with his usual precision, Wright had achieved by
this demonstration of determination and endurance exactly what he wanted. Doubt was
no longer possible; quibbles, earlier insinuated, were almost universally suppressed. On
1 January, Georges Prade, one of the French journalists most skeptical of Wright's
achievements before August 1908, gave voice to reluctant feelings of awe and admiration that were widely shared in France.

> The year finishes with a new burst of thunder. One more time, the eagle has taken
> flight and has astonished us by the power of his wings. It really seems that this
> mysterious man likes to surprise us . . . With this flight of 75 miles, his sudden climbs
> to more than 300 feet in the clouds, his eternal and disconcerting circling above the
> heather of Auvours by dint of his prowess, he remains the man of the year, and I
> apologize for having found such a miserable epithet to characterize the man who will
> very likely be the man of the century.[4]

But if Wright's flights at Le Mans demonstrated, beyond a shadow of a doubt, the

39. Blériot sets forth across
the Channel.

40. A photographic portrait
of Bleriot wearing his pilot's
helmet.

41. Wilbur Wright's hangar at Auvours.

42. Wilbur Wright's workshop and living quarters at Auvours. (When not flying, Wright used a bicycle for transportation.)

43. A highly concentrating Wilbur Wright about to take Mrs Hart O. Berg up for a flight.

brothers' primacy over the French, they also provided a tremendous stimulus to the development of French and – in a large sense – European aviation. Wilbur, for all his famed taciturnity, turned out to be a formidable propagandist for the cause of heavier-than-air flight. During his four months at Auvours, Wright took aloft a long string of passengers, among them Louis Barthou, the French Minister of Public Works; Paul Painlevé, an eminent mathematician and politician; various journalists, industrialists, and military officers; and several carefully chosen women. His purpose was to demonstrate that flying machines could be safe when handled by an experienced operator. These flights made a huge impression on those who experienced them. As the correspondent of *Le Figaro* wrote after going up with Wilbur, "I have known today a magnificent intoxication. I have learnt how it feels to be a bird. I have flown. Yes, I have flown. I am still astonished at it, still deeply moved."[5]

In February 1909 Wright left Auvours and transferred his base of operations to Pau, a small, charming town at the foot of the Pyrenees. Life in Le Mans had been good to him: in addition to earning hundreds of thousands of francs and acquiring several gold medals and a nomination to the Legion of Honor, the craggy Wright had gained sixteen pounds on the solid cuisine of the Sarthe. In Pau Wright completed the training of the three French pilots, required by his contract with the Weiller syndicate.[6] Once the Count de Lambert, artillery Captain Lucas Girardville, and Paul Tissandier had soloed and demonstrated their ability to control the Wright Flyer, it became more difficult to claim that only a "prodigious acrobat" like Wright could hope to fly. When not in the

air, Wilbur, now accompanied by Orville and his sister Katherine, received the visit of kings, queens, and aristocrats, who made the pilgrimage to Pau from the luxury of Biarritz to witness the miracle of flight and to have themselves photographed with Wright. Thus, despite Orville's serious accident at Fort Meyer and Wilbur's occasional forced landings and broken struts and spars, the conviction spread that flight was not a quixotic dream and that its development was only a matter of time.

Yet how would that development proceed? In a small book written before Wright's 1908 flights in France – and subtitled evocatively *From Crest to Crest, From City to City, From Continent to Continent* – Captain Ferber had predicted that competitions for monetary prizes would begin to play an important role in the technical progress of aviation and suggested that a flight across the English Channel, from Calais to Dover, was relatively easy and would soon tempt "the daring." Such a flight, Ferber suggested, would have an immense impact by diminishing "the insular inviolability" of Great Britain.[7]

By the time Ferber's book appeared in 1909, this prediction, unlike others he made, no longer seemed to apply to some distant future that his contemporaries were unlikely to see.[8] Indeed, as early as December 1906 a well-known champagne producer, Ruinart père et fils, had offered a prize of 12,500 francs ($2,500) for the first heavier-than-air flying machine that succeeded in crossing the Channel under its own power. No contenders for this dangerous undertaking presented themselves in 1907. But in the wake of the Wright brothers' spectacular flights in the fall of 1908, the idea of a Channel flight was given fresh life when Lord Northcliffe's mass circulation *Daily Mail* announced its own prize of £500 ($2,500) under conditions that were considerably more inviting than those imposed by Ruinart.[9]

Northcliffe was not the first newspaper man, nor would he be the last, to play an important role in the history of aviation. But no newspaper owner ever took up the cause of aviation with greater passion, nor had a greater impact on the air policies of his country, than this self-made millionaire who grasped the powers of the press in an age of increasing literacy and sought to reign over the minds of his readers like an imperious king. Just two years older than Wilbur Wright and, like him, an enthusiast of technological innovation and an avid reader of popular scientific literature, Northcliffe, born

47. Lord Northcliffe (left) with Orville Wright at Pau in February 1909.

44. Alfonso XIII, King of Spain, sitting in the Wright Flyer at Pau in February 1909. Alfonso later explained that as a sportsman and a man of soldierly temperament, he had to exercise extraordinary restraint in order to respect the promise he had made to his mother not to go aloft with Wright.

45. Dignitaries lifting the disks needed to catapult the Flyer: the third person from the front is the former Premier of Great Britain, Arthur Balfour.

46. Wealthy spectators watching Wilbur Wright fly at Pau from the comfort of their automobiles.

48. The young Alfred Harmsworth (far right) with fellow bicycle enthusiasts.

Alfred Harmsworth, made his first breakthrough in journalism as the editor of *Bicycling News*. Taking shrewd advantage of the bicycle boom, and exploiting the interest of cyclists in the increasingly popular practice of photography, Harmsworth raised the circulation of the *News* eightfold and went on to launch a series of publications that made him one of the richest and most powerful men in England. By 1898, his recently created newspaper, the *Daily Mail*, had a circulation of half a million copies, twice that of its closest competitors. With journalistic success came the temptation to intervene directly in politics. Yet in the electoral arena, Harmsworth's touch proved less golden, and he was rebuffed in his effort to enter parliament in 1895. Nonetheless he became a force to be reckoned with in the Conservative Party; in recognition of his achievements he was awarded a knighthood, then elevated to the peerage as lord Northcliffe in 1905.[10]

It was understandable that an enthusiast of bicycles and automobiles like Northcliffe would follow with impassioned interest the development of aviation. It followed also that, as an acute interpreter of the reading public's mind, he would see that flight could provide a rich and up-to-the-present relatively untapped source of news. By April 1906 Northcliffe had decided to engage a full-time aviation correspondent, whose exclusive task would be to follow developments in the air. "Make no mistake," Northcliffe told the young Harry Harper upon hiring him, ". . . the future lies in the air."[11] Aviation would produce what Northcliffe called "splash stories," the kind that kept the public on tenterhooks and sold newspapers.

Northcliffe's interest in flight, however, went far beyond a professional and business investment in generating and reporting news. Deeply concerned with questions of national and imperial defense, Northcliffe was keenly aware of the military implications of aeronautical technology for British security. And this awareness was further galvanized by events taking place on the continent in the fall of 1906.

It was one of the paradoxes of the early history of aviation that, though powered flight was first achieved in the United States, the capital of aviation before the First World War was indisputably Paris. No other Western city prized aviators more highly, nor responded to their exploits with more intense enthusiasm. This was in great part due to the Parisian tradition of balloon flights that went back to 1783, a tradition that had been revived and consolidated in the late nineteenth century, making Paris the lighter-than-air capital of the world. But the popularity and visibility of aviators also owed a great

49. Alberto Santos-Dumont, dashing aeronaut and elegant man about town.

deal to the example set by the Brazilian expatriot and dandy, Alberto Santos-Dumont, who dominated the Parisian aeronautical scene during the first six years of the twentieth century.

Born in 1873, Santos-Dumont grew up on an immense and highly mechanized coffee plantation in the province of São Paolo. From childhood he was fascinated by machinery. At the age of seven, he was driving a steam-powered tractor; by twelve, he had graduated to the plantation's railway engines. Six years later, he would acquire and import one of Brazil's first automobiles, a three-and-a-half horsepower Peugeot. Any machine that moved intrigued him. Yet the medium through which he longed above all to circulate was the air. An enraptured reader of Jules Verne and an admirer of his aviation novel *Robur-le-Conquérant,* in which Verne predicted the imminent realization of heavier-than-air flight, Santos-Dumont later remembered lying in the shade of his house's veranda and gazing "into the fair sky of Brazil . . . musing on the exploration of the vast aerial ocean."[12] When asked as a young boy what he wanted to be in life, he replied without hesitation: "a flying man." Though people often mocked him for it, he never changed his mind.[13]

A bizarre accident suffered by his father when he fell off his horse while inspecting his coffee machines provided Santos the means with which to pursue his fantasy of aerial navigation. No longer able to manage his property, his ailing father sold his plantation, gave the eighteen-year-old Santos-Dumont a fifth of his substantial fortune, and sent him to Paris with the exhortation to study physics, chemistry, and electricity. A dutiful son but an uninspired student, the young Brazilian chose to advance his scientific education in Paris with a private tutor rather than preparing himself to gain entrance to one of France's outstanding technical schools. At loose ends after five years of desultory studies and rich enough to be able to finance his caprices, he took up the fashionable sport of ballooning and quickly became proficient enough to compete successfully in races.

Santos was captivated by the sybaritic and aesthetic delights of ballooning. One can understand why. An eccentric by temperament, living in a city that fancied dandies, he enjoyed a life that others could only dream about, lunching and sipping champagne while drifting high across the French countryside. There was nothing comparable to such an experience, he wrote when describing his first ascent and the emotions it inspired in him. "What dining room offered more marvelous surroundings? . . . I was finishing a glass of liqueur when the curtain suddenly fell on this admirable stage setting of sun, clouds, and blue sky."[14] Indeed, Santos-Dumont was so fond of taking his meals *dans l'air* that he ordered a special dining room table two meters high for his apartment: "His servant – in uniform and tall like a bean stalk – climbed a tiny ladder with two steps in order to serve his master and his guest, for the table, which was quite small, could only contain two place settings."[15]

It turned out, however, that the Brazilian was more serious about flying than his dandyish behavior may have suggested. By 1898 he had tired of being at the mercy of the wind and, encouraged by the recent development of the internal combustion engine, he had begun to design dirigibles, a type of motorized and steerable balloon that had for decades been imagined and depicted by science fiction writers and their illustrators. Santos-Dumont produced a series of fourteen dirigibles and flew them over and around Paris, delighting turn-of-the-century *flaneurs* with his combination of Latin eccentricity, sartorial elegance, and aeronautical daring. What Parisian could resist the charms of an "aeronaut" who had the chic to crash-land his dirigible in the Baron de Rothschild's lovely garden where one of his admirers, the very aristocratic Countess of

50. An airship imagined by Albert Robida in 1883.

51. The airship Albatros imagined by Jules Verne in his novel *Robur-le-conquérant.*

52. Santos-Dumont's aerial dining table at his Parisian apartment on the rue de Washington.

Eu, arranged to have him served a delicious lunch high above the ground while waiting to be disentangled from one of the Baron's chestnut trees?[16]

A little man of fierce determination and unpredictable moods, Santos was determined to gain recognition as the leading aeronaut of France. To encourage the development of aeronautics, the rich petroleum magnate Henry Deutsch de la Meurthe had created a prize of 100,000 francs ($20,000) to be awarded to the first person who flew successfully from the Parisian suburb of Saint Cloud to the Eiffel Tower, rounded it, and then returned to Saint Cloud in a total time of thirty minutes or less. In September 1901, after several failures, the Brazilian won the prize and (much to the chagrin of the prize's downer) established his primacy over his French rivals.

For the next few years, Santos was satisfied to enjoy his fame and to titillate the Parisian public by landing his dirigible in front of his house just off the Champs-Elysées or at his favorite restaurant in the Bois de Boulogne. In 1906, however, the Brazilian surprised the Parisian aeronautical world by announcing that he intended to become a contender for the prizes being offered for heavier-than-air flight. Just two years before he had suggested that the conquest of the air by means of heavier-than-air machines *might* occur – if it did – a half century hence.[17] But, as news of the Wright brothers' experiments appeared in French aeronautical journals, Santos began to wonder if the future were not closer at hand. When he saw Gabriel Voisin soar briefly above the waters of the Seine in an aircraft of his own design, he was prompted to act. Inspired by Voisin's use of box-like structures to provide stability, Santos designed one of the strangest and least promising flying machines ever seen, which he christened the 14bis to indicate its continuity with the fourteen dirigibles that had preceded it. On the afternoon of 23 October 1906 the Brazilian succeeded in rising to a height of three

53. Santos-Dumont making an emergency landing in Edmond de Rothschild's garden.

54. Eugène Grasset's representation of Santos-Dumont rounding the Eiffel Tower. Grasset adopts an aerial perspective in order to portray Paris as he imagined that it looked to Santos-Dumont from an altitude of 300 meters.

meters, which he maintained over a distance of two hundred feet, thereby winning the Archdeacon prize for the first heavier-than-air flight of more than 25 meters. By the standard of what the Wright brothers had achieved by this date, Santos's uncontrolled hop, which ended in the collapse of his undercarriage, was scarcely a milestone in the history of aviation. But the onlookers, who had gathered at the Bois de Boulogne, were transfixed and convinced that they had witnessed the world's first airplane flight. "The stupefied crowd had the impression of a miracle; struck dumb with admiration at first, they shouted with enthusiasm at the moment of the landing, and carried the aviator away in triumph."[18]

A frequent visitor to France, where he went to escape the chill of British winters and the severity of British speed limits, Lord Northcliffe was present at Santos's flight on 23 October. On 12 November, after fitting the 14bis with primitive ailerons,[19] Santos flew again, extending his distance covered in the air to 722 feet. The next morning, when Northcliffe read the *Daily Mail's* brief and matter-of-fact account of this flight, he was furious. "He immediately telephoned the editor to say that the news was not that 'Santos-Dumont flies 722 feet,' but, 'England is no longer an island. There will be no sleeping safely behind the wooden walls of old England with the Channel our safety moat. It means the aerial chariots of a foe descending on British soil if war comes.'"[20] In the next edition, the *Daily Mail* announced ominously that the flight of Santos-Dumont had an international significance. "The air around London and other large cities will be darkened by the flight of aeroplanes . . . They are not mere dreamers who hold that the time is at hand when air power will be an even more important thing than sea power."[21]

57. Santos-Dumont about to fly. Note the ailerons between the wings of the 14 bis.

Meanwhile Northcliffe had dispatched his aviation correspondent to Paris to interview Santos-Dumont. In the course of the interview, Santos scolded the English for not offering financial inducements to aviators, as the French industrialists and newspapers had done. "You English are practical, but you don't encourage inventors or beginners. You wait to reap the fruit of other people's brains."[22] Santos invited the English to offer a prize of £10,000 for the first aviator to fly the Channel. Northcliffe responded immediately to the suggestion of a prize to encourage aeronautical progress, but changed the itinerary suggested by Santos and increased the distance to be traversed by a multiple of almost eight. The *Daily Mail* announced that it would offer £10,000 ($50,000) for the first nonstop flight between London and Manchester. "We desire to remove the impression that England is not in the van of progress in the new science, and we are anxious that the business of constructing aeroplanes, which will no doubt in the future be as large as that of motor-car making, shall be assisted as rapidly as possible."[23] The point of the competition, the *Daily Mail* made clear, was to encourage the British to adapt themselves to a technological transformation before they fell dangerously behind in the race to conquer the air.

In November 1906, the 186-mile flight from London to Manchester was well beyond the capabilities of any flying machine, as the British newspapers did not hesitate to point out. Ridiculing Northcliffe's gesture, the London *Star* renewed its offer of £10 million for the first flying machine to fly to any destination ten miles from London and to return to its point of departure. "One offer is as safe as the other."[24]

Nor did the British military leadership show itself in any hurry to invest in aeronautics. What changed their minds eventually were not Santos-Dumont's hops in France but developments in Germany. On 1 July 1908 Count Zeppelin flew two hundred and forty miles in his rigid airship. He quickly announced his intention to make even longer flights. Germany was swept by "Zeppelin fever," as the Kaiser's government gave signs

44

of intending to embark on the construction of an aerial fleet, even more threatening than the battleships they already possessed.[25] The frightening vision of airships "dripping death" from the skies over a helpless London, conjured up in H. G. Wells's recently published novel *The War in the Air*, passed from fantasy to the horizon of reality – if not true today then possibly so tomorrow. British public opinion was alarmed; and Lord Northcliffe seized the occasion to ram home once more his message about the need for Britain to commit itself to a program of aeronautical development. Discounting the most alarmist warnings about the possibility of an imminent attack of Britain by air – which it nonetheless published – the *Daily Mail* concluded that at present Count Zeppelin's airships were no threat to British security; but it added forebodingly that their successors might well be. In view of this, the British Admiralty and War Office "would be well advised to appropriate money to enable us at least to keep abreast of Continental enterprise."[26]

At the very moment when these polemics were under way in London, Wilbur Wright was assembling the Flyer in Léon Bollée's automobile factory in Le Mans. Like many Europeans who followed aeronautical developments, Northcliffe had been skeptical about the Wright brothers' claims. But the events of August 1908 quickly changed his mind. Commenting on Wilbur's flight of 8 August, the *Daily Mail* wrote that "The scoffer and the sceptic are confounded . . . A bird could not have shown a more complete mastery of flight."[27]

Later that month Northcliffe approached Wilbur Wright and sought to interest him in undertaking the flight between Manchester and London. When Wright prudently demurred, he then took up Santos-Dumont's original suggestion and proposed that Wright should fly the Channel. Officially, he told Wright, he intended to offer a prize of $2,500; but privately, he would guarantee him another $7,500 if he attempted and won the prize.[28] To this would be added half the net receipts obtained by the exhibition of the Flyer at a great hall in London.

58. The Zeppelin II leaving its hangar on the Lake of Constance.

Wright was briefly tempted. Early in November, he wrote Orville: "If I felt sure of decent weather I would go for it as such an exhibition would practically end the necessity of further demonstrations next year, and cause all the parliaments of France, Germany & England to vote credits [for the Flyer] at their winter sessions."[29] But Orville was not convinced that Wilbur's engine was reliable enough to make the Channel crossing; and Wilbur himself disliked the idea of competing for prizes, on the grounds that "exceptional feats" were ill-suited to the image of the "inventor," with which the Wrights were determined to identify themselves.[30] Thus, though the Wrights welcomed Northcliffe's visit to Pau in February 1909 and carried on a cordial correspondence with him, they took themselves out of the competition for the Channel flight, preferring to return to the United States, where they were forced to endure elaborate celebrations of their feats, first in New York, then in Dayton.

59.   The Wrights fly home to Uncle Sam.

The decision of the Wrights to return to the United States in the spring of 1909 opened up an opportunity for the French. Though overshadowed by the Wrights during the months between August 1908 and May 1909, the French aviators had not been idle. Indeed, much as he disliked being thought of as a mere sportsman, one of the reasons Wilbur Wright had decided to stay in France over the Christmas holidays of 1908 was because he believed that he could not afford to lose the much coveted Michelin prize for distance to one of his French rivals. "If I had gone away the other fellows would have fairly busted themselves to surpass any record I left," Wilbur explained to his father in a letter he wrote on 1 January 1909. "The fact that they knew I was ready to beat anything they should do kept them discouraged."[31]

Who were the "other fellows" that Wright had in mind? By January 1909, Santos-Dumont had been decisively superseded as France's premier aviator by Henry Farman, a turn of events that suggests how rapidly the world of aviation was changing. A "sportsman" rather than an "inventor," Farman illustrates the type of pilot who would increasingly dominate the coming phase of aviation. As a young man growing up in Paris, where his father was correspondent for the London *Standard*, Farman displayed both artistic and athletic gifts. When it came to deciding on a career, however, the lure

60. "The Flying Man" Henri Farman posing with his Voisin biplane in November 1907.

61. Henri Farman's flight of 13 January 1908, when he flew the first officially monitored kilometer in a closed circuit.

of sport won out over the aesthetic and Bohemian enticements of the Ecole des Beaux Arts. Farman, like so many of his younger contemporaries, had fallen in love with the bicycle, *la petite reine* of fin-de-siècle France.[32] Endowed with formidable qualities of endurance and balance, he took up racing in 1892 and, after becoming one of France's leading cyclists, he then went on to motor cars, finishing second to Marcel Renault in the Paris-Vienna competition of 1902. By 1907 Farman had accumulated a considerable fortune of half a million francs, primarily by selling automobiles in partnership with his brother Maurice. This money, along with his undisputed courage, his "methodical patience," and his expert knowledge of vehicles and machines gained over a period of fifteen years, gave him a definite advantage when he decided in 1907 to turn his talents and ambition to aviation.[33]

Once embarked on his new course, Farman progressed with extraordinary swiftness. Commissioning a biplane from the Voisin brothers and fine-tuning it step by step to suit his individual needs and abilities, he beat Santos-Dumont's record for distance in October 1907 and won the Deutsch-Archdeacon Grand Prix for the first (officially recorded) kilometer in a closed circle in January 1908, just a few months before Wilbur Wright returned to France to begin his demonstration of the Flyer at Le Mans. By far his most significant achievement from an aeronautical point of view, however, came on 30 October 1908, when he completed the first cross-country flight between Bouy and Rheims.

To be sure, when Farman accomplished this exploit, the Wrights had flown longer; but they had done so in the relative security of an enclosed and carefully defined space. By venturing forth into the countryside, where safe landing sites were less predictable, Farman and the other French pilots who quickly followed in his path were definitely raising the stakes of aeronautical progress.[34]

The Wrights having taken themselves out of the running, Farman became the favorite to fly the Channel and win the *Daily Mail* prize. Other possible contenders were Farman's great rival, the sculptor Léon Delagrange, and Wilbur Wright's pupil, the Russian-born Count Charles de Lambert. The first aviator to attempt the Channel crossing, however, was an even more recent recruit to aviation, the debonair Hubert Latham.

Born in 1883, Latham came from an old and very rich family of Le Havre shipowners, who maintained British passports to go with their English surname, despite three generations of residence in France. After studying law at Balliol College, Oxford, and completing military service in France, Latham indulged himself in some of the distrac-

62. Members of the Aéro-Club de France measure the distance of Farman's flight of 13 January 1908 with the omnipresent bicycle.

Le premier Voyage en Aéroplane

FARMAN, sur son appareil Voisin, va du camp de Châlons à Reims, à la vitesse de 75 kilomèt. à l'heure

C'EST LE TRIOMPHE DE L'ÉCOLE FRANÇAISE D'AVIATION

Récit de l'émouvante prouesse

FARMAN NOUS TÉLÉGRAPHIE
SES IMPRESSIONS

[PAR DÉPÊCHE DE NOTRE ENVOYÉ SPÉCIAL]

Reims, 30 octobre.

Le rêve qui flotta depuis des siècles dans l'esprit des hommes, ce rêve qui fut si longuement caressé par la multitude des humains, vient d'être réalisé. La machine volante est née ! Par un exploit triomphal, dû à son courage, à son énergie, à sa volonté d'abord, puis à son merveilleux aéroplane, Henry Farman vient d'accomplir une magnifique prouesse.

Se jouant des accidents de terrain, des arbres même les plus hauts, des rivières, des routes, des lignes de chemin de fer, des maisons, des villages, il a, dans un vol étonnant, éblouissant, franchi la distance qui sépare le camp de Châlons de Reims. Tous les adjectifs les plus éloquents, les plus dithyrambiques, les plus emphatiques, je puis les employer ici sans aucune hésitation.

Farman a été le premier homme qui, avec un appareil plus lourd que l'air, avec une machine génialement agencée au moyen de bois et de toile, poussée par une hélice, ait accompli cette formidable randonnée.

Pour un pareil événement, ma vive émotion paraîtra bien compréhensible. Il faut avoir vu cette cellule avancer dans l'air avec une aisance parfaite, il faut l'avoir vue planer au-dessus des bois, se découper à quelque cinquante mètres de hauteur dans une atmosphère limpide ; il faut l'avoir vue aller dans le soleil inondant l'air pur, pour se faire une idée du spectacle magnifique qui s'offrit à mes yeux.

Le voyage de Reims est décidé rapidement. Aux environs de quatre heures, Farman et Gabriel Voisin, ayant senti le vent, décident d'un commun accord

Itinéraire du voyage aérien de Farman

deux fils, a fait le merveilleux voyage tout à fait gratuitement. Maurice embrasse Farman. Nous l'acclamons, et bientôt accourent une foule de gens, de soldats, de paysans, qui foulent sans pitié le terrain d'atterrissage.

les peupliers grandissent de façon surprenante ; les corbeaux qui tenaient une assemblée criarde s'enfuient épouvantés à mon approche. Ah ! ces peupliers de trente mètres ! Fallait-il les passer à droite ou à gauche ? Mon in-

63. The course of Farman's cross-country flight as it was depicted on the front page of *Le Matin.* "It's the triumph of the French school of aviation."

64. Traditional rural society and the new air age meet in this artist's representation of Farman's flight.

49

tions available to Edwardian men of means – lion and elephant hunting in Africa, exploration in Indo-China, automobile and speedboat racing in France, a balloon journey across the English Channel – before taking up the ultimate turn-of-the-century sport: heavier-than-air aviation. Provided with one of the best and most beautiful aircraft then available, an Antoinette IV driven by a light and powerful Levavasseur engine, Latham taught himself to fly in February–March 1909 and within a few months had set a new French duration record and had carried off a major prize for speed.

Latham became an overnight sensation with the crowds who followed aviation. His English-tailored clothes struck exactly the right balance between sporty casualness and man-about-town elegance and distinguished him clearly from inventor-engineers like the Wrights or the designer of his airplane, Léon Levavasseur. Careful to cultivate his dashing image, Latham became famous for the answer he gave to the French President Armand Faillères when asked what profession he had practiced before becoming an aviator. "*Un homme du monde*,", he replied. But, oh, how he could fly! After fifty years of aviation journalism, Harry Harper thought that he had never seen a finer pilot.[35] In June 1909 Latham announced his decision to try for the *Daily Mail* prize.[36]

Unfortunately for Latham, by the time he had installed himself in Calais and assembled the Antoinette, the weather over the Channel had turned unseasonably turbulent. Rain fell incessantly and the wind whistled across the cliffs at Sangatte, where Latham had established his camp. By 12 July the quaint roofs of the houses in Calais resembled "polished metal mirrors" and the ground had become a "pool of mud." Pounding rain, however, had not dampened the enthusiasm of the city's inhabitants or their visitors. A peasant woman was overheard explaining the principles of flight to her friends in the marketplace. The local fishermen agreed that, being French and not knowing the meaning of the word "impossible," Latham would certainly reach the *Chaikispeer* (Shakespeare) Cliff. Even an old priest, who thought the heavens should be left to God's angels, confessed that he wouldn't consider missing Latham's flight.[37]

Finally, on 19 July, after days of waiting for the winds to subside, Latham took off from the cliffs of Sangatte while a crowd of admirers watched. The correspondent for *L'Auto* attempted to capture in words the emotions that these onlookers experienced as they watched the tiny Antoinette disappear into the distance:

> By the sheer force of his daring skill, dominating matter already enslaved by science, a human being piloting a mechanical bird launched himself from the top of the cliff bordering the sea. Then, diving into the light fog that blurred one's view of the uncertain horizon, he swooped into the distance, with the speed of a modern steed of the air, over the swells of a mysterious grey sea, while some enormous sea gulls, croaking in the sky, escorted this new Icarus with the beating of their wings.[38]

Alas, the "matter" of Latham's machine was not as "enslaved" by science as *L'Auto*'s correspondent so poetically imagined. Seven miles out into the Channel, just as he was preparing to take a photograph of the torpedo-boat *Harpon* that the French government had assigned to follow him, Latham's engine began to cough and sputter, then stopped. Unable to restart it in the damp and heavy air, Latham then calmly glided to land on the

66.   Latham's Antoinette at Sangatte. The onlookers who had made their way to Sangatte by bicycle, automobile, and foot were numerous enough that they had to be cordoned off from the plane.

67. Latham disappears over the Channel.

68. The cliff at Sangatte.

Channel swell, the first pilot to ditch an airplane over water. When a launch from the *Harpon* finally reached him, he was propped up on the back of his seat smoking a cigarette and looking supremely nonchalant.[39] Such elegant behavior, described in careful detail by the newspaper correspondents gathered in Calais, touched his admirers' hearts.

Given a hero's welcome in Calais, Latham proclaimed his determination to try again. Before he could do so, however, he had been upstaged and robbed of the glory both he and his admirers thought was destined to be his by yet another French aviator, who seemed, among the possible contenders, to be the one least likely to succeed.

In a period when the French were reduced to applauding Brazilian and American aviators and when the leading French pilots had either been born abroad or had suspiciously English-sounding names, the Frenchness of Louis Blériot was reassuring. Dark, solidly built, with an aquiline nose, a determined glance, and a moustache he wore drooping at the ends *à la gauloise*, Blériot brought to aviation an extraordinary passion, credentials as a well-trained engineer at one of France's leading technical schools, and a substantial income of 60,000 francs a year that he derived from the selling of headlights and accessories for the rapidly growing French automobile business.[40] About the same time that the Wrights first went to Kitty Hawk, Blériot began to experiment with flying machines, turning out a series of aircraft between 1900 and 1906 that had in common primarily their inability to fly.

With the Blériot VI, which he tested in July 1907, the determined engineer finally got into the air. His progress was henceforth steady, even if punctuated by frequent crashes. The day after Farman's cross-country flight between Bouy and Rheims, Blériot made the first round-trip airplane journey, flying from Toury to Artenay and back and covering a total distance of 28 kilometers. Driven to overtake his rivals, he succeeded on 13 July 1909 in flying from Etampes to Orléans, a distance of 42 kilometers, in under 45 minutes, thereby winning the Aéro-Club de France's Prix du Voyage of 14,000

70. Louis Blériot.

53

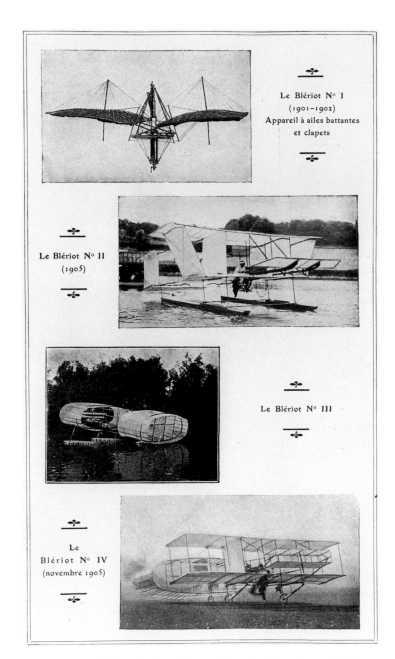

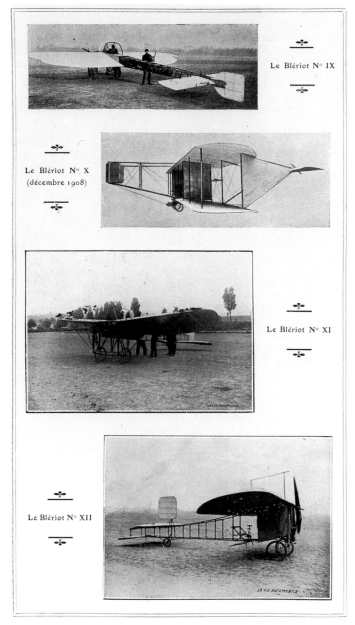

71, 72. Eight, of Blériot's first twelve aircraft, including no. XI, the plane in which he flew the Channel.

francs. For the first time, Blériot could present himself as a credible candidate for the 38-kilometer crossing of the Channel.[41]

The problem was that Latham had already established a camp along the Channel coast; moreover Blériot was now on crutches, as a result of severe and painful burns suffered during one of his recent flights. For the moment, then, Blériot could do nothing more than stand by and await the result of Latham's flight. But when he received news of Latham's failure on 19 July, he immediately notified the *Daily Mail*'s Paris office of his intention to undertake the Channel crossing. With luck, he could make the flight before Latham was able to repair his badly damaged machine or replace it with a new one. Aware that Blériot now planned to try for the prize, Latham and his crew worked day and night to assemble another Antoinette; by the 23rd, the new plane was ready. Blériot, meanwhile, had set up his own camp at a small farm not far from the cliffs of Sangatte. Neither man, however, could attempt the flight because winds of gale force were blowing.

The question became who would dare to fly first: the dashing Latham or the dogged Blériot.[42] Understandably, both men leaned heavily on the counsel of their advisors. Aviation by now had already taken on some of the aspects of a team sport. Pilots were surrounded by engineers, mechanics, journalists, and the equivalent of public relations men. All stood to gain if their man won.

To Latham's dismay, it was Blériot's team that proved to be the more aggressive. Rising a little after 2:00 a.m. on the morning of 25 July, Alfred Leblanc, Blériot's business associate and close collaborator, saw that the winds had calmed and rushed to the hotel to wake Blériot and urge him to make the flight. Blériot himself was at first hesitant, as was his anxious wife. But his spirits perked up considerably after his machine performed smoothly during a brief warm-up flight.[43] Persuaded by his mechanics that his engine would carry him safely across the Channel, Blériot prepared for take-off and awaited sunrise, the earliest starting time according to the *Daily Mail*'s conditions for the winning of the prize. At 4:35 a.m., on a signal from Leblanc, Blériot lifted his monoplane, loaded with seventeen gallons of gasoline, into the air and was off, as Latham watched with tears in his eyes.[44] Thirty-six and a half minutes later, after a battle with adverse winds, down-drafts, and a motor prone to overheating, the exhausted pilot landed on a meadow near Dover Castle, falling "straight upon the land from a height of sixty-five feet," breaking one of his propeller blades and his undercarriage.[45] Given his reputation as a pilot hard on airplanes, it was only appropriate that Blériot's epoch-making flight should end with a crash.

73. Blériot atop his plane on the morning of 25 July 1909, as he is towed to his take-off spot.

L'itinéraire suivi par Blériot et la vue des falaises de Douvres

Cliché de l' " Illustration "

74. The route followed by
Blériot in his historic flight, as
reconstructed by *L'Illustration*,
31 July 1909.

As a sheerly technological achievement, Blériot's flight was of limited significance.
Other aviators had flown longer and further. Just a few days before, Henry Farman had
stayed aloft for an hour and twenty minutes. Not to mention Wilbur Wright, who at
Auvours on the last day of 1908 had flown for two hours and twenty minutes.

To be sure, Blériot had the courage to venture over the Channel, with no visible
points of reference to guide him. To judge by his own accounts, the minutes during
which he lost the French coast from sight and left his destroyer escort behind in the
impenetrable Channel fog were the most frightening and disorienting in the entire
flight.[46] Still, Blériot's navigational procedures could scarcely serve as a precedent for
future pilots flying over large bodies of water. Just before taking off, he asked Leblanc
to point him in the direction of Dover; when he first reached the English coast, he was
miles northeast of his destination, and perilously close to losing his way in the Channel
mist.[47] It is hard not to conclude that Blériot was propelled into history as much by luck
and sheer tenacity of spirit as he was by Alexandre Anziani's engine.[48]

Leaving aside the technical aspects of Blériot's flight, however, its significance and
implications as a *symbolic* act were enormous. Both the French and the British immediately understood this. Most commentators from these two countries agreed that 25 July
would mark an historic and unforgettable date in the annals of science and civilization.[49]
The French press took special pride in the fact that the deed had been accomplished by
a French aviator in an airplane of French design. Discovering belatedly the superiority
of Blériot's monoplane over Wright's biplane – the "French" solution to aircraft design
– they conveniently forgot that Farman's much-praised Voisin had two wings. As the

Parisian daily *Le Matin* succinctly summed up the meaning of the exploit: with Blériot's flight, French genius had carried off yet one more victory.[50]

The British papers, while saluting Blériot and praising his courage, could not repress their concern that Blériot's flight would have dire implications for British security. The *Daily News* wrote: "A rather sinister significance will, no doubt, be found in the presence of our great fleet at Dover just at the very moment when, for the first time, a flying man passed over that sacred "silver streak' and flitted far above the masts of the greatest battleship."[51] Indeed, ironically, it had been Blériot's sighting of British warships steaming along the coast that had permitted him to correct his navigational error and turn southwest toward Dover.

The most reflective journalists realized that this was no mere "sporting feat" similar to the swimming of the Channel by Captain Matthew Webb in 1875 and wondered, as Gaston Calmette, editor of *Le Figaro* did, what the future held in store, now that man could dominate the seas, the continents, and the mountains. "What will become of men's laws, their customs barriers, the vain efforts of their industrial protectionism, their commercial exchanges, their defenses, their relations, their intercourse, on the day when man can, by the action of his will alone, pass in a few hours beyond all horizons across all the oceans and above all the rivers . . ." Calmette had no doubt that "within the foreseeable future, the conditions of human life will be profoundly changed."[52]

While journalists pondered the meaning of Blériot's flight, both London and Paris prepared to celebrate him. Never before in Europe or America had an exploit by an aviator unleashed such popular enthusiasm. Indeed, this enthusiasm, though deeply felt, was by no means spontaneous; Lord Northcliffe was not a man to leave anything to chance. To ensure instantaneous coverage of the Channel flight, he had installed near Latham's camp at Sangatte a Marconi wireless station, which permitted his correspondent Harry Harper to receive weather reports from Dover and to transmit to Dover blow-by-blow accounts of the preparations for flight on the French side. From the Lord Warden Hotel in Dover, Harper's reports were relayed to the *Daily Mail* newsroom by

75. Blériot is greeted by admirers on his arrival in London.

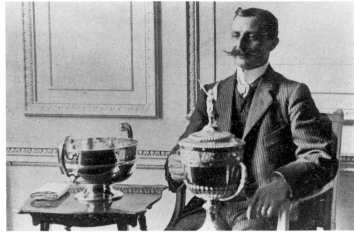

76. Blériot paired with the British explorer Sir Ernest Shackleton during the banquet organized by Lord Northcliffe at the Savoy Hotel.

77. Blériot savors his trophy and his check from the *Daily Mail*.

telephone.[53] While waiting for the first successful flight, the *Daily Mail* had carefully fanned the flames of public interest, featuring interviews with the leading contenders and carefully building the dramatic intensity of the occasion. The *Daily Mail*'s campaign was emulated by other European and American newspapers. Here was a story that no newspaper dared to neglect. Their readers followed day by day, with mounting enthusiasm, events in Calais. By the time of Blériot's flight, both Calais and Dover were thronged with journalists and curiosity-seekers from all over Europe and the United States.

Once having crossed the Channel, Blériot could not wait to return to France. Indeed, he embarked the same afternoon on the French destroyer *Escopette* after an informal lunch with his wife, the captain of the vessel, and a few close friends. He does not seem to have grasped straight off that his exploit had far-reaching political and cultural implications. But those in his immediate entourage knew better; they convinced him that he would have to return to England the next day to receive his prize from the hands of Lord Northcliffe and to participate in the celebration that the English were organizing in his honor. At a banquet held at the Savoy Hotel in London, attended by 130 hastily assembled guests, Northcliffe awarded Blériot his £1,000 (25,000 francs) in prize money and, in a "vibrant speech" that emphasized the solidity of the Entente Cordiale, celebrated the heroic qualities of the French and the English, the two peoples, he added diplomatically, who had done the most for civilization.[54] As living symbols of these qualities, Blériot and Shackleton, the British "conqueror of the South Pole," were seated side by side and much photographed together. To further emphasize the ongoing triumphs of the new technologies, Guglielmo Marconi sent his compliments by wireless from mid-Atlantic, the first message of its kind ever transmitted by this method.[55]

The following Wednesday Blériot returned to Paris to receive the most elaborate and carefully planned reception that any aviator had yet received.[56] A hundred thousand Parisians had flocked to the Gare du Nord, where Blériot's train was expected to arrive in the late afternoon. All along the path of his train, from Calais to Paris, one could hear, like the roll of a giant drum, the clamor of hero-worshipping voices. In Paris, peddlars hawked portraits of Blériot along the boulevards and wandering singers sang songs to his glory:

> *Blériot, c'est notoire*
> *En quittant Calais*
> *Entra dans l'Historie*
> *Sans sceptre ou palais.*[57]

> Blériot, it's no mystery
> When leaving Calais behind
> Became a part of History
> Without a sceptre or a palace.

On arriving at the station, Blériot and his wife were mobbed by the overflowing crowds. "*Ce fut du délire,*" wrote one journalist who covered the scene.[58] "It was crazy." Rescued with difficulty by two police agents specially assigned for the occasion, they were then whisked off to the station's customs room, which had been decorated for the occasion with French and English flags. Once there and surrounded by invited dignitaries, they received a delegation of workers from the Blériot factory, who presented their *patron* with a statuette called *Le Cri de la gloire* by the well-known sculptor Grisard. The purpose of this "spontaneous" gesture was, of course, to celebrate the indissoluble union of capital and labor.

After being greeted by the Minister of Justice Louis Barthou, in the name of the government, Blériot then proceeded by carriage to the Aéro-Club of France on the Champs-Elysées, while the crowds on the boulevards pressed against police cordons to get a glimpse of the man who, with a single *coup de ses ailes* (beating of his wings), had eliminated the age-old barrier of the English Channel. There, in an "intimate" reception attended by the *crème de la crème* of French aviation, the vice-president of the Aéro-Club announced that the club had decided to award Blériot its most prestigious prize – the gold medal – and to commemorate his "superb" flight with a monument erected on the site near Calais from which he had departed. For three more days the ceremonies continued, overshadowed in the press only by the bloody repression of the workers' uprising in Barcelona, the so-called "tragic week."

Lord Northcliffe could pride himself on having created one of the great news stories of the new century. But the English press magnate was after more than news. His intention was to use Blériot's exploit to bring pressure on the British government to commit itself to the rapid development of an air arm. The *Daily Mail* lost no time in drawing the lesson from Blériot's crossing of the Channel. British insularity had vanished; expensive dreadnoughts would be useless against swarms of relatively cheap and quickly manufactured airplanes; sea power was no longer a shield against attack. "Men who navigate the air know nothing of frontiers and can laugh at the 'blue streak' [the British navy]."

Northcliffe's purpose was not to spread panic among the British public but to goad the British government into action. Taking issue with H. G. Wells's contention that Blériot's flight had proved the English to be a "slacking," "dull," "rather soft and backward" people – in an article which the *Daily Mail* had commissioned, then prominently displayed – Northcliffe's newspaper recalled reassuringly that when the British do wake up to danger "it is our habit to act with vigour and earnestness."

Northcliffe's message was clear. Blériot's flight had brought to the fore a British problem that went far beyond temporary leadership in the development of a new technology. British decline was a real danger; but it was not inevitable and could be prevented by energetic action. Among other evidence, the *Daily Mail*'s campaign was itself a sign that the British were beginning to rise from their indolent slumber and become conscious of a complacency induced by "long supremacy" and "unrivalled success." Contrary to what some commentators claimed, there was no immediate cause for alarm. An invasion of the British Isles by air was not yet practicable. Nonetheless, the British must be made to understand that they could no longer count on the fleet for

78. Blériot and Fontaine besides Blériot's wrecked aircraft soon after his landing. This photograph was carefully staged by *Le Matin*'s photographer to extract the maximum patriotic effect and to symbolize the union of *Le Matin* (in the form of Fontaine to the right), Blériot in a determined pose, and France, symbolized by the flag.

79. Fontaine holds the unfurled tricolor high, as Blériot's procession makes its way along the boulevards of Paris.

their security. Britain's future depended on the development of a "navy of the air." "We have time to act, but we have no time to wait."[59]

The *Daily Mail*'s call to action was heard. Within a week of Blériot's flight, the Liberal government's Minister of War, R. B. Haldane, found himself under savage parliamentary attack in what one historian has called "the beginning of air power politics in Britain." Out of this debate came the demand for an independent air service that would eventually culminate in the Royal Flying Corps and its illustrious successor, the Royal Air Force.[60]

In Paris it was *Le Matin* that got the most press mileage from the Blériot story. This newspaper's correspondent, Charles Fontaine, penetrated the inner circle of the Blériots before the flight took place and scouted out the clearing in England where Blériot finally landed. Fontaine was waiting on the relatively low ground of North Foreland Meadow near Dover Castle early in the morning when Bleriot's monoplane first emerged from the mist. Seeing the opportunity to turn the flight into a patriotic occasion and underline the national character of Blériot's exploit, he signalled his location to the aviator from the ground with a French flag flapping in the gusty winds that swept in from the Channel. Indeed, Fontaine's flag became an important constituent of the ensuing celebrations. In London and in Paris, Fontaine was constantly at Blériot's side, carrying with him the tricolor which, waving in the morning breeze, had given the signal for the landing of *le bel oiseau de France*.[61]

Lest anyone overlook the intimate connection between *Le Matin* and Blériot, the paper's influential editor, Henry de Jouvenel, gave a banquet in his honor. In his speech, de Jouvenel was careful to delineate the crucial role his newspaper had played in the flight.[62] "We have asked ourselves if we deserve the honor that you do us in dedicating to us your first outing in Paris. But we think that what has brought us this honor is not the fact that we sent two or three more reporters than the other newspapers, but rather the fact that we perhaps believed in you more than the others." Acknowledging the support provided by Blériot's wife and his *amis de la première heure,* de Jouvenel concluded on a note that indicated the central role that newspapers had come to play in aviation. "We are behind, at the back of the scene," de Jouvenel said disingenuously, contradicting the photographic evidence that had figured prominently in *Le Matin*'s accounts of Blériot's flight. "We represent the enthusiastic confidence of the French masses."[63] To symbolize the close union *Le Matin* had achieved with France's aviator-hero, Blériot's airplane hung outside the windows of the newspaper's headquarters for the next three days.

Nor did *Le Matin* restrict itself to this gesture. Fontaine had the further idea of writing a full-blown account of Blériot's crossing of the Channel. This was yet one more contribution to a growing genre of books that sought to capture in literary form and transform into a spiritual adventure what was essentially a technological event. Lacking the aeronautical knowledge and poetic flair of François Peyrey, Fontaine substituted patriotic fervor. Attempting to describe for his readers the man Blériot, Fontaine could think of no better comparison than an ancient Gallic chieftain. "When . . . he appears in an aviator's suit, coiffed with the round mantle that covers his head and ears and dressed in a short blue workman's blouse drawn in at his waist, with his energetic head, his rounded forehead, his direct and honest look, and above all his long and powerful drooping whiskers, you could easily take him for one of those robust defenders of ancient Gaul called Ambiorix or Vercingetorix."

Of course, continued Fontaine, everyone was aware of Blériot's charm, his simplicity,

80. In this caricature by Mich, Blériot recognizes his image in a statue of the Gallic hero Vercingetorix.

Comment Blériot
a traversé
la Manche

par

CHARLES FONTAINE

Seul témoin oculaire de l'atterrissage

Récit de la traversée
par
Louis BLÉRIOT

Conclusions
de M. Paul PAINLEVÉ
de l'Institut

E. DEWINTER

LIBRAIRIE AÉRONAUTIQUE
32, Rue Madame, PARIS

his modesty, his ready smile, his affability, his dedication to science, his courage, his sang-froid, and his audacity. What were less well known were his patience, his perseverance, and his stubborn determination to succeed after so many disappointments and failures. He had spent a fortune on aviation – as much as 800,000 francs ($160,000) – but what was a fortune for an "apostle" like Blériot? Fontaine left no doubt in the minds of his readers that the qualities he ascribed to Blériot were not so much personal to him as quintessentially French.

With a journalist's intuition for the deepest desires of his readers, Fontaine had grasped the potential significance of Blériot's flight and sounded a theme that would be repeated by others in a score of variations. A nation that was capable of producing a Blériot was not a nation in decline, as so many pessimists were claiming.[64] Here was "one of these modern heroes, soldiers of science and progress, and victors over the hostile forces of nature in whom was combined the double superiority of character and intelligence."[65] And if the French public responded with such wild enthusiasm to the flight of the reserved and dour engineer from Cambrai, it was because French wings over Dover had finally redeemed the depressing series of setbacks in aviation the French had suffered during the previous decade and held out the promise of their resurgence in the face of the German threat. What a relief it was that the crossing of the Channel,

81. Charles Fontaine, *Comment Blériot a traversé la Manche* (Paris: Librarie Aéronautique, 1909).

82. This inexpensive bronze medal commemorating Blériot's flight sold for 10 francs and emphasized his Gallic traits.

L'appareil exposé devant le *Matin*

Un souvenir de la traversée

Clichés du " Matin "

Vue prise de l'hôtel du *Matin*

83. Blériot's airplane hanging outside the headquarters of *Le Matin*.

84. The Channel as it appeared to Blériot when he left the coast behind and headed out over water.

a deed that required energy, spirit, faith, sang-froid, daring, calm, perseverance, and a capacity for improvisation should have been accomplished by a Frenchman. Indeed, there were those who thought that only a "French brain" could have realized this exploit. Now France could pride itself on having taken the lead in aviation, just as it had earlier taken the lead in automobiles, dirigibles, and submarines.[66] Now no one could pretend to argue that the country of Claude Bernard, Louis Pasteur, the Curies – and Blériot – was aging or decadent.[67] "Come on, one is still proud to be French, even while looking at something other than ancient ruins."[68]

Blériot seems to have been genuinely surprised by the popular response to his flight. Replying to Lord Northcliffe's eulogy during the banquet at the Savoy Hotel, he remarked that the reception he was receiving was out of all proportion to the effort he had made.[69] Two days later, when he stepped out on the balcony of *Le Matin* to receive the acclamation of the crowd that was impatiently awaiting his appearance, he was overwhelmed, even startled, by the violence of their hurrahs. "Before the ovation of the public, the bird that flew from France to Dover withdraws and loses his grip, as if he were frightened. 'It's too much!' Blériot murmured. 'Never, never, not even the other day in London did I feel anything like that. It's wonderful and it's frightening.'"[70]

As Blériot struggled to find words and a political rhetoric adequate to the occasion, taking refuge wisely in the tactic of taciturnity developed to perfection during the previous year by Wilbur Wright, what he did not suspect was that he had participated in the creation of a new form of mass spectacle: the long-distance flight, what in French would come to be called a *raid*. Or to be more accurate, he had participated in the creation of an aeronautical variant on a theme already developed by explorers, bicyclists, motor-car drivers, and balloonists – but one that was especially suited to the new technology of aviation.[71]

A raid was a flight between two well-known points of reference, usually major cities, that had never been successfully completed before. The most spectacular raids – and therefore those that captured most fully the public's imagination – were those that took place over large and historically significant bodies of water. The sight of the aviator and his plane disappearing into the vastness of the sea or ocean, perhaps never to be glimpsed again, produced emotions in the public that no flight over land ever could. There was something about the limitless horizons and terrifying depths of the oceans and the seas that evoked feelings of awe and wonder, reminiscent perhaps of the ill-fated flight, known to all students of Greek mythology, that Daedalus's son Icarus undertook from Crete.

The most visible protagonist of the raid was of course the pilot, but he was in fact only one of many actors in a complex drama. Before he could attempt a raid, a team of engineers and mechanics had to create an airplane capable of carrying out the deed. The permission and often the assistance of the affected governments had to be sought, as had been the case with both Latham and Blériot. Accurate weather reports had to be ensured. Members of the press had to generate popular enthusiasm for the flight, building up the drama of the occasion before the flight took place and later, after it was completed, describing it and explaining its significance. Photographers had to be on hand to record the event for the newspapers and the illustrated magazines. Nor should one forget the crucial role of the public, because how they responded to the press and the pilot would determine the duration, the intensity, and the psychological success of what was not simply an individual exploit but a mass spectacle in which thousands, or even millions, of people would participate. Finally, in this print-oriented and very literary culture of the early-twentieth-century West, it was necessary to take all these elements and to transform them into a narrative that could be published as a book.

Thus, when Blériot crossed the Channel on 25 July 1909, he was doing more than demonstrating the virtues of a monoplane with a tractor propeller, exposing the vulnerability of England to invasion from the air, or showing the world – and his countrymen – what French scientific genius combined with French élan and sang-froid could accomplish. He was the central actor in a social drama, which would be played out time and again throughout the twentieth century by a long series of aviators ranging from Roland Garros to Charles Lindbergh and Howard Hughes. He was the first to claim the legacy of Icarus and show that human beings could traverse large bodies of water by means of wings. As Blériot himself succinctly put it, it was above all by conquering the sea that aviators would advance the conquest of the air and excite the enthusiasm of crowds.[72]

85. "Again I felt that overpowering rush of excitement which I find almost everyone has experienced who has seen a man fly. It is an exhilaration, a thrill, an ecstasy. Just as children jump and clap their hands to see a kite mount, so, when the machine leaves the ground and with a soaring movement really flies upon its spreading wings, one feels impelled to shout, to rush after it, to do anything which will relieve the overcharged emotion." (Harry Harper in the *Daily Mail*, 26 July 1909, describing Blériot's departure for Dover.)

66

3

War in the Air

No place is safe – no place is at
peace. There is no place where a
woman and her daughter can hide
and be at peace. The war comes
through the air, bombs drop in the
night. Quiet people go out in the
morning, and see air-fleets passing
overhead – dripping death – dripping
death!

H. G. Wells, 1908[1]

IN 1908–1909 intrepid aviators, like the Wrights, Farman, and Blériot, proved that airplanes could be made to fly. Their example inspired other – and usually younger – men to "navigate the air." Flight schools were organized to give aspiring pilots more systematic training. Workshops began to produce flying machines and offer them for sale. Publications devoted exclusively to aviation appeared. The first *aérodrome*, ancestor of our airports, was constructed at Juvisy on the outskirts of Paris.

Commenting on the impact of Blériot's flight in France, the aeronautical enthusiast Etienne Taris thought that he detected a change in the way that aviators were perceived by both the general public and the educated elite. Formerly the aviator appeared "as a slightly whimsical figure, generally a nice young man in love with the outdoors and violent exercise, a dare-devil, etc." Now suddenly the aviator's image had changed. The aviator had been promoted professionally to the rank of engineer and industrialist while at the same time people ascribed to pilots the virtues of the sportsman, namely someone who possessed great physical courage, with all the prestige that this implied. Most important of all, Taris thought, Blériot's exploit had captured the imagination of the masses in a way that Wilbur Wright's flights, witnessed primarily by rich and idle people, had never done. This was why Taris – and others – thought that the cause of aviation was now won. Henceforth no one would dare to scoff at those who dedicated their lives to realizing the dream of flight.[2]

The military metaphor used popularly to encapsulate these developments, to give them a meaning that could be easily grasped by the airminded and the terrestially bound alike, was "the conquest of the air." This phrase was designed to appeal to a young generation whose fathers and older brothers had only recently completed the conquest of the globe. The new empire to be subjugated lay in the sky. In 1909 what twenty-year-old male living within the confines of the triumphant and technologically dominant West could fail to feel the grandeur of this challenge? Indeed, a poll taken that year in France among six hundred secondary students revealed that those who responded admired aviators more than any other historical or contemporary personalities. Napoleon was less popular among these *lycéens* than Blériot.[3]

Yet the stirring rhetoric of "the conquest of the air" concealed a dilemma, which the promoters of aviation now had to face. What practical purposes could airplanes serve? One possible use, of course, which the Wrights and other aviation pioneers had been

86. The bombing of New York (detail) as imagined by H. G. Wells's illustrator A. C. Michael in *The War in the Air* (London: George Bell and Sons, 1908).

87. H. G. Wells around 1900.

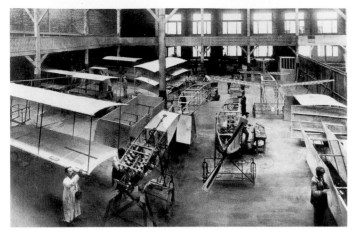

88. The Voisin aircraft factory in 1908.

89. A sketch of Port-Aviation at Juvisy: this *aéro*drome was modeled on the *hippo*drome at Longchamp and had grandstands capable of accommodating seven thousand people.

quick to point out, was military. Flying machines, many were arguing, would revolutionize the art of war. As Captain Ferber explained in a memorandum he prepared for the French War Department, the possession of a fleet of airplanes would give a general the possibility of knowing the moves and countermoves of the enemy. "No matter how quickly the enemy might mobilize his resources, not even the most rearward reserves would escape notice. . . . Under these conditions, victory is certain."[4]

In January 1906, though, when Ferber wrote these lines, the generals and admirals who shaped military budgets remained to be convinced that flying machines could be effective instruments of war. They made no effort to hide their skepticism.[5] Into the breach opened up by their indifference or hostility to the new invention rushed men of letters. Giving their imagination full rein, they speculated freely on the impact that powered flight would have on the way that nations made war. Circulated in large editions, picked up and commented on by newspapers and reviews, discussed by governmental committees, some of these visions of aerial warfare reached large and influential audiences. Read today, they reveal feelings and attitudes widely shared within the national groups from which their authors came and help us to understand the intensity of the emotions unleashed by Blériot's flight.

The most famous of these prophecies – and the one best remembered today because of the notoriety of its author – came from the furiously busy pen of the Englishman H. G. Wells, a prolific essayist and best-selling novelist who specialized in "scientific romances" and visions of the future which were translated and read eagerly throughout the countries of the West. The first installment of Wells's adventure tale, *The War in the Air*, appeared in the *Pall Mall Gazette* in January 1908. The twelve segments, vividly illustrated by A. C. Michael, were published as a book later that year. Wells's large following, his highly placed connections, and his reputation as the author of *Anticipations*, a series of reflections on the impact that science and technology would have on life and warfare, ensured that the book would be widely read – and even more widely discussed.

Wells was no ordinary spinner of romances: he thought of himself as an educator whose task was to enlighten the public about the dangers arising from technological inventions and the increasing complexities of life. A Fabian Socialist who deplored the inefficient and irrational organization of society, he believed that he should do everything he could to aid "moral intelligence" to overcome the "acquisitive egoism of the individual," though he was honest enough to remain dubious about the outcome of the struggle, even before the catastrophe of the First World War.[6]

One thing Wells was not dubious about was the nature of his talent. Himself a product of the lower middle class and scornful of the old "aristocratic" literature, "full of subtle meanings, hinting quotations, faint allusions," he deliberately sought to reach the masses of new readers from the lower social orders with "loud bawling books" that combined popularized science with rousing adventure and colloquial speech.[7] Though Wells's status as a major novelist may be questioned today, he had a powerful presence in the culture of the pre-1914 period.[8] Captain Ferber, for example, believed that Wells was "a great philosopher" who would have "the greatest influence" on the future of France "because the coming generation, imbued with his ideas, will favor the evolution he foresees."[9]

Wells first addressed the aviation issue in 1893 when he declared that "the advent of the flying man" was "an inevitable occurrence." Inevitable, perhaps, but not around the corner. Prudently giving himself a century's leeway, Wells predicted that Londoners would be commuting to their homes in the suburbs in winged flying machines by the year 2000.[10]

Wells's 1895 short story "The Argonauts of the Air" reminded overly optimistic readers that the conquest of the air would not come easily. Wells dismissed visions of a flying machine "with a nice open deck like a liner, and all loaded up with bombshells and guns" – such as the one that Jules Verne had offered in *Robur-le-Conquérant* – as "the easy dreaming of a literary man." To learn how to navigate the air would require "infinite labour and infinite danger." The cost in lives and treasure, Wells said, might "even exceed all that has been spent in man's conquest of the sea. Certainly it will be costlier than the greatest war that has ever devastated the world." And indeed, the two protagonists of Wells's story – the millionaire inventor Monson and his assistant Woodhouse – lose control of their bird-like aircraft, after they succeed in leaving the ground, and crash into the solid masonry of the Royal College of Science, producing a "flame of blazing paraffin that shot heavenward from the shattered engines of the machine."[11]

Yet scientific fact was overtaking scientific fiction.[12] As hyperactive and far-reaching as Wells's imagination was, it could not keep step with the breathless pace of technological innovation. In 1901 he once more predicted the realization of powered flight – "long before the year A.D. 2000, and very probably before 1950."[13] Two years later the Wrights left the ground in their first powered flight at Kill Devil Hill. Eager to turn a profit on their invention, they lost no time in trying to confirm Wells's prophesy that once flight had been achieved, the new technology would "be most assuredly applied to war."[14]

The direct inspiration for *The War in the Air*, however, was not so much the breakthrough of the Wrights – which was still regarded with skepticism by informed European aeronautical specialists when Wells wrote his book – but the widely viewed and highly publicized flights of Count Zeppelin in his giant airship, the LZ3, which in 1907 had demonstrated its ability to stay aloft for nearly eight hours and traverse a distance of 220 miles while carrying a numerous crew and a substantial load of water ballast. The personal interest Kaiser Wilhelm took in Count Zeppelin's experiments – he had contributed 100,000 marks to the construction of the LZ3 as a sign of his appreciation of the Count's persistence – suggested that the German Empire was on the verge of producing a formidable new engine of war capable of delivering men and bombs to faraway destinations.[15] For the British public, already anxious about German ambitions and Kaiser Wilhelm's decision to build a navy equal to Britain's, the rumors coming out of Count Zeppelin's base near Friedrichshafen on Lake Constance could only be alarming. People claimed that Zeppelin was constructing an even more gigantic

90. Count Zeppelin with the Kaiser.

91. The Zeppelin LZ2 above the Lake of Constance.

airship that would be capable of remaining twenty-four hours in the air. This was the type of literary opportunity that Wells was uniquely equipped to exploit.[16]

The War in the Air is the story of Bert Smallways, "a vulgar little creature," who "had lived all his life in narrow streets, and between mean houses he could not look over, and in a narrow circle of ideas from which there was no escape. He thought the whole duty of man was to be smarter than his fellows, get his hands, as he put it, 'on the dibs,' and have a good time."[17]

Bert is a worshipper of Progress. He works in a bicycle shop, smokes cheap cigarettes, buys a motorbike on credit, and thrills to the latest developments in aeronautics. In short, he is a thoroughly modern man. Bert is an excited witness of the inventor-aviator Butteridge's return to London after his epoch-making flight over England and Scotland in the world's first practical airplane. In love with speed and machines, an unthinking supporter of a firm foreign policy, Bert never considers the possibility that aeronautical progress may have a negative effect on his life, his country, and civilization in general.

After an improbable but amusingly narrated series of events, Smallways is swept across the Channel on a runaway balloon. By chance, he comes upon a secret German base filled with huge whale-like airships. Smallways tries to pass himself off as Butteridge who, we are told, had been negotiating (like the Wrights) to sell his invention to the Germans. The Germans are about to embark on an attack against the United States. Sure of their superiority in airships, they are anxious to gain control of Butteridge's airplane, so as to neutralize any danger to their own flying machines, which they call *drachenflieger* (dragon-fliers). When Bert's ruse is revealed, the infuriated German commander, the "big and blond and virile, and splendidly non-moral" Prince Karl Albert, decides to take the *Englander* along — *als Ballast*. The sinister implication is that Bert can be disposed of at any time to improve the balance of Prince Karl's airship, the *Vaterland*.

The German air fleet first sees action in the North Atlantic where a battle is raging between German and American dreadnoughts. As the battle hangs in the balance, Prince Karl sends his airplanes against the American ships. Bert saw "queer German drachenflieger, with their wide flat wings, their wheeled bodies and their single man riders, soar down the air like a flight of birds," dropping bombs and sowing destruction on the American flagship *Theodore Roosevelt*. "Smash! came a vast explosion in the forward part of the flagship, and a huge piece of metal-work seemed to lift out of her and dump itself into the sea, dropping men and leaving a gap into which a prompt

72

92. Butteridge circles Trafalgar Square in his flying machine. The illustrator, A. C. Michael, has a very vague notion of what a 1908 flying machine looked like. There are three wings, set in tandem, with pusher and tractor propellers and no evidence of an elevator or rudder.

"HIS RETURN TO LONDON . . . WAS AN OCCASION OF UNPARALLELED EXCITEMENT."

93. Smallways discovers the German air base.

"HE WAS DRIFTING HELPLESSLY TOWARDS THE GREAT IMPERIAL SECRET, THE IMMENSE AERONAUTIC PARK."

drachenflieger planted a flaring bomb."[18] Then a string of a dozen airships swept down "with unhurrying speed" to finish off the American fleet. "They kept at a height of two thousand feet or more until they were over and a little in advance of the rearmost ironclad, and then stooped swiftly down into a fountain of bullets, and going just a little faster than the ship below, pelted her thinly protected desks with bombs until they became sheets of detonating flame."[19] It was thus, Wells prophesied, that these "cheap things of gas and basket-work" would make an end of the dreadnoughts, "the weirdest, most destructive and wasteful megatheria in the whole history of mechanical invention."[20]

Flying at a speed of ninety miles an hour, the German air fleet reaches New York before news of the American naval disaster had arrived. Panicked by the sight of these monsters in the sky dropping high explosives, the city government surrenders. But the people of the city ignore the directives of their leaders and, enraged, fight on. Unable to pacify New York because he carries no land troops, Prince Karl decides to bomb its inhabitants into submission. From his vantage point on the *Vaterland* thousands of feet above Broadway, Bert Smallways watches as the German airships pour death and destruction on the buildings and crowds below:

> As the airships sailed along they smashed up the city as a child will shatter its cities of brick and card. Below, they left ruins and blazing conflagrations and heaped and scattered dead: men, women, and children mixed together as though they had been no more than Moors, or Zulus, or Chinese. Lower New York was soon a furnace of crimson flames, from which there was no escape. Cars, railways, ferries, all had ceased, and never a light led the way of the distracted fugitives in that dusky confusion but the light of burning.[21]

Simultaneously horrified and fascinated by the spectacle, Smallways realizes suddenly that such disasters could occur not only in "strange" and "foreign" places like New York but also in Bun Hill, the sleepy London suburb where he lived and worked. Britain's immunity was at an end: "nowhere in the world was there a place left where a Smallways might lift his head proudly and vote for war and a spirited foreign policy, and go secure from horrible things."[22]

The force of Wells's novel and its impact on its readers derived from his insight that the rapid development of aeronautical technology would erase the age-old distinction between combatants and civilians. Wells believed that once navigation in the air had been mastered it was inevitable that great cities would be destroyed. Killing from the sky was all too easy; because aviators were in little danger from ground fire and people seen from the air lost their humanity. Smallways finds comic the agitated movements of a man on the ground jumping to flee a falling bomb – until the bomb explodes and the man disappears in a flash of fire, vanishing absolutely.[23]

Guernica, the Blitz, Dresden, Hiroshima, and Nagasaki were all prefigured in Wells's prose and the images that his illustrator prepared for him. But the novelist's vision even exceeded the horrors of twentieth-century experience. For he went on to argue that, though aircraft would be capable of wreaking terrible destruction on civilian populations, they would be unable to bring wars to a decisive close. Neither airships nor airplanes could transport or land an occupying force. They might bring a people to its knees, but they could not consolidate their victory. Air wars would thus have a tendency to drag on indefinitely.

Moreover, a nation under attack by air could always respond by bombing the enemy's cities. Beneath the ruins of their cities, the survivors would produce fresh

94. The Battle of the North Atlantic: German airships and flying machines attack American dreadnoughts.

95. The German air fleet devastates the city of New York.

"AS THE AIRSHIPS SAILED ALONG THEY SMASHED UP THE CITY AS A CHILD WILL SHATTER ITS CITIES OF BRICK AND CARD."

airships and explosives. There was no way of preventing retaliation by air. Given their inability to carry heavy artillery, airships would be ineffective against one another and "air-fleet admirals" would avoid aerial combat, preferring to seek "the moral advantage of a destructive counterattack."[24] Such counterattacks were bound to be effective. Unlike the earth, the sky contained an infinite number of routes of access to a country's cities and centers of strength. Cheap as airships were in comparison to dreadnoughts, no nation could afford to build an aerial fleet numerous enough to protect its people. A war fought in the air, therefore, would be interminable, would spread throughout the world involving the Chinese and Japanese, and would lead to social disorganization and the collapse of civilization – not gradually, as had been the case with Rome, but in "one swift, conclusive smashing and an end."[25]

Wells left no doubt that such an outcome was inevitable unless the leading nations somehow acquired the will to master the machines they worshiped and develop values adequate to the times in which they lived. In his novel, the Germans launch the air war because of their development of a powerful engine capable of propelling their airships across the North Atlantic. Though Wells portrayed the Germans predominantly as arrogant, mechanically disciplined, ruthlessly efficient, unscrupulous, and cruel – all stereotypes common in the British and French literature of the period – he saw no cause for optimism in his own country. The half-educated Smallways of Britain lived only for speed and vulgar pleasure, which they deified under the name of Progress, and took no notice of what was going on in the rest of the world. The prospect for the British, therefore, was dismal indeed. As Wells was to write the following year, when explaining to the readers of the *Daily Mail* the meaning of Blériot's flight, "I look out upon the windy Channel and think of all those millions just over there, who seem to get busier and keener every hour. I could imagine the day of reckoning coming like a swarm of birds."[26]

When describing the aggressive and "unmoral" mentality of the Germans in his novel, Wells had mentioned the role of Rudolf Martin, noting that his writings had helped to prepare the German imagination for war in the air.[27] A low-ranking official in the Imperial Statistical Office, Martin fell out of favor with his superiors when he insisted on publishing opinions considered incompatible with the discretion required of his administrative post.[28] Prussian bureaucrats were supposed to confine themselves to implementing the ideas of their political masters. The Kaiser had decided that Germany should challenge Great Britain's mastery of the world's seas. This meant massive investment in expensive warships, and had as a corollary a policy of confrontation with Germany's chief imperial adversaries in colonial territories outside Europe. From the point of view of Germany's security, the most serious consequence of the Kaiser's policy had been to align Great Britain with France and Russia, Germany's probable enemies in a future war.

Though always respectful of the Kaiser, Martin had his own vision of Germany's future. One essential aspect of it – indeed its underlying theme – was his passionately held conviction that Germany's future lay not on the ocean but in the air. He was persuaded that man's ability to navigate the air was a turning point in world history, more important than any other invention in modern times. In the future people would divide the history of humanity into the period before and after the conquest of the air.[29] Airships and flying machines would transform culture, society, politics, and the way that nations made war. Martin believed that Germany was particularly well placed to benefit from the new technology. If properly exploited, it would make possible the creation of a German Empire that extended from Holland in the west to Mesopotamia and Persia in the east and large African holdings in the south, including Morocco.

Martin developed these ideas in two works published during the first five months of 1907. The first of these, *Berlin-Bagdad*, he termed a "novel." It might more accurately be called the mad fantasy of a German imperialist. In it Martin wove together uninformed intuitions about the immediate future of aeronautics with expansionist dreams and dangerously wishful thinking about the possibilities for European peace. The action of *Berlin-Bagdad* begins in January 1910 when the Kaiser requests and obtains from the Reichstag an appropriation of a billion marks for the purpose of building a fleet of 30,000 flying machines and 400 airships. Once in possession of these aircraft, Germany would be capable of transporting a heavily armed force of almost half a million men to England in the course of a single night. England's maritime superiority would thus be overcome. As the Kaiser concludes in an imagined speech to Germany's assembled military leaders, "Behind us lies the last period of German weakness and inferiority. The future of Germany is in the air!"[30]

Martin is careful to emphasize the peaceful intentions of Germany. Thus the series of events that leads to an expansion of the German Empire comes not as the result of German aggression but as the unexpected consequence of a war between Japan and Russia. Because of its superior air fleet, Japan, "the youngest daughter of technology," defeats Russia. In the resulting chaos, the Romanov dynasty is overthrown and the Russian Empire collapses, disintegrating into hundreds of independent states.

In 1913 a dictator emerges in Moscow; with the aid of German engineers, he assembles a fleet of Zeppelins – each capable of carrying a thousand men and their armaments – with which he plans to reconquer the Central Asian provinces of the former Russian Empire. The soldier he appoints to carry out this mission, Michael Suvorov, is a ruthless and ambitious aeronaut. Martin emphasizes that, despite his Russian surname, Suvorov is of German origin. Why? Because only a German could be so at home in the air. Deploying a combination of attack and transport airships, Suvorov stages a daring raid against the insurgent Emir of Bukhara, ruler of Central Asia. After a brief but murderous bombardment, which takes thousands of lives and levels much of his palace, the Emir capitulates. Suvorov then lands a battalion of airborne soldiers, who occupy and pacify the city. He repeats this process throughout the rebellious cities of Russian Central Asia, accomplishing in one day what had taken the Russian army centuries in the past. As Martin lightheartedly observes, two or three torpedoes, dropped over a period of five to ten minutes, were sufficient to inspire in local populations the necessary respect for Moscow's power.[31]

A fanatical aeronaut who eats, sleeps, and governs aloft, Suvorov uses his air fleet to overthrow his former master and become the new ruler of the Russian state. When Suvorov sets out to reconquer the Western territories of the old Russian Empire, he comes into conflict with Germany, the world's leading air power. Germany's thousands of airships and flying machines prevail over Suvorov and force him to take refuge in the mountains of Central Asia – but not before he succeeds in carrying out a successful bombing raid against Berlin that takes the lives of 25,000 soldiers and 16,000 civilians and leaves 70,000 wounded. Martin revels strangely in the description of the imagined destruction, as the Russian airships, fanning out "like a flight of fantastic dragons," drop huge torpedoes on the German capital from the sky.

Yet in the structure of Martin's narrative, the bombing of Berlin serves an essential purpose. From this unhappy experience the chastened Germans learn a needed lesson: in the age of air power, it is vital to expand their frontiers as far as possible so as to render the country's heartland and capital safe from enemy bombardment. Fortunately, Germany's strategic necessities correspond to the innermost desires of her neighbors. In Martin's vision, German expansion takes place through a combination of conquest and confederation. In the war against Suvorov's Russia, Germany had occupied Poland, Austria-Hungary, the Ukraine, Turkey, and the Caucasus provinces of Russia. Once in Poland, the Germans remain. According to Martin, the German occupation works to the benefit of the Poles; liberated from Russian control and their absurd nationalist ambitions, they prosper as citizens of the German Empire. Meanwhile, Austria, Hungary, and Turkey – recognizing German's overwhelming military superiority – apply for membership in a greater German Confederation. The members of the Confederation colonize Mesopotamia, transforming Bagdad into one of the urban glories of modern civilization, a city ruled by Germans and Austrians whose wealth derives from plantations farmed by Anatolians and Persians and supervised by Poles and Central Europeans.

Expansion feeds expansion. Given the strategic requirements of its air fleet, the German Confederation has no choice but to annex Holland, Flemish Belgium, Switzerland, and Morocco. When Great Britain refuses to acknowledge the legitimacy of these territorial changes, the German Chancellor reminds the British Ambassador that Germany is capable of landing an army of two million men in England by air. The crowning British humiliation comes when the British government is forced to ask for German assistance after Suvorov attacks India by air, routing the British forces there. This turn of events opens the way to further imperial expansion by those nations with major air fleets. The German Confederation conquers Persia in a day; Japan and Russia partition China. As conceived by Martin's fertile imagination, Americans vacationing in the new German city of Bagdad cannot understand why the Germans waited so long to accomplish their civilizing mission in Asia Minor. After all, the Germans were only doing what the British, Russians, and Americans had done long before. Why should anyone mind?

Time and again, Martin reminds us that all these marvelous events were made possible by the development of aeronautics and radio technology. Berlin in 1930 has become the capital of an empire with no internal problems. The new chancellor – like Michael Suvorov an aeronautical enthusiast – has created a corporate state in which conflict between workers and their employers has been eliminated by compulsory arbitration of disputes. A national-socialist party has arisen to champion the policies of the Chancellor and now dominates the Reichstag with the aid of newly granted women's votes. The Social Democratic Party has declined because German workers, transported throughout the German Confederation in airships, have come to realize how absurd and impractical the Marxist idea of giving equal rights to half-savage peoples like the blacks of Africa and the bedouins of the Middle East would be. Returning to Germany, workers are often heard asking why their country had not yet expanded into Persia, Afghanistan, and China. Capitalism was intact, social distinctions among classes had not changed, but imperial expansion had brought increased prosperity for all. The Poles were especially happy in this airminded confederation where the King of Prussia ruled, everyone spoke German, and military aircraft were piloted and manned exclusively by ethnic Germans.

Berlin-Bagdad contains some amusing pages on the ways in which the air age would transform everyday life. In Martin's vision of 1930 Berlin, flying machines were omnipresent. There was scarcely a high-school student who had not mastered the art of flying a plane. Workers had easy access to their favorite parks where gardens and tennis courts floated high above the ground. Members of the lower middle classes were whisked off to the Alps in airships for refreshing weekend vacations. Aerial thieves were pursued by aerial police. Tuberculosis was treated in hospitals suspended fifteen thousand feet above the city. Rich industrialists and real estate speculators, whose numbers had doubled since 1910, lived in distant suburbs and commuted to the capital in private flying machines along giant airways, the aerial equivalent of *Autobahnen*. Their villas had flattened roofs from which they launched their airplanes and cupolas in which they housed their airships. The upper classes fled the city in the evening during the summer months, flying toward northern latitudes and returning to Berlin the next day. Life in the air had profoundly transformed the character of the Berliners. There was no longer a foreign writer to be found, Martin fantasized, who would have dreamt of making an unfavorable comparison between the Germans and the supposedly superior Anglo-Saxons – presumably a common occurrence when Martin wrote his book, or so he seems to have thought.[32]

96. An aerial shopper.

Such scenes are reminiscent of the drawings that Albert Robida had published in France a quarter century before.[33] But unlike Robida, Martin was not satisfied to amuse. His primary purpose was to show how aircraft would change warfare and alter the balance of power among the world's Great Powers. *Der Zeitalter der Motorluftschiffahrt* (The Age of Aerial Locomotion), a series of essays published in the same month that Wilbur Wright arrived in France to sell his Flyer, spelled out his views on these matters in more prosaic language and less far-fetched detail. Like H. G. Wells, Martin understood that the inhabitants of cities would soon be at the mercy of aerial attack from airships capable of dropping torpedoes from high altitudes. Unlike Wells, however, he also foresaw the possibility of using airships against ground troops and predicted that entire armies would be transported by air at night for the purpose of outflanking the enemy or assaulting it from the rear.[34] This would make possible surprise onslaughts and lightning victories. An era of *Blitzkrieg* was at hand.

The nations who stood to gain the most from the new technology were those, like Germany, the United States, and France, that were inventive, industrial, sports-loving, and possessed a large potential pool of soldiers.[35] Smaller peoples would have to put themselves under the protection of their more powerful neighbors. The case of England was less clear. Once equipped with a fleet of airships, the British would have greater

97. The air age imagined by Albert Robida in 1883: an airship station atop Notre Dame Cathedral in Paris.

98. The air gendarmerie maintains order in the skies.

control over their empire and would possess the capacity to intervene on the Continent. But the price they would pay for these gains was the loss of their insular invulnerability. Moreover, Martin believed that aircraft would always be more effective over land than sea where the English had their strongest military forces. Weighing all these factors, he concluded that the advent of the air age would given Germany a decisive advantage over England.[36]

Such views, especially coming from an imperial official and coinciding with the successful experiments of Count Zeppelin, were bound to attract the attention of the British press. In July 1908 Lord Northcliffe instructed his Berlin correspondent, the American journalist Frederick Wile, to interview Martin. Among other things, Martin told Wile that Germany possessed the capability to transport an army of 350,000 men across the English Channel in half an hour. The new Zeppelins could comfortably carry fifty men from Calais to Dover. The Zeppelins now in the planning stage would transport twice that number. The paradoxical conclusion Martin drew from these undeniable "facts" was that the development of aerial navigation would lead towards a perpetual alliance between England and Germany. "The British Fleet will continue to rule the waves, while Germany's airships and land armies will represent the mightiest Power on the continent of Europe."[37] In other words, the condition for peace between Germany and England was England's acquiescence in German domination of the European Continent and the Middle East. Martin had no doubt that England would make the wise and prudent choice.[38]

Martin, like Wells, was inclined to subordinate the military role of flying machines to airships. Airships, he thought, were quieter, safer, and capable of carrying vastly larger loads of troops and explosives. In *Berlin-Bagdad*, flying machines have the same relationship to airships that torpedo boats had to battleships and cruisers within a naval armada: the giant Zeppelins wreak destruction from the air, while airplanes buzz around and nettle the opposing forces. In his writings of 1907, Martin's concept of an up-to-date flying machine was the 14bis with which Santos-Dumont had made his first heavier-than-air flight. Not surprisingly, Martin found it easier to imagine the airplane as an engine of pleasure, suited to charming excursions, than as an instrument of war.

It was Wilbur Wright's flights at Le Mans in 1908 that led him to reconsider his

99.   The German airship *Vaterland* under attack by an American airplane. Like Martin, Wells imagined air war in terms of naval precedents. The American airplane rams the *Vaterland* and its crew then attempts to board the airship.

UNE MENACE ALLEMANDE QUI FAIT RIRE L'ANGLETERRE. — Projet d'un débarquement d'aéroplanes imaginé par le conseiller Rudolf Martin.

position. In September, after Wright had demonstrated that he was capable of staying in the air for periods up to and beyond an hour, Martin, now president of the newly formed German Air Fleet League, evidently played with the thought of going to Le Mans. Once there he hoped to induce Wright to undertake a flight across the Channel which he would accompany by speedboat. He would then embody his impressions in a brochure describing the landing of a German army in England by means of airships proceeding to Dover from Ostend and Calais and the simultaneous bombardment of British warships by German aerial artillery.[39] One can imagine what the American's response to such a proposal would have been. Apparently, however, the meeting never took place. Wilbur was not an easy man to approach; nor did he readily tolerate foolish propositions. Nonetheless, Martin was so excited by the military implications of Wright's machine that he sought to mobilize public opinion in Germany in favor of its purchase. At the end of 1908 he suggested that, given the relatively inexpensive cost of the Flyer and the facility of its construction, it would be possible to invade England with a fleet of 50,000 airplanes, each carrying two men.[40] Though the English press scoffed at this idea, the joke lost some of its humor when Blériot successfully flew the Channel seven months later.

Martin was persuaded that the development of aviation would enable the technologically leading nations of the West to expand and consolidate their domination of colonial peoples. Flying machines would diminish the importance of distance and lead toward the unification of the world. This would work to the advantage of those peoples capable of navigating the air. The French novelist Emile Driant provided a spectacular example of Martin's contention in his exciting adventure tale of 1909, *L'Aviateur du Pacifique*.

Emile Driant is seldom read today. This was not the case, however, in 1916 when, just before his death at the Battle of Verdun, he seemed likely to succeed to Alfred de Mun's chair in the Académie Française. Young readers consumed his fantasies of war in near and distant lands as quickly as he could produce them. Nor did he lack for admirers among the custodians of the Third Republic's literary culture.

100. H. W. Koekkoek's rendering of a German invasion of England by troops carried by Wright Flyers, as imagined by Rudolf Martin. The French caption reads: "A German threat that makes England laugh."

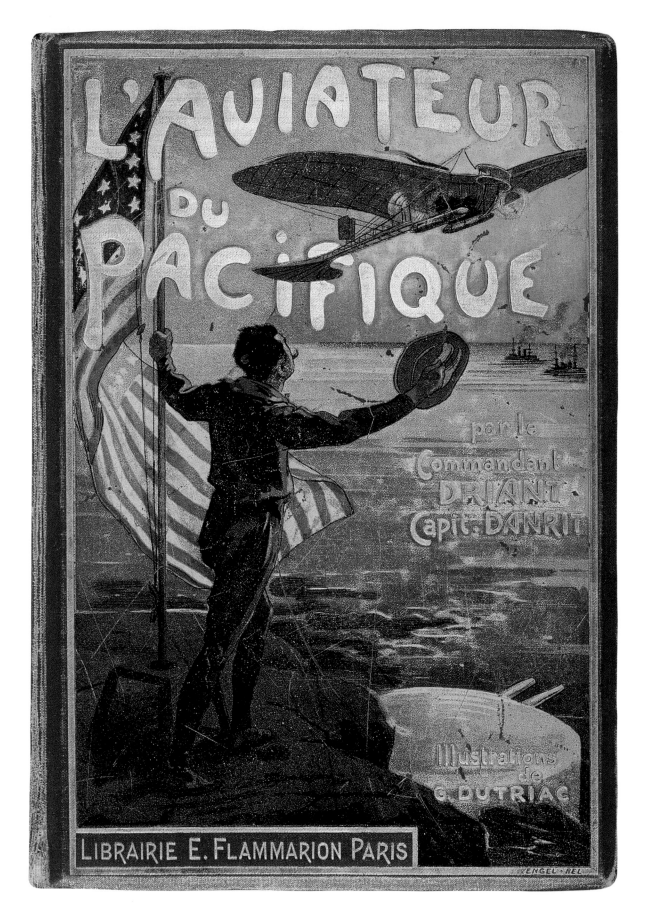

Writing was not the career Driant had set out to pursue. A graduate of the French military academy at Saint-Cyr and an exemplary infantry officer and teacher, Driant rose to the rank of major before resigning from the army in 1905 in frustration at his inability to obtain promotion. The anticlerical generals who ran the Ministry of War in the aftermath of the Dreyfus Affair approved neither of Driant's conservative political and religious convictions, nor of his friendship with the nationalist poet Paul Deroulède who staged an abortive coup d'état against the Republic in 1899. It was rumored also that some high-ranking generals could not forgive his close relationship with the charismatic General Boulanger, under whom he had served at the height of Boulanger's popularity and whose daughter he had wed in 1888.[41] After leaving the army, Driant had sought his revenge in a series of virulent articles in the nationalist press. Challenged to a duel by General Percin, whom he suspected of having blocked his promotion, Driant demonstrated his skills as a marksman, wounding his assailant twice. A devout Catholic, he then promptly paid a visit to the Bishop of Troyes, who embraced and absolved him.[42] Such were the complexities of the cultural politics of early twentieth-century France.

Driant believed that the West was on the verge of entering an era of savage wars. His novels, consciously inspired by the example of Jules Verne, related voyages to exotic places, described in painstaking and accurate detail the new technologies of war, and exalted traditional values of honor, duty, sacrifice, and love of the *patrie*. Their purpose was to provide French youth with an image of their nation – in Driant's novels universally admired for its courage, ardor, élan, and generosity – and to prepare them for the inevitable war they would have to fight. Driant made no attempt to hide the horror of technological war as he foresaw that it would be fought in the twentieth century. On the contrary, his novels abound in scenes of terrible carnage made possible by the new machines. In Driant's view, force, not right, justice, or law, would be decisive in the coming conflict. "A pox on the weak and shame on the vanquished – such is the last word of civilization."[43]

Written in the direct aftermath of Blériot's flight and interwoven with references to it, *L'Aviateur du Pacifique* was Driant's first novel to feature flying machines. We are introduced to Driant's hero, Maurice Rimbaut – an aeronautical engineer and (like Blériot) a graduate of the Ecole Centrale – on board a ship en route to Midway Island, where he is supposed to deliver to the American garrison a dirigible ordered from his firm. Though a dirigible expert, Rimbaut makes evident from the novel's first page his preference for the airplane. "It's simple, it's fast, consequently it's the future."[44] Rimbaut carries with him the plans for an airplane he has designed. Curiously, this aircraft, as imagined by Driant and depicted by his illustrator Georges Dutriac, had more in common with the Wrights' Flyer and Latham's Antoinette than it did with Blériot's single-engined monoplane.

When Rimbaut's ship is torpedoed and sunk by perfidious Japanese "bandits," he and a companion, the American lieutenant Archibald Forster, survive by using the cabin of Rimbaut's dirigible as a boat and succeed in reaching Midway. There they find a formidable workshop of war mounted by the Americans: "dynamos whirling in a circular movement so dizzy that their polished flywheels seemed immobile, gas motors running noiselessly, hydraulic platforms that raised effortlessly to the summit of the rock the gun turrets and their monstrous twin cannons, work benches, machine tools of all forms, machines for recharging the metallic cartridges used in rifles and machine guns."[45]

Learning that Midway is under siege by the Japanese and having fallen in love with

101. Emile Driant, *L'Aviateur du Pacifique* (Paris: Flammarion, 1909).

83

102. The Katebird.

103. Lieutenant Spark observes with wonder the departure of Maurice Rimbaut from the island of Midway in his airplane.

the American commandant's daughter Kate – who, he discovers to his delight, comes from French and probably Alsatian stock – Rimbaut volunteers to build an airplane, based on his design, and to fly it across the Pacific to alert the American fleet presently off the coast of California. Driant portrays the young and patriotic Rimbaut as motivated by a combination of factors. Here was a chance to save his fiancée from certain death, to help the gallant Americans – potential allies of France in a future war – against the treacherous "Japs," and at the same time to realize his dream of making a record-breaking flight that would establish France's primacy in aviation before the admiring eyes of the world. If his mission is successful, there will still be time for the fleet to reach Midway before the garrison's water supply runs out.

While Maurice assembles his flying machine, the Japanese try to enter the fort with the aid of a traitor, a stock figure in Driant's novels. The Americans respond by massacring the invaders with their machine-guns. "In less than two minutes, nothing remained on the platform but a pile of outstretched bodies, tossing about, writhing under the curtain of lead that continued to sink upon them without interruption."[46] When the surviving Japanese attempt to return to their ships, the Americans dispatch them with a combination of bayonets and machine-gun fire. " 'No prisoners!' Captain Broadway had said. And indeed there were none."[47]

This respite gives Rimbaut a chance to launch his now completed airplane by catapult. As he is about to take flight, his American rival for Kate's affections, Lieutenant Spark, feels an irrepressible urge to provoke Maurice to a duel. But then Spark's "soldier's conscience reawoke." Admiration for the aviator Rimbaut and gratitude for his generous act took precedence over personal considerations. How could a mere earthling think of killing the man who had conceived this marvel and who alone knew how to fly it?[48] Rimbaut triggered the rockets he had attached to the rear of his plane, revved the two propellers to 1800 rpm, ordered the restraining rope cut, and "with a prodigious rapidity" shot into the air: "his speed accelerated; the noise of his motor disappeared in the distance; his long fuselage shrank; once a sea-gull it now became a sea-swallow, then a tiny speck of foam, vanishing into the rays of the rising sun."[49]

Skimming over the Pacific at a height of 150 feet aboard their "great yellow bird," Rimbaut and his passenger Archibald Forster reach Honolulu after twenty-two hours of flight, only to find out that the island of Oahu had been captured by the Japanese in a sneak attack against the American base at Pearl Harbor. Avoiding the Japanese fleet, Rimbaut diverts to Maui where he has to overfly the terrifying volcano Kilauea in order to reach the hotel where he hopes to refuel. Leaving Forster behind so as to maximize the range of his machine, he avoids a Japanese patrol by catapulting himself into the crater's mouth and continues on to San Francisco where he tells his story to the Admiral of the Fleet. After a bloody battle, Midway is rescued from the Japanese. Rimbaut is reunited with his American-French love and, as the American fleet set its course toward Japan and "the merciless conflicts of the West," Rimbaut and his fiancée, their ordeals now finally over, hastened eastward, "toward France, toward Happiness."[50]

Driant's powerful and bellicose imagination foresaw the Japanese attack on Pearl Harbor, over thirty years later, and divined the critical role that flying machines would play in the conflict for control of the Pacific. Elected to the Chamber of Deputies in 1910, he became a fervent enthusiast of aviation and urged on the French military a

104. The Katebird sets out across the Pacific: this carefully detailed drawing demonstrates that Driant's illustrator, Georges Dutriac, was familiar with the Wright Flyer.

105. Maurice Rimbaut and Archibald Forster skim above the Pacific. The Katebird is equipped with pontoons for landings on water. No flying machine had yet successfully landed on water when Driant wrote this novel.

more extensive use of aircraft. An aviator accompanied by a good marksman, he argued, could strike down a general in the midst of his troops, thus disorganizing the enemy's command at the beginning of a battle. He could land behind the enemy's lines, destroy his armaments and supplies, attack his railways, and cut his telegraph and telephone communications.[51] Flying machines could transport powerful engines of destruction and soldiers who, depending on the circumstances, would have the choice of fighting from the air or on the ground.[52] They could supply troops in the field with food and munitions, relieve a besieged vanguard, or transport diplomats and envoys. They were, in brief, "a fourth arm whose speed would render it infinitely precious."[53]

Driant thought that aircraft would be especially valuable in colonial warfare because of their ability to reach, *par la voie des airs*, positions inaccessible to other forces. In his 1911 novel *Au-dessus du continent noir*, Driant described a lightning raid by air across the Tchad desert and mountains to carry out a reprisal against dissident and evil natives. The aircraft imagined by Driant for this mission had little in common with the flying machine that Maurice Rimbaut had piloted across the Pacific. A combination of monoplane and helicopter equipped with pontoons, the *Africain* had a range of a thousand kilometers and an air speed of 140 kilometers per hour. Its pontoons and

106. Emile Driant, *Au-dessus du continent noir* (Paris: Flammarion, 1911).

86

107. *L'Africain* attacks dissident tribesmen in their mountain retreat, "sowing death in a second."

108. The *Africain* uses its rotor blades to land vertically on a mountain crevasse.

adjustable wings allowed it to land on any type of surface. Viewed from afar, ground troops at first confused it with one of those enormous vultures that circled in the African sky, waiting for helpless prey; as it came nearer, it assumed the aspect of a giant dragonfly with its wings extended – one that some "mysterious entomologist" had pinned to the firmament.[54] Watching this "winged monster" land, Driant's hero, the Alsatian Captain Frisch, could only exclaim: "How beautiful it is! . . . Here is the most marvelous instrument with which science and human audacity have endowed us."[55]

Driant had grasped that, in addition to their other military uses, airplanes could be a powerful factor affecting the morale of ground troops. Surrounded by bloodthirsty native warriors, two days' march from the closest relief force, knowing that they must die, Frisch and his men take heart at the sight of the *Africain*. When the aviators on board the plane display the French tricolor as they execute a graceful turn, the troops down below tremble with emotion and pride at the thought that France led the world in aviation and dominated the African skies. Unable to restrain themselves, they burst out into spontaneous applause. "And these French soldiers, whom nothing could save, forgot their isolation and became a fervent community inspired by admiration for their race and love for their country, a country that, though it could not help them, at least sent them its most daring sons to be present at their final effort and to salute their supreme sacrifice."[56]

Implicit throughout *L'Aviateur du Pacifique* and *Au-dessus du continent noir*, explicit in Dutriac's illustrations, was the idea that within fighting forces aviators were bound to become the elite of the elite. The risks they took, the technical skills they had mastered, the courage their job required, their position high above the ground – all these qualities

would command respect and admiration from earthbound combatants. Moreover, it was not just fellow soldiers who would be impressed by aviators. As a former commander of colonial troops and a dedicated imperialist, Driant believed that French airplanes over Africa would symbolize in the eyes of the subject populations the overwhelming superiority of their white masters. *Au-dessus du continent noir* is full of references to the awe native Africans feel for French aviators. When the *Africain* takes off from Captain Frisch's beleaguered camp, the attacking Arabs are too astounded by the spectacle to shoot.

Rudolf Martin and H. G. Wells also thought that airplanes would create a new hierarchy among fighting men. Pondering the meaning of Blériot's flight, Wells concluded that the flying machine would bring to an end "the days of natural democracy." The time was coming when men would be sorted out into "those who will have the knowledge, nerve, and courage to do these splendid, dangerous things, and those who will prefer the humbler level. I do not think that numbers are going to matter so much in the warfare of the future . . . The common man with a pike . . . could chase the eighteenth-century gentleman as he chose, but I fail to see what he can do in the way of mischief to an elusive chevalier with wings."[57]

Reading Wells, Martin, and Driant today, one is struck by the rapidity with which European minds nationalized, then militarized aviation – long before general staffs were willing to take flying machines seriously as a means of waging war. The protagonists of *The War in the Air*, *Berlin-Bagdad*, and *L'Aviateur du Pacifique* and *Au-dessus du continent noir* are not individuals so much as nations. Bert Smallways, Prince Karl, Michael

109. The besieged French colonial officers rush to greet the arriving aviators.

110. Amidst fire from the attacking Africans, Captain Frisch rises in admiration to salute the departing aviators.

111. As the princess he serves ascends into the sky, an African looks up in disbelief.

Suvorov, Maurice Rimbaut, and Captain Frisch are representations and distillations of their respective countries. Characterization is forgotten by these authors in an attempt to penetrate to the national core. All these books explore the relationship between the new technology of aeronautics and the future of the major European powers. They are filled with the imagery of expansion and decline. All vibrate with the emotions generated by the certainty of an impossible war. As Wells brilliantly put the paradox of these years, "The strength and heart of the nations was given to the thought of war"; "the apparatus of war, the art and method of fighting, changed absolutely every dozen years in a stupendous progress toward perfection"; yet "people grew less and less warlike, and there was no war."[58]

To be sure, there were many, like the French senator Baron d'Estournelles de Constant, who believed that man's ability to fly would reduce the likelihood of war. They reasoned that governments would hesitate to risk war when they knew that their civilian populations, their general staffs, and they themselves would face certain retaliation by aerial attack.[59] Most commentators in this period, however, agreed with Wells, Martin, and Driant that aerial weapons would be used and that the coming war would be fought in the sky as well as on land and sea. Indeed, while professing his optimism about the chances for peace, Estournelles de Constant mounted a campaign to persuade

90

the French government to invest in aerial weaponry and was critical of French leaders for failing to keep pace with Germany in aeronautical development.[60] The paradoxes of deterence were already evident long before 1914.[61]

The writings of Wells, Martin, and Driant also suggest the different attitudes with which the French, the Germans, and the British viewed the prospect of aerial war. Driant perceived aviation as a quintessentially French science and considered it unlikely that the Germans could ever adapt themselves successfully to combat in the third dimension: "this instrument is not in the genius of their race, which is prudent and methodical. To take advantage of it, one needs daring, a quality that is above all French."[62] Blériot's flight gave Driant grounds for thinking that the French had taken the lead in aeronautics.[63] Believing as he did that war with Germany was inevitable, he never doubted that this technological primacy could be translated into a military advantage for France. And indeed, there is reason to believe that the tremendous enthusiasm for aviation and aviators that swept over France during the 1910–14 period derived at least in part from the conviction (or hope) that aviators would help France to triumph in the case of a war with Germany.[64]

Martin viewed the advent of the air age with breathless enthusiasm tempered by latent anxiety. The Germans had an opportunity to dominate the air because of their scientific and technological expertise, their dynamism, and their geopolitical position in the center of the European continent. This offered Germany "the most brilliant opportunity in world history."[65] Once masters of the skies, the Germans could create an empire equal to their talents and their energies. The airship was "tailor-made" for German soldiers.[66] But the air age also brought its perils. Germany was surrounded by industrial powers capable of developing airship fleets and populated by aeronautically gifted peoples. Writing in 1907, Martin had to acknowledge that the French led the Germans in heavier-than-air flight and would be capable of administering punishing, and perhaps decisive, air attacks against German infantry units in the case of war between the two countries. A year and a half later he predicted that Germany would prevail in an air war against France.[67] But German cities might suffer bombardment, and smaller nations now had a means of retaliating by air against a larger and more powerful adversary like Germany. It was also true that Britain would have the capability of transporting airborne troops to the continent, adding to the danger of German encirclement. Thus Martin, like his emperor Wilhelm II, wavered between feelings of aggressive expansionism and fears of encirclement and powerlessness in the face of Germany's enemies.[68]

From Wells's British perspective, the development of aeronautics was just one more nail in the coffin of a people gone hopelessly soft. The British had not contributed to the development of airships or airplanes and could only look forward to being the victims of aerial attack by their continental and Asian enemies. *The War in the Air* evokes a mysterious world of national and racial adversaries, laboring in hidden factories to devise aerial weapons with which to deliver their enemies a knockout blow. No nation could be sure of what weapons its enemies possessed because flying machines, unlike dreadnoughts, could be developed in secret and were relatively easy and cheap to produce. Hence in Wells's macabre vision of a world gone mad, it turns out that the most effective airplanes belong not to the Germans, the French, or the Americans, but to the Asiatic Confederation. His fanciful description of these machines and their pilots was designed to strike terror into the hearts of his British readers. They carried one man and were

built very lightly of steel and cane and chemical silk, with a transverse engine, and a

"THE AIRSHIP STAGGERED TO THE CREST OF THE FALL—AND
VANISHED IN A DESPERATE LEAP."

flapping sidewing. The aeronaut carried a gun firing explosive bullets loaded with oxygen, and in addition, and true to the best tradition of Japan, a sword . . . The wings of these flyers had bat-like hooks forward, by which they were to cling to their antagonist's gas-chambers while boarding him . . . These light flying-machines were carried with the fleets . . . and were capable of flights from two to five hundred miles according to the wind.[69]

Indeed, a growing awareness of the seriousness of the "yellow peril" is one of the leit-motifs of Wells's book. Martin and Driant also wrote at length on this theme and foresaw bloody conflicts between the West and East; but they were inclined to think – or they persuaded themselves – that the West would prevail because of its technological superiority. Wells did not share their optimism. One of the most striking scenes in Wells's novel portrays the destruction of the German airship *Hohenzollern*. Outmaneuvered by the sleeker and faster Asian airships, severely damaged by the superior Japanese airplanes, "which hovered and alighted like a swarm of attacking bees," the *Hohenzollern* bursts into flames, collapses, and is swept over Niagara Falls. Watching this scene, Bert Smallways instinctivly identifies with his German captors against the yellow invaders. For him, Wells tells us, the destruction of the *Hohenzollern* "meant – what did it not mean? – the German airfleet, [his German friend] Kurt, the Prince, Europe, all things stable and familiar, the forces that had brought him, the forces that seemed indisputably victorious. And it [the *Hohenzollern*] went down the rapids like an empty sack and left the visible world to Asia, to yellow people beyond Christendom, to all that was horrible and strange!"[70] After defeating the Germans in the air, the Japanese pilots pursue their helpless adversaries on the ground, using their razor-sharp swords to slice them up – like sausages.

Driant's unalloyed enthusiasm for aeronautics and Martin's ambiguity therefore stand

112. The German airship *Hohenzollern* is swept over Niagara Falls after being disabled by Japanese airplanes.

113. The Japanese pilots pursue German survivors of the *Hohenzollern* with their samurai swords.

out in sharp contrast to Wells's pessimism and apprehensions. Whatever hopes he harbored, Wells commented darkly in another novel of 1909, were not identified with the British Empire or "any of the great things of our time."[71] Could mankind have prevented the war in the air and the subsequent collapse of civilization? This question, Wells suggested, was as idle as asking whether mankind could have prevented the slow decay of Assyria, Babylonia, and the Roman Empire. "They could not because they did not, they had not the will to arrest it."[72] He might have added that they did not arrest it because there were many, like Martin and Driant, who thought their nations might benefit from the use of these new weapons.

Martin lived to read about the Zeppelin raids against London and Paris that he had predicted eight years before. When he died in 1916, the Russian Empire was indeed on the verge of disintegration. The Communist state that replaced it would, like Suvorov's in *Berlin-Bagdad*, give a high priority to aviation, as would the Nationalist Socialist regime that came to power in Germany in 1933. "We must become a nation of flyers," the ex-ace Hermann Goering said repeatedly in his radio broadcasts; and, like Martin, what he had in mind when he exalted aviation was not just a faster means of transportation or an instrument of national defense but a technological discipline that would foster the development of the values necessary for survival and domination in the hard and ruthless conditions of twentieth-century life.[73]

As for Driant, he got the opportunity to experience at first hand the war he had so long predicted, and it was every bit as bloody and costly in human lives as he had imagined it would be. He died in February 1916 – and won the place in French military history he had always coveted – at the head of his beloved Chasseurs while valiantly trying to repulse the first attack of what came to be known as the Battle of Verdun.[74] That battle, like so many Driant had described, was merciless; and hundreds of thousands of men fell victim to the new machines of war that he had depicted with such relentless fascination, among them airplanes which were deployed by the hundreds with telling effect.[75] How many people, walking down the quiet street that bears his name in the center of Paris behind the beautiful gardens of the Palais Royal, suspect that this hero of Verdun was also one of France's leading prophets of war in the air? Indeed, France's most famous ace – Georges Guynemer – had been an avid reader of Driant's aerial romances. Perhaps he had dreamed as a young boy of emulating Maurice Rimbaut's exploits. Fiction into fact.

114. Colonel Driant at his command post in the Bois des Caures near Verdun in January 1916 just before the German attack.

L. Sabattier

4

Poets of Space

A new civilization, a new life, new
skies! Where is the poet who will be
capable of singing this epic?

Gabriele D'Annunzio, 1910[1]

ERONAUTICAL TECHNOLOGY lagged well behind the visions of Wells, Martin, and Driant. But as they wrote and published, war in the air was quickly losing its utopian quality and imposing itself as a topic of discussion among civilian and military leaders. It was in 1909, the year when Driant's novel *L'Aviateur du Pacifique* appeared, that the United States and the European Great Powers embarked on the development of aerial fleets. From this point on, the military would exercise an increasingly significant influence on the development of aviation. The threat and fear of war generated funds for the purchase of aircraft that would not otherwise have been available. This demand, in turn, both accelerated and shaped technical innovation. As Ferber predicted, military leaders quickly came to prefer airplanes to airships and dirigibles because they were faster, more maneuverable, and easier to hangar. Their civilian masters supported them in this preference because airplanes were also cheaper, hence easier to justify to legislators looking for ways to cut fiscal corners. Though generals like Britain's Douglas Haig and France's Ferdinand Foch discounted the military value of airplanes, no Great Power dared to be without an air arm. By the summer of 1914, when war came, Europe was ready to fight in the air. In a mere five years, some of Wells's more far-fetched prophecies were on the verge of becoming realities.[2]

These five years, however, mark an entire epoch in the history of aviation. In 1909 military investment in aviation was still halting and halfhearted. When thinking about the future of aviation, even a professional military officer like Ferber thought primarily in terms of the flying machine's civilian uses. He believed that the invention of the airplane would give rise to a new industry with a mass civilian clientele. Writing in 1909, he predicted that soon airplanes capable of carrying three or four persons would be built. Flying would become fashionable, just as cycling had in 1893 and motoring had a decade later. It was then, and only then, that the aviation business would truly take off: those aircraft manufacturers who had been able to hold on through the early years would begin to pay dividends to their shareholders, and more conservative investors would be drawn toward a new and potentially profitable industry.[3]

Ferber did not go so far as Santos-Dumont, who had recently predicted that it would not be long before everyone would possess his own airplane.[4] Rather he suggested that,

115. The *beau monde* at the Rheims air show in August 1909. By Louis Sabbatier.

116. Pegasus, the favorite flying machine of poets.

given the airplane's ability to transport a relatively light load at high speeds, it would play the role of the old stage-coaches that transported precious goods, urgent messages, high civil servants, and affluent people in a hurry. Since busy travelers were more and more numerous, the airplane had a natural and growing clientele just waiting to be tapped.[5]

The prospects were dazzling; the profits were potentially great. Before this new industry could develop, however, Ferber believed that the airplane would have to demonstrate its practicality. This would require, as it had in the case of the bicycle and the automobile, a transitional period when wealthy amateurs used the new machines for excursions in the countryside and airminded sportsmen competed in races sponsored by newspapers. These races would capture the imagination of the masses and would have important economic consequences by eliminating, in a Darwinian struggle for existence, those producers incapable of refining and simplifying their designs. The exploits of aviator-sportsmen would advertise the virtues of the machines they flew, bring orders and investment capital to their builders, and push them to extract from their creations ever greater performance, and especially ever higher speeds. "We'll go from 150 to 200 kilometers an hour, we'll go even further, we'll try to attain 300 kilometers an hour, which for the airplane will be as difficult to obtain as 100 was formerly for the automobile. That will put Marseille three hours away from Paris, Moscow a day away from Paris, Peking forty-eight hours from Paris!"[6]

A better prophet than aircraft designer or pilot, Ferber had foreseen with uncanny prescience the outlines of the intermediary period that would fall between the realization of powered flight and its exploitation as a weapon of war or a means of transporting goods and people: a period when airplanes would be flown by "sportsmen" and aviation would be perceived by the general public as a thrilling but peculiarly dangerous type of spectator sport. For the next five years, aviators would risk life and limb, seeking to outfly their rivals and break record after record. If their exploits did not immediately create a mass market for airplanes, as Ferber had predicted, it was because airplanes remained more expensive than automobiles and the challenge of flying an airplane was considerably more daunting (and dangerous) than that of driving a car.[7]

In the long run, of course, Ferber was to be proved right. People in a hurry – *les gens pressés* – would learn to travel by air even if they disliked it. But curiously, what Ferber did not anticipate was the impact that this new sport would have on European culture – and especially that form of European culture generally called modernism. Asked in July 1909 by the newspaper *L'Auto* what uses the airplane would be put to five years hence, Paul Adam, the well-known writer and partisan of sport as a builder of character, expressed doubts that bourgeois souls, attached to their security, could be persuaded to entrust themselves regularly to this new and perilous form of transportation. The flying machine, he predicted, would remain "a kind of marvellous Pegasus" that only "poets of space" would dare to mount.[8] One wonders if Adam realized, when he wrote these lines, that it was also true that many Western men of letters – including himself – would find the poetry of flight an irresistible theme. Indeed some would go so far as to identify flight with poetry, and one Russian Futurist would even temporarily give up the writing of poetry in favor of the practice of flight.

Poets, however, found themselves responding to events that, on their face at least, seemed far removed from the world of literature. For aviation, as it developed between 1908 and 1914, was a product of inventors, professional sportsmen, and entrepreneurs, all driven by a complex of motives in which the dream of conquering the air was mixed inextricably with patriotism, the competitive spirit, and the expectation of financial gain. The armies of capitalism marched hand in hand with the avant-gardes of technology and sport.

To be sure, it was not the best-financed inventors who succeeded in achieving powered flight. The Frenchman Clément Ader and the American Samuel Langley, though well supplied with government subsidies, failed.[9] The Wright brothers developed their Flyer with an investment of a few thousand dollars, money generated from their modest bicycle business. They resisted Chanute's attempt to find them wealthy backers and chose instead to perfect their invention alone and at their own pace. In France, Ferber received encouragement but little else from his military superiors. His disciple Gabriel Voisin launched the world's first aircraft factory on a shoestring. As Ferber wittily – and perhaps somewhat bitterly – put it in 1909, aviation had issued "without capital investment from the ideas and work of a very small group of people who, through the opaque curtain of ignorance, had been blinded by the evidence" [that nothing prevented human beings from flying].[10]

Still, alluring as this vision of the genesis of aviation is – resplendent with the romance of lonely and inspired inventors surrounded by a curtain of "opaque ignorance" – it omits some important facts. In France, the people who created the aviation industry possessed the "capital" of higher and often technical education, along with familial experience and connections in the world of business and finance.[11] Some, like Santos-Dumont, Louis Blériot and Henry Farman, had ample funds with which to underwrite their folly. Moreover, they had behind them an organization – the Aéro-Club de France – whose well-heeled leaders had the enthusiasm, the patriotic spirit, and the generosity to invest in aviation in the form of hundreds of thousands of francs' worth of prizes that they created between 1904 and 1909.[12] They were joined by newspaper publishers, like Lord Northcliffe and the American expatriot James Gordon Bennett who established an annual prize of $5,000 for the fastest pilot in the world. One of the leaders of the Aéro-Club later claimed that by the beginning of 1909 aviation had at its disposal financial incentives such as no other industry and no other scientific effort had ever had.[13]

In France, at the beginning, prizes were given for individual exploits performed under carefully specified conditions and, whenever possible, monitored by the leaders of the national Aéro-Club: exploits such as the first flight of twenty-five meters or more made by Santos-Dumont in October 1906; the first flight of one kilometer in the form of a closed circuit with turns by Henry Farman in January 1908; and Wilbur Wright's record for time spent in the air on the last day of the same year. The stimulus to Blériot's Channel flight had also been a prize: the thousand pounds offered by Lord Northcliffe's *Daily Mail*. These exploits had all attracted excited crowds; public enthusiasm for the new invention was clearly there, dry tinder waiting for the match capable of igniting it. Why not, then, offer the public aerial spectacles in which people could participate more directly, thereby transforming the public's enthusiasm into a source of profits? In short, there was every reason to believe that flying, like other sports, could be made to pay.

Always alert to the financial possibilities of their invention, the Wrights had played with the idea of flying exhibitions for Barnum and Bailey's three-ring circus, fresh from a great success in touring Europe's major cities. Because of the technical problems involved in such an enterprise and the lack of enthusiasm of the brothers, the deal fell through. Farman flew some exhibitions in the United States in 1908, with disappointing results. Eventually the Wrights and others would organize teams of aviators which would tour major cities throughout Europe and the United States.

But exhibitions held less promise than tournaments in which well-known aviators would come together to compete for prizes of various types. The first of these meetings

117. The fusion of champagne and the Wright Flyer against the background of Rheims cathedral.

118. A popping champagne cork provides lift for Henri Farman's flying machine.

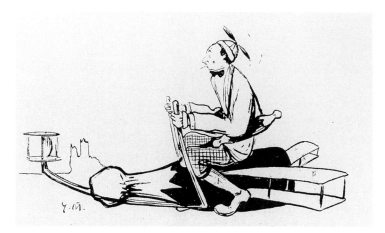

– or meets, as they were called in the United States – was scheduled to be held in Monaco in the spring of 1909; but in spite of the substantial prizes being offered, no aviator volunteered to compete.[14] Other meets, scarcely more successful, were organized in the French cities of Douai and Vichy. Still, the new entrepreneurs of the air were not discouraged. They sensed that advances in aviation technology and flying skills were catching up with their vision of a tournament of aeronautical champions. Events proved them right. In this area of aviation, as in so many others, the French showed themselves to be innovators. During the last week of August 1909, just one month after Blériot flew the Channel, the world's leading aviators gathered at Rheims, an old cathedral city to the east of Paris. No one who attended this event would ever forget it. As Wilbur Wright had demonstrated the previous year at Le Mans, aeronautical technology had an uncanny ability to transform itself into spectacle and art.

The Rheims meeting had been carefully organized by a group of investors who gathered together under the name of the Compagnie Générale de l'Aérolocomotion. The company's stock was floated on the Paris Bourse in May 1909 at a price three times their 40,000 franc initial investment, an indication that the company's directors had ambitions that went well beyond the contribution to "aeronautical progress" that they emphasized in their prospectus.[15] The officers of the company no doubt felt encouraged by the fact that the Aéro-Club de France had agreed to lend its prestige to the event and to monitor the competitions.[16] They could also take heart in the fact that the very grand Marquis (soon to be Prince) de Polignac had assumed the presidency of the committee organizing the event. As the head of the house of Pommery, he was well placed to tap the resources of the major champagne producers of the Marne, who contributed the lion's share of the nearly 200,000 francs in prize money and the additional 225,000 francs judged necessary for the preparation of the site.[17] The combination seemed inevitable. Just as champagne was the quintessential French drink, so aviation seemed destined to become the typically French means of locomotion. Both embodied the qualities of the French "race": élan, esprit, audace.[18]

   The site chosen for the meet was the plain of Bétheny, three miles to the north of Rheims on the road toward Neufchâtel. It was here, on this great clearing with occasional clumps of trees and a distant horizon bordered by rolling hills, that the President of France, Félix Faure, had invited the Russian Tsar in 1901 to witness a review of the French army and to consecrate the recent Franco-Russian alliance. The organizers of the meet had spared no expense to provide the spectators an experience with all the comforts and distractions of a world fair. A railroad track had been laid to

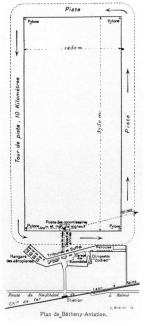

119. Bétheny-Aviation.

transport the spectators from Rheims to Bétheny, and a station christened Fresnay-Aviation had been erected to receive them. Three hundred meters from the terminal, four grandstands, with elegantly outfitted boxes, had been built to accommodate three thousand people. A large and well-stocked buffet restaurant, decorated with festoons of electric lights in the form of pearls, was created to satisfy the appetites of those able to afford it. Bars dispensed the finest champagne. Fifty cooks and 150 waiters had been mobilized to prepare and serve *les gens aisés* over two thousand meals a day.

Such a setting demanded spectators of uncommon quality, and the Marquis de Polignac's committee was able to produce them. The President of France Armand Fallières himself agreed to grace the meeting with an official visit. He came accompanied by leading members of the government and made a display of heartfelt enthusiasm for the aviators, who risked their lives in dismal weather to entertain him, shouting "Bravo, Bravo" each time they flew past his box.[19] Dignitaries from a score of countries, including the Roosevelts, David Lloyd George, and the future king of Belgium, were glimpsed among the cheering crowds. High ranking military observers, like General John French of Great Britain, came to see what flying machines could actually do. More practical, the Japanese sent engineers to observe *how* planes flew. Hotel rooms in Rheims were in such demand that they fetched the extraordinary sum of a hundred francs per night – if you could find one.

Despite its aristocratic cachet, the meet at Rheims was designed from the beginning to be a popular festival that brought together the classes in a celebration of the new and

120.   The grandstands at Bétheny-Aviation as Latham saw them from an altitude of 450 feet. (this photograph was taken from the dirigible Zodiac).

121.   One of the restaurants at Rheims.

122. A painting by Albert Brenet evoking the visit of President Faillières to Rheims on 22 August 1909. The artist's rendering of the festive atmosphere neglects to record the dismal weather. Because of gusty winds and heavy rain, Faillières saw more flying machines in their hangars than in the sky.

very French technology. In this respect, the organizers followed a pattern that was already well established at the great race tracks of Longchamps and Auteil in Paris: folk unable or unwilling to afford grandstand seating were allowed for a cheaper admission fee to take up quarters on the open grounds. They made their way from Rheims and the surrounding villages on foot or in horse drawn wagons and endured the jostling and milling crowds on the road to Bétheny "with cheerful eagerness."[20] Once within the enclosure, their colorful and extraordinarily diverse costumes created a striking contrast with the elegantly costumed ladies and gentlemen in the boxes. High and lowborn could wander about the stands that sold toy dirigibles and helicopters and listen to the musicians who played fashionable songs, like the pleasantly ribald "Dans mon aéroplane." Harry Harper, who accompanied Lord Northcliffe to Rheims, found the meet's atmosphere like Derby Day, with a touch of Ascot and Cowes Week thrown in. "An air of delightful gaiety pervaded the whole scene."[21]

The Grande Semaine de l'Aviation de la Champagne had been announced as the world's first international flying meeting. In reality, all the entrants, except for the Englishman George Cockburn and the American Glenn Curtiss, were French. This fact reflected the leading role that the French, in the space of a few short months, had come to achieve in aviation. It also revealed the inability of the organizers to recruit *le grand absent*, Wilbur Wright. Orville had wanted to participate, convinced that he could "beat

the pants'' off the competition. Instead, Wilbur insisted that Orville should travel to Berlin, where he flew exhibitions before crowds as large as the ones at Rheims and concluded a deal with the Germans similar to the one that the Wrights had earlier made in France. Wilbur meanwhile was busy filing a suit against Glenn Curtiss for infringement of the Wrights' wing-warping patents. Trophies were one thing, business another.[22]

The meeting at Rheims got off to an unpromising start on Sunday, 22 August. Torrential rains had turned the field into a sodden quagmire. Gusty winds out of the

123.   The President of France (lower center) and his suite watch Louis Paulhan fly on 24 August 1909.

124.   Spectators standing alongside the race course at Rheims.

Chansons de FRAGSON

Dans mon Aéroplane

Paroles de Christiné-Christien
Musique de H. FRAGSON

CHANT SEUL NET 0.35
PIANO & CHANT NET 2 Fr.

CHRISTINÉ Éditeur - PARIS
33, Faubourg St Martin

Tous droits d'exécution publique, de traduction, de reproduction et d'arrangements réservés pour tous pays y compris la Suède, la Norwège et le Danemark

Copyright in the United States of America by CHRISTINÉ
International Secured ... "All rights of public performance reserved"

LE PETIT PARISIEN
Le plus fort tirage des journaux
du Monde entier

Grande Semaine aéronautique
DE LA CHAMPAGNE
Du 22 au 29 Août 1909

M. FARMAN   M. BLÉRIOT   M. WILBUR WRIGHT

M. LATHAM   M. SOMMER

PROGRAMME

par le PETIT PARISIEN à ses Lecteurs

125. The fashionable 1909 song *In my airplane*. The composer H. Fragson is pictured above. The lyrics, by Christine-Christien, begin innocently enough but become more and more erotically suggestive.

Not long ago little old Suzanne
Said to her lover
Oh! How bored I am
I don't like cars any more,
I don't like horses
I want something new.

He answered: Darling,
The other day
I got you a gift.
It's something really swell
That I bought from Monsieur
  Wright.

Oh! come, oh! come,
Come up in my airplane
It's just like a bird
It stays up in the air as it should.
Oh! come, oh! come,
Come on, little old Suzanne
You'll go crazy honey
When you've seen my little bird.

126. The promoters of the Rheims meeting evidently did not give up hope that Wilbur Wright would compete until the end. The cover of the program published by *Le Petit Parisien* portrayed Wright among the most famous aviators scheduled to participate in the event.

127. Orville Wright being congratulated by the German Crown Prince after his exhibition flights at Potsdam in August 1909.

128. Those "without wings" were forced to endure the mud during the first days of the meet.

southwest made flight impossible. The twenty thousand people who made their way to Bétheny on the opening day were greeted with a downpour apt to dampen the most ebullient spirits. The only heroic sight to be seen was the Marquis de Polignac gliding above the mud on his handsome horse, struggling to maintain some modicum of order. Not even those privileged to have boxes in the grandstands were spared. Ladies grumbled as their elegant satin shoes sank in the mud and were discolored. "What a lot of grimaces!" wrote the correspondent of *Le Petit Parisien*, who made no attempt to hide that he found the plain of Bétheny a sad and depressing place to be in the final days of summer.[23]

Then, toward the end of the day, the weather finally cleared. White flags appeared on the distant hangars showing that flight was imminent. The Wright Flyers, piloted by Paul Tissandier, the Count de Lambert, and Eugène Lefebvre, were catapulted into the air. They competed for the right to represent France in the speed race for the Gordon Bennett Prize that would be held on the next to last day of the week-long meet. Lefebvre, a recent recruit to aviation, left the crowd grasping with his graceful figure eights and his sharp turns around the pylons, almost scraping his wings on the ground. The great revelation of the afternoon was to see two, three, and even four airplanes flying at the same time. When Lefebvre ascended to three hundred feet, dived to within a few feet of the ground, and then climbed while the Count de Lambert flew beneath him, the correspondent for *L'Intransigeant* felt that he and all those present had been treated to a preview of "the wonders that the near future has in store for us."[24]

Excitement built as the days passed. Record after record was broken. Even the weather improved. On the fifth day, the wind calmed and the August sun came out. The wait between flights became shorter. On the sixth day, as blazing sun gave way to lingering twilight and nightfall, Henry Farman set a new world's record for distance by flying 112 miles and won the Grand Prix de la Champagne. Known for his avoidance of heights, Farman had hugged the ground as he completed more than eleven circuits

129. Eugène Lefebvre banking around a pylon at Rheims.

130. Latham, Paulhan, and Farman being photographed as they fly around the course at Rheims. The hangars are to the right and the stands to the left. Latham was known for his willingness to fly higher than other aviators of the period.

131. Henry Farman on the flight with which he won the Grand Prix de Champagne for the longest distance traversed without landing: Notice how low Farman is flying.

of the course before running out of fuel. The following day the American Glenn Curtiss defeated Louis Blériot and won the Gordon Bennett Prize in a thrilling race to see who could cover twenty kilometers in the fastest time. Accelerating and then leaning into the turns like the motorcycle champion he was, Curtiss bettered Blériot's time by 5.6 seconds and became the fastest man in the air, as he already was on the ground. On the last day he beat Blériot again over a course of thirty kilometers, reminding the French that, despite the absence of the Wright brothers, they still had to take into account the Americans.

But as usual it was the adored Hubert Latham – living symbol of the *style belle époque*

– who gave the crowd its strongest emotions.[25] Gertrude Bacon, a veteran balloonist, later remembered Latham's pursuit of Louis Paulhan as one of the most thrilling moments of the meeting. Paulhan was in the air, making his way around the ten kilometer course. To Bacon, Paulhan's Voisin flying machine seemed like a "big weary bird swaying with strong but tired wings" as it arduously rounded the white pylon two miles away and headed back toward the grandstands. When Paulhan drew level with the stands, the crowd began to cheer. Then the cheers became delirious:

> A sudden, mighty rush and into the air plunged another bird – but such a bird! – a fierce hawk, or better simile, a dragonfly – a darting, graceful, immensely powerful dragonfly, instilled with the true beauty of flight, with boundless reserves of strength and speed, steady as a rock, graceful exceeding with its long shapely body and its single pair of outstretched wings. "Latham! Latham!" shrieked the ecstatic crowd, waving hats and handkerchiefs and programs in wild applause, while high over the toiling, lumbering Voisin soared the lovely monoplane; and off like a dart round the track, before the background of a rising thundercloud against whose black the beautiful white wings and the flashing propellers stood out as a dream of pure loveliness.[26]

On the last day, Latham tried for the altitude prize. Ascending into the sky in leisurely circles, he climbed past the heights that had earlier been reached by Paulhan and Farman until he attained the extraordinary altitude of 508 feet. No one had ever come close to flying so high before. The spectators watching him with binoculars had the impression that he was about to disappear, a small speck in the sky. They no longer heard the sound of his engine. They no longer saw the blur of his propeller. To the correspondent of the Berlin *Illustrierte Aeronautische Mitteilungen*, it must have been thus in prehistoric times that monster and now extinct birds had flown after their prey. "And stronger than ever came upon us the longing inherited from our forefathers after freedom and independence." Certainly Farman, Curtiss, and the others could claim to have accepted, in their imperfect machines, the battle with the elements. But their achievement dwindled in significance as this German journalist watched Latham's giant bird ascend, "a picture more beautiful in its harmonic forms that one can imagine."[27]

From every point of view, the Grande Semaine de l'Aviation de la Champagne was judged to be a great success. Five hundred thousand people paid attendance, two hundred and fifty thousand on the last day alone. Hundreds of thousands more watched from the surrounding hills. The stockholders of the Compagnie Générale de l'Aérolocomotion made a clean profit of close to 800,000 francs, over twenty times their initial investment.[28] So much champagne had been consumed that it was rumored that the champagne manufacturers had more than doubled in profits what they had donated in prizes.[29] As for the pilots, they could scarcely complain. They carried away 188,500 francs in rewards for their prowess and courage. Among the most successful were Farman with 60,000 francs; Latham with 55,000; and Curtiss with 38,000. For them, Rheims boded well for the future. Like championship tennis players at Wimbledon, they now prepared to scatter throughout the world and to pursue their fortune elsewhere.

The big winner, though, was the cause of aviation. No longer was it possible to doubt that the airplane had come to stay. In one week twenty-two aviators had taken to the sky over a hundred times in airplanes of ten different types. Altogether they had flown 2,462 kilometers, the distance from Paris to Moscow.[30] Every record set by the Wrights during the past year had been broken.[31] Watching one aviator after another take to the sky and traverse the ten-kilometer circuit around the course at Bétheny, *Le Petit Parisien*'s correspondent thought back to the situation a year ago, when Wilbur Wright began his flights at Hanaudières, and wondered if the last 365 days had been a dream. "Yes, to be honest, everything that has happened astonishes you, surprises your imagination, leaves you deeply moved and disconcerted, your head a bit dizzy as if you'd had too much to drink".[32] His colleague from *L'Auto* had similar thoughts but ended by asking himself where all this crazy progress in aviation would lead: "Will our life be better? Will we ourselves be better?" Leaving his questions unanswered, he concluded that the week at Rheims would have incalculable results for the future of human transportation. In five years people would commute by aerial buses and would be able to purchase small planes that could average 25 kilometers an hour and fly two or three meters above the ground.[33]

132, 133. Glenn Curtiss races past the grandstand in pursuit of the Gorden Bennett prize while Louis Blériot watches anxiously.

134. The return from Bétheny.

135. Georges Scott's rendering of the race between Paulhan and Latham.

136. Blériot's crash at Rheims.

137. The popular aviator Eugène Lefebvre at the controls of his Wright Flyer. Just before his fatal crash, Lefebvre had told his family and friends: "Yes I will succeed and I'll make some money, unless I break my neck." (quoted by the *Le Petit Parisien*, 9 September 1909.)

Miraculously, despite several potentially fatal crashes – two alone by the accident-prone Blériot – no one had been killed or seriously injured during the week at Rheims. Just eight days after the meeting ended, one of the crowd's favorite pilots, the young engineer Eugène Lefebvre, was killed while testing a Wright Flyer at Juvisy. Lefebvre, who had taught himself to fly only a few months before, lost control while making a low turn and crashed in front of a restaurant where he had just eaten with some friends. He was the first Frenchman to die in an airplane. Shortly before taking off, Lefebvre had been informed that the organizing committee at Rheims had awarded him a special prize of a thousand francs for his exploits during the meeting.[34]

Commenting on the circumstances of Lefebvre's death, Ferber explained why the young engineer's death would be followed by others. The first aviators – the Wrights, Farman, Delagrange – never forgot that they were flying a half ton of metal miraculously suspended in the air. They avoided high altitudes and cross-country flights. The more recent pilots, like Lefebvre, were less prudent. They took risks in order to win the favor of the public. Lefebvre, in particular, had distinguished himself by his penchant for climbing and then plunging toward the ground, reascending just as it appeared than he was about to crash. A year ago, Ferber said, Lefebvre's death would have temporarily halted the progress of aviation. Now it would not delay the movement for a single day: "we are too thirsty for air, for space, and for speed to delay the realization of a discovery that history has been waiting for such a long time!"[35] Two weeks after writing these lines, Ferber was killed during a meeting at Boulogne after stalling while making a turn only eight meters above the ground.

Ferber once again was right. The West was much too intoxicated by speed and the exhilaration of flight to refuse the sacrifice of human lives that the conquest of the air would demand. Indeed, the danger of flight enhanced its attraction to the public. The day after Lefebvre's death, yet another meeting opened, this one at Brescia, a small Italian city east of Milan. Blériot was there, as was Curtiss. Also entered in the

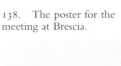

138. The poster for the meeting at Brescia.

139. The course at Brescia.

I. CIRCVITO AEREO-BRESCIA
SETTEMBRE 1909. — 100000 LIRE DI PREMI

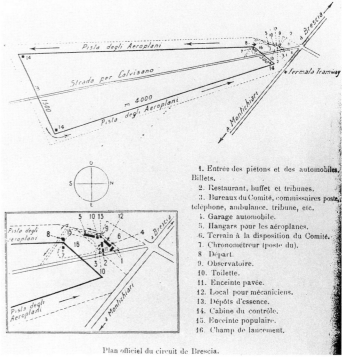

1. Entrée des piétons et des automobiles. Billets.
2. Restaurant, buffet et tribunes.
3. Bureaux du Comité, commissaires poste, téléphone, ambulance, tribune, etc.
4. Garage automobile.
5. Hangars pour les aéroplanes.
6. Terrain à la disposition du Comité.
7. Chronométreur (poste du).
8. Départ.
9. Observatoire.
10. Toilette.
11. Enceinte pavée.
12. Local pour mécaniciens.
13. Dépôts d'essence.
14. Cabine du contrôle.
15. Enceinte populaire.
16. Champ de lancement.

Plan officiel du circuit de Brescia.

competition were the French pilot Henri Rougier and Mario Calderara, an Italian army officer whom Wilbur Wright had taught to fly in Rome the previous May.

Among the thousands who flocked to Brescia was the young Franz Kafka, who was vacationing with his friends Max and Otto Brod at Riva, a spa on the shores of Lake Garda. None of them had ever seen a flying machine. When they read that an aviation meet was going to take place in Brescia, they enthusiastically decided to attend, despite the fact that they were running low on cash.[36] Kafka, it appears, was especially keen to make the trip, perhaps because he was in search of new impressions to stimulate his literary imagination, which had been stagnant during the previous months. An inwardly turned young man of fragile nerves given to fits of depression, Kafka had come to doubt his literary gifts. He felt his talent was seeping away and complained of a pressure in his stomach, "as if the stomach were a person and wanted to cry."[37] Anxious to rescue his friend from the doldrums, Max Brod challenged him to a contest: both would take notes on the aviation meet; when it was over, they would compare their texts to see who had done the better job. Or so he wrote later in life. If the story is true — and there is no reason to doubt it — we can only be grateful that he had the good idea of urging Kafka to write "The Aeroplanes at Brescia."[38]

In Kafka's sketch, Brescia was teeming with people. The local paper reported proudly

140. Franz Kafka in 1908.

that the town was so overcrowded with visitors – some from as far away as Naples! – that prices were rising splendidly and the militia was needed to protect the buffets. On the first day of the meeting, in addition to those in the grandstands, fifty thousand people had paid a smaller entrance fee to watch from the field. It was thus with a mixture of courage and *Angst* that Kafka and his friends set off to join the crowds at Brescia. Courage, he wrote, because "where there is such a dreadful mass of people, usually everything proceeds in a nicely democratic way, and where there is no room one needn't look for it. *Angst* – *Angst* because of the way Italians organize such undertakings . . ."[39]

In Brescia Kafka and his friends were directed by the organizing committee to an inn that, on first glance, was the dirtiest he had ever seen. They spent the night in a room that Brod later remembered as having a hole in the middle of the floor through which they could look down to the bar that lay beneath.[40] The next day, after an hour-long ride on a "wretched train," surrounded on all sides by laughing people and showered by soot and dust, they arrived at the aerodrome where they were greeted by prancing cavalry. "Order and misadventures seem equally impossible."[41]

Once inside the enclosure, they visited the hangars: with their curtains closed, they looked "like the closed-up stages of a touring dramatic company." Over each flew the flag of the aviator's country; on each was written the aviator's name. "*And Blériot?* we ask. Blériot, of whom we have been thinking all the time, where is Blériot?" Instead they came across Glenn Curtiss, sitting alone and patiently reading the *New York Herald*, waiting for the moment when the wind would fall sufficiently so that he could fly. When they returned half an hour later, Curtiss was still staring at the same page.

Turning his attention to the field, Kafka found it large, featureless, dusty, an "artificial desert" in an almost tropical land. The few objects to be seen on it seemed "forlorn." It had none of the charming features to be found on other sports fields. "One misses the lovely hurdles of racecourses, the white lines of tennis courts, the fresh turf of soccer matches, the stony up-and-down of automobile and cycle tracks."[42] Consigned by lack of money to the mass of standing spectators, Kafka suddenly realized that viewed from the expensive, tall grandstands which loomed behind him, the crowd of which he was a part must appear to melt imperceptibly into the "empty plain."[43] In the eyes of the Italian aristocracy and the "sparkling ladies from Paris," he was no more human than the guide posts that defined the course or the distant signalling mast.

Suddenly Kafka and his friends caught sight of Blériot leaning against one of the wings of his yellow flying machine. They recognized him at once by the way his head sat so firmly on his shoulders – an impression they had no doubt formed by seeing the French aviator's image reproduced repeatedly in Prague's newspapers before leaving for their vacation in the south. Could it be, they wondered, that Blériot was going to go up in this tiny and fragile thing? His courage seemed extraordinary. The first seafarers had had it easier. "They could practice first in pools, then in ponds, then in streams, and not venture out to sea until much later, for this man there is only the sea."[44] As Bleriot looked on paternally, his six mechanics prepared his plane for flight. It all appeared so natural; and yet everyone knew that something extraordinary was about to happen. Kafka thought that it was this combination of Blériot's matter-of-factness and the crowd's expectations of something miraculous that defined the special aura that surrounded the famous aviator. Blériot was already a master at that nonchalance that was becoming *de rigueur* for famous flyers. One wonders if he had learned it from watching Wilbur Wright at Hanaudières and Auvours.

Finally, after a long struggle to start his engine, leaving the onlookers more exhausted than those taking direct part, Bleriot got into the air.

One sees his straight upper body over the wings, his legs are deeply planted as if they were a part of the machinery. The sun is sinking, and under the baldachin of the grandstands, it throws its light on the soaring wings. Devotedly everyone looks up at him; there is no room in anybody's heart for anyone else. He flies a small circle and then appears almost directly above us. And everyone looks with outstretched neck as the monoplane falters, is controlled by Bleriot, and even climbs. What is happening? Here above us, there is a man twenty meters above the earth, imprisoned in a wooden frame, and defending himself against an invisible danger which he has taken on of his own free will. But we are standing below, pushed away, without existence, and looking at this man.[45]

The signalling mast now indicating a decrease in wind velocity, Curtiss decided to try for the Grand Prix of Brescia. His engine roared; his plane raced across the field; in seconds he was in the air, flying toward trees that had suddenly become visible in the distance. "He disappears from sight, we see the trees, not him. From behind some houses, God knows where, he comes out at the same height as before, and races toward us; when he climbs, you can see the under surfaces of the biplane dipping darkly; when he descends, the upper surfaces glisten in the sun. He makes a turn around the signal mast and, indifferent to the roar of welcome, turns straight back to where he had come from, only to become rapidly tiny and lonely again."[46]

Five times around the ten-kilometer course in just under fifty minutes, and the American won the 50,000 lira prize, easily beating the other contestants.[47] Yet what Kafka chose to record were not the details of Curtiss' winning flight but the cruel indifference of the spectators. "And while Curtis is working there alone above the woods, while his wife, whom everybody knows, worries about him, the crowd has almost forgotten him." They were too busy complaining to pay him any attention: complaining because neither Rougier nor Calderara had flown and the promised dirigible had yet to arrive. "The rumors running around about Calderara's accident are so full of his glory that one is ready to believe that the love of the nation would raise him into the air more securely than his Wright Flyer."[48]

142. The grandstand at Brescia.

Just as Curtiss was finishing his winning flight, the earlier night of Italian autumn started to fall. The last coaches had begun to leave for Brescia. As Kafka and his friends boarded their horse-drawn carriage, they felt the breaking of the bond that united them with the aviators, still flying in the lingering light, and became once more their earthbound independent humdrum selves. At a turn in the road, they looked upward and saw the Frenchman Rougier who was trying for the altitude prize. Like the other carriages, theirs stopped, while the drivers and passengers watched Rougier's flight. The French aviator "appeared so high in the air that one thought that soon his course would have to be determined only by the stars that were about to show themselves in the sky, which had already grown dark. We couldn't stop turning around; Rougier was still climbing straight up, but our way led with finality deeper into the *campagna*."[49]

Kafka was only twenty-six years old when he wrote this sketch. As a writer, he was scarcely known, a promise rather than a literary reputation.[50] But there is no other text that captures in such fineness of detail and with such spare elegance of language the atmosphere of the first aviation meetings: the featureless immensity of the aerodrome compared with other sports fields; the contrast between the impersonality of the plebian grounds and the parade of smartly dressed personalities in the grandstands, who preferred walking and being seen to sitting and watching; the fatiguing tedium of the wait for the aviators to leave the ground; the God-like aura that surrounded famous pilots like Blériot; the impression of desperate fragility the flying machines gave; the spectators' sense of being confined to earth as the aviator soared toward the heavens; the merciless egotism of the crowd; and the inevitable passage from the miraculous world of the sky – in which the aviators lived and which the spectators had momentarily and vicariously shared – to the mundane world of the plain. In twelve brief pages Kafka got on paper what hundreds of thousands had experienced in August and September of 1909 but were unable to express.

While waiting impatiently for Blériot to fly, Kafka observed from afar the Italian aristocracy walking up and down the gangways of the grandstands. "They say good day to each other, bow, recognize each other once again, they embrace each other."[51] Among the personalities he glimpsed was the Italian poet Gabriele D'Annunzio, whom he described as "short," "weak," and "shyly" dancing attendance on Count Oldofredi, one of the most important men on the organizing committee.[52]

Shyness was a strange quality to attribute to D'Annunzio, the most celebrated man of letters in Italy whose well-known string of feminine conquests vied for public attention with his already long list of brilliant literary works. Not given to modesty, he prided himself on his valor and his indomitable will. Just nine months earlier he had written to his mistress, describing himself as a hero whose toughness of spirit was greater than the most resistant cold-forged iron.[53] Nor was D'Annunzio a man inclined to flee the gaze of crowds. Unlike Friedrich Nietzsche, whose thought he had done so much to popularize in Italy, he shunned solitude and dedicated his febrile energy to the cultivation of his public persona, believing that the greatest creation of an author was his life. For him, the Nietzschean Superman was not a distant evolutionary ideal but a project whose goal lay within his grasp.

D'Annunzio was in Brescia for a purpose. He had come to gather material for a novel he was writing, his first in ten years. If he favored Count Oldofredi with his attention, it may have been because he hoped the count would be able to arrange his "baptism in the air." What is certain is that, by one means or another, D'Annunzio succeeded in persuading Glenn Curtiss and Mario Calderara to take him up for brief flights. On returning to earth, *Il Poeta* – as he was customarily called in Italy – announced to the correspondent of Milan's *Corriere della Sera* that flying was a "divine thing." "Divine and for the moment inexpressible." Famous for his inexhaustible appetite for women, D'Annunzio was naturally inclined to compare his experience of flight to intense erotic pleasure, one of those "unforgettable" moments of "supreme happiness" that stand out like "luminous points" as we look back on our lives. Returning to earth had been like "*una voluttà troncata*," a typically D'Annunzian way of alluding to the interruption of sexual intercourse before orgasm. It was not surprising therefore that all he could think of now was his next flight. Flying had become "a new need, a new passion."[54]

D'Annunzio expanded on these thoughts in an interview he gave to the airminded Parisian newspaper *Le Matin* in 1910. Contrary to what many people believed, aviation

143. D'Annunzio with Curtiss in his airplane during the Brescia air show, elegantly dressed as ever.

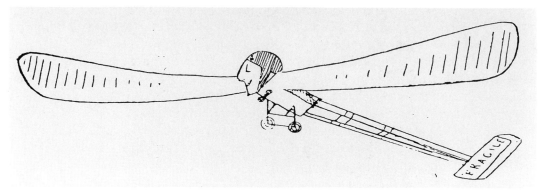

144. A winged D'Annunzio as seen by a caricaturist in 1911.

was not a "bizarre and perilous game," devoid of all practical importance and limited to acrobats and madmen. It carried within it "the promise of a profound metamorphosis of civic life" that would have far-reaching consequences for aesthetics as well as for war and peace. Already arms manufacturers and legislators were talking about the new danger that came from the skies. High in the sky, above the clouds, customs barriers, property rights, and frontiers lost their meaning. Aviation would create a new civilization and a new life. New idols, new laws, and new rituals would appear. Relations among nations would be transformed. The "Republic of the Air" would exile the wicked and the parasites and would open itself to "men of good will." The "elect" would abandon their "chrysalis of weight" and take flight. "A new civilization, a new life, new skies! Where is the poet who will be capable of singing this new epic?"[55]

Forse che sì forse che no (Perhaps Yes, Perhaps No), published in February 1910 and quickly translated into French and other European languages, was D'Annunzio's answer to this question. In many respects, *Forse che sì* was reminiscent of D'Annunzio's earlier novels. Illustrated with motifs and symbols that identify it as a product of the same sensibility that gave rise to art nouveau, it is a story of decadence, passion, voluptuousness, incest, suicide, and madness narrated in a breathless prose, full of esoteric classical allusions, that piles adjective upon adjective and page upon page, leaving the reader both exhilarated and exhausted.

In summary the plot scarcely seems robust enough to sustain the dense narrative of over five hundred pages. The protagonist Paolo Tarsis is consumed by desire for the voluptuous, perverse Isabella Inghirami. Isabella enjoys the game of flirtation – especially when it yields pain; but she is inclined for the moment to put off Paolo's advances. Isabella's melancholy and virginal sister, Vana, is desperately in love with Paolo. To save him from her sister, Vana reveals that Isabella has had an incestuous relationship with their effete, still adolescent brother, Aldo. When Paolo turns away from Vana in revulsion after hearing her confession, she ceremoniously prepares for death and stabs herself with an inlaid Turkish dagger. Vana's act drives Isabella over the emotional precipice on which she had been living into insanity. She is found wandering aimlessly around the streets and is mistaken for a prostitute. Overwhelmed by the ugliness of life, Paolo saves himself from the abyss of this disintegrating emotional world by committing a heroic – if useless – act that confirms his superiority to the other human beings around him. He finds life by courting death. The phrase *la morte, la morte* runs like a refrain throughout the novel.

All this was vintage D'Annunzio. Admirers of *Il Piacere* (Pleasure), *Il Trionfo della morte* (The Triumph of Death), and *Il Fuoco* (The Flame) would not be disappointed. There was one essential difference, however, between Paolo Tarsis and the tormented fin-de-siècle heroes of D'Annunzio's previous novels. Paolo Tarsis was an aviator and a

116

FORSE CHE SI FORSE CHE NO · ROMANZO DI GABRIELE D'ANNUNZIO.

ALTAM · SVPRA · VOLAT · ARDEA · NVBEM

PRESSO I FRATELLI TREVES IN MILANO. MCMX.

14.° migliaio.

— Forse — rispondeva la donna, quasi protendendo il sorriso contro il vento eroico della rapidità, nel battito del suo gran velo ora grigio ora argentino come i salici della pianura fuggente.

— Non forse. Bisogna che sia, bisogna che sia! È orribile quel che fate, Isabella: non ha alcuna scusa, alcuna discolpa. È una crudeltà quasi brutale, un'offesa atroce al corpo e all'anima, un disconoscimento inumano dell'amore e d'ogni bellezza e d'ogni gentilezza dell'amore, Isabella. Che volete voi fare di me? Volete rendermi ancor più disperato e più folle?

— Forse — rispondeva la donna, aguzzando il suo sorriso che il velo pareva confondere

D'ANNUNZIO, *Forse che sì forse che no.* I

"builder of wings." He was no mere scribbler of words but instead a master of machines. With his companion and fellow *volatore* Giulio Combiaso, he had come to Brescia to compete in an international aviation meeting.

D'Annunzio contrasts the sickness of Paolo's feelings for the "temptress" Isabella with the "great virile sentiment" that binds him to "loyal" Combiaso. D'Annunzio's brief history of their relationship is an ode to war, violence, adventure, and the fraternity of men who share extreme situations. The friendship of Paolo and Giulio, D'Annunzio tells us, had been born on the bridge of a warship when they served together in the peacetime Italian navy, longing for that day when they could aim their guns at real targets. It had been cemented "in the hell of submarine battles" amidst "the fumes of burnt oil, the vapors of gasoline, the mixture of hydrogen and oxygen produced by electric generators."[56] Unwilling to submit themselves to external discipline, they had abandoned the navy and travelled the world in search of adventure. In Cairo they had met a French ornithologist who turned their sense for navigation in three dimensions, developed in the submarine corps, towards the sky.[57] Together they had built a light and powerful flying machine, which they named Ardea because of their ambition to fly high. They became part of that "small aristocracy" of aviators who dressed alike and spoke alike and had their own cabal.[58]

As D'Annunzio portrays them, Paolo and Giulio are moved by a pure and noninvidious desire to emulate and surpass each other. "If you win, I win; if I win, you

145. The title page from *Forse che sì forse che no*: The emblem reads: "Altam Supra Volat Ardea Nubem." (Ardea flies high above the clouds.)

146. The first page of the text of *Forse che sì forse che no*, with its elaborate art nouveau emblems.

117

win," is the code according to which they live. Their friendship is based on equality: equal force, equal liberty, equal fidelity. Each measured his own worth by the worth of the other. There was no task so hazardous or so difficult that both were not equally capable of accomplishing it. One's exploit acted as an incentive to the other, pushing him to demand more of himself. Their goal was "to surpass the companion, all the others, and themselves."[59]

This was a form of unselfish fraternity no woman could understand. With their "glittering nails" women undid the toughness of men and dragged them down to earth. When Vana urges Giulio to be careful, he replies: "Prudence is worthless. All that matters is instinct, courage, and fate."[60] For aviators, death was always lurking around the corner. But death was "the companion of every game that's worth playing."[61]

Yet in D'Annunzio's vision, women, not death, were the real danger. They swarmed around aviators, evoking with their feminine dress and lascivious glances the nightmare of "an enormous invisible Vice with a hundred visible heads."[62] In her drive to manipulate men and her shrewdness at achieving her ends, Vana is as dangerous as the other women who are drawn to aviators by the prospect of "fire and blood." Just before Giulio is about to fly, Vana gives him a rose. Caught in her spell, his leonine eyes shining like phosphorous, Giulio promises to carry it higher than any man has ever flown, far above the clouds.

When D'Annunzio arrived in Brescia on 10 September he was depressed by the meanness of the spectacle. The weather was bad; there were few flights; all one heard were "the whistles and shouts of an angry crowd." In short, the meeting at Brescia was a "failure" and a "flop."[63] Transmuted by D'Annunzio's imagination in the novel, however, the dreary setting took on the quality of a vibrant armed camp. "The competition was like a war council. The place had the aspect of an arsenal and citadel." On top of the aviators' sheds, flags and pennants fluttered like a "full dress naval ceremony." "And, like the ancient standards of the infantry of the medieval communes, the fronts of the roofs were painted joyfully with the colors of the nations, the emblems of the workshops, and the names of the celestial helmsmen."[64]

D'Annunzio's real interest, however, was not in describing a place he had found depressing but in evoking states of mind. To do that he had to get his aviators into the air. The wind having fallen, Paolo and Giulio take off. For Paolo, entering the air was a liberation from "the tormented ground." "He left behind him the turbulence of his passion, Isabella's agitating smile, the adolescent [Aldo's] feverish and hostile glance, the vanity of his friends, the stupidity of those around him, all that intruding throng that had assaulted and oppressed him. He rediscovered his silence, his desert, his task."[65]

Paolo's first thought is for Giulio Combiaso. "Brother, brother, we are alone, we are free . . . How virile is the sky today!"[66] Cheered on by the delirious spectators in the race to see who can make the longest flight, Paolo has the sensation of becoming one with his plane. He felt as if the ribbing of his wings was penetrated with the air of his lungs. He was no longer a man but a man-machine who flew out of sheer joy. Paolo sees the signal announcing his victory. He glimpses "the grey mass of the crowd with their pallid faces and their outstretched hands."[67] "He leaned forward, banked, and sped by in a thunder of triumph, in a flash of splendor, white and weightless, sparkling with spars and steel, ringing with vibration, the messenger of a vaster life."[68]

Inspired by his friend, Giulio then tries for the altitude prize. Even after the mast signals his victory, he continues to climb. Winning was not enough. He had to go beyond. "*Ancora! Stravinci.*" The hysterical crowd, sensing danger, drives him on. Their "spasm" was "like the incessant pulsing of a collective fever that communicated itself

147. D'Annunzio (center) visiting the hangars at Brescia.

through the unfeeling air and reached those human wings."[69] Suddenly one of Giulio's propeller blades broke and began to fall toward the ground. The earthbound masses watched silently and breathlessly, as Giulio's machine lost its equilibrium and plummeted to the ground. After the crash, the spectators rushed toward the field, "avid to see blood, to look at lacerated flesh."[70] Restrained by cavalry, they swayed and pressed against the horses, trying to get a glimpse of the dead aviator. That night in Brescia, D'Annunzio wrote, was like the evening that follows battle. "The appearance of fire and blood in the heroic game had exalted even the humblest lives."[71]

The next day, after spending the night beside the body of his dead friend, Paolo attempts to win the altitude prize. As he attains the height reached by Giulio the previous day when his propeller broke, Paolo feels the presence of his friend. "Do you want to go higher? Do you want to?" Giulio's specter asks. At that moment, Paolo, "carrying to the summit of his courage the immortality of his pain," sees a brilliantly colored rainbow in the form of an arch of triumph. It is at the same time the symbol of his victory and the sign of the friend who will never leave his side.[72]

When Isabella realizes that Paolo has chosen to stand vigil next to the body of his dead companion rather than to seek consolation from her, she is "inflamed by an insane jealousy against that great sorrow that was usurping her dominion."[73] She gives herself to Paolo, only to reassert her power over him and to seek revenge against her male rival, the shadow of Giulio Combiaso, even more of a threat to her dead than he was when alive.

Paolo finally saves himself – many hundreds of torment-filled pages later – by flight. Having discovered that "the face of love was as obscene as that of a drunken clown," he decides to attempt the crossing of the Mediterranean from the western coast of Italy to the island of Sardinia, one hundred and thirty-five nautical miles.[74] "The builder of wings," who has been "chained to the earth" by his passion for Isabella, will take to the air.

119

In undertaking this perilous flight across the Thyrrenian Sea, Paolo responds to the siren call of Blériot's example. Even when making love to Isabella, he could not forget the details of Blériot's exploit and the acquiline profile of his heroic Frankish face. The brief journalistic account Blériot had given of his flight sounded within him "like the successive blows of wind on sails that threaten to capsize a boat." The vision of Blériot's monoplane alone above the Channel lit up his mind "like flashes of lightning."

Paolo's intentions were at first suicidal: he sought union with his friend Giulio through death. But once in flight, he regained his will to live. The hands with which he gripped the controls of his machine appeared like a symbol of the ideal life toward which he yearned. He left behind the shore below. He had the sensation of a journey now completed. The sun suddenly appeared. "His wings were resplendent with their protruding ribbing; the metal shone; the waters below signalled a dazzling path."[75] In a moment of revelation not unlike a religious conversion, Paolo Tarsis wonders if death can become life; if the day of his immolation could instead become the day of his transfiguration. As at Brescia nine months before, when trying for the altitude prize, Paolo heard Giulio's specter ask him: "Do you want to? Do you want to?" Within himself, he felt the desire to live, "the will to live in order to triumph."[76] Looking for death, he had found life.

The coast of Sardinia – victory – was now within sight. Making of his will an "iron dart," Paolo endures (as Blériot had before his Channel flight) the pain to his left foot caused by burning gasses escaping from a ruptured exhaust pipe and lands "as in a dream, as if by miracle" on a strip of sandy soil beside the breaking waves. There he was met not by the clamor of crowds but by "savage silence" and "the word of the secret wet-nurse who knows life and death and that which must be born and that which cannot die and the time of everything: 'Son, there is no god but you.'" "He sat on the solitary bank; and he began to remove what remained of the charred leather from his burnt foot. Since he had exhausted all his strength and could not bear the agony, he slid down to the shore; and kept his foot immersed in the water."[77]

Critics have been harsh on D'Annunzio's novel. They comment unfavorably on the turgidness of its language, the excess of its similes, and the inappropriateness of the classical and mythical allusions with which D'Annunzio seeks to elucidate the meaning of the new technology of aviation.[78] To be sure, it is hard to suppress a smile when reading D'Annunzio's summary of the history of flight. In two pages he takes us from the crib of Prometheus, "arduous like the very nest of superhuman desire suspended in the Unknown," to the story of "two silent brothers, *figli del placido Ohio* . . . who to push the winged machine had added the force of two propellers to the stubbornness of two hearts."[79] Had he read this, Wilbur Wright would no doubt have been perplexed and amused. These Europeans were capable of making such strange things out of something as straightforward and rational as flight.

It is easy, however, for a contemporary reader to miss the power D'Annunzio had achieved over his numerous admirers and the long-lasting legacy of the ideas he wove into the fabric of this novel. For Henry Bordeaux – who himself would make a notable contribution to the literature of aviation – D'Annunzio's novels offered "all the treasures of the Renaissance, all the daring of the written word, all the iridescence, the flashiness and the sumptuousness of the fabrics that the galleys of Venice used to bring from Byzantium. The richness of his vocabulary was incomparable, as was the virtuosity of his style and the phosphorescence of his imagination." Reading D'Annunzio was like watching "never-ending fireworks, or the spurting upwards of a shining stream of water that would never agree to descend."[80] *Il Poeta* would not have disapproved of this very D'Annunzian description of his way with words.

D'Annunzio himself believed that *Forse che sì* contained some of the most perfect pages he had ever written. Many of his readers agreed. The Italian composer Ildebrando Pizzetti wrote D'Annunzio that he believed that no previous poet had ever achieved with words the power of lyrical and epic expression that shone forth from the new novel. He feared that most critics would not grasp the musical composition of the work, in which words obtained their effect not just by their meaning but by their placement and repetition.[81] Even critics who regretted the typically D'Annunzian emphasis on the tortuous relationship between Paolo Tarsis and Isabella Inghirami were overwhelmed by the mastery and virtuosity of his style. Proclaiming D'Annunzio "the greatest Mediterranean tragic poet of the moment," the avant-garde critic Ricciotto Canudo praised him extravagantly for his evocation of the heroic flights of Paolo Tarsis and Giulio Combiaso at Brescia, "this incomparable poem in prose about our modernity."[82]

What did readers like these appreciate so much in D'Annunzio's prose? Take, for example, his baroque description of Paolo Tarsis taking off for the distance trials at Brescia.

> Just as an eagle in a sandy valley does not leap into flight but starts with a rapid step, runs accompanying the run with a growing quivering of feathers, leaves behind its own shadow as it rises at a weak angle, and finally soars on the vastness of its wings, flying against the flow of wind: just as at first the claws leave deep imprints, then little by little lighter ones until they seem to barely graze the sand, and the last trace is invisible: thus the machine left the ground, its three light wheels racing amidst the clear blue smoke from the exhaust, almost as if the dry grass of the field were burning beneath it.[83]

Here a new technology has been artfully assimilated into the poetic discourse of a preindustrial age.

Post-Second World War Italian critics have complained that D'Annunzio sought to put the airplane in the service of a reactionary ideology. A recent biographer accuses him of using the flying machine to recycle yet one more time his dream of an escape from "the painful and negative reality of the present."[84] This is no doubt true. Images of violence abound in *Forse che sì* and aviators are reduced to racial stereotypes not unlike the ones used contemporaneously by Wells, Martin, and especially Driant. When Paolo Tarsis wins the prize for distance over his English rival, his triumph is represented by D'Annunzio as the victory of *il Latino* over *il Barbaro*. By a supreme effort of will, the aviator-superman transforms himself into "an unbendable dart" and exalts his people. "An entire race was new and joyful in him."[85]

Yet to dismiss D'Annunzio as someone moved by a nostalgia for a nonexistent past is to overlook his conviction that flight was capable of providing a new dream and a new myth for a new century. What he sensed in the crowd at Brescia was a heightening of its vitality, as it watched and applauded "that graceful and terrible game, that elegant and daring competition, that gay duel between two flyers of the same species. All the force of dreams swelled the hearts of those earthlings turned toward the Assumption of Man."[86] Flight would make possible the rebirth of myth and the revitalization of culture; man once more would be able to dream.

Wells, Martin, and Driant had all sensed that aviation would produce a new aristocracy. But none of them had been able to articulate this idea as powerfully as D'Annunzio. The Italian poet was persuaded that, by means of flight, man could elevate himself morally and spiritually. "The new instrument seemed to exalt man above his fate, to endow him not only with a new dominion but with a sixth sense." Those willing to face the terrible risks of flight and laugh at death, as Tarsis and Combiaso had learned to do, would be transfigured and transformed into heroes. By becoming one with their machines, the new elect of aviators could create a religion of speed and escape the limitations of everyday life. The way to spiritual transcendence led through the conquest of the air, a realm in which man would always be at the mercy of his adversary, Death. "The struggle was unending, the danger ever present. Like the bloody Ortia of the ancient Tauride, the Unknown was not seated but upright on the altar demanding the sacrifice of human lives. The victims dared to look him in the eye unflinchingly, up to the threshold of Darkness."[87]

This, to D'Annunzio, was the profound meaning of the aviation meeting he had witnessed at Brescia. "The crowd flocked to the spectacle as to an ascension of its species. Danger seemed the axis of the sublime life. All foreheads had to turn up-wards."[88] Others would translate D'Annunzio's ideas into different idioms and cultural forms, but their core would remain remarkably unchanging. The aviator was "the messenger of a vaster life." He was a technological superman whose bones and flesh had been transmuted like the wood of his propeller into "an aerial force" whose mission was to triumph over nature.[89] The earthbound would have to settle for the vicarious identification they could feel with these "celestial helmsmen" who looked down on those below with a scornful smile.[90]

148.   The Gordon Bennett trophy for speed in aviation dedicated to the heirs of Icarus.

5

A Rendezvous with Death

Take possession of the air, submit
the elements, penetrate the last
redoubts of nature, make space
retreat, make death retreat.

Romain Rolland, 1912[1]

D'ANNUNZIO was by no means the only eminent poet who was tempted to sing "the new civilization, the new men, the new skies." Edmond Rostand, author of the acclaimed plays *Cyrano de Bergerac* and *L'Aiglon*, and in the eyes of many the leading interpreter of the French spirit, also found the metaphors of aviation irresistible.[2] Deeply moved by the sight of flying machines in the sky, Rostand set out in the summer of 1911 to translate into poetry the feelings that the achievements of his country's aviators had aroused in the populace at large.[3] No living poet in France had a better command of the classical alexandrine form in which French poets had traditionally chosen to write, nor a better ear for the sonorities of the French language. Moreover, as a member of the Académie Française – the youngest ever to be elected – Rostand had access to the pages of the widely read weekly *L'Illustration*. Thus *Le Cantique de l'aile* (The Hymn of the Wing), the long poem he published in July 1911, reached a large and receptive public which had been bombarded during the previous five years with a series of striking images recording the conquest of the air.

When composing *Le Cantique de l'aile*, Rostand sought to interpret and, at the same time, respond to the gamut of emotions that the new technology had inspired in a country that was deeply divided politically and nervous about the possibility of war with Germany. He could count on receptive readers. In the summer of 1911 the enthusiasm of the French public for aviation had never been greater. The previous year flying machines had progressed to the point where cross-country races could be staged between European cities. To the great delight of his countrymen, a French aviator won the first of these. Competing against a resolute British adversary who risked his life in a daring night flight, Louis Paulhan became the first person to fly from London to Manchester within a period of twenty-four hours, thereby earning the £10,000 ($50,000) prize that Lord Northcliffe had created four years before. Both pilots flew French-made Farmans powered by French-manufactured 50-horsepower Gnôme engines. By dint of superior skill and greater experience, Paulhan overcame a driving wind that forced his opponent Claude Grahame-White to abandon the struggle. As Grahame-White graciously acknowledged, the better man had won; and, as the French newspapers were quick to point out, the better man was French.[4] There was every reason to believe that the French aviators had now definitively outdistanced their foreign competition, including the Americans; and this sense of national technological achievement was reflected in Mimi Pinson's *Les Ailes de l'amour* (The Wings of Love), a popular play performed in Paris at the Trocadéro theater a few months later, in which a rich American woman was led to follow a glorious French aviator *dans la voie des airs*.[5]

The following year, in 1911, city-to-city races were organized on a grander scale. In

149. Georges Scott's evocation of Georges Chavez's fatal crash after the Peruvian had successfully overflown the Alps.

150. Edmond Rostand in the robes of an academician.

125

151. Paulhan's English adversary, Claude Grahame-White, in his aviator's garb at the time of the London-Manchester race.

152. Grahame-White's mother anxiously attaches a rose to the strut of his Farman before his departure for Manchester.

153. Grahame-White about to take off in his unsuccessful effort to win the *Daily Mail* prize, 27 April 1910.

154. Louis Paulhan departs Lichfield for Manchester on 28 April 1910. The *Daily News* later evoked the awe-inspiring splendor of the flight as it appeared to an observer on the ground. "Gracefully balanced in mid-air, dipping gently forward and backward, the aeroplane went travelling at a speed of nearly a mile a minute. In the oncoming twilight of this soft April day, the sky assumed a fairy-like aspect. Against the clouds of dazzling white, or deep blue or lurid scarlet, as they were suffused in turn by the rays of the sinking sun, the biplane appeared indeed a thing of beauty and wonder. All along the route groups of rustics and labourers had gathered to watch this great man-made insect of wood, iron and canvas flying and buzzing over the hills and streams of the countryside." (Quoted by Wallace, *Claude Grahame-White*, p. 68.)

May a group of eight aviators left Paris for Madrid in a competition sponsored by *Le Petit Parisien*. Three hundred thousand spectators flocked to the airfield at Issy-les-Moulineaux to observe the spectacle of their departure. The race soon became a contest between three French pilots and was won by Jules Védrines after he survived an encounter over the Pyrenees with an eagle – or so he claimed. Whether true or fanciful, Védrines's account of his historic flight, during which he spent almost fifteen hours airborne over a period of three days, made for great newspaper copy and inspired commercial artists.[6] Védrines was decorated by the Spanish king and feted by the Madrid aeronautical community. The next spring he exploited his new celebrity by running for and almost winning a seat in the French parliament; campaigning in his flying machine, he argued that the presence of an aviator in the Chamber of Deputies was indispensable at a time when it was vital that France should maintain its mastery of the air.[7]

By then, however, Védrines's celebrity had been partially eclipsed by the achievements of one of his countrymen, who became the European aviation sensation of 1911. At the end of May *Le Petit Journal* sponsored a race between Paris and Rome. The leading contenders were again Frenchmen flying French machines. Four days after the race's start, Jean Conneau, a lieutenant in the French navy competing under the pseudonym of André Beaumont, landed before a cheering crowd gathered in the Parioli quarter of Rome. Not even the Pope could resist witnessing the epoch-making spectacle. He watched through a telescope from his terrace as Conneau appeared on the

155. An intrepid aviator defying the attacks of an eagle.

127

156. Jules Védrines campaigning in March 1912.

157. Jean Conneau being cheered by a crowd in Parioli after winning the Paris-Rome air race. Conneau later described his arrival in Rome. "I alighted within a few yards of a line formed by an enthusiastic crowd, frantic with pleasure . . . . The gate-keepers were powerless against the mob invading the aerodrome and rushing toward my machine. Here I was lifted out of my seat and carried shoulder high. I had become their property, and was unable either to utter a word or protect myself. Tossed about, dragged in every direction, I felt bruised and sore by the contact of thousands of hands trying to touch me, whilst wild shouts were filling the air" (André Beaumont (Jean Conneau), *My Three Big Flights*, p. 42).

horizon of the Roman compagna and was said to have blessed the French aviator as he passed over the Vatican. Along with other poets, Edmond Rostand was moved to write verse celebrating the occasion:

158. Conneau comes within sight of St Peter's dome as he nears Rome.

159. Spectators applaud Conneau, as he lands to win the Circuit of Britain in July 1911. French aviators were astounded by the small crowds that aviation races drew in Great Britain during this period.

> Tout fut beau: la Victoire et le cri qui la nomme,
> Et la Ville Eternelle, et le jeune saison,
> Et le Captif sacré quittant son oraison
> Pour voir l'Aile franchir les collines de Rome!
>
> Everything was beautiful: the Victory, and the cry that names it,
> And the Eternal City, and the young season,
> And the sacred captive leaving his prayer,
> In order to see the Wing cross the hills of Rome![8]

Conneau went on from this victory to win the grueling Circuit of Europe and Circuit of Britain. His renown was such that he was deluged with registered letters, requesting his autograph and financial aid. "One asked for a bicycle, another money for a month at the seaside, a third wrote asking for furniture for his daughter's marriage, still another the sum of $27\frac{1}{2}$ francs to settle a bill." Conneau was astonished by the variety of the propositions he received. "Lunatics did not forget me; I received the most extraordinary congratulations from them, naturally some 'crazy' verses and proposals that scarcely differed from those of the others."[9]

Shrugging off such requests, Conneau took advantage of his celebrity by writing a

160. Conneau leaving Buckingham Palace after a reception given by the Royal Family.

161. Conneau was able to translate his aviation exploits into commercial advantage. This advertisement reads: "In the big air races, bring a little less gasoline, but take along a bottle of Mariani wine, and you'll double your chances." Claude Grahame-White attributed his endurance in the London-Manchester race to the nip of brandy he had taken after becoming faint from the cold.

M. André BEAUMONT,
(Enseigne de vaisseau J. CONNEAU),
Aviateur,
Triomphateur de la course *Paris à Rome*
du *Circuit Européen*
et du *Tour d'Angleterre* (les mille Milles),
Cliché Eug. Pirou, phot., Paris.

162. Charles Rolls appearing anxious before his round-trip Channel flight. Looking at this photograph, one can understand why early airplanes were called flying "machines."

clever and amusing book based on his experiences that became an international bestseller. *Mes Trois Grandes Courses* (My Three Big Flights) struck just the right note, portraying the aviator as a mixture of technician and athlete who had won entry to a magical realm of "aerial mysteries" and "fairy-like scenes" and who was transformed by the miracle of flight. "He is free. He follows a path free of any limitation. At his pleasure, he can ascend, descend, maneuver; he meets no obstacle. He is truly free. He has conquered the air as formerly he conquered the ocean. And the victorious machine that he has created obeys his every movement with the lightness of a bird. The danger? But danger is one of the attractions of flight. If man loves flying so much, it is because every leap forward he makes toward [the conquest of] space threatens his existence. He is not adverse to gathering his laurels next to cypress trees."[10]

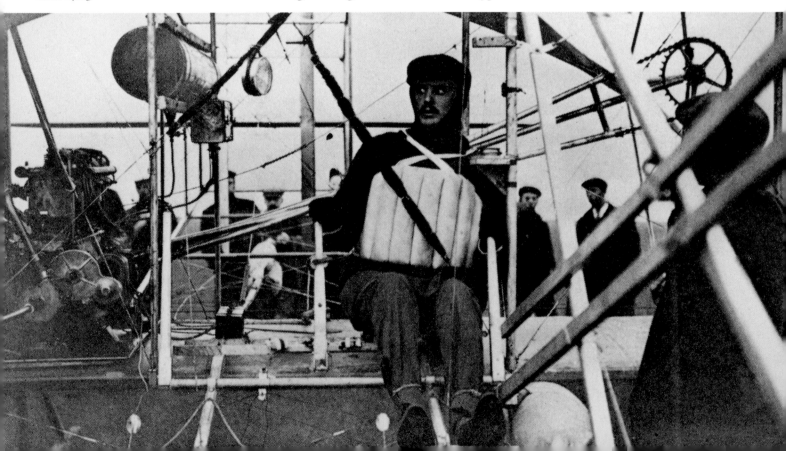

By July 1911, then, the French had ample reason to pride themselves on their contributions to the "preeminently French science of aeronautics."[11] But stretching the capability of flying machines and giving crowds the thrills they craved had begun to take a toll in human lives, as D'Annunzio and others had foreseen. In July 1910 the car manufacturer Charles Rolls became the first Englishman to die in an aviation accident when the new experimental rear elevator in his Wright Flyer snapped at an altitude of 150 feet during a precision landing contest at an air show in Bournemouth.[12] Seeing that he was going to undershoot the hundred-yard landing zone, Rolls tried to gain altitude by pulling up on the elevator lever. The elevator was unable to withstand the increased load and splintered with a crack that could be heard by the horrified spectators. In a matter of instants, the biplane tilted into an uncontrollable vertical dive, striking the ground "with a dreadful thud."[13]

Rolls was no beginner: shortly before his death, he had successfully flown the Channel from England to France and returned nonstop.[14] If as level-headed a pilot as Rolls was unable to control his machine during a landing under good weather conditions, one had to wonder whether the Wright Flyer was safe.

Similar questions were raised about the Blériot XI. On 23 September 1910 the Peruvian aviator Georges Chavez crashed while landing in the Italian town of Domodossola after having successfully flown over the 6,600 ft. Simplon Pass. The crowd gathered to applaud his spectacular exploit watched in horror as he fell to the ground "like a stone" from a height of sixty feet. A fellow aviator and friend of Chavez, who witnessed the crash, said that the Blériot's wings had been so weakened by the struggle with the Alpine up and down drafts that they folded like a dove's during his descent into the improvised landing area.[15] Others believed that Chavez had been so numbed by the cold that he lost the use of his hands and was unable to control his machine while landing. Claude Grahame-White thought it possible that the Peruvian had "suffered some sort of an attack of faintness after his swift rush over the Alps at such a great height."[16] Nothing remained of his machine except a formless heap of wreckage. Chavez, who had not lost consciousness during the crash, died four days later from internal injuries.

163. Rolls just before his fatal crash. Note the newly installed rear elevator to the right of the photograph.

164. Georges Chavez about to depart on his flight over the Alps.

In this growing list of air fatalities, the French played a leading role: of the thirty aviators killed during the first six months of 1911, sixteen were French. Three had died on a single day at the end of June during the beginning of the Circuit of Europe, won by the tenacious Jean Conneau.[17] Small wonder, then, that aviators had become identified in the minds of many French people as flying fools and death-defying risk-takers who valued the thrills offered by the air over the bourgeois comforts of life.

Moreover, aviators were increasingly viewed not only as reckless daredevils likely to kill themselves and their passengers, but as a danger to people on the ground. In May 1911, at the moment of the departure of the contestants in the Paris-Madrid race, one of the machines went out of control and killed the French Minister of War, while severely injuring the Prime Minister and the leading patron of French aviation, Henry Deutsch de la Meurthe. Artists began to imagine ways by which earthlings could defend themselves from falling aviators and their flying machines, and the first steps were taken to regulate air traffic. Responding to a campaign in the press that portrayed flying machines as the toys of irresponsible millionaires and a danger to public safety, the French Minister of Public Works appointed a commission charged with the dual task of protecting the public "against the disturbance or the risks that air traffic can occasion" and aviators "against the dangers caused by their imprudence, their daring, or the defects of their machines."[18]

Le Cantique de l'aile was Rostand's response to those who condemned aviation as an affront to God and Nature and a threat to law-abiding citizens on the ground. Rostand made no attempt to conceal the dangers of flight nor the cost in human lives entailed in mastering the air.

> Depuis que cette chose impérieuse existe
> Qui veut qu'on aille aux cieux,
> La France est le pays des mères à l'oeil triste. . . .

165. Chavez above the Simplon Pass. The previous year Latham had won the altitude prize at Rheims by ascending to a height of 508 feet.

166. Spectators gather grimly around the wreckage of Chavez's Bleriot. Commemorating Chavez's death, the poet E. A. Butti wrote:
> . . . Rejoice, Man, that the avenging Alps
> could only give you a single death!
> And what a death they gave you! A death that renders you immortal,
> A death that consecrates, a death that makes sublime,
> A death that protects from the low clamor of fame,
> and crowns with myrtle the statues of heroes!

167. A contemporary artist reflects on the dangers that flying machines posed to the general public. "There are three sorts of falls: the fall of the aviator. The fall of the airplane (very rare). The fall of everything (much more frequent)."

Since this imperious thing exists
That desires that we should go to the skies,
France is the country of mothers with sad eyes. . . .[19]

Rostand's purpose, however, was not to lament but rather to justify and celebrate these victims. If French mothers had sad eyes, they also had "glorious foreheads." The response of French youth to aviation had disproved those "flute players" and prophets of despair who were mourning the country's death. The French had shown their "profound strength" by taking so avidly to the skies. French youth had responded to the "cry" of the Wright brothers like "an immense covey of impatient birds."[20] They had understood that the new invention required daring young men who were adroit and willing to die. And how lightheartedly France's "young and headstrong sons" had gone to meet their fate in the air. As winds of gale force whistled about them, "They bid us goodbye with a shake of their helmet, then they raise their hand." For the young Frenchmen of today were just as willing to die for "the azure" as the ancient Hellenes had been willing to die for Greece.[21]

Contrary to the detractors of aviation, Rostand went on, the great mass of the French people had intuited the meaning of flight and its implications for the nation's future. They realized that the young men in their flying machines had forced them to raise up their eyes toward the heavens above and away from the mud below. They felt uplifted and transformed, as they watched their aviators from the roofs and fields of France. Dazzled by the exploits of "these exciters of divine enthusiasm," the "crowd" no longer saw "the merchants of irony or hate."[22] They had regained their hope, their pride, and their courage and they had become more generous of heart, so that now they opened more often those "rudimentary wings which were only arms." They had risen above their divisions and low intrigues and turned away their eyes from those who blackened the asphalt and the pavement with their lies. The people grasped instinctively that aviation was more than a "frivolous game." They understood that it was *l'âme même* – pure spirit. How otherwise could one understand the emotions that an aviator in the sky aroused?

> Cet homme crierait-il quand, dans un ciel paisible,
>   Cingle ce vaisseau pur,
> S'il n'avait pas senti que c'est Psyché visible
>   Qui traverse l'azur?

> This man, would he cry when this pure vessel
>   Navigates the peaceful sky,
> If he had not felt that it was Psyche come to life
>   That traverses the blue?

Then, striking a titillatingly erotic note that Rostand knew the sensibility of the period would prize:

> Entendrait-on, d'amour, lorsque passe cette aile,
>   Cette femme gémir,
> Si cette aile, en passant, ne faisait pas en elle
>   Une autre aile frémir?

> Would one hear this woman moan from love,
>   When a wing passes in the sky,
> If this wing, while passing, did not cause
>   Another wing to shudder in her?

And finally, returning to a classical allusion that placed aviators on a level with the gods of ancient mythology:

> L'âme s'agite au fond de celui qui contemple
>   Une aile dans l'air bleu,
> Comme un dieu prisonnier qui sent, au fond d'un temple,
>   Passer un autre dieu!

> It stirs, the soul of he who contemplates
>   A wing in the blue air,
> Like an imprisoned god who senses, from the depths of a temple,
>   The passing of another god![23]

When evoking the public's response to wings in the air, Rostand spoke from personal and deeply felt experience. A few months before writing these lines, he had watched Jean Conneau from the beach at Biarritz as he battled treacherous down-drafts that made it impossible for him to land safely. Miraculously saved from an accident that may well have been fatal, Conneau regained control of his machine and found himself alive on the ground.

Very moved and without will, I remained immobile, satisfied to look around me.

Was it an illusion? There was no one in that place where a few minutes before hundreds of onlookers had been swarming. Yes, however, there was one man who had remained on the beach where I could have crushed him but where his courage had retained him. He came toward me. I jumped nimbly on the ground and we shook hands with emotion. This intrepid man was Edmond Rostand. I thanked him for the solicitude that he had shown me after such a nerve-wracking flight and promised myself that I would dedicate my first pages on aviation to his heart and his calm audacity.

Mes Trois Grandes Courses was indeed dedicated to Rostand, "in remembrance of our emotional meeting at Biarritz."[24]

In seeking metaphors that would do justice to France's aviators, Rostand drew upon a wide variety of images to which his classically educated readers could be expected to respond. Beginning with an epigraph from Homer – "taking pride in their wings, the fields resounded" – Rostand went on to call France's pilots "great heroes," "unsullied athletes," the "sons" of Napoleon's soldiers, "archangels" who had been destined to appear ever since the moment when humanity first left the mud behind, and "a band of knights" determined to surpass one another.[25] If no trace had been found of some of those who had disappeared in flight, it was perhaps because they had "ascended, ascended, ascended" directly into heaven without ever returning to the ground. However they died, France's flying heroes deserved to be praised by those whom they had served:

> Batailles de l'espace! ineffables conquêtes!
> Triomphes sans remords!
> Gloire à tous ceux par qui ces choses furent faites!
> Gloire à ceux qui sont morts!

> Battles of space! ineffables conquests!
> Triumphs without remorse!
> Glory to all those by whom these things were done!
> Glory to those who are dead![26]

The prophets of despair and the doomsayers had complained that the twentieth century lacked passion and that materialism would leave the "soul" without transcendent tasks. How wrong they had been. Suddenly courage of the ancient mold had come to life, and the exploit had been reborn. Aviation was responsible for the miracle; or, as Rostand put it in a series of verses that combined classical and contemporary allusions: the modern hero, having withdrawn into his tent like a Greek champion, had ripped the cloth from his walls and used it to fly away. It was in vain that the spectre of Icarus should try to attach itself to the frail fuselage of today's planes, and breathe into their pilots the fear of repeating his fate. "Man is afraid of nothing."[27]

> Aile, arrache la roue au baiser gras de l'herbe,
> Et monte au ciel d'été
> Dans la gloire du risque et le dégoût superbe
> De la sécurité!

> Wing, tear your wheel from the thick kiss of the grass,
> And ascend into the summer sky
> In the glory of risk and the proud disgust
> For safety.[28]

The scorn for personal safety and the determination to achieve a great exploit, regardless of the cost, was what gave a transcendental meaning to Blériot's flight. When Blériot had hobbled to his flying machine and flown into the Channel mists "despite his burning ankle," he had taught the French

> Comment on peut changer en aile une béquille,
> Et la chair en esprit!

> How one can transform a crutch into a wing,
> And flesh into spirit![29]

Technology, in other words, need not be an enemy of culture.

This was the central message of Rostand's stirring poem. No epoch was more marvelous than the one in which man had learned how to use the wings that he had carried for all these centuries hidden in his heart, and no people was greater than the French who, to demonstrate their horror at weighing on the world, had learned to fly above it.[30] Thus far from taking refuge on the ground and turning their eyes downward toward the urban pavement, the French should take to the air.

> Plus haut! toujours plus haut, pilote! et gloire aux hommes
> De grande volonté!
> Gloire à ces dérobeurs de flamme que nous sommes!
> Gloire a l'Humanité!

> Higher! ever higher, pilot! and glory to men
> Of great will!
> Glory to those stealers of the flame that we are!
> Glory to Humanity![31]

For those dead aviators whose only thought when plunging toward the ground was anxiety about those below whom they might alarm, Rostand had these consoling words:

> Quittez la seule peur qu'en tombant vous connûtes:
> L'homme vole. Dormez!

> Put away the last fear that you knew while falling:
> Man flies. Sleep![32]

Rostand made only a veiled reference to the German menace – calling the French a people "whose wounds all open toward the East"[33] – and none to the potential use of airplanes for military purposes. Indeed, he emphasized that the French "knights" of the air had the happiness of knowing that the only blood they had on their hands was their own.[34] But other writers, like Blériot's collaborator, the engineer and pilot Alfred Leblanc, were quick to make explicit that justification of the new sport at which Rostand had only poetically alluded. "The more flying men we have, the stronger we will be and the less we will fear the attacks of other powers since we will have mastery of the air."[35] Or, as the nationalist writer René Bazin put it with greater literary flair in his comments on the approaching Circuit d'Anjou of June 1912, in which French airplanes would be tested for potential military uses: if the French applauded their aviators so enthusiastically, it was not only because they appreciated their daredevil exploits, but also because they realized that they were risking their lives for France. "Because of that, when you appear, all of France is moved. And it loves you, it applauds you, it thanks you, because in you, who are fearless, it rediscovers the knights who made it what it is, a vanguard nation, elegant in the face of peril."[36] Who would have been able to predict what a long life Rostand's metaphor of a knighthood of the air was going to have?

Rostand portrayed aviation as a realization of the dreams of humanity, reformulated poetically in the nineteenth century by poet-prophets like Eugène Lamartine and Victor Hugo. Through the use of metaphor and simile, he established an equation between the French aviators of the present and the Greek heroes and medieval knights of the past. The effect of his seductive verse, so deeply imbedded in French literary tradition, was to connect aviation with a known past, to make the strange familiar. Yet another response to aviation, though, was to see it as the harbinger and agent of a new and fundamentally different machine-driven civilization that would definitively divorce humanity from its past, leading it in unexpected and disturbing directions. In propagating and diffusing this second image of aviation, no one was more single-minded nor inventive than the Italian poet Filippo Tommaso Marinetti, founder and leader of the Futurist movement.

168. F. T. Marinetti in 1907.

Born in Egypt of Italian parents, educated in France and Italy, Marinetti settled in Paris, where the considerable fortune he inherited allowed him to pursue his literary ambitions untroubled by financial constraints. Photographs of him taken in this period reveal a balding turn-of-the-century dandy with an upward-swirling mustache and a determined, provocative glance. Marinetti's first poems, written in French and influenced by the reigning school of Symbolism, already betrayed a fascination with technology – especially fast cars – and a strong attraction toward metaphors of ascent. "We are tired," he wrote in 1902, "of sleeping in the depths of blue grottos, embedded like colossal gems in the stones . . . The hour has come to conquer space and to ascend toward the assault of the Stars."[37]

To be sure, the function of space, the heavens, and the stars in this early poem was highly metaphorical. The stars in their firmament stood for the heavy weight of the past, which must be overcome by means of will, energy, and violence. But Marinetti soon showed that he was sensitive to the new technologies – technologies that, he believed, were transforming the way that people perceived the world and thus laying the foundation for a new culture based on speed and the negation of space.[38] And if it was mere coincidence, it was certainly a symbolically suggestive one that the publication of the first Futurist manifesto in February 1909 came only six weeks after the completion of Wilbur Wright's triumphant season of flights at Le Mans.

In this manifesto, Marinetti announced the end of one age and the beginning of another. "We stand on the extreme promontory of the centuries! Why look behind us at a moment when we must break down the mysterious doors of the Impossible?"[39] Mythology, the traditional fund of imagery for poets, had been overtaken by technology. Surrounded by symbols of modernity – electric lights, double-decker streetcars, "famished automobiles" – Marinetti summoned his friends to embark on a journey of discovery. "Let's go, I say, my friends! Let's be off! At last, mythology and the mystical Ideal have been surpassed. We are going to be present at the birth of the Centaur and we will see the first angels fly."[40]

The new age demanded a new morality and a new type of art. "The only beauty is in struggle." Poetry must become "a violent assault" against unknown forces in order to compel them to yield to humanity's commands.[41] The old conceptions of time and space were dead; they had died yesterday. "We already live in the absolute, since we have already created omnipresent eternal speed." The new beauty was a beauty of speed. The subjects of the new art would be creations of technology. A racing car, "its hood embellished with great exhaust tubes like snakes with explosive breath," was more beautiful than the *Victory of Samothrace*. Among those symbols of modernity that the Futurists intended to celebrate, Marinetti included (and concluded with) "the gliding flight of airplanes, whose propellers whirl through the air like flags and attract the applause of enthusiastic crowds."[42]

To an even greater extent than D'Annunzio, Marinetti made an explicit connection between flight and war.[43] While vacationing in the south of France a few months after having published the manifesto, Marinetti imagined the destruction of his literary enemies in a bloody attack by air. *Tuons le clair de lune* (Let's Kill the Moonlight), is far removed from the scientifically-based anticipations of Wells, Martin, and Driant. Marinetti shows little interest in or knowledge of the construction of contemporary aircraft. Instead he wishes to evoke the fusion of metal and living flesh, human beings transformed into flying machines. As their motors "applaud with joy," the Futurist fleet that he imagines himself to be leading spits machine-gun fire at its adversaries, symbols of the official culture that Marinetti and his Futurist friends had pledged themselves to destroy. The allegory ends, as the poet enjoys his victory over his slaughtered foes, promiscuously mixing images of coitus, death, and rebirth.[44]

Marinetti's novel *Mafarka le futuriste* (Mafarka the Futurist), written the same year, projected his fascination with flight onto the level of a cosmic fantasy. *Mafarka* can be read on many levels. Much of it takes the form of an African adventure novel with bloody battles, hair-raising escapes from certain death, traitors, summarily dispatched, and elaborate scenes of "African" barbarousness and sensuality, a tale similar in many respects to the contemporary narratives of Emile Driant. Marinetti's preface makes clear

GRANDS POÈTES INCENDIAIRES!

O MES FRÈRES FUTURISTES!

GIAN PIETRO LUCINI,

PAOLO BUZZI, FEDERICO DE MARIA,

ENRICO CAVACCHIOLI,

CORRADO GOVONI, LIBERO ALTOMARE,

ALDO PALAZZESCHI!

Voici le grand roman boute-feu que je vous ai promis.

Comme notre âme à nous, il est polyphonique. C'est à la fois un chant lyrique, une épopée, un roman d'aventures et un drame.

Je suis le seul qui ait osé écrire ce chef-d'œuvre, et c'est de mes mains qu'il mourra un

VIII   MAFARKA LE FUTURISTE

jour, quand la splendeur grandissante du monde aura égalé la sienne et l'aura rendue inutile.

Quoi qu'en disent les habitants de Podagra et de Paralysie, il claque au vent de la gloire comme un étendard d'immortalité, sur la plus haute cime de la pensée humaine. Et mon orgueil de créateur en est satisfait.

Ne le défendez pas : regardez-le plutôt bondir en éclatant, comme une grenade bien chargée, sur les têtes craquées de nos contemporains, et puis dansez, dansez la ronde guerrière, en pataugeant dans les flaques de leur bêtise, sans en écouter le clapotis monotone!

Quand je leur ai dit : « Méprisez la femme! » ils m'ont tous lancé des injures ordurières, comme des tenanciers de maisons publiques après une rafle de la police! Et pourtant ce n'est pas la valeur animale de la femme que je discute, mais son importance sentimentale.

Je veux combattre la gloutonnerie du cœur, l'abandon des lèvres entr'ouvertes qui boivent la nostalgie des crépuscules, la fièvre des chevelures

169, 170. Marinetti's preface to *Mafarka le futuriste*, addressed to "Great Incendiary Poets," exhorts his "Futurist brothers" not to defend his novel but to watch it bounce while exploding, "like a well charged hand grenade, on the broken heads of our contemporaries . . ."

139

that *Mafarka* is also meant to be understood as an attack on the cult of romantic love and monogamy. "I wish to vanquish the tyranny of love, the obsession with the one and only woman, the great romantic moonlight that bathes the bordello's facade."[45]

But if these elements are present in Marinetti's novel – and their presence is what makes it such a densely textured work – *Mafarka* is also intended to be a celebration of the liberating powers of aviation and an allegorical representation of its implications for the renewal of Western culture. Mafarka sacrifices his life in order to give birth to a higher form of being, a beautiful winged giant capable of mastering nature and subjugating the sun and stars. Similarly, Marinetti declares, Futurism could only create by first destroying its adversaries – all those who remained wedded to the past. Setting forth his philosophy, Mafarka proclaims that Death was not an enemy to be fled but a mistress to be courted. "I glorify violent Death at the end of youth, a Death that harvests us when we are worthy of its deifying caresses."[46]

When Marinetti wrote *Mafarka*, he had not yet flown. In September 1910 he took a brief flight over Milan in a Voisin biplane with the record-breaking aviator Jean Bielovucic, as the sun was setting. Remembering that flight five years later, he wrote that he had felt "his chest open like a great hole into which the entire horizon of the sky flowed deliciously, smooth, fresh, and torrential." He felt "the ferocious and flushing massage of the crazy wind." "Increasing weightlessness. An infinite sense of voluptuousness. You descend from the machine with a light and elastic jump. You have removed a weight from your back. You have triumphed over the stickiness of the road. You have triumphed over the law that forces man to crawl."[47]

Marinetti later claimed that his first flight transformed the way that he felt about literature and propelled him toward a new type of writing.[48] Certainly, ample traces of his aerial experience can be found in the long prose poem he wrote in 1911 and published in January of the following year, *Le Monoplan du pape* (The Pope's Monoplane), a work unlike anything that he had written before.[49] In some ways, this poem can be understood as a response to the verse written by Edmond Rostand and others celebrating Jean Conneau's flight over the Vatican and Rome in May 1911. But it also reflected the emotions aroused in Italy by the war the Italian Liberal government had undertaken that year against the Ottomans for control of Libya, a war which the Pope, a self-described prisoner in the Vatican and unyielding adversary of the Italian state, opposed.[50]

Indeed, while in the process of writing *Le Monoplan du pape*, Marinetti went to Libya and witnessed the first use of airplanes in combat. His lyrical account of the battle for the city of Tripoli, which appeared as articles in the Parisian evening newspaper *L'Intransigeant*, singled out the exploits of Captain Carlo Piazza who, flying at a height of a thousand feet in his Blériot, had signalled to the Italian artillery the location of the enemy. "Higher, more handsome than the sun, Captain Piazza soared, his bold, sharp-edged face chiseled by the wind, his little mustache crazy with will." His two wings "slicing brutally" through the halo of sunset, Piazza sang joyfully as he directed "rounds of lead in the torrential sea of the enemy army."[51]

Marinetti made no attempt to conceal his envy for the god-like aviator. "Oh! The infernal joy that you must have felt during this glorious morning." Unable to bear the servitude of a purely terrestial existence, the poet-journalist-combatant imagined himself as Piazza overflying the battlefield. "My heart crazy with enthusiasm carries my motor ever higher, scaling the steps of the blue."[52] What a sense of joy it gave to follow the Italian troops from a height of fifty meters as they hunted out the "treacherous" Arabs in their thickets and wells with "sinister" and "precise" bullets.[53] Marinetti identified himself as "the roaring heart of the nation, whose wild beating applauds you!

Aquile Romane e Aquile Italiane.

Romba sfavilla - motor d'Italia,
balza dal suolo - librati al ciel,
garrulo trilla - fulgido ammalia
rapido al volo - magico angel!

Là dove un giorno l'aquila antica
spinse il suo volo, pose il suo spron,
l'uom fa ritorno - genio e fatica
prodigo al suolo - reca qual don!

Non la galea triste di schiavi
curvi sul remo pel mare va
non la plebea schiera d'ignavi
figli di Reno più marcerà!

Non la gioconda macchina inquieta,
lo scappamento più guiderà,
non la rotonda palla di seta,
schiava del vento timida andrà;

ma, in mezzo ai nembi dell'uragano,
contro dell'uomo, del ciel furor,
di estremi lembi, l'aereoplano
non vinto o domo, sarà signor!

Contro scirocco che freme e frulla
l'aerea prora la nave dà,
come lo stocco caro a Fanfulla
che fiede ancora ombre e viltà.

Avanti, avanti terra promessa
dal sol baciata, cinta dal mar,
fra inni e canti sempre la stessa
all'avanzata devi restar!

Guidi Colombo, Spagna fedele
alla fortuna seguendo il sol,
Venezia ha un rombo, sciolga le vele;
incontro al sole va Marco Pol!

Spingan le prore fra i ghiacci eterni
Cagni e Savoja col tricolor;
sol d'equatore, col gel s'alterni
mai non si muoja l'Italo fior!

Suol che sei viato, flutto domato
di nebbie il velo non invidiar;
di lauri cinto - soldato alato
di Libia il cielo - ecco solcar!

171. A postcard with the image of Piazza and other Italian military aviators.

172. The words of a popular song praising Italian military aviators based on the music from the opera *Norma*. The song celebrates the triumph of man over the forces of Nature, affirming that, "unconquered" and "unsubdued," the airplane will dominate the "heaven's fury."

173. The cover of a volume of D'Annunzio's poems celebrating Italy's heroes of the ground, sea, and air; one of these poems praised Piazza and other Italian aviators who "in the danger of the wind" were poised above the unsuspecting enemy.

I leap over you to go finish off the victory by climbing step by step the ladder of the sky!"[54]

A little more than a month after writing these lines, Marinetti completed *Le Monoplan du pape* in the Italian trenches at Sidi Messri. In this long poem, subtitled a "Political Novel in Free Verse," Marinetti imagined himself as a human flying machine, driven to escape from the clinging earth by his hatred of the walls that surround him "like a coffin."

The first lines of the poem celebrate, excitedly, the fusion of poet and machine.

> Je vibre en dansant sur mes roues raisonneuses
> giflé par le vent fou de mes fantaisies.
>
> I vibrate while dancing on my reasoning wheels
> slapped by the crazy wind of my fantasies.[55]

Leaving behind the urban disorder of Milan, the poet flies down the west coast of Italy, heading for Sicily, "the great heart of Italy." Having arrived there, he greets the inhabitants of Palermo from the air, declaring that he is one of theirs because like them he has nothing but scorn for society and its laws. He then flies on to confront the great volcano Etna, demanding to know his destiny and the duties that belong to his race. The fiery volcano responds with a violent diatribe against the Italians, whom he accuses of adoring their ancestors and sleeping "under the calm leaves of Peace."

The poet now understands the mission that his father, the volcano, is assigning him. Italy must be regenerated by war; otherwise its frontiers will disappear from the map. Only those who are willing to destroy can create. Death is the price we pay for life. Violence is a form of creativity. Italy has no choice but to attack Austria.[56]

After a hazardous flight over the Sahara where he observes the "filthy mess" of African villages, the poet flies toward Italy, only to hear cries announcing the outbreak of hostilities with Austria. He comes upon a group of peasant women who are gathering along the railroad tracks in order to block the troop trains rushing toward the northern frontier. They cry that they intend to create "an immense mattress of human bodies."[57] Enraged at the sight of this "vast clamor of messy women" who are incapable of understanding the grandeur and necessity of war, the poet decides to launch an aerial attack. Skimming the surface of the ground, he decapitates a hundred women with his right wing, then, banking, makes another pass, decapitating another thousand lined up along the "vibrating rails."[58]

Just as Jean Conneau had recently done, the poet now arrives in Rome, "the solemn intersection of celestial roads"; but instead of receiving the blessing of the Pope, he lowers a strong metallic crane attached to his undercarriage and carries the Pontiff away like a great fish, as his engine vomits oil in disgust. Heading toward the northeastern frontier with his papal prey dangling helplessly from his wheels, the poet reaches Monfalcone in time to witness the defeat of the Austrians by the Italian forces. As he drops his "aerial bait" in the Adriatic sea, the Austrian fleet hurls shells and shrapnel at him from afar. Turning himself into a battery of artillery, he fires furiously at the now defeated enemy. "Destroy! We must destroy! We must go on destroying forever!"[59]

In comparison with Marinetti's Futurist writings of 1909, *Le Monoplan du pape* is intensely and explicitly political, reflecting the antagonisms that surfaced in Italy in 1911 as a response to the Libyan War. The enemy Marinetti denounces is no longer the Parisian literary establishment, hopelessly attached to the techniques and themes of the past, but the coalition of Italian clericals, socialists, syndicalists, and anarchists who oppose war. Marinetti uses the term "war" not merely or even principally as a metaphor for conflict and strife, but as a word signifying the heightened state of being that he had experienced in Libya, an episode he later described as "the most beautiful aesthetic spectacle of my existence."[60] War, he cries, will be a "vacation of fire and blood and red lunacy" which will unite the Italians in an orgy of destruction. Anyone who dares to oppose or obstruct the war will be swept aside by Marinetti's courage and his pistol.

The figure of the monoplane plays a vital role throughout the poem. In addition to its metaphorical uses – as a means of liberation from the past, from the poet's former self, from women, from the deadening tedium of peace – the flying machine is portrayed as an engine of war, capable of terrorizing civilians, dropping bombs, destroying submerged submarines, and also, interestingly, as a factor of morale for ground troops.

> O soldats d'Italie,
> Il nous faut résister pendant une heure encore!
> Je suis sur vous, inébranlable,
> comme un phare,
> dont la lentille souveraine
> groupe les moindres feux épars de la détresse
> et les mue en faisceaux de courage.

> Oh soldiers of Italy!
> We have to hold on for one more hour!
> I am above you, unyielding,
> like a beacon
> whose sovereign lens
> collects the smallest scattered signals of distress
> and transmutes them into bundles of courage.[61]

But what attracted Marinetti above all in the flying machine was its potential for liberating humanity from its two great enemies, time and space. By consuming and thus killing space, the propeller frees man from the servitude of time and makes it possible for him to multiply infinitely his life, thus transforming him into a god.[62] There was no better example of man's rebellion against the divinities that had for so long enslaved him than his determination to conquer the air.

Marinetti celebrated the flying machine as a means of escaping from the constraints imposed by nature. For him, flight was a realization of man's age-old Promethean dream of conquering the elements and achieving godhood. While waiting for the coming war with Austria, there was nothing more interesting on earth than "the beautiful death" of aviators.[63]

It would be a mistake to think that Marinetti had written his Futurist allegories with tongue in cheek. He took them – and meant them to be taken – seriously. In his view, technology did not merely offer a new topic for literature; it had replaced literature and rendered the romantic and sentimental sensibility of the nineteenth century obsolete. Men would merge with motors. Their will would become like steel. Their vital organs would become as interchangeable as a flying machine's spare parts. The motor was man's "perfected brother" because it was capable of eternal youth. "We believe in the possibility of an incalculable number of human transformations, and we say without smiling that wings sleep in the flesh of man."[64]

Nonetheless, Marinetti had doubts about his ability to realize his aspiration toward infinity. In *Le Monoplan du pape*, he acknowledged bitterly that his flying machine flew forever "in the eyes of a woman."[65] Moreover, he knew that his vocation was not for flying but for spectacle:

Je suis l'artiste, l'être nombreux et fourmillant,
la rixe pullulante
la soirée de première,
la salle comble où tout est pris. . . .

I am an artist, a being numerous and in over supply,
the swarming brawl,
opening night,
the packed house in which every seat is taken. . . .[66]

In short, Marinetti knew himself to be a showman whose favorite form of action was to shock and provoke a willing audience. His genius lay above all in the business of promotion – the promotion of himself, to be sure, but also those he judged, rightly or wrongly, to be his disciples.

But as Marinetti himself had suggested in the first Futurist manifesto of February 1909, a truly Futurist culture could only be created by artists who were willing to give up books in favor of technology. The invention of objects, with a life of their own, had overtaken myth and romantic dreams. When the next generation of Futurist poets came to overthrow their elders, Marinetti had warned, they would find us not in academies or libraries but "in the country, under a hangar pounded by the monotonous rain, crouched next to our vibrating airplanes, heating our hands over the miserable fire made by the books we are writing today."[67] Or as Marinetti put it in an interview while trying to clarify the intent of the first Futurist manifesto: "We want to replace in people's imagination the silhouette of Don Juan as an ideal with that of Napoleon, Andrée, and Wilbur Wright."[68]

One avant-garde poet who also sensed that technology was overtaking art but who,

174. A drawing by Umberto Boccioni of Marinetti and other Futurists performing in June 1910.

144

unlike Marinetti, was willing to take this insight to its logical conclusion was the Russian Futurist writer, Vasily Vasilyevich Kamensky. In 1910, soon after publishing his first novel, Kamensky abandoned literature in order to devote himself single-mindedly to aviation. Recalling this moment in his life, he later wrote that he felt irresistibly drawn toward

> the wings of airplanes . . . I wanted to participate in the great discovery not merely with words, but with deeds. What are poems and novels? The airplane – that is the truest achievement of our time. The aviator is the man of worthy heights. If we are really Futurists . . . if we are people of the motorized present, poets of universal dynamism, newcomers and messengers of the future, masters of action and activity, enthusiastic builders of new forms of life – then we must be, we have no choice but to be, fliers. Henceforth let the smell of gasoline and burnt motor oil and the flat expanses of airdromes and machines ready for take off be our life.[69]

Kamensky was only one of a number of Russian intellectuals and artists who displayed an interest in aviation during the years before 1914. Their curiosity, often verging on obsession, reflected the enthusiasm that the new science of aeronautics generated in government and military circles, and among the Russian public at large. Though Russian scientists had been active in aeronautical research and though ballooning had been popular among aristocrats in the late nineteenth century, it was not until Louis Blériot's flight across the Channel in July 1909 that the Russian government began to patronize heavier-than-air flight.[70] The central figure behind the government's interest in the new technology was the Grand Duke Alesandr Mikhailovich, a member of the imperial family, who had been vacationing in France at the time of Blériot's flight and who had quickly grasped the military uses of aviation. On returning to Russia, the

175. Grand Duke Alesandr Mikhailovich and other Russian dignitaries posing in front of a flying machine.

176. The front page of the St Petersburg newspaper *Gazeta-Kopeika*, which features the St. Petersburg–Moscow air race and its participants.

Grand Duke pleaded the case in military circles for the development of an aerial fleet, organized a committee to raise money for the purchase of French flying machines, and arranged to have Russian officers sent to France to receive flight training.

As in France, the supporters of military aviation understood that the quickest way of developing a strong air arm was to encourage interest in flying among the civilian population. Flying had to become popular, and there was no easier way to accomplish this than to promote aviation as a sport. As in France also, the key agent in this process became the capital's Aero Club, an institution which united high political figures, such as the Prime Minister Pyotr Stolyin and the former Finance Minister Count Witte, and less prominent sportsmen and technicians anxious to advance the cause of aeronautics. In 1909 the All-Russian Aero Club was granted imperial status, thus guaranteeing it court patronage and the prestige and support that this brought with it. The Imperial All-Russian Aero Club oversaw the granting of pilot licenses and organized races, air meets, and exhibitions of flying machines. With its encouragement, air strips were built; flying schools were established, principally at Gatchina outside St. Petersburg, in Odessa, and near Sebastopol; and magazines devoted to flying and the science of aeronautics began publication. A group of aviators emerged whose names and photographs appeared frequently on the first pages of the empire's newspapers.[71]

Kamensky first flew with one of these pioneers in 1910. He would never forget the thrill of feeling his flesh and spirit fused with the metal and wood of a flying machine, as Vladimir Aleksandrovich Lebedev introduced him to the domain of the air.[72] A champion cyclist and racer of motor cars, Lebedev had been sent to France by the

Imperial All-Russian Aero Club in 1909 to learn the art of aviation; while there he studied with Henry Farman before returning to St. Petersburg to organize the Club's flying school.[73] Known like his French teacher for his avoidance of unnecessary risks, Lebedev left dangerous competitions like the crash-ridden St. Petersburg-Moscow race of July 1911 to other less cautious aviators and instead dedicated his efforts to flying instruction and the promotion of aviation as a business. It was through Lebedev, who had opened an aviation firm in St. Petersburg, that Kamensky arranged to buy his first flying machine, a Blériot XI.

While waiting for the delivery of the Blériot, Kamensky took the advice of a friend, the famous sportsman and aviator Sergei Utochkin, and decided to go to Paris, where he hoped to learn to fly. Once in Paris, Kamensky presented himself to Blériot who put him to work learning the intricacies of the Anziani and Gnôme engines that his machines used. Finally, armed with a letter from his supervisor testifying to his progress in the care and repair of engines, Kamensky was taken up for a brief flight over Paris by Blériot himself, who gave him some basic instruction in the use of the controls, saying: "It's all very simple – you just have to know how to do it."[74] After six flights, Kamensky was allowed to taxi around the field at Issy-les-Moulineaux outside Paris in order to get a feeling for the control of the Blériot's tail; but he decided to abandon his training and return to Russia when he was asked to put up a sizeable deposit of money against possible damage to the machine.

A discouraging beginning, no doubt, for a fledgling aviator determined to learn how to fly.[75] Still, if anything, Kamensky's Parisian interlude reinforced his feeling that aviation had important cultural implications. While at the airdrome, he saw some of the reigning luminaries of European intellectual life – among them Anatole France, Pierre Loti, Maurice Maeterlinck, Emile Verhaeren, Gerhardt Hauptmann, and Henri Bergson – who made the pilgrimage to Issy-les-Moulineaux to see the new invention. Flight in France was taking on the aspect of a new religion whose adepts performed their rituals in the sky.

Before returning to Russia, Kamensky made a brief trip to London to visit an aeronautical exposition with Lebedev and Henry Farman. Kamensky was astonished by the dominance the French had achieved over the British in the field of aviation. Three-fourths of the machines he saw in London had been built by Farman. Travelling to St. Petersburg by way of Milan, Rome, Florence, Venice, Vienna, and Berlin, Kamensky noticed the general European enthusiasm for aviation. The newspapers and illustrated weeklies were full of photographs of flying machines and aviators. "The heads of all humanity were raised to the sky and stiff with astonishment at the conquest of the air." Every day brought reports of new records, new achievements, and the deaths of fearless heroes. "My soul throbbed when I heard the buzzing of a plane: why not I rather than another lucky fellow."[76]

By the time Kamensky had returned to St. Petersburg, the Blériot was waiting for him at the Gatchina airdrome. The problem was that there was no one there who was capable of teaching him to fly it; thus like many other aspiring aviators of the period, he had no choice but to teach himself. After receiving some basic theoretical instruction from Lebedev – who as a Farman pilot prudently declined to take the Blériot off the ground – Kamensky began to taxi around the field with the tail raised, as he had been taught to do in Paris. Then one day he ventured to pull back on the stick. The machine rose unevenly into the air; Kamensky fought for control; somehow he managed to guide it shakily back to earth, after cutting the engine, as Lebedev had taught him to do.

The sound of the chassis settling onto the field and the wheels racing across the grass

177. Kamensky (right) and Lebedev pose in front of Kamensky's newly acquired Blériot in St. Petersburg in 1911.

were music to Kamensky's ears. He could not believe that he was still safe and sound. His joy was so great that he leaped to the ground, transfixed with happiness. He rushed back to his apartment to announce the news to his roommate, the writer Arkady Averchenko, who grabbed his most recent book of stories from the shelf and inscribed it to "celestial Vasily" from the "earthbound Arkady." Kamensky later wrote that no record-breaking aviator could feel prouder than he did on the first day his wheels left the ground.[77]

178. Kamensky standing in his Blériot in Perm in June 1911; surrounding him are local admirers come in the hope that they would see him fly.

In June 1911 Kamensky shipped the Blériot to his home town of Perm in the Ural mountains and attempted some flights from the local racetrack. But Kamensky's failures were more frequent than his successes; and knowing that he needed more instruction, he decided to go to Warsaw in order to pursue his flight training at the Mokotow airdrome, where there was a flight school and a group of accomplished aviators.

Kamensky was one of a group of eight student pilots; together they spent all day at the airdrome. "In our eyes: airplanes taking off. In our ears: the sounds of motors. In our nose: the smell of gasoline and burnt oil. In our pockets: insulating tape. In our dreams: the flights we would make."[78] They studiously avoided the topic of accidents, except sometimes to joke: "If you intend to smash yourself to smithereens today, lend me 50 rubles."[79]

At the beginning of November 1911, the Imperial All-Russian Aero Club sent a representative to Warsaw to supervise the examination of Kamensky and his fellow students. The examiner stood on a horse-drawn cab and signalled to Kamensky with a red flag the maneuvers he expected him to execute. To Kamensky the examination seemed to drag on forever. He could only think about his engine and what would happen if it should stop. Finally, the examiner signalled to him to cut his engine and to land. He glided to within a few feet of the examiner's wagon, was pronounced an international pilot–aviator, and embraced his instructor, as he was ready to embrace the entire world.[80]

After passing their exams, most of Kamensky's fellow students went abroad to make their fame and fortune by competing in international competitions. Kamensky stayed in Warsaw and, when spring came, he began to participate in air meetings, fly exhibitions, and give passengers "joy rides." In April 1912 he embarked on a tour of Polish provincial towns where few people had ever seen an airplane. He lectured on "contemporary aviation" and flew his Blériot, while military bands played music to keep up the spirits and patience of the expectant spectators who were often forced to wait for hours before they saw Kamensky leave the ground.

All went well until he arrived in Czestochawa, a large town southwest of Warsaw whose inhabitants turned out in force to watch Kamensky fly. The field that had been chosen for the exhibition was located near a railway station, ominously just beyond the

179. Kamensky about to take off in Warsaw in 1912.

180. A poster announcing a flight and lecture by Kamensky on "contemporary aviation" in March 1912.

Авіаторъ ВАС. КАМЕНСКІЙ

Въ Воскресеніе 18 марта 1912 г.
состоится
ПОЛЕТЪ
НА АЕРОПЛАНѢ
авіатора
В. Камеискаго.

Начало полета въ 5½ час. веч.
Въ день полета съ 4½ час. вечера будетъ играть хоръ музыки 8-го Стрѣлковаго полка.

Въ СУББОТУ 17 марта с. г.
въ залѣ Общ. Ремесленниковъ и Торговцевъ
ДВѢ ЛЕКЦІИ:
1) „ОСНОВЫ АВІАЦІИ"
прочтетъ на польскомъ языкѣ инженеръ М. КРУЛЬ.
2) „СОВРЕМЕННАЯ АВІАЦІЯ"
прочт. на русскомъ языкѣ пилотъ-авіаторъ В. КАМЕНСКІЙ
Начало въ 8 час. вечера.
ПОДРОБНОСТИ ВЪ АФИШАХЪ.

city's slaughterhouse. By five o'clock in the afternoon, a thick crowd had gathered there and people were standing on the roofs of the nearby houses. The flying field was enclosed by ropes guarded by soldiers on horseback. As was the custom in such events in Poland, the governor arrived with his suite, proceeded by the chief of police. Two orchestras were playing military marches and walzes. Kamensky was in the middle of the field with his Blériot. When the time came for him to fly, the wind blew up and threatening black clouds appeared. It began to thunder, and flashes of lightning could be seen in the sky.

Kamensky prudently decided to postpone his flight until the weather cleared, but the chief of police informed him sternly that the governor insisted that he fly immediately; otherwise he would cancel the event and send the impatient and increasingly angry crowd home. Torn between his instincts as an aviator and his awareness that the cancellation of his flight could have serious financial consequences, Kamensky decided to go up. His take-off into the wind went smoothly enough; but he soon lost control of the Blériot as the wind began to toss his machine about like a piece of cork in a raging sea.

> I clenched my teeth, screwed myself into a ball, multiplied my will power, adjusted and sought to level the airplane every which way. But it was all in vain: while banking, a gust of wind hit the underside of my wing – from a great height I turned topsy-turvy in my machine. The motor stopped working. Death awaited me. The chill of helplessness gripped me and images of my childhood flashed instantaneously like sparks before my mind's eye.[81]

When Kamensky woke up eleven hours later with multiple fractures, two local newspapers had already announced his untimely demise. One lucky spectator won a hundred rubles by predicting that he would be resurrected after death. Only the muddy bog into which he had crashed had saved his life.[82]

Advised by his doctor to find a peaceful place in which to recover, Kamensky collected what remained of the Blériot and returned to his home town of Perm. There, with the earnings from his exhibition flights, he bought a piece of land in the country, built a house, and dabbled in aviation design. In 1913 he tested a machine designed to take off from and land on water or snow.[83] A surviving photograph suggests why the

181. Kamensky at the controls of his hydroplane before attempting an unsuccessful test of the machine's ability to fly.

experiment was a failure. Kamensky's contraption looks more like a primitive paddle steamer than a hydroplane. Wisely, he never sought to fly again.

182. The "Futurist" David Burlyuk in 1914.

By this time, however, Kamensky was being drawn toward a different type of adventure: the developing literary war between the Russian avant-garde and their Symbolist and Decadent adversaries. Throughout his aviation career, Kamensky had never lost contact with his old friend David Burlyuk, artist, poet, organizer, and ideologue of the Russian avant-garde. In 1912, while Kamensky was in Warsaw, Burlyuk wrote him about his discovery of a poetic genius: the eighteen-year-old Vladimir Mayakovsky, a student of art in Moscow. In the autumn of 1913, at Burlyuk's urging, Kamensky went to Moscow, where he met Mayakovsky and allied himself with a group of poets, artists, and musicians, all moving loosely in Burlyuk's orbit, who had begun to call themselves Futurists.[84] Like Marinetti, Burlyuk believed that the very nature of art had to be redefined. Art was not something that could be created in the loneliness of a poet's garret or an artist's studio. As "revolutionaries" the Futurists must take art and literature into the streets and squares and provoke the masses. Art must "invade" life and become a form of action. "Henceforth we should derive our enjoyment from provoking the bourgeoisie."[85]

Both Kamensky and Mayakovsky showed themselves to be well endowed with the talents necessary for carrying out Burlyuk's injunctions. In November the three poet-artist-performers held a recital in the Polytechnic Museum in Moscow. The event had been carefully publicized by Burlyuk, and all seats had been sold. A noisy crowd of young people, unable to purchase tickets, had to be restrained by mounted police outside the hall.

Kamensky was presented to the audience by Mayakovsky, attired "futuristically" for the occasion in a yellow blouse and a black top hat that he wore at a rakish angle. In lieu of an ordinary introduction, Mayakovsky flamboyantly read one of Kamensky's poems in which the "pilot-aviator" declared himself to be a "warrior of song" who had "screwed" through the sky with his "elastic propeller" and challenged the "flabby courtesan Death" with a defiant gesture of disgust.[86]

The topic of Kamensky's lecture was, naturally enough, "Airplanes and Futurist Poetry." Resplendent in a cocoa-colored suit trimmed with gold brocade, he held forth about the impact of the new technologies on the writing of poetry. When asked why he had an airplane painted on his forehead, he responded that it was a sign of his "universal dynamism." In reply to a charge by someone in the audience that the Russian Futurists were merely imitators of Marinetti, Kamensky went to lengths in order to distinguish himself and his companions from the Italians. Unlike Marinetti's group, he pointed out, the Russian Futurists did not want to destroy museums; nor did they believe that the only "hygiene of the world" was war. Their purpose was to preside over the funeral of the old Russian literature and art – by which Kamensky meant, of course, the literature and art that had dominated Russia at the turn of the century. "We Futurist poets are alive, throbbing, up-to-date, working, like motors, in the name of youth's enthusiasm and for the glory of Futurism; we would be very happy to arm you, friends of contemporary life, with our splendid ideas."[87]

The spectacle at the Moscow Polytechnic Museum was only the first in a series of performances that Burlyuk, Mayakovsky, and Kamensky gave throughout Russia's provincial capitals. Their purpose was to provoke, shock, and convert to their vision of modern culture the audiences that flocked to applaud and denounce them. In the process, they also managed to make themselves a bit of money.

Since officials were reluctant to authorize their performances and the distribution of

183. Vladimir Mayakovsky in his yellow blouse.

184. The text of Kamensky's poem *Vyzov* (Summons) read by Mayakovsky at the Polytechnic Museum in November 1913.

ВЫЗОВ ———

КАК**Ф°**Нію ДУШи
МоТОрОВ *симфонію*
—— фррррррррр
это Я это Я
футур**ж**Ст-ПЕСНЕБоёЦ и
ПИЛОТ-АВІАТОр *)
ВАСИЛІЙКАМЕНСКІЙ
вЛаАсТичНыМ пРопеЛерОм
ВВИНТИЛ *О*БлАкА
киНув Т А М
за визит
ДряБлоЙ смерти КОКОТКш
из ЖалоСти сшитоѕ
ТАнгОВое МаНтО и
ЧУЛКИ с
ПАнТАЛОНАМИ

their posters, Kamensky was able to use his official title as a "pilot-aviator of the Imperial All-Russian Aero Club" to good effect. On one occasion in Kharkov, when the local governor was reluctant to approve the distribution of their posters, he showed him his certificate on which it was written that the authorities should provide him with all possible cooperation. The governor asked to see the poster. Noting that Kamensky intended to speak on "Airplanes and Futurist Poetry," he asked innocently: "What is Futurism?" Kamensky explained maliciously that Futurism celebrated with images the achievements of aviation. The governor then inquired whether Burlyuk and Mayakovsky were aviators; to which Kamensky replied: "Almost." The governor asked why the names of the Futurists were always surrounded by scandal. Kamensky answered that it was all the fault of the newspapers which sought to create sensation in order to sell their filthy rags. The governor agreed with this disapproving characterization of the press and authorized the distribution of the posters.

The Kharkov performance was a great success, especially among young people who relished the way the Futurists boldly disparaged the reigning priests of literature and art. After explaining that the principles of Futurism were intuition, personal freedom, and abstraction, the "poet-aviator," as Kamensky billed himself, declared that he was ready to dance a "tango with cows" and denounced some unsuspecting spectators as "hornless philistines," "geese," and "cattle dealers." Poetry, he announced with Futurist exuberance, was the "wedding feast of words."[88]

During another performance in Odessa, after Kamensky had read some of his aviation poetry, a general in the audience rose and said: "The entire world kneels before the heroes of the air. And this so-called Futurist Kamensky declaims revolting poetry about aviators. If this Futurist had once sat in an airplane, he would not dare to write such indecent verse and link aviation with Futurism. It's unacceptable." The audience warmly applauded the general, but Kamensky displayed his aviator's diploma, which

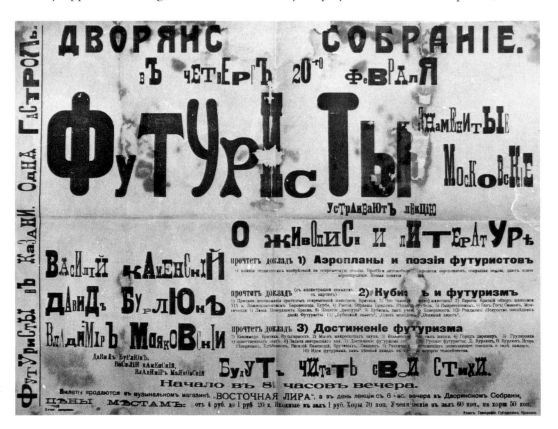

185. A Futurist poster from February 1914 announcing a performance by Kamensky, Burlyuk, and Mayakovsky in Kazan. Kamensky was to speak on "Airplanes and the Poetry of the Futurists."

152

bore his photograph. The general came up to the stage, verfied the authenticity of the document, and apologized. The theater then gave Kamensky an ovation. Burlyuk took advantage of the situation to cry to the audience: "That's why you'll also come to accept as true the ideas of Futurism."[89]

186. Kamensky in 1914.

A man of passionate enthusiasms, Kamensky threw himself headlong into the realization of the new literature and art. Among the poems he wrote between 1913 and 1918, many sought to convey the emotions of flight and evoke a Futurist vision of a new airminded world. Some of these poems are exciting visually because of the way they play aesthetically with the size and arrangement of words, especially "The Flight of Vasya Kamensky in an Airplane over Warsaw" in which the shape of the text – a pyramid that is meant to be read from the bottom to the top – suggests the disappearance of the aviator from sight into the vastness of the sky.[90]

Yet curiously Kamensky achieved literary success and remained best known not for his air poetry but for his 1915 novel about the famous seventeenth-century Cossack rebel Stepan Razin and for his pastoral poetry about the countryside near Perm, where he built his house and chose to spend much of his time. Seeing the direction that Soviet cultural policies were taking in the 1920s, Kamensky abandoned experimental poetry – at which he had been a genuine innovator – and did his best to be a good Soviet writer, going so far (at the height of the purges in 1938) as to write a book entitled *Country of Happiness*.[91] The first authentic aviator-poet, Kamensky died honored as a creator of earthbound verse.

187. The poem "The Flight of Vasya Kamensky in an Airplane over Warsaw."

Not all Western poets and intellectuals greeted the coming of the flying machine with the unqualified enthusiasm of D'Annunzio, Rostand, Marinetti, and Kamensky. One of the sharpest critics of the new technology – and of those who embraced it – was the Viennese journalist Karl Kraus, a maverick who prided himself on thinking against the current of the times in which he lived. Kraus feared that his contemporaries were becoming prisoners of their own inventions. People had been clever enough to create sophisticated machines, but they lacked the intelligence to use them properly. Speed had become an end in itself rather than a means to some kind of human end. Unlike the balloonists of the previous century, the aviators of the present had no reverence for the air and invaded the heavens like intruders, in order to attack the earth. Flight represented a danger to those who remained on ground. Because the air had been conquered, the earth was condemned to be bombarded. Of all the disgraces that had occurred on earth, Kraus believed that the greatest was the use that was being made of the ability to fly. Instead of raising humanity toward the stars, aviation had only extended man's misery to the air, "as if it did not have ample room below."[92]

The British novelist John Galsworthy also deplored what he called "the prostitution of the conquest of the air to the ends of warfare." "If ever men presented a spectacle of sheer inanity it is now," he wrote in 1911, "when, having at long last triumphed in their struggle to subordinate to their welfare the unconquered element, they have straightaway commenced to defile that element, so heroically mastered, by filling it with engines of destruction. If ever the gods were justified of their ironic smile – by the gods, it is now!"[93]

Yet Kraus and Galsworthy were exceptions. Even intellectuals who denounced the building up of nationalist tensions and the cult of violence in pre-1914 Europe could not suppress their enthusiasm for the conquest of the air. Romain Rolland is an interesting example, all the more so because in the years following 1914 he became an icon of the left and a living symbol of pacifism in France. In *La Nouvelle Journée,* the last installment of his long and influential novel sequence *Jean-Christophe*, written during the years

188. Kamensky at work in 1946 amidst rural surroundings.

153

189. Romain Rolland in 1912.

directly preceding the outbreak of the First World War, Rolland gave an unsparing portrait of the younger generation in France. Georges Jeannin, the son of Jean-Christophe's old friend Olivier, is portrayed by Rolland as shallow, egotistical, inconstant, and easily duped by the rhetoric of his time. A practitioner of every popular sport from football to automobile racing, Georges is inclined "by the vigor of his muscles and the laziness of his mind" toward the nationalist and royalist doctrines of the Action Française.[94] For all his talk of the need for action and order, however, Georges remains at heart a pleasure-seeker who believes in nothing. To save Georges from himself and the false messiahs who offer him salvation in royalism, religion, and war, Jean-Christophe urges him to take up aviation, the new sport which, for the first time since the dawn of the Great Revolution, had caused the "huddled masses" to lift their eyes up toward the sky.[95] "Take possession of the air, submit the elements, penetrate the last redoubts of nature, make space retreat, make death retreat."[96] Urged by the young man's mother to dissuade her son from flying, Jean-Christophe confesses that "He did not believe himself permitted . . . to impede the healthy and normal play of young beings who, had they been compelled to inaction, would have turned toward self-destruction."[97]

It was naive of Rolland – though at the same time deeply revealing – to believe that the self-destructive impulses driving young men like Georges Jeannin would be sublimated or deflected into more constructive forms of action through the practice of flight. He himself had noted with dismay in the same novel that "the new generation, robust and warlike, aspired after combat and had, before their victory, the mentality of conquerors." How curious that he did not go one step further and identify the enthusiasm for aviation with this bellicose mentality that celebrated "the anvil of battle on which one day the action of bloody fists would reforge French power."[98] Kraus, Galsworthy, and H. G. Wells were closer to the mark when they warned that aviation itself had become a dangerous outlet for feelings of aggression that would ultimately result in flying machines dripping death from the air.

To acknowledge this is to raise a disturbing but necessary question about the deeper meaning of aviation in the early twentieth-century West: could it be that the desire to conquer the air carried as its unconscious corollary a Luciferian ambition to escape from the last of human limitations – to annihilate those age-old adversaries space and time through the worship of speed, to "make death retreat" by agreeing to yield to its "deifying caresses," and to attain to something approaching godhood through fusion with machines? Read in this light, Marinetti's bellicose and phallic fantasies of flight, destruction, and mechanical reincarnation take on a larger meaning that cannot be restricted to what (some might be inclined to argue) was an isolated and unrepresentative avant-garde. The Italian poet was by no means alone in believing that wings slept in the flesh of man. But few were willing to acknowledge as honestly as he did that the price to be paid for the dramatic "human transformations" he so confidently predicted was a rendezvous with death.[99]

190. Georges Scott's drawing 'La Passagère' (The Passenger).

154

6

Painters take Flight

I have ripped through the blue
lampshade of color. I have come out
into the white. Follow me, comrade
aviators, sail on into the depths – I
have established the semaphores of
Suprematism.
                    Kazimir Malevich, 1919[1]

ON 3 December 1913 three of Vasily Kamensky's Futurist friends staged an opera in St. Petersburg's Luna Park that alternated over a period of four nights with a tragedy by Vladimir Mayakovsky in which the poet discoursed in free verse about his life. The opera was called *Victory over the Sun* – a title that Marinetti, who was due to arrive in Moscow the following month, would have savored – and it was consciously meant to be "a slap in the face of public taste."[2] Come watch and listen, the opera's prologue invited, as we men of the future "take flight."

To press home the provocation, the opera was acted and sung by a group of amateurs, whose faces were disguised by masks and whose bodies were enclosed in cardboard costumes. The characters they played were given generic names, such as "The Strong Men," "The Ill-Intentioned One," "The Traveler," "The Fat Man," "The Coward," "The Attentive Worker," and "The Sportsmen." They moved in front of sets painted in starkly contrasting squares and triangles whose shapes created an impression of infinite space. Spotlights crisscrossed the stage, constantly changing the perspective from which the action was being viewed, saturating the objects with color, and slicing the figures apart. The effect was that of a Cubist painting coming to life on stage.

Instead of addressing one another, the actors declaimed before the audience like disembodied abstractions who had nothing but a tenuous connection with the human race. Their monologues, dialogues, and choruses, pronounced in staccato rhythm, each syllable distinctly separated from the one that preceded and followed it, crackled with unmotivated violence and metaphors of war:

> Start a fight with machine guns
> Crush them with a fingernail
> . . . Let the red-hot horses
> Trample
> And the hair curl
> At the smell of skin![3]

In the middle of the opera's sixth and final scene, the roar of a propeller is heard behind the set. A young man appears and sings a song that declares his intention not to fall prey to the snares and vulgar tricks of beauty, symbolized by the now defeated sun. Sportsmen enter and proclaim defiantly the existence of Futurist lands in which everything moves without the resistance of gravity and paths lead in all directions, vertically as well as horizontally. Suddenly, as the roaring of an engine is heard, the broken wing of an airplane falls on the stage. The actors rush toward the wing and utter a series of

191. Robert Delaunay, detail from *L'Hommage à Blériot*, Öffentliche Kunstsammlung, Basel.

192. Newspaper photograph of the first performance of *Victory over the Sun*.

193. Malevich around 1913.

invented words that evoke images of a somersault and a man falling into a bog. Behind the set another figure identified as "The Pilot" laughs and steps out onto the stage, announcing with amusement that he is safe and sound. The opera ends as the actors sing:

> All's well
> That begins well,
> And has no end.
> The world will vanish but we will have no end![4]

On this futuristic note, the curtain falls.

With its reference to Kamensky's nearly fatal accident and its identification of the aviator as a prototype for the man of the future, *Victory over the Sun* was but one more example of the extent to which metaphors of flight had captured the imagination of the Russian avant-garde. Provided with a relentlessly dissonant score by Mikhail Matyushin and a libretto by Aleksei Kruchenykh that bordered on nonsense, everything in the production was intended to provoke the audience, and its authors succeeded brilliantly in their objective, eliciting a chorus of shouts, hisses, boos, and insults that periodically interrupted the performance and added to its scandalous allure. Yet if *Victory over the Sun* is remembered today, it is not because of its dialogue or its music – not even because of the uproar it produced, just one more Futurist battle after all in a long campaign – but because of its arresting sets and costumes, created by an artist whose reputation during the past two decades has itself begun to soar.[5]

The thirty-five-year-old designer of *Victory over the Sun*, Kazimir Severinovich Malevich, presents a fascinating and revealing example of the way an avant-garde painter could react to the phenomenon of flight during the pioneering years of aviation. A quirky and passionate man whose Polish parents had fled their country in the aftermath of the insurrection of 1863, Malevich grew up in the southern Ukraine where his father worked as a foreman in sugar refineries. His earliest memories were of the "hissing" and "groaning" of the machines in his father's factory, but unlike the young Santos-Dumont it was not toward new technologies but toward the depiction of nature on canvas that he was drawn as a young man. Aware that he needed systematic training if he were properly to develop his artistic talents, he set off in 1904 for Moscow, where he vainly applied for admission to the Academy of Painting and worked in Fedor Rerberg's studio, considered in Russia the most avant-garde of its time.[6]

Malevich's rise as an artist was scarcely meteoric. Unaccustomed to the rhythm of life in a big city and chronically short of money, he floundered and returned frequently to paint the countryside around his home town of Kursk before settling permanently in Moscow. By the end of 1910, though, the provincial from the Ukraine had established himself sufficiently in the Moscow art world so that he was invited to show three paintings at the famous "Jack of Diamonds" exhibit, which included works by Vasily Kandinsky, Mikhail Larionov, and his wife Natalia Goncharova, all artists in the forefront of the Russian avant-garde. A self-portrait by Malevich done about this time projects the image of an intense but carefully groomed artist gazing into the distance with a severely focused glance and framed by a background of coarsely sketched female shapes which emanate an aura of threatening eroticism and lava-like passion (Pl. 195).

By the time of the "Jack of Diamonds" exhibition, Malevich had moved far away from the plein-air Impressionist style of painting to which he had shifted after 1903 (Pl. 196). As he gained greater confidence in his own artistic vision, he embraced a version of neo-primitivism, which expressed itself in a wilfull distortion of form and perspective and the extravagant use of brilliant colors to suggest internal states of mind (Pl. 197).

194. Malevich in Kursk around 1900.

195. Malevich, *Self-Portrait*, 1908–09, State Tretiakov Gallery, Moscow.

What now interested him, he later wrote, was no longer the duplication of nature but the creation of forms that flowed only from his own emotional needs and the stimulus provided by the art of painting. Painting should be an end rather than a means; its truth should be contained in its forms.[7] Influenced by Larionov and Goncharova's rural paintings and inspired by his discovery of Russian icons, Malevich produced a series of works in 1911–12 that combined his pursuit of "pure painting" with a fascination for the Russian people in their most plebian activities: going swimming; having their nails clipped; polishing a floor; carrying water from a well; transporting earth; attending church; accompanying a coffin to its final resting place. Though clearly derivative of French artists, such as Cézanne, Matisse, and Gauguin, in their form, color, and composition, Malevich's images are nonetheless unmistakably Russian, and they reflect a powerful imagination informed by a first-hand knowledge of Russian peasant life (Pl. 198).

The paintings Malevich did in this period recall the rural themes of Kamensky's novel, *The Mud Hut*, published two years before. Yet just as Kamensky had felt the irresistible pull of technology in 1911 when he decided to become an aviator, so too in the same period Malevich began to mechanize his landscapes and human figures.[8] *The Woodcutter* of 1912 is a metallic robot whose body appears to be made of prefabricated cones welded together (Pl. 199), and the two peasant women of *Morning after the Snow Storm* are inserted into a madly heaving Cubist setting in which the snow, the buildings,

159

196.   Malevich, *On the Boulevard*, 1903, Location: State Russian Museum, Moscow.

197.   Malevich, *On the Boulevard*, 1911, Stedelijk Museum, Amsterdam.

198. Malevich, *Peasant Women at Church*, 1911, Stedelijk Museum, Amsterdam.

the trees, and the human figures are all made of nonorganic shapes, the vision of a non-Euclidian geometer rather than the naturalist observer who had left Kursk only eight years ago (Pl. 200). Recognizable details of the human face now became more difficult to discern in Malevich's paintings, and he began to portray the body cinematically and sequentially as a machine in motion. Though Malevich may have known little at this time of Marinetti's writings, aside from the original 1909 manifesto, he had in fact already realized on canvas the Italian poet's project of a fusion of man and machine (Pl. 201).

Given the enthusiasm for flight in Russia and especially in Russian avant-garde circles during these years, it was not surprising that Malevich would be drawn toward the aviation theme. But unlike other Russian intellectuals, he was not attracted toward airplanes as aesthetic objects possessing a new kind of beauty or toward aviators as a race of superior men who defied death. Nor was he frightened, as his friend the poet and visionary Velimir Khlebnikov was, by the prospect of a machine that might end by enslaving humanity through its domination of the skies.[9] What fascinated him was the notion of ascent, of take-off, of escape from the earth. In his imagination, flight became a metaphor for the transformation of consciousness, its liberation from the constraints of normal day-to-day existence, and the redefinition of time and space.[10]

199. Malevich, *The Woodcutter*, 1912, Stedelijk Museum, Amsterdam.

200. Malevich, *Morning in the Country after Snowstorm*, 1912, Solomon R. Guggenheim Museum, New York.

To understand the power and resonance this metaphor came to have for Malevich, one must reconstruct the mentality of the intellectual world in which he moved during the year immediately preceding the production of *Victory over the Sun*. In 1912 Malevich met the violinist, composer, and artist Mikhail Matyushin and the artist-turned-poet Alexei Kruchenykh. Both men would exercise an important intellectual influence over the painter and would act as conduits and mediators for ideas that were circulating throughout the Russian avant-garde.

Matyushin was a man of enthusiasms. In 1913 his great obsession was the notion of "the fourth dimension," especially as it had been developed in the writings and lectures of Peter Dimianovich Ouspensky.[11] Ouspensky believed that the world, as we perceived it in three dimensions, was only a pale and reduced version of the world that actually existed. To escape from the prison of the three-dimensional world, to experience space and time in all their complexity, it was necessary to cast off the "chains" of conventional logic. This was "the first, the great, the chief liberation toward which humanity must strive."[12] It was in art, Ouspensky thought, that the signs of this liberation would first become visible. "Art in its highest manifestations," he concluded his book *Tertium Organum*, "is a path to cosmic consciousness."[13]

Much taken by Ouspensky's ideas, Matyushin interpreted Western European Cubism

163

201. Malevich, *The Knifegrinder*, 1913, Yale Art Gallery, New Haven.

as a long-awaited breakthrough in perception onto a higher level of reality. The Cubists, he believed, had used intuition to go beyond the limited capacities of the human eye. In breaking with Renaissance rules of perspective and trying to visualize objects simultaneously from all sides, they had understood that the task of art was not to *reproduce* what ordinary people saw but to *reveal* what the clairvoyant artist intuited about the world and its visual forms. The price artists would have to pay for their liberation from pictorial conventions was that their work would be incomprehensible to those who could not, "with a single stroke of their wings," lift themselves up to unknown dimensions and breathe the pure air of radical change.[14]

164

Kruchenykh took a similar approach to language. Poetry, he believed, must be freed from its bondage to reason and comprehensibility. Since conventional thought and speech could not keep up with the emotions of someone in a state of artistic inspiration, poets should feel free to express themselves in a personal language that transcended analytical reason, a language that Kruchenykh called *zaum*. "This absolutely new way will be the combination of words according to their inner laws, which reveal themselves to the wielder of words, and not according to the rules of logic or grammar as was the case before us."[15]

Kruchenykh made an explicit connection between *zaum* and Cubism. Contemporary painters, he said, had discovered that the use of irregular perspective opened a new fourth dimension of visual perception. Similarly, contemporary poets had realized that irregular structuring of a sentence in terms of its logic and word formation generated movement and a new perception of the world.[16] How, asked Kruchenykh, could one have any sympathy for those who insisted on clinging on to the old conventions? "Is there any comparison between the joy of existing in the new dimensions and whatever wretched consolation one may find in the previous worlds?"[17]

In July 1913 Matyushin, Kruchenykh, and Malevich met at Matyushin's dacha north of St. Petersburg in Uusikirkko, Finland. Khlebnikov had planned to join them but through misfortune he lost the money Matyushin sent him for the trip, "those earthly wings," with which he hoped to "fly from Astrakhan to you."[18] Despite the recent death of Matyushin's wife, the poet Elena Guro, the atmosphere in Uusikirkko appears to have been lighthearted and resolutely optimistic. While there, Kruchenykh and Malevich drafted an aggressively worded manifesto in which they proclaimed their intention to destroy the "clean, clear, honest, resonant Russian language . . . the antiquated movement of thought based on laws of causality," and "the elegance, frivolousness, and beauty of cheap artists and writers who constantly issue newer and newer

202. Matyushin, Malevich, and Kruchenykh in Uuisikirkko, Finland, during the summer of 1913.

works in words, in books, on canvas and paper." This declaration of cultural war was accompanied by a list of projects they and their Futurist friends were contemplating, including the opera *Victory Over the Sun*. "Better to sweep away the old ruins and erect a skyscraper as tenacious as a bullet!"[19]

The proclamation of "The First All-Russian Congress of Poets of the Future," as Matyushin, Malevich, and Kruchenykh grandly called their meeting, promised that beginning on 1 August 1913, new Futurist books would be "taking off." The first of these, *Troe* (The Three), published in September, contained an important literary manifesto by Kruchenykh titled "New Ways of the Word" that summed up his views of language and literature. Previously poets had proceeded from thoughts to words; "we," the men of the future, arrive at unmediated comprehension through the word. The three units of psychic life – sensation, representation, and ideas of concepts – were about to be extended by a fourth unit: "higher intuition." "THE WORD IS BROADER THAN THE THOUGHT."[20]

This was a program that appealed to Malevich's deepest feelings about the nature of art. "Art," he wrote to Matyushin, "is that which not everyone can penetrate in a thing, and what is left over is only for the monsters of time."[21] Transformed by the spiritual intuition of the artist, any object, no matter how ordinary, could become beautiful.[22]

One of Malevich's contributions to *Troe* was a powerful untitled drawing whose topic was the faceless figure of a pilot hurtling through space. Already, earlier in the year, Malevich had sought, using Futurist techniques, to depict "the simultaneous death of a man in an airplane and at the railway." In this drawing, prepared for another book by Kruchenykh called *Vzorval'* (Explosivity), the opposing trajectories of an airplane and a locomotive intersect, giving rise to in a burst of cosmic energy[23] (Pl. 205). Done only a few months later, the drawing for *Troe* is distinctly more abstract. Malevich's major interest had changed from the portrayal of movement in terms of lines of force to a Cubist analysis of space[24] (Pl. 204). Once more, as in *The Woodcutter* of 1912 and *The Knifegrinder* of 1913, the pilot, in so far as one can make him out in the subtly modulated tones of black, grey, and white, is portrayed in conical sections as a piece of machinery, no different from the fuselage of the airplane which cuts through the pictorial space

203. Malevich, cover for *Troe* by A. Kruchenykh, V. Khlebnikov, and E. Guro (Moscow, 1913): the figure resembles the costumes that Malevich designed for the Futurist Strongmen in *Victory over the Sun*.

204. Malevich, untitled drawing, originally published in *Troe*, 1913, The British Library.

205. Malevich, *Simultaneous Death of a Man in an Aeroplane and at the Railway*, originally published in *Vzorval'* (Explosivity) by Alexei Kruchenykh *et al.* (St. Petersburg, 1913).

from the upper-left-hand corner of the drawing. The real topic of this work, though, is not the pilot, who is fused with the metal pieces of his flying machine, but free-floating cubes and planes, which are juxtaposed and warped in such a way so as to give the impression of a new perception of space. The mysterious Russian letters, the musical notes, and the numbers in the lower-right-hand corner of the picture suggest that we are being introduced to a radically different dimension of human perception where the relationship between words, music, and numbers is not what it was in the old, pre-Futurist world. Malevich's image lends a new and deeper meaning to a line of poetry by Elena Guro that appears on the facing page:

> the visionary who has been set on fire with such terrible,
> sonorous light.[25]

In "New Ways of the Word" Kruchenykh had declared that the aim of Futurists was not to discover new objects or new themes but to see and feel things in a new way. "A new light cast on the old world *can produce a most fantastic effect.*"[26] It was precisely this program that Malevich set out to realize in his sets for *Victory over the Sun*, which he first sketched in the summer of 1913. His drawings suggest a world in which perspective no longer governed visual perception and the eye was drawn into vistas vibrating with a sense of the unknown. Smaller squares were set within larger squares, giving the viewer the impression of gazing out into infinitely receding space (Pls. 206–10). Colored light was used not to silhouette but to break up and reconstitute form, thus creating the sensation of a world in ceaseless flux.

The artist and poet Benedikt Livshits, who was present at the first performance, later recalled the visual effects Malevich's techniques achieved. For the first time, he said, a painted solid geometry was realized on a stage. Using the new technology that made it possible to control projectors from a single panel, Malevich dissolved human bodies into geometric shapes.[27] "Abstract form was the only reality, a form which completely absorbed the entire Luciferan futility of the world . . . This was a *zaum* of painting . . ."[28]

206–10. Malevich, drawings for the sets of *Victory over the Sun*, 1913, St. Petersburg State Museum of Theatrical and Musical Arts.
  206: Act 1, Scene 1. 207: Act 2, Scene 2. 208: Act 1, Scene 3. 209: Act 2, Scene 5. 210. Act 2, Scene 6.

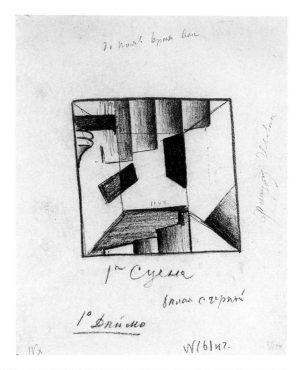

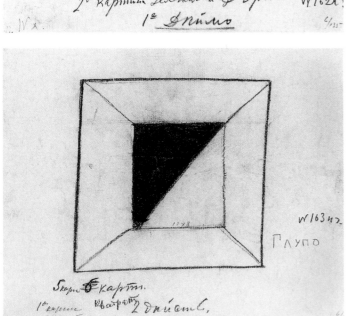

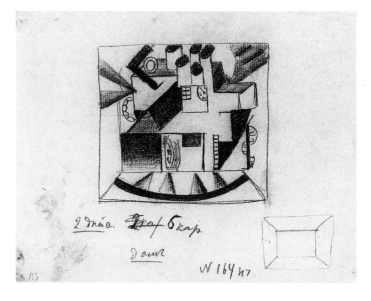

When Malevich did the sets for *Victory over the Sun* he had already begun to experiment with what he called "alogical" painting, an interpretation of Cubism in which objects were juxtaposed within a painting with the aim of creating a sense of unfamiliarity, shock, and absurdity. These works were constructed in such a way, Malevich later wrote, "that the unexpected confrontation of two forms would produce a dissonance of maximum force and tension."[29] During this alogical phase, which extended throughout the year 1914, Malevich returned to the theme of flight and produced a painting called *Aviator*, which was first exhibited in March 1915 (Pl. 212).

On first viewing, this work seems to have nothing to do with aviators or with flight. It portrays a stiff, metallic, one-eyed man wearing a top hat who is suspended in Cubist space. The man's body is composed of cylinders that gleam like highly polished machinery. His right and left foot are reversed, which emphasizes the strangeness of the visual world the painting invites us to enter. In his left hand the man holds an ace of clubs. Superimposed and flattened against him is a large white sturgeon with saw-like contours whose head is soaring upwards. An arrow extending across a whisk or eggbeater points towards the number zero, which is affixed to the man's top hat. From the zero emerges a cone of pale yellow light, which contrasts with the stark white of the fish and directs the eye of the viewer toward the letters APTEKA, spread across the upper-right-hand section of the canvas. The teeth of a greyish-blue saw, running down the central axis of the picture and situated behind the man's left arm, have severed the A from the other letters, while a green plane floats, like a flying carpet, behind the central figure.

No painting by Malevich more than this one reveals the extent to which his art was influenced by the avant-garde poets and painters with whom he surrounded himself.[30] Kruchenykh had written that "language should first of all be *language*, and if it reminds one of anything then it should be a saw or the poisoned arrow of a savage." Both a saw and an arrow play an important iconographical role in Malevich's painting, as they did in another alogical work he did in 1914 called *Englishman in Moscow*.[31] In the two cases, these objects are used to suggest the dissection or destruction of the past. The figure of the fish also appears in *Aviator* and *Englishman in Moscow*. The fish is a well-known Christian symbol of resurrection. Malevich identified it with the attempt of intellectuals to escape from the confined world in which they lived. Artists, he wrote in one of his more important essays of the period, were caught "in the nets of the horizon, like fish" and now had the opportunity to escape.[32] APTEKA (pharmacy) signified commerce, convention, and the pettiness of everyday life; the word "pharmacist" was used by Malevich's avant-garde friends as a pejorative term to refer to people with professions who were not intellectuals or artists.[33] As Mayakovsky wrote in his poem *Chelovek* (Man),

> Pharmacist
> let me lead
> my soul
> painlessly
> out into the space.[34]

Indeed, the formal clothes worn by the man in this painting are not unlike the dress adopted by Mayakovsky to mock the bourgeois public during the Futurist tour, which he, Kamensky, and Burlyuk had made the same year this painting was conceived and executed.[35]

The KA in APTEKA, which is clearly separated from the other letters, may refer to a poem of that name which Malevich's friend Velimir Khlebnikov was writing in March

211. Vladimir Mayakovsky as Futurist performer.

169

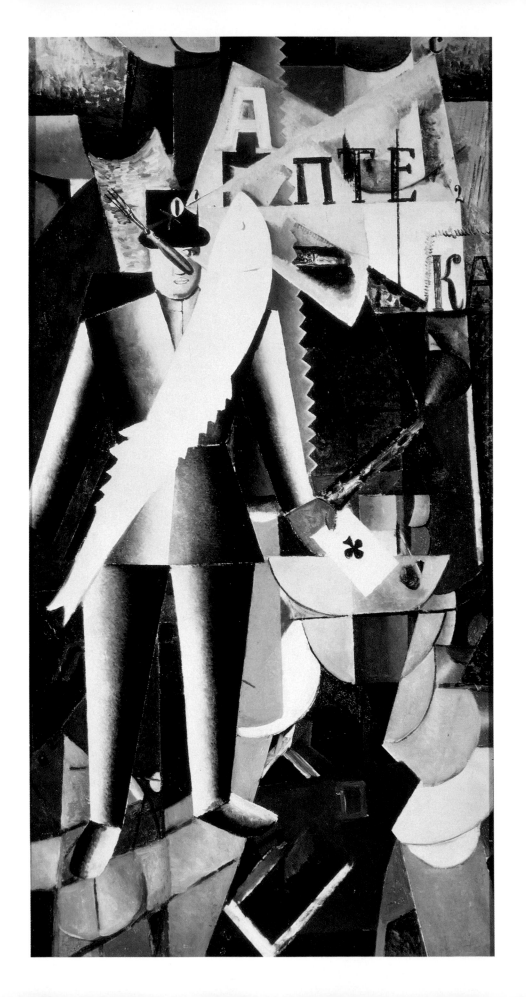

1915, when *Aviator* was first exhibited. As employed by Khlebnikov, *ka*, a term he took from ancient Egyptian religion, meant a force or principle capable of abolishing the conventional divisions of time and space.[36] The zero at the apex of the figure's top-hat was a concept with especially powerful meanings for Malevich. One was infinity; another was the boundary separating the three-dimensional from the four-dimensional world; a third was self-transcendence. In May 1915 he wrote to Matyushin: "We are organizing a journal and beginning to discuss various points. In view of the fact that we intend to reduce everything to zero in it, we have decided to call it *Zero*. We ourselves will then transcend zero."[37] Finally, the ace of clubs, which the aviator holds in his left hand, suggests that he had drawn a card that would make possible his imminent liberation from the world of stultifying conventions of bourgeois "pharmacists."[38]

212. Malevich, *Aviator*, 1914, State Russian Museum, Moscow.

The flight of Malevich's aviator, then, was a metaphorical escape from everyday life and an ascension toward a new system of perception. The jarring dissonances of the painting, its sharply contrasting colors, the flatness of its surface, and the lack of any perspective from which one can read its space undermine the viewer's sense of reality and open up, in the image of the soaring fish portrayed in white – a color to which Malevich ascribed transcendency – the prospect of resurrection from the pharmaceutical poison of conventional life and a breakthrough toward infinity. In Malevich's mind, as in *Victory over the Sun*, the aviator was a symbol for the man of the future who would liberate himself from the limitations of gravity and earthly space. Hence the letter A (for *Aviator*) painted in white that stands above the fish's head on the axis of the saw with which the old world will be destroyed.

Malevich continued to produce alogical paintings throughout 1914. Influenced by the work of Picasso and Braque, which he knew through reproductions and private collections in Moscow, he experimented with collage, inserted realistic representations of objects from everyday life, and cancelled out symbols of conventional politics and art, suggesting the bankruptcy of the past (Pl. 214). But whatever his fascination with this style, which foreshadowed the later development of Dadaism and Surrealism, Malevich was being irresistibly drawn toward a very different form of art. He felt the need to liberate himself from the tyranny of things, as we perceive them, and to create forms that corresponded to his intuition of the world. In December 1915 he seized the opportunity of a joint exhibition of avant-garde artists at the Dobychina Gallery in Petrograd to show a group of works in which no human figures appeared. Brightly colored squares, rectangles, circles, and triangles float freely in white space. The manifesto which Malevich prepared in order to explain the origin and purpose of these paintings announced that he had transformed himself into "the zero of form" and proclaimed the creation of a new school of art. "Believing that Cubo-Futurism has fulfilled its task, I am crossing over to Suprematism, to the new realism in painting, to objectless creation."[39]

Though fated to go down in history as a milestone in twentieth-century painting, "0.10: The Last Futurist Exhibition" – as it was called – was not a success. Of the six thousand people who came to view the paintings, only one was moved to buy; and the newspaper *Petrogradskiye vedomosti* called the painters "savages" playing at "anarchism in art."[40]

Undaunted by the snickers of the critics and the lack of enthusiasm shown by some of his friends, Malevich made clear that he had no intention of abandoning his exploration of abstraction. As he explained in a letter to Matyushin, there was no turning back. Suprematism had led him to the discovery of a world that lay beyond ordinary perception. "My new painting does not belong to the earth exclusively. The

213. 0.10: The Last Futurist Exhibition.

ЧАСТИЧНОЕ

ЗАТМЕНІЕ

ПЕРЕДАЕТСЯ КВАРТИРА

въ Москвѣ

Малевичъ

earth is thrown away like a house eaten by termites. And, in fact, in man, in his consciousness, there lies a striving towards space, the pull of a 'take-off' from the earth."[41] Planes of painted color on a white canvas, he continued, gave a strong sensation of space, which engaged the consciousness directly with no need for the mediation of objects. "I am transported into endless emptiness, where you sense around you the creative points of the universe."[42]

No doubt about it, Malevich's Suprematist 1915 paintings are abstract and disturbingly reductive, if judged by the standard of what other artists were painting in 1915 and what he himself had painted the previous year. Geometry and color are all that remain. But if one looks at them as a group – and adds to them the paintings and drawings he did during the next three years – it is clear that many, if not all, of these Suprematist works were inspired by objects present in Malevich's world. Among these, the most important was the flying machine: as their titles unambiguously suggest, many of these paintings and drawings are attempts to convey pictorially the experience of flight. This is true of the painting *Suprematist Composition: Airplane Flying* of 1915; the drawings *Formation of Aerial Suprematist Elements with Sensations of Flight* of 1915, *Suprematist Composition Conveying a Sense of the Universe* of 1916, and the 1916 *Suprematist Formation. Sensation of Movement and Resistance*; and even the designs for Suprematist fabrics done in 1919, to mention just a few of the many works he created in those years with wing-like images (Pls. 215–219). In 1924, when Malevich turned his attention from painting to architecture, he was careful to include among his plans a building for pilots (Pls 220–221). And as late as 1928, his painting *Head of a Peasant* sets its mask-like and inscrutable subject against a background of earth and sky in which airplanes ascend gracefully through the whiteness of celestial space; while lower in the picture a row of schematically depicted peasant women remain embedded in green soil, oblivious to the airborne symbols of the new age in the distance[43] (Pl. 222).

Malevich was keenly aware that his painting during the decade 1910–20 had been inspired by breakthroughs in technology. Explaining the origins of Suprematism in 1916, he wrote that "the new life of iron and the machine, the roar of motorcars, the brilliance of electric lights, the growling of propellers, have awakened the soul, which was suffocating in the catacombs of antiquated reason and has emerged at the intersection of the paths of heaven and earth."[44] Once he began to shift the emphasis in his

214. *Composition with Mona Lisa*, 1914. Private collection. The famous face of Leonardo's painting, an icon of Western art, is crossed under the ironic title (in the upper righthand corner) or "Partial Eclipse."

215. Malevich, designs for Suprematist fabric, State Russian Museum, Moscow.

216. Malevich, *Formation of Aerial Suprematist Elements with Sensations of Flight*, 1915, Öffentliche Kunstsammlung, Basel.

217. Malevich, *Suprematist Composition Conveying a Sense of the Universe*, 1916, Öffentliche Kunstsammlung, Basel.

218. Malevich, *Suprematist Composition Conveying the Feeling of Movement and Resistance*, 1916. Öffentliche Kunstsammlung, Basel.

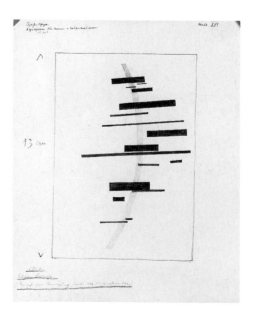

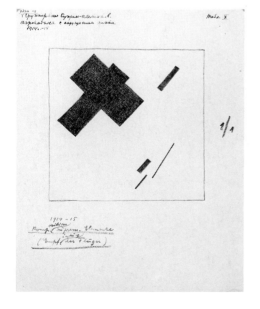

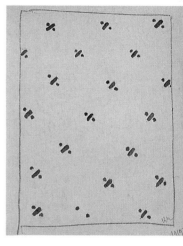

creative activity from making art to writing about it, which happened around 1918, metaphors of ascension occurred frequently in his essays. The path to abstraction, he wrote in 1927 in a book designed for Western European readers, had been like the ascent of an airplane. "The familiar recedes ever further and further into the background . . . The contours of the objective world fade more and more and so it goes, step by step, until finally the world – 'everything we loved and by which we have lived' – becomes lost to sight."[45] In the same book, Malevich distinguished carefully between the rural scenes that stimulated the Academic painter, the urban settings to which the Futurist responded, and the aerial views of winged formations that inspired the Suprematist (Pls. 223–226).

Yet what attracted Malevich was not so much the sky through which real airplanes moved as an imaginary planetary space where motors, wings, wheels, and fuel would not be necessary and spacecraft would be built "from various organisms, creating one whole."[46] A deeply reflective man whose writings abound with religious references and metaphors,[47] Malevich could not bring himself to believe that technology was driven by utilitarian considerations. It was an emotion – the yearning for movement, speed, and flight – that had brought about the birth of the airplane. "For the airplane was not contrived in order to carry business letters from Berlin to Moscow, but rather in obedience to the irresistible drive of this yearning for speed to take on external form."[48]

Thus, for Malevich, the airplane had been important because for the first time in history man was liberated from earth and catapulted into space on an adventure whose outcome no one could foresee. It was not in vain that "little aeroplanes" had emerged "from the bowels of the earth." "Everything was striving to leave the globe, and to make its way further in space . . ."[49] Once humanity had achieved unity – and Malevich believed it was on the path to doing this – it must reconcile itself with the technology with which it was presently engaged in a deadly struggle. "The pilot conducts unending war with his aeroplane; he wants to overcome it and to graft onto himself this new-grown body, to fuse it inseparably with his organism: the operation must be conducted with pain and blood so long as we consist of bones, flesh, and blood."[50]

Everything in this passage, written in 1919, suggests that Malevich foresaw the day when man and the machine would become one. A process of unification was leading toward the fusion of humanity, the material objects it had created, and the elements like wind and water against which man had traditionally fought. "Man," Malevich concluded, "is an organism of energy, a grain striving to form a single center. All the rest

219. Malevich, *Suprematist Composition: Airplane Flying*, 1915, The Museum of Modern Art, New York. "Their bodies fly in aeroplanes, but art and life are covered with the old robes of Neros and Titians. Thus they are unable to see the new beauty of our modern life." (from "From Cubism and Futurism to Suprematism: the New Realism in Painting," trans. and reproduced in Malevich, *Essays on Art, 1915–1928*, 1, p. 21.

220. Malevich, *Future Planits for Leningrad. The Pilots' Planit*, 1924, The Museum of Modern Art, New York.

221. Malevich, *Design for an Airport*, Sammlung Museum Ludwig, Cologne.

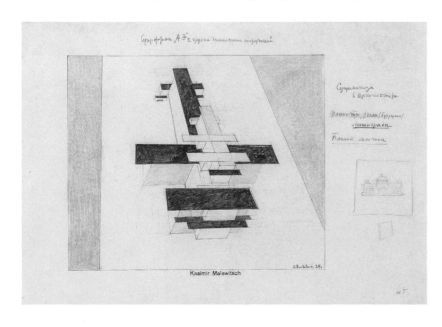

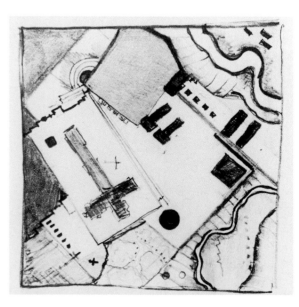

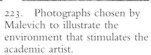

223. Photographs chosen by Malevich to illustrate the environment that stimulates the academic artist.

224. Photographs chosen by Malevich to illustrate the environment that stimulates the Futurist artist.

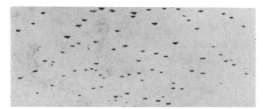

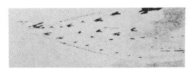

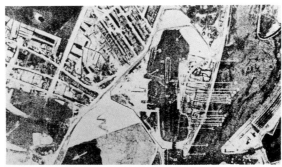

225, 226. Photographs chosen by Malevich to illustrate the environment that stimulates the Suprematist artist.

222. Malevich, *Head of a Peasant*, ca. 1928. State Russian Museum, Moscow.

227. Malevich, *Sensation of Universal Space*, 1916, Öffentliche Kunstsammlung, Basel. "Our century is a huge boulder aimed with all its weight into space." (from an unpublished manuscript that Troels Andersen dates 1916–17: Malevich, *The Artist, Infinity, Suprematism*, p. 34.)

is simply pretence."[51] And the direction of that striving was upwards so that sight could be liberated and human beings could become lighter and less earthbound, hence infinitely freer[52] (Pl. 227).

228. Robert Delaunay at 18.

During the decade between 1915 and 1925 Malevich wrote at length about all those Western artists who had inspired him and who had contributed to the movement toward non-objective art. Yet in none of the many essays he wrote did he ever mention the French painter, Robert Delaunay. This is curious in that among European avant-garde artists Delaunay was, along with Malevich, the one who responded most enthusiastically to flight during the years before 1918. The absence of any reference to Delaunay by Malevich is all the more surprising given the fact that the Frenchman was in frequent contact with Russian painters living in or visiting Paris through his Russian wife Sonia Terk, who was herself a gifted avant-garde artist; and Delaunay's paintings were known and discussed in Russia during the years before the war.[53] Had Malevich known the full range of Delaunay's work – and it is inconceivable that he was not aware of some of it – he would have discovered an artist who shared his passion for the new twentieth-century technologies, metaphors of ascension, and the aesthetics of soaring wings.[54]

Seven years younger than Malevich, Delaunay's climb to artistic prominence was much more rapid. Living in Paris was certainly an advantage; but Delaunay's panache, his unshakable confidence in his own genius, and the support of his high-living and artistically endowed mother, the Countess Berthe de Rose, also helped to smooth his way, as did the fortunate circumstance that he was under no financial compulsion to sell his paintings. Nor did Delaunay waste his time in an art academy absorbing lessons that he would later have to unlearn. After being expelled from a series of lycées, he did a two-year apprenticeship with a Belleville studio that specialized in the creation of theater backdrops; then he struck out on his own as a professional painter and showed his first canvases – colorful landscapes done in an Impressionist style influenced by Monet – in the Salon des Indépendants when only nineteen.[55]

It was an exciting time to be a young painter, and Delaunay took full advantage of the stylistic innovations that talented and ambitious artists were introducing, as they vied for primacy in the avant-garde. By 1909 Delaunay had worked his way through the Impressionism of Monet, the Symbolism of Gauguin, the color experiments of the Fauves, the pointilism of Seurat, the structural and spatial interests of Cézanne's still lives, and had begun to play with the techniques of Cubism as they were being developed by Picasso and Braque (Pl. 230). But the painter who most enchanted him and of whom he would speak with unfaltering admiration for the rest of his life was Henri Rousseau, known as Le Douanier because of his employment with the customs service from which he was retired when Delaunay met him in 1906.

Rousseau brought Delaunay into contact with the painters Picasso, Léger, and Vlaminck and the poet and art critic Guillaume Apollinaire, a charismatic figure who would come to play an important role in the development of Delaunay's ideas and art. Delaunay, in turn, introduced the Douanier to his mother, whose stories of her travels in India inspired Rousseau to do a jungle painting, *La Charmeuse de serpents* (The Snake Charmer), which the Countess bought and hung prominently in her elegant apartment on the Avenue de l'Alma.

Though drawn toward the techniques of other, more sophisticated painters like Cézanne, Delaunay appreciated the authenticity of Rousseau's art and was inspired by his example. The Douanier was the incarnation of the "people," always true to himself, and overflowing with the self-confidence of his race, despite his lack of formal artistic training.[56] By temperament suspicious of cerebral art and himself someone who worked by intuition, the younger painter envied the ease with which the older man had produced a unique artistic vision without having to agonize over its theoretical foundations. And it may be, also, that Rousseau's work encouraged Delaunay to create paintings organized around symbols of modernity. The image that would always be associated with Delaunay, the Eiffel Tower, had earlier appeared in a picture by Rousseau; and already in 1907 Rousseau had begun to insert dirigibles and flying machines into the sky of his suburban landscapes[57] (Pl. 231).

Yet, even if Delaunay was influenced in his choice of subjects by Rousseau, his means of representing them show the unmistakable influence of Cézanne and the Cubists. His first study of the Eiffel Tower, an engagement present for the woman who would soon become his wife, portrays it in somber brown and mauve colors, seen from the side of the Trocadero hill (Pl. 232). As he often did, Delaunay took his image from a picture postcard, in this case a photograph of a Voisin biplane circling the Tower as it began its

229.   Countess Berthe de Rose in her apartment on the Avenue de l'Alma.

230. Delaunay, *Self-Portrait*, 1909, Musée National d'Art Moderne, Centre Georges Pompidou, Paris.

return to the airdrome at Issy-les-Moulineaux. Delaunay eliminated the biplane from his com-position, but retained the aerial perspective to emphasize the upreaching thrust with which the Tower appears to violate the sky. If Rousseau could not figure out from which street Delaunay had done the painting – "*Tu es allé dans quelle rue? . . . Et après, tu l'a vue de quel côté?*" – it was because he had portrayed it as it could only be seen from well above the level of the highest ground.[58] Defying any attempt on the viewer's part to put the image in a recognizable perspective, the Tower seems to tilt away from the river towards the Champ de Mars.

The words Delaunay inscribed in the upper-left and right-hand corners of the small painting leave no doubt about the powerful significance this edifice had for him, as he entered into a lifelong relationship with Sonia Terk: "Exposition Universelle 1898, La

Tour à l'Univers s'adresse; mouvement profondeur 1909 France Russie'' (Universal Exposition 1898, The Tower addresses itself to the Universe; movement depth 1909 France Russia). The universality of modern society in which a radio signal launched from the Tower could be heard simultaneously throughout the world; the centrality of Paris, where universal exhibitions were held; the military and cultural alliance of France and Russia (symbolized by the relationship between himself and Sonia Terk) and beyond this, in a phrase meant for his lover alone, a coded sexual reference to the male's movement and the female's depth.[59]

Delaunay produced another small painting about the same period that showed his inclination to combine the Tower with the theme of flight (Pl. 235). Again the inspiration was a picture postcard – an image of the dirigible *République* either landing or about to ascend – but here instead of eliminating the aircraft, as he had done in the previous painting, he now integrated it with a view of the Tower whose stalactitic form is partially obscured by the massive hulk of the dirigible and the branch and foliage of a tree. The effect is a haunting integration of the forms of nature, as Delaunay had learned from Cézanne to represent them, and two of the preeminent objects created by

231. Henri Rousseau, *Les Pêcheurs à la ligne avec aéroplane*, 1907–08, Musées nationaux, Paris. Mme. Jean Walter Collection.

181

232. Delaunay, *Tour, Première Etude*, 1909, Private collection.

233. The postcard that inspired Delaunay's first painting of the Eiffel Tower.

modern technology: the Tower and the dirigible, both symbols of French achievement and power. Nature blends imperceptibly into technology, suggesting that both are products of a higher law governing the movement of the universe. Note also that the contrast, so central to the photograph's effect, between the immensity of the dirigible and the ant-like beings who swarm below it has been replaced in Delaunay's image by a harmony that reigns between the undulating forms of nature and the elliptical forms of man's machines. Technology and nature are transformed by the imagination into a

234. Postcard of *La République*.

235. Delaunay, *Dirigeable et Tour*, 1909, Private collection.

painting that exudes a charming, almost innocent, optimism about humanity's future in the modern world: the naivete of the Douanier Rousseau with the spatial sensibility of Cézanne.[60]

With his first studies of the Tower, a new period began in Delaunay's art and life. He worked on a grander scale and experimented with architectural forms showing, in his paintings of the Saint-Séverin cathedral, how the eye distorted the lines of the church's nave like a wide-angle camera lens, bending columns into curves (Pl. 236). He explored the Eiffel Tower from every angle, representing it from above, below, in the middle, and from every conceivable side, merging it into surrounding buildings, breaking it apart with light[61] (Pl. 237). He executed panoramic views of the city, pictured from the heights of the Arc de Triomphe and the spire of Notre Dame cathedral, gazing down upon the river as if suspended in the sky (Pl. 238). He broke the rooftops of Paris into a somber Cubist mosaic out of which the form of the Tower soared, points of red light in a heaving sea of green and grey (Pl. 239).

And with these paintings, that increasingly blurred the boundaries between objects and deformed space, came friends, support, and the taste of success. Delaunay sold his first paintings at the *Blaue Reiter* show in Munich in December 1911; he enjoyed his first retrospective exhibition in Paris two months later; and he was emboldened by these

236. Delaunay, *Saint-Séverin. No. 2*, 1909, The Minneapolis Institute of Arts.

237. Delaunay, *Champs de Mars: The Red Tower*, 1911, The Art Institute of Chicago.

238. Delaunay, *La Flèche de Notre Dame*, 1909,

signs of public recognition to undertake for the Salon des Indépendants in March 1912 a major painting that celebrated the city of Paris and combined a vision of the Tower with allegorical representations of the Three Graces (Pl. 240). The critics were enthusiastic, one going so far as to describe Delaunay's painting as a "veritable symphony of colors."[62] But none was so unqualified in his praise as Guillaume Apollinaire. Writing in the pages of the newspaper *L'Intransigeant*, the poet-critic pronounced *La Ville de Paris* the most important work of the salon and declared that what Delaunay had achieved went far beyond a mere artistic event.

> This picture marks the advent of a conception of art lost perhaps since the great Italian painters. And if it sums up all the efforts of the painter who composed it, it also sums up, without any scientific apparatus, all the efforts of modern painting. It is broadly executed. Its composition is simple and noble. And no fault that one might find with it will go against this truth: it's a picture, a real picture, and it's been a long time since we've seen one.[63]

Such extravagant praise encouraged Delaunay to press on with his studies of color and light. He knew, however, that *La Ville de Paris* was nothing but a step toward the kind of art that he aspired to do.[64] During the course of 1912, as Delaunay worked on a series of paintings called *Les Fenêtres* (The Windows), he became convinced that he had discovered a new way of making art that had nothing to do with the techniques of the Cubists, the Futurists, or the German Expressionists, who had become champions of his work (Pl. 241). The secret, he believed, was to abandon line in favor of color because, whereas line was necessarily static, scientifically modulated color contrasts held the key

239. Delaunay, *La Ville No. 2*, 1910, Musée National d'Art Moderne, Centre Georges Pompidou, Paris.

240. Delaunay, *La Ville de Paris*, 1912, Musée National d'Art Moderne, Centre Georges Pompidou, Paris.

to understanding the movement of the world. "*A line is a limit. Color creates depth* (not in perspective, *not in sequence*, but *simultaneously*) *both in form and in movement*."[65] Since light was in a continual state of flux, it engendered forms that were quite independent of the objects we are aware of seeing.[66] Unlike Vasily Kandinsky (with whom he had recently initiated a correspondence), Delaunay was adamant in rejecting any art that aimed toward the representation of internal states of mind. He sought to expand the bound-aries of perception by making us see in new ways. "The *eye* is our highest sense, the one that communicates most directly with our *brain*, our *consciousness*. The idea of the vital movement of the *world* and its *movement is simultaneity . . . Let's try to see*."[67]

Reflecting on the differences that separated him from his newly found German friends, like the Expressionist August Macke, Delaunay emphasized the importance of observing the movement of colors. He accused Macke of not being in a direct relationship with nature, which he insisted was the source of beauty. Of all the sources of inspiration in nature, the one that moved him most deeply, he wrote Macke, was the sun. The sun combined explosive and ever-changing color and the circular form whose rhythms he found endlessly fascinating. Do not forget, he reminded Macke, that the purpose of painting was representation, the creation of objects that resemble reality. "That's the essential and deepest thing about art."[68]

It would be understandable if Macke had been puzzled by this letter. The truth is that for all his talk of observing nature and "objectifying" reality, Delaunay was moving in the direction of greater abstraction. Art, he wrote in the summer of 1912, must never become enslaved to the object. It must never attempt to imitate what ordinary people see.[69] And indeed the *Windows* series, which he was painting at this time, were experiments in color contrast in which recognizable objects played a less important signifying role. Yet Delaunay continued to resist the idea of non-objective painting. The subject, he wrote, was indispensable – provided of course that the subject was strictly visual and a "pure expression of human nature."[70] It was in search of such subjects that Delaunay turned toward aviation images in his major paintings of 1913–14.

In doing so, Delaunay may well have been influenced by Guillaume Apollinaire, with whom he developed an intense friendship in the course of 1912. Apollinaire and Delaunay were especially close during the last months of the year, when the poet stayed in the Delaunays' apartment while recuperating from the trauma of being imprisoned for alleged involvement in the theft from the Louvre of Leonardo's famous painting, the *Mona Lisa* – a favorite target of Futurist derision.

An influential art critic and a brilliantly inventive poet, Apollinaire was experimenting in this period with verse that juxtaposed traditional and modern imagery to produce dissonant and unexpected effects. One of his most famous poems, "Zone", which Delaunay, like Apollinaire's other friends, would have known and which he may have heard Apollinaire recite, is full of aviation metaphors.[71] It begins:

A la fin tu es las de ce monde ancien
Bergère ô tour Eiffel le troupeau des ponts bêle ce matin
Tu en as assez de vivre dans l'antiquité grecque et romaine
Ici même les automobiles ont l'air d'être anciennes
La religion seule est restée toute neuve la religion
Est restée simple comme les hangars de Port-Aviation.[72]

In the end you are tired of this old world
O shepherdess Eiffel Tower the herd of bridges bleats this morning
You've had enough of living in Greek and Roman antiquity
Here even the automobiles have an old-fashioned look

241. Delaunay, *Les Fenêtres simultanées sur la Ville, première partie, deuxième motif, première réplique*, 1912, Hamburger Kunsthalle. This painting inspired Guillaume Apollinaire to write a poem that ends: "The window opens like an orange/The beautiful fruit of light."

242. Guillaume Apollinaire in the hands of the law.

244. Delaunay, *L'Equipe de Cardiff*, 1912–1913, Stedelijk van Abbemuseum, Eindhoven.

> Only religion has remained brand new religion
> Has remained simple like the hangars of Port-Aviation.

Intent on celebrating Christ, Apollinaire placed him with aviators in the air:

> Et changé en oiseau ce siècle comme Jésus monte dans l'air
> Les diables dans les abîmes lèvent la tête pour le regarder
> Ils disent qu'il imite Simon Mage en Judée
> Ils crient s'il sait voler qu'on l'appelle voleur
> Les anges voltigent autour du joli voltigeur
> Icare Enoch Elie Apollonius de Thyane
> Flottent autour du premier aéroplane.

> And turned into a bird this century like Jesus takes to the air
> The devils in the abyss raise their heads to watch him
> They say that he is imitating Simon Magus of Judea
> They cry that if he knows how to fly [*voler*] he should be called a thief [*voleur*]
> The angels hover around the graceful acrobat [*voltigeur*]
> Icarus Enoch Elijah Apollonius of Tyana
> They float around the first airplane.[73]

Being himself a lover and catcher of birds, Delaunay would certainly have responded to these lines in which Apollinaire evoked the fraternity of birds and planes:

> Et tous aigle phénix et pihis de la Chine
> Fraternisent avec la volante machine

> And all of them the eagle phoenix and Chinese *pihis*
> Fraternize with the flying machine.[74]

Zone was first published by Apollinaire in December 1912; the following month he and Delaunay travelled to Berlin where the German avant-garde journal *Der Sturm* had organized an exhibition of Delaunay's works. One of the pieces that Delaunay exhibited in the German capital was a large painting called *L'Equipe de Cardiff* (The Cardiff Team) (Pl. 244). Delaunay had completed it under pressure just before leaving for Berlin. Inspired at least in part by a newspaper photograph of a rugby match, *L'Equipe de Cardiff* brought together in an explosion of carefully modulated colors, reminiscent of the *Windows* series, a number of the most important images and forms that Delaunay had come to associate with modernity. In the foreground, slightly to the right of center, a faceless rugby player, portrayed in red, encircled by teammates and adversaries, leaps up to catch a ball. The ball, in turn, is contained within the half circle of a red Ferris wheel, behind which we see the soaring form of the Eiffel Tower, colored green and surrounded by wispy clouds. As our eye follows the curve of the Ferris wheel, it is led to a boxy Voisin biplane, whose wings reflect sunlight breaking through a dark blue sky. Stretching across the center of the canvas is a band of advertising billboards. The central panel in yellow with red letters advertises ASTRA, the French manufacturer of Wright Flyers. To the left we see an L and part of an A, which a contemporary French viewer of the painting would read as the last two letters of *Le Journal*, one of the Parisian newspapers most active in promoting aviation. To the right, appearing to bend off at an angle, is a red sign with white letters on which appear the words MAGIC (in English) and PARIS. Assaulted by this wealth of imagery, which we are supposed to assimilate *simultaneously* as a whole, we understand intuitively that Paris is the capital of technology – the modern magic – and that the twentieth century is one of ascension and movement upwards toward the stars – *ad astra*.

243. The newspaper photograph on which Delaunay based *L'Equipe de Cardiff*. Note that he has sketched a Ferris Wheel in the upper righthand corner.

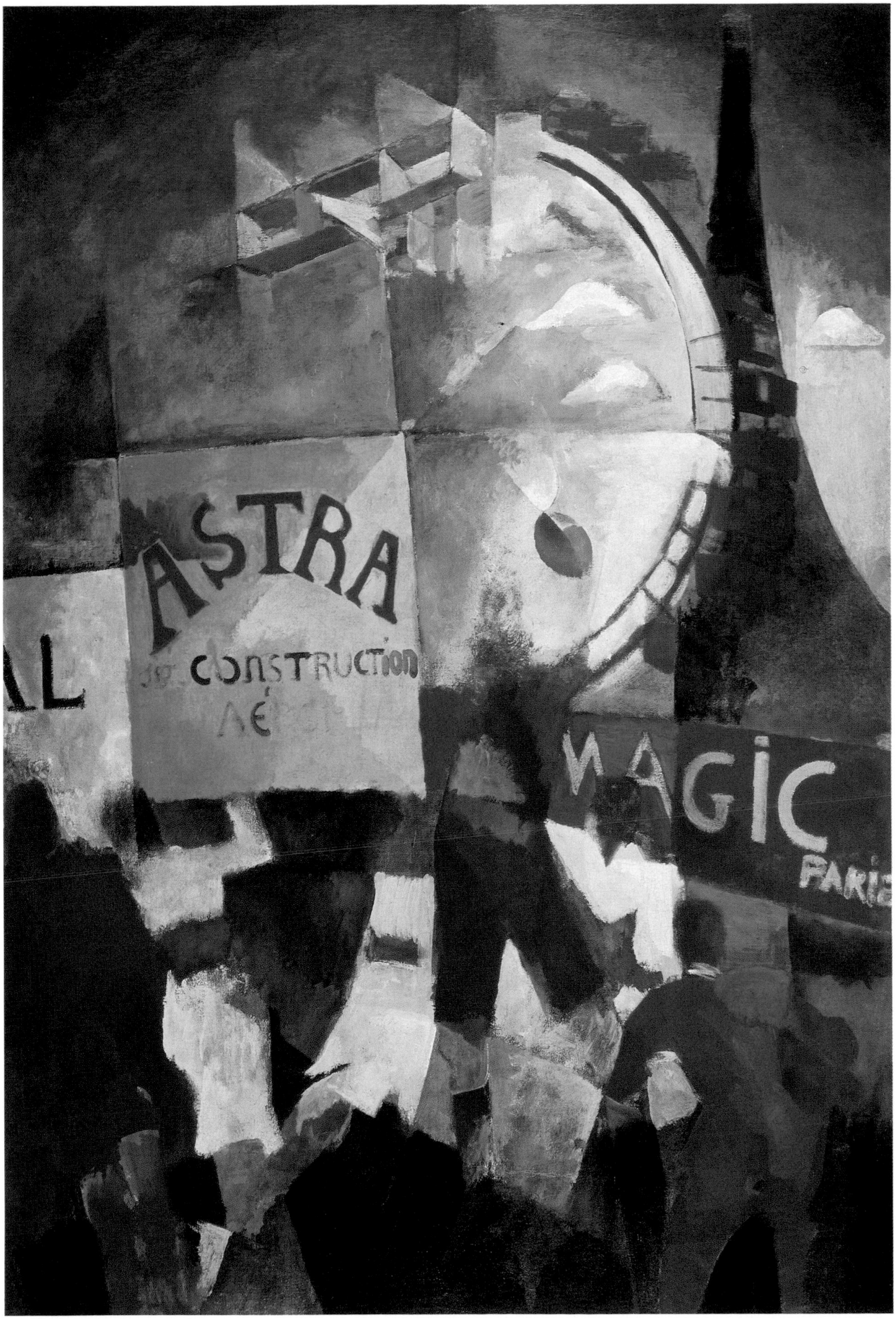
ASTRA
CONSTRUCTION
MAGIC

Delaunay thought so highly of this picture that he decided to produce a new version of it for submission to the Salon des Indépendants in March 1913. The result was an even larger painting, over ten feet high, that differed in important respects from the original (Pl. 245). Delaunay retained the basic pattern of rectangular panels, broken by the curve of the Ferris wheel and the leaping dynamism of the human figures. He now, however, delineated the features of the rugby players – whose forms were simply blurs of color in the earlier version – and individuated their uniforms, replacing the red of the central figure with tones of purple, brown, and green to distinguish him more clearly from his teammates and adversaries. Delaunay divided the Eiffel Tower into a base of bluish-purple and a spire of green, not unlike his earlier *Flèche de Notre Dame*, and lightened the blue of the sky through which the flying machine cruises, even more prominent than in the earlier version but now appearing bifurcated into the biplanes and tail. The surface of the painting was speckled with flecks of white paint to give the impression that the whole composition was an advertising billboard; and instead of bearing the word MAGIC, the right-hand panel, now in a cool green rather than the vulcanic red of its predecessor, was lettered DELAUNAY on top with the letters W-YORK-PARIS- below, suggesting (in contrast to the its more ethnocentric predecessor) the simultaneity of life in the world's great capitals and perhaps, also, the international reach of Delaunay's reputation. What had begun as an advertisement for sport and Paris – the Tower, the Ferris Wheel – had become an advertisement for Delaunay, whose reputation was now soaring like the airplane that glided above the rugby game, giving the whole scene the seal of modernity.[75]

A work as bold as this one was and so unabashedly ambitious was bound to provoke dissenting reactions. Reviewing it in *Montjoie!*, an avant-garde journal, Apollinaire proclaimed *L'Equipe de Cardiff* "the most modern picture in the Salon." There was nothing sequential in this work; every tone called forth and illuminated the other colors of the prism. This, he said, was simultaneity: "Suggestive and not only objective painting which acts on us in a way similar to nature and poetry! Light is here in all its truth." Apollinaire also applauded Delaunay's success in having escaped from intellectual art and created a work that had a "popular character." "I think this is one of the greatest compliments one can pay a painter nowadays."[76]

The accessibility of *L'Equipe de Cardiff* – what Apollinaire meant by its "popular character" – may have been precisely what caused Delaunay's German friend and admirer, Franz Marc, to dislike the painting. Sent a photograph of *L'Equipe de Cardiff* by Delaunay, Marc responded with brutal candor:

If this is one of your most recent pictures, then I must confess that I expected a development diametrically opposed to its style. This is actually the sheerest Impressionism, instantaneous, photographic motion. . . . The only thing that struck me about the picture is that it is very Parisian, very French, but very far removed from my ideas. The picture I saw in your studio last fall, the long picture with the tripartite view [*La Ville de Paris*] excited me much more.[77]

Delaunay was unmoved by Marc's criticism and believed, on the contrary, that he had now taken a major step forward in achieving on canvas what Apollinaire and other avant-garde poets, like his recently acquired friend Blaise Cendrars, were trying to realize in their poetry: the depiction of the simultaneity of actions and the transformation of the sense of time typical of modern urban life. Though Delaunay was incapable of expressing his purpose unambiguously in prose, he knew exactly what visual effect he was striving to achieve. Replying to Marc by return mail, he reiterated his belief in the importance of *L'Equipe de Cardiff*. "With this picture, which is the most perfect and

245. Delaunay, *L'Equipe de Cardiff. Troisième Réprésentation*, 1912–1913, Musée d'Art Moderne de la Ville de Paris.

beautiful subject, I have outdone myself . . . It is the most important, the very newest picture theme in my art and at the same time the most representative in its execution."[78]

Delaunay never wavered in his opinion that *L'Equipe de Cardiff* was a trailblazing work – "the surface of the picture is living and simultaneous; the entire picture is an ensemble of rhythms" – and he returned to the theme in later years. He was especially delighted with the way that he had integrated elements of modern technology into the overlapping mass of rugby players who represent the poetic dynamism and vitality of human life. "Their relative spaces, their movement enter into the general movement of the picture; there are no dead or descriptive parts that come to destroy the breath of life given by the general vision of the work."[79]

Delaunay took *L'Equipe de Cardiff* to the first German Autumn Salon where it was highly appreciated, especially for its vivid colors.[80] He and his wife, with over forty works on show between them, were among the stars of this internationally acclaimed exhibition of the European avant-garde. The largest part of Delaunay's contribution consisted of sun and moon paintings, which he had been working on ever since the Salon des Indépendants in March. These works, which he chose not to exhibit in Paris, again demonstrated his strong impulse toward abstraction; they also confirmed his liking for circular shapes. The subject of these paintings, Delaunay later explained, was "form itself created by the contrasts of colors in simultaneous vibration . . . It's the form in movement, static – and dynamic."[81]

Yet when Delaunay began to look for a theme suitable for a painting to be submitted to the 1914 Salon des Indépendants in Paris, he decided in favor of a large canvas dedicated to the achievement of Louis Blériot. Some art historians have been puzzled by what they see as Delaunay's retreat from abstraction and a return to figurative painting. They are inclined to account for this by Delaunay's "intellectual weakness" or the literary company he kept during this period of his life.[82]

There is no doubt that Delaunay was capable of stumbling into contradictions when trying to set forth his aesthetic theories. It was true also that, like his wife, he was much taken by the brilliant young poet Blaise Cendrars, whose verses crackled with electric images of modern life. It may also be that Delaunay hoped by a Blériot painting to reach a larger public. He certainly knew that the sun and moon paintings he had exhibited in Berlin had not enchanted his Parisian friends. Moreover, he was well aware that Roger de la Fresnaye had enjoyed success in the Salon d'Automne of 1913 with his patriotic work *La Conquête de l'air*, a painting Delaunay believed quite rightly to have been influenced by *L'Equipe de Cardiff*[83] (Pl. 246). For anyone in search of a popular subject, aviation had an obvious appeal. Crowds thrilled to the sight of soaring wings.

In late 1913, however, Delaunay saw no contradiction between his experiments with color and the depiction of airplanes.[84] The flying machine, with its outstretched wings and whirling propeller, satisfied his requirements for an artistic subject that could be reduced to pure form and light. How otherwise account for the fact that one of the paintings Delaunay exhibited in Berlin in September 1913, along with his abstract works, was *Soleil, Tour, Aéroplane* (Sun, Tower, Airplane), in which the biplane of *L'Equipe de Cardiff* was combined with a sun exploding in a rainbow of propeller and disk-like forms? In this work, the red and mauve rectangles of the airplane merge imperceptibly into rotating circles of light (Pl. 247).

Furthermore, we know that the enthusiasm Delaunay displayed for aviation was long-standing and deeply felt. In July 1909 he and Sonia had followed "day by day" the preparation of Blériot's flight across the English Channel. After its successful completion, they had been on the boulevards to welcome the triumphant aviator home.

246. Roger de la Fresnaye, *La Conquête de l'Air*, 1913, Museum of Modern Art, New York. Mrs. Simon Guggenheim Fund.

192

Delaunay had even written Blériot a letter of congratulation, to which Blériot had courteously responded. Later that fall Delaunay had sketched flying machines on exhibit at the Grand Palais during the first Salon de l'Aéronautique. In 1913 Delaunay and his wife often trudged by foot from the railroad station at Versailles to the airdrome at Buc in order to watch the planes take off and land in the late afternoon light. "By foot," Sonia later remembered, "like the pilgrims of old. He [Robert] watched the take-offs with joyous eyes."[85] Though Delaunay did not record his impressions in writing, another avant-garde artist Lyonel Feininger has left a description of what he perceived and felt while watching a similar sight:

> For a long time I watched the airplanes fly over the airport. I cannot find the words to describe the beauty of the landscape to the west which in the mist of evening appeared unreal. Some puddles of water in the field, after the rain of the night before, shined like gold at twilight and the only dark spot was formed by the mass of two immense hangars below. The hills around Paris, from Montrouge to the left to Saint-Cloud to the right, disappeared as night fell. Through the mist, innumerable factory smokestacks with their serpentines of smoke appeared totally deformed. Little by little, the sun, like an enormous ball of fire, disappeared in the clouds to the west and that extraordinary landscape seemed to me to be the perfect decor, worthy of the miracle of flying man. Furrowing the sky with long trains of smoke, the monoplanes and biplanes, in groups of two and three, climbed, descended, turned like dragonflies on sparkling wings, disappeared behind the apartment buildings, and reappeared in order finally to descend in gliding flight toward the ground, pitching, balancing, and vacilitating before alighting.[86]

It was this setting and the emotions it inspired in him that Delaunay set out to capture in *L'Hommage à Blériot,* completed in February and first exhibited at the Salon des Indépendants in March 1914 (Pl. 248).

The title Delaunay gave to his painting can easily be misleading. Its subject was above all light: as Delaunay later explained, the picture provided an "analysis of the solar disk at sunset in a clear, deep sky" and portrayed "multiple [electric] disk prisms that flood the earth, from which airplanes depart."[87] In so far as Delaunay's work celebrated Blériot, it was not the daring aviator who flew the English Channel whom the viewer was invited to admire but the inventive industrialist, symbol of collective human effort, who through his ingenuity made it possible for other men to fly. This becomes clear when one realizes that it was not Blériot but his aircraft which are figured in the painting; and to the extent that human beings can be glimpsed through the swirling circles of light, they are laboring members of the ground crew rather than fearless pilots gripping the controls.[88] Did Delaunay identify himself in some way with the achievements of Blériot? Did he think that the new art he was creating demonstrated the leading role of France in painting, just as Blériot had done in the new technology of aeronautics? Perhaps, because in later life he persistently referred to this period in his art as one of "construction," following the "destructive" phase of the Cubist Tower paintings; and the painting is dedicated "au grand constructeur Blériot" (to the great builder Blériot), with the two names Blériot and Delaunay linked visually together.

The rest of the inscription is less clear. The cryptic words *premiers disques solaires simultané forme* (first solar disks simultaneous form), which Delaunay placed in large letters along the lower edge of the painting, appear not to take into account the many paintings of suns and disks that Delaunay had executed during the previous year. But the phrase may have indicated to Delaunay himself that this was the first time he had

247. Delaunay, *Soleil, Tour, Aéroplane,* 1913, Albright-Knox Art Gallery, Buffalo.

successfully integrated these images within a large and complex composition, a picture in the grand style that was worthy of comparison with his most recent submissions to the Salon des Indépendants, *La Ville de Paris* of 1912 and *L'Equipe de Cardiff* of 1913.[89]

Ten years later, in notes he made about his paintings, Delaunay described the visual imagery that *L'Hommage à Blériot* evoked in his mind:

> Simultaneous solar disk. Forms.
>
> Creation of the constructive disk. Solar fireworks. Depth and life of the sun. Constructive mobility of the solar spectrum; birth, flame, flight of airplanes.
>
> Everything is roundness, sun, earth, horizons, intense plenitude, of poetry that cannot be put into words – Rimbaudism. The motor in the picture.
>
> Solar power and power of the Earth.[90]

Delaunay was right. No verbal description can do justice to the painting: more than any other of his canvases, it exemplifies his belief that the mission of art was to capture the movement of light and space.[91] The setting is sunset as planes prepare for take off on the ground and maneuver in the sky. The giant red and mauve propeller of a monoplane dominates the lower-left-hand corner of the canvas and is encircled by disks of bright blue, red, green, and yellow light. To the right, from the colors of another, bluer disk, emerges the figure of a mechanic who, with the help of two other members of the ground crew, is pushing a second monoplane into position for take-off. The plane seems headed toward the center of a disk made up of rings of alternately hot and cold colors that radiate energy and light. Directly above the monoplane's right wing and the mechanic who is holding it level is the rose-colored Eiffel Tower, reflecting afternoon sunlight, now a small and distant structure seen from high in the air. The blue curve of the Seine caresses the Tower's base and undulates toward the west, forming the outer ring of the central disk. An intensely red biplane flies above the tower, its wings enclosed in an uneven ellipse of purple and golden sunlight. A third monoplane – what appears to be an Antoinette – ascends toward the upper border of the canvas on the vertical axis emanating from the white circle of yet another disk. The red flame of the setting sun merges with the yellow glow of electric arc lamps. The effect is a Dionysian dance of light and color, a blazing hymn to humanity's ingenuity and will, a visual symphony in which the upward thrust of the Tower, the soaring wings of the biplane and the monoplane, and the electrically charged preparations for take-off on the ground all suggest the ascension of humanity towards a higher spiritual realm.[92]

If Delaunay's intention in painting *L'Hommage à Blériot* was to attract attention, he was successful, more so than he could have hoped – or feared. Even unadventurous critics found Delaunay's work impressive and sent their readers to contemplate it, though one admitted with a puzzled air that he found it difficult to place it in the tradition of nineteenth-century French art. "It doesn't resemble anything by Carrière, nor anything by Courbet, nor anything by Delacroix, it really doesn't resemble anything at all."[93]

Ever the champion of the avant-garde, Apollinaire could be expected to single out and praise Delaunay's work; but he did so in such a tortuous and ambiguous way that the artist was deeply offended. One can hardly blame him. In the few lines that Apollinaire devoted to Delaunay's painting in *L'Intransigeant*, he situated Delaunay within the movement launched by Marinetti that had now attracted a group of talented Italian painters, including Umberto Boccioni, Giacomo Balla, Gino Severini, Carlo Carrà, Luigi Russolo, and Ardengo Soffici. Observing that Delaunay was perfecting his experiments in color, Apollinaire drew attention to "the labyrinths of swirling Futurism" that he discerned in his painting.[94] To compound his summary treatment of

248. Delaunay, *L'Hommage à Bleriot*, 1914, Öffentliche Kunstsammlung, Basel.

Delaunay's painting, Apollinaire had earlier declared Alexander Archipenko's sculpture to be the high point of the Salon and devoted an entire article to its virtues.[95]

Delaunay's angry reply appeared two days later in *L'Intransigeant*. Apollinaire, he wrote, was free to make himself the apostle of Futurism in France, if he so desired; but the readers of this newspaper should realize that French artists regarded Marinetti's movement as foreign and of no interest to themselves. As for his own relationship to Futurism, Delaunay stated unequivocally: "I am not and I have never been a Futurist; no critic has any reason to mistake himself on this account. I am surprised by the ignorance of M. Apollinaire concerning the simultaneous contrasts that form the basis and novelty of my craft."[96]

The Italian Futurists were only too happy to enter what was shaping up as a bruising encounter of egos. Apollinaire had given them the ammunition they were longing for. What could better serve their purposes than an admission by the leading spokesman of the Parisian avant-garde that Delaunay was marching in the Futurists's footsteps? On 8 March 1914, a letter from Carrà, Soffici, and Papini, the last two coeditors of the Florentine Futurist journal *Lacerba*, appeared in *L'Intransigeant*: "The Futurist character of the compositions of M. Delaunay has been pointed out many times . . . we challenge M. Delaunay to prove the priority of his works over ours."[97]

Delaunay's response to this letter could scarcely have been more insulting.[98] In addition to discounting the value and novelty of their work, Delaunay, a tall man of commanding presence, even went so far as to insert a demeaning reference to the Italians' physical stature: "To the ridiculous accusation made by these little Italian gentlemen anxious to advertise themselves in the usual Futurist manner, I respond that it would have been difficult for me to plagiarize the big art-school paintings they call Futurist."[99]

249.   The Futurist painters in Paris in 1912. From left to right: Luigi Russolo, Carlo Carrà, F. T. Marinetti, Umberto Boccioni, Gino Severini.

Delaunay was not the only artist exhibiting at the Salon des Indépendants to be put off by Apollinaire's review. Offended by Apollinaire's suggestion that the improving quality of his work was somehow due to Delaunay's influence, Henry Ottmann also wrote to the editor of *L'Intransigeant*, accusing Apollinaire of "dishonesty" and working to discredit "living and sensitive French art" by misleading public opinion. Distraught to the point that he forgot the most elementary French grammar, Ottmann managed to suggest that Apollinaire was both corrupt and an agent of absurd foreign artistic tendencies.[100]

This was more than Apollinaire felt that he could and should stomach. Annoyed by Delaunay, outraged by Ottmann's letter, and displeased by the way *L'Intransigeant*'s editor had presented his enthusiastic review of Archipenko's sculpture, Apollinaire resigned from the newspaper and sent his seconds – André Billy and Fernand Léger – to demand an apology from Ottmann.[101] The chill in the relations between Apollinaire and Delaunay is shown by the fact that Delaunay agreed to serve as one of Ottmann's intermediaries. A terse communique in *L'Intransigeant* on 11 March stated that the incident was now closed.[102]

For all its apparent triviality, this tiff among painters and their poet-critic was revealing. In addition to exposing Delaunay's haughtiness and stormy temperament, it gives some idea of the ways in which the world of art had been infiltrated by nationalist passions; and it also demonstrates the pressure that avant-garde artists had come under to associate their production with a movement or an up-to-date aesthetic theory. No longer was it enough to *do* art; it was now equally important to manipulate public opinion and cultivate one's reputation as a person whose work was always on the cutting edge of the modern movement. Artists were claiming priority for their aesthetic *discoveries* with the same stubbornness that Wilbur Wright had displayed in pressing his claim that he and Orville had *invented* the airplane. In both cases, the resulting controversies distracted talented people from productive activity and concealed the extent to which leading figures in aeronautics and the arts had learned from one anothers' efforts.[103]

This exchange also had a lasting consequence for Delaunay. The growing rift between the artist and Apollinaire now became an irreparable break, and Delaunay lost the most faithful, eloquent, and visible champion of his work. The book that Apollinaire had promised to write about Delaunay and the Orphist painters would never be done.[104] Falling into a black hole of neglect made even blacker by his self-imposed exile from France during the First World War, Delaunay lost the momentum that the innovative masterpieces done during the years 1912–1914 should have given him. When he died in 1941, few people were aware that he had been a leader of the prewar avant-garde.

Delaunay would spend the rest of his life laboring to distinguish his achievements from those of the Cubists and the Futurists.[105] But there was an irony in the Futurist attack on Delaunay that the Frenchman never seems to have grasped. For all the talk of their machine civilization – and for all the claims by Marinetti that the Futurists would celebrate "the gliding flight of airplanes whose propellers whirl through the air like flags" – Futurist painters showed little interest in this quintessentially modern theme. They preferred to portray bicycles in motion, the glow of electric arc lights, the hustle and bustle of a twentieth-century street, the whirling feet of a dog, or the blur of a galloping horse. It took Delaunay, a painter often accused of traditionalism, to produce a truly modern aviation painting that combined the new language of abstraction with a portrayal of the visual beauty of airplanes. A rich and vital Futurist *aeropittura* (aviation painting) would develop in Italy, but it would come more than ten years after the execution of *L'Hommage à Blériot*.

One of the directions Futurist *aeropittura* would take, however, was prefigured in a work that Carlo Carrà did in the summer of 1914 (Pl. 250). Carrà belonged to that group of "little Italian gentlemen" that Delaunay had scornfully dismissed in his letter to the editor of *L'Intransigeant*. Seeking to give an "abstract" impression of "urban tumult" without the use of human figures, Carrà produced a collage now sometimes called *Manifestazione interventista* (Interventionist Demonstration), but originally entitled *Dipinto Parolibero (Festa Patriottica)* (Free-Word Painting (Patriotic Festival)). This striking work evoked by means of newsprint the emotions of a demonstrating Italian crowd seen from an aerial perspective.[106] The very form of the collage suggests at the same time the arc of a spinning propeller and the view of a Milanese piazza seen from a spiralling airplane, and shows that Delaunay was only one of many avant-garde artists during this period to be attracted toward circular forms.[107] That this aeronautical interpretation was intended by the artist is further indicated by the words one finds in the center of the collage around which the oblique axes rotate: ITALIA (Italy), *aviatore* (aviator), *battere il record* (to beat the record), *eliche performanti* (high performance propellers). In the second ring, the words EEVVIIIVAAA IL REEE (LOOONG LIIIVE THE KIIING) and EVVIVAAA L'ESERCITO (LOONG LIIIVE THE ARMY) sound a shrill nationalistic and military note, as does the patriotic cry ABBASSOOOO (DOWN WITH [Austria]), further emphasized by the irredentist slogan W TRIESTE ITALIANA MILANO (LONG LIVE ITALIAN TRIESTE MILAN) set against the background of an Italian flag. In the third ring, along its outer border to the upper right the word TOT refers explicitly to an widely advertised anti-heartburn pill manufactured in Milan but also suggests – because of its meaning in German, "dead" – approaching bloodshed, mourning, and the imminent destruction of the Habsburg Empire. Along the central axis, beneath the innermost circle, appears in large capitals the word SPORTS (in English), and throughout the intersecting circles and thrusting axes fragments of newspaper headlines convincingly evoke the sounds of crowds demanding war and shouting irredentist slogans.[108]

In a single striking image, Carrà succeeded in bringing together *simultaneously* several of the distinctive characteristics of the European mentality he and others perceived in the summer of 1914: the uncontrollable tumult of urban crowds heated to fever's pitch by the rhythms and sounds of city life and the propaganda of newspapers; the passion for sport, and especially for the sport of aviation; the lust for blood; and the irresistible power of patriotic slogans.[109] All this was conveyed through the medium of newspaper print of varying sizes and color contrasts that ranged from the bright green, white, and red of Italy's flag to the ominous black of the interventionist slogans and the word TOT.[110]

Marinetti was quick to grasp the significance of Carrà's collage and its potential value in demonstrating the leading role of Italian Futurist painters in the European avant-garde. On 21 July he wrote to the coeditor of *Lacerba*, Ardengo Soffici, instructing him to publish Carrà's work on the cover of the next issue. "The urgency is due to our desire to establish immediately that Carrà and Severini were the first to make this absolutely original fusion of visual dynamism and words in liberty. This in order to prevent the usual Delaunays and other plagiarizers from taking the credit for our discoveries."[111]

Festa Patriottica was published on the front cover of *Lacerba* on 1 August 1914.[112] A few days later Europe went to war. At first neutral, Italy would soon be swept into the conflict by interventionist demonstrations not unlike the one that Carrà had tried to portray using the aeronautical image of a mass meeting that had spun out of control. Out of the bloody conflagration would come yet another icon of the aviator – not the inventor of Wilbur Wright nor the sportsman of Hubert Latham; not the death-defying superman of Gabriele D'Annunzio nor the Promethean hero of Rostand; not the dreamy seer portrayed by Malevich nor the triumphant builder celebrated by Robert Delaunay – but the ace. It would become one of aviation's most long-lived images.

250. Carrà, *Dipinto Parolibero (Festa Patriottica)*, 1914; also known as *Manifestazione interventista*. Mattioli Collection, Milan.

7

Aces

So it was that war in the air began. Men rode upon the whirlwind that night and slew and fell like archangels. The sky rained heroes upon the astonished earth. Surely the last fights of mankind were the best. What was the heavy pounding of your Homeric swordsmen, what was the creaking charge of chariots, besides this swift rush, this crash, this giddy triumph, this headlong sweep to death?

H. G. Wells, 1914[1]

I N 1914 the dominant image of the aviator was the "sportsman"; after 1915 it became the flying "ace," an airborne knight armed with a machine-gun who jousted in the sky.[2] Curiously, no prewar intellectual had imagined the ace, though Marinetti had anticipated one aspect of the ace's psychology in his portrait of Captain Piazza, as he pursued Ottoman troops in his Blériot: "higher, more handsome than the sun . . . his bold, sharp-edged face chiseled by the wind, his little mustache crazy with will."[3] All Marinetti's imagined airmen are driven by a fatal attraction toward the embrace of death, "the Death that takes us when we are worthy of its deifying caresses."[4] Most high-scoring aces would come to know that feeling.

The first person to experience the transition from sportsman to ace – indeed, the person who can be said to have *created* the figure of the ace in a brilliant burst of improvisation during the first nine months of the First World War – was the great French aviator Roland Garros, known today almost exclusively because the tennis stadium in which the French Championships are played every spring bears his name. An understandable if ironic connection because, though a memorable competitor in many sports, Garros never achieved eminence with a racquet.

Of all the French pilots of the prewar period, Garros was the most complex and versatile, sensitive to an extreme and "moved by everything that was beautiful and great," as one of his contemporaries remembered him.[5] All those who saw Garros fly were struck by his virtuosity and elegance. He himself believed that beyond all the obvious endowments needed to excel as an aviator – courage, will power, physical resistance, presence of mind – there was a further quality that, for want of a better word, he called "style." No one who had watched Garros carving delicate turns or performing aerobatics would dispute that he possessed the "instinctive comprehension of flight" to an extraordinary degree. "A bird turned into a man!" one of his admirers wrote, admitting that he was unable to describe in words the feelings he had while watching Garros fly.[6]

Born in 1888 on the French island of Réunion in the Indian Ocean and brought up in Saigon, Garros was sent as a young boy to pursue his secondary studies in Paris.[7] His adolescence could serve as a prototype for what Romain Rolland and others were writing about the generation of 1914 during the years preceding the outbreak of the First World War.[8] An indifferent student frequently accused by his teachers of day-

251. A German ace wedded to his Fokker, his gun sight an extension of his eye. Note the Pour le mérite medal in the upper left hand corner.

252. Roland Garros atop the plane with which he made the first Mediterranean crossing by air in September 1913.

dreaming, Garros cared for nothing but his bicycle and the new sports imported from England.[9] He captained his soccer team and won the interscholastic bicycle championship of France in 1906. He played tennis, participated in running races, and lifted weights. With a friend, he undertook a long motorcycle journey through France. His real passion, however, was for flight. An avid reader of Jules Verne, he dreamed of flying in the depth of the night above a lighted city, usually Nice where he had been sent as an adolescent to recover from double pneumonia: "I stop at balconies and the skylights of garrets, I startle lovers."[10] Later, in 1906, he was watching at the Bois de Boulogne when Santos-Dumont attempted to raise his first flying machine from the ground.

After graduating from the Ecole des Hautes Etudes Commerciales, Garros bought an automobile agency with money borrowed from the father of a classmate and began to sell a sporty version of the Grégoire motorcar. This first venture into business earned Garros some money and with it the financial independence he craved. Yet the dream of flight would not go away. In August 1909 he was among the crowds who flocked to Rheims for the great air meet. He was transfixed by what he saw there. "I would have gambled my life to be like 'them,'" he later remembered. By the last evening, "everyone was delirious, women cried." There was no reason, he acknowledged, to believe that he was any more enthusiastic than the others.[11] Except, perhaps, that a month later, after several nights of "feverish hesitation," Garros ordered a Demoiselle, a light and inexpensive flying machine adapted from the model recently developed by Santos-Dumont and exhibited at the Salon de l'Aéronautique.

Garros taught himself to fly and after three hours in the air (and one potentially fatal accident) he embarked on a career as a professional aviator. During the following four years he experienced almost every sensation the new sport had to offer. He risked his life providing thrills for crowds throughout the United States and Latin America in the equivalent of an aerial circus. He flew city-to-city races for the Blériot team in Europe in 1911, finishing second to Jules Védrines and Jean Conneau in the demanding Paris-Madrid and Paris-Rome contests. He set a new altitude record of 17,000 feet in Tunis in December 1912. And on 23 September 1913, he accomplished a feat that not even D'Annunzio's fertile imagination had dared contemplate: taking off from Fréjus-Saint-Raphaël, he successfully crossed the 800 kilometers of water separating the French Riviera from the Tunisian coast. He landed at the French military base of Bizerte with a heavily vibrating engine and only a little over a gallon of fuel left in his tank. Why had

254. A lean and muscular Gavros holds fast to his prize-winning bicycle in 1906.

255. Garros attempts a backhand. Few tennis instructors would advise his technique today.

253. Garros photographed by Jacques Lartigue as he banks above the airdrome at Issy-les-Moulineaux 1911.

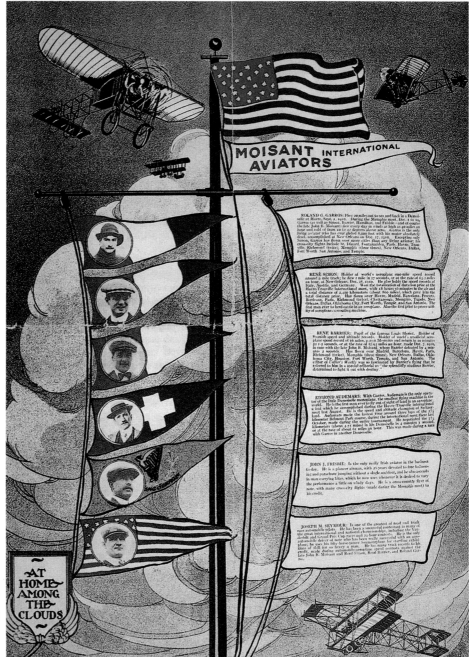

256.   Garros in his Demoiselle in 1910; the Demoiselle cost only $1500 when Garros bought it.

257.   Garros wearing the shoulder belts he used to control the Demoiselle.

258.   The flyer announcing Moisant International Aviators. In his *Mémoires*, Garros wrote that the crowd paid to see the Moisant aviators risk their lives and sometimes grew violent, firing shots and threatening them with death when they declined to fly because of bad weather. To attract customers, they posted the portraits of their pilots who had been killed while performing. It was the month after the death of their leader, John Moisant, that they did their best business.

he pushed on after his engine began to show signs of failing? "To indulge myself, to live a beautiful adventure, even at the price of death."[12]

Garros was in Vienna, competing in an air meet, when the Archduke Ferdinand and his wife were assassinated in Sarajevo. No one, he thought, seemed particularly affected by the death of the heir to the Habsburg crown. They expressed sadness only at the fate of the Emperor who had suffered so many tragedies. "And it never occurred to any of us, I believe, that this event, which left the masses indifferent, would be the spark that set Europe aflame."[13] Indeed, after leaving Vienna, Garros went on to fly an exhibition in the German city of Mannheim. Toward the end of July he embarked on an automobile tour of German aircraft factories at the invitation of a newly acquired friend, the celebrated German aviator Hellmuth Hirth. Watching the care with which engines were assembled in the Mercedes plant, he thought bitterly that Hirth would never have to worry that his engine would break down on the eve of a big race.[14] He had just returned to Paris when war between France and Germany was declared.

Garros volunteered immediately and was assigned as a private to the MS 23, a squadron flying Morane Parasols, the fastest French military aircraft then in use. Sent with his unit to the area around Nancy in the east of France, he flew his first reconnaissance mission already on 19 August, as the brunt of the German army was forcing its way through Belgium into northern France. With him as observer was a captain from the general staff. Cruising in the vicinity of Saarbrücken at 5500 feet, Garros spotted a German aircraft with large black crosses on the wings. His observer took a shot with his carbine from a little less than 300 feet, but there was no evidence that he had done the German aircraft any damage. Fired on by German ground troops who mistook it for a French Farman and surrounded by puffs of shrapnel, the German Euler dived and headed for home. Garros was not impressed by his first experience of aerial warfare. He noted in his diary: "My observer sees nothing, not even what I show him. Return after two hours missing one cylinder."[15]

Determined to give himself a better chance of downing German aircraft, Garros arranged to fly with an officer who was renowned for his marksmanship. On 26 August they caught sight of an enemy plane heading in the direction of Lunéville. Garros pursued the Albatros, placing the German to his left and about five feet beneath him. His observer fired, then fired again, but they were forced to veer off to the right when their adversary responded with a machine-gun. Before they could make another pass, the Albatros had descended, disappearing in the clouds. Garros's terse commentary in his diary on this mission conveyed his frustration: "After two and a half hours of flight, we return, as usual with one cylinder not functioning. Our armament has shown itself to be insufficient."[16]

Disappointed by these early attempts at aerial combat, the French Command instructed its pilots to confine themselves to reconnaissance flights and whenever possible to avoid encounters with the enemy. But Garros took away from his experiences in August 1914 the conviction that the Parasols could be armed with a machine-gun, operated by the pilot, that would fire along the axis of the plane. Before this could be accomplished, however, it would be necessary to find a means of firing through the path of the propeller without destroying its blades or undermining the controllability of the aircraft. The obvious solution to the problem was synchronization; but the Hotchkiss machine-guns used by the French army contained a firing mechanism that could not be stopped once in movement.

Another alternative was to reinforce the propeller blades to the point that they were capable of deflecting the relatively low percentage of cartridges that would not pass

freely through the propeller's path. The designer of the Parasol, Raymond Saulnier, had tried to interest the French military authorities in such a device during the spring of 1914, but had been discouraged by the failure of his experiments and doubts expressed by army experts who questioned whether any pilot could fly and operate a machine-gun effectively at the same time.

Assigned to the aerial defense of Paris in November 1914, Garros set out to solve this problem. He began with Saulnier's drawings. After a series of demoralizing failures, he and his mechanic Jules Hue devised a mechanism that armed the propeller effectively and deflected bullets striking its blades away from the propeller's path.[17] When Garros was ordered to proceed to Dunkerque in March 1915 he possessed an aircraft with which he could spit deadly fire throught the blades of his propeller. No German aviator had ever had to cope with such an adversary before. Of the four German planes downed by French pilots up to that point, all but one had all been disabled by observers firing carbines.[18]

Garros achieved his first victory on 1 April.[19] Cruising at 4,500 feet en route to bomb a railway station at Bruges in Belgium, he noticed an enemy Albatros about a thousand feet to his left. Waiting until he was within a hundred feet of the German, he fired four bursts of twenty-four bullets each. The German pilot's observer responded with carbine fire, putting a bullet through Garros' wing. The German plane dived, seeking to escape. Garros followed:

the chase became more and more chaotic; we were now no higher than one thousand feet; at that moment an immense flame burst from the German engine and spread instantaneously. What was curious, the plane didn't fall, but descended in an immense spiral. The spectacle was frighteningly tragic, unreal. The descent became more pronounced for 25 seconds and ended with a fall of 100 feet and a horrible crash. I watched for sometime to convince myself that it wasn't a dream, I carefully marked the spot, and returned.[20]

Upon landing, Garros immediately set out by automobile for the scene of the crash. The burnt and bleeding bodies of the pilot and his observer were in a horrible state. Though disgusted by what he saw, Garros confessed to a family friend the "satisfaction" and "joy" he felt at having "created alone, and in spite of all the risks of the unknown in aviation, the instrument that brought me success." He also noted with evident pride

208

LA GUERRE 1914-1915
EN IMAGES
Faits, Combats, Épisodes, Récits

ROLAND GARROS
GLOIRE DE L'AVIATION FRANÇAISE
L'UN DE SES DERNIERS EXPLOITS

Illustrations de O'GALOP
PELLERIN & Cie, imp.-édit.
IMAGERIE D'ÉPINAL, N° 95

Né à LA RÉUNION en 1888, dès l'adolescence il montra un goût très vif pour les sciences exactes et pour l'aventure. Aussi s'adonna-t-il avec passion à l'Aviation. C'est en 1911 qu'il s'est affirmé comme aviateur. Cette année-là, en effet, il se classa second dans Paris-Madrid, dans Paris-Rome et dans le Circuit Européen. En 1912, il conquérait le record de la hauteur en atteignant l'altitude de 5.601 mètres. Cette même année, il gagnait en outre le Grand Prix d'Aviation et effectuait ensuite la traversée de la Méditerranée, de Tunis à la Sicile. En 1913, il dominait cette mer une fois encore, volant victorieusement de Fréjus à Bizerte.

Quand la guerre éclata, Garros était déjà Chevalier de la Légion d'Honneur. Engagé volontaire et nommé sergent, il fut de suite un des plus redoutables adversaires des avions ennemis. Bientôt sous-lieutenant, il poursuivait ses exploits; et, c'est après avoir accompli le plus brillant, alors que seul à bord, à la fois pilote et mitrailleur, il venait de descendre trois appareils allemands — l'un de ceux-ci représenté piquant embrasé vers le sol — qu'un vulgaire accident, une banale panne de moteur, se produisant, hélas! au-dessus des lignes ennemies, l'obligea d'atterrir. Par là seulement ROLAND GARROS pouvait tomber vivant aux mains des Allemands.... 19 avril 1915 !!!

261. Garros sketched by Jean
Cocteau just before his capture
by the Germans in April 1915.
In 1916 Cocteau wrote a series
of poems dedicated to Garros,

My pirate friend
     with the heart of
  Roland
     with the heart of
  Tristan
He hunts
The Valkyries.

the fact that his combat had been witnessed by thousands of allied and enemy troops and that his victory had created a "sensation" in Dunkerque.[21] Less than two weeks later, however, Garros felt compelled to write to another younger and closer friend apologizing for the enthusiastic and breezy account he had given him of his first victory. "I recounted in a humorous vein my first successful combat: the thing was instead tragic and scarcely lent itself to jokes. It was horrible and I remained traumatized for some time. It was in this period of numbness that I wrote you nonsense in bad taste in order to react against my own mood."[22]

Garros downed two more German planes with his machine-gun before he was himself forced down and taken prisoner on 18 April. By then, however, Garros had set a pattern that other talented First World War aviators would follow. He fought alone and on terms chosen by himself; he modified his plane to fit his own specifications; and he noted carefully and in detail the circumstances of his victories, going so far as to visit the site of his adversaries' crashes and photograph his victims. Despite French Army policy forbidding the singling out of individual combatants for praise, it was impossible to keep news of Garros's victories out of the press. General Foch himself cited Garros's exploit in a communiqué on 4 April, proclaiming him to be a pilot "as modest as brilliant," who "has never ceased to give the example of the most admirable spirit."[23]

What Foch was willing to grant, the press could not be expected to withhold. Commenting that the principle of anonymity in combat had been infringed – "rare privilege!" – L'Illustration emphasized the lonely nature of Garros's exploit. "He piloted the plane he himself created, a Morane monoplane, ingeniously, lovingly adapted and perfected by him, a light and beautiful machine, similar to a lark, delicate and tiny in comparison to the hawk it had to attack, but formidably armed with a machine-gun. And Roland Garros mounted alone this machine, his child."[24] The ace had been born.[25]

262. Oswald Boelcke as a cadet before the war.

263. Max Immelmann, the "eagle of Lille," in 1916.

About a month after Garros's capture, Ensign Max Immelmann arrived in the occupied French city of Douai with the newly constituted Section 62, a squadron of the German flying forces consisting of six pilots and supporting ground personnel. Exceptionally well endowed with those qualities necessary for success in the phase of the air war that was just now beginning, Immelmann was not yet twenty-five years old, an excellent athlete and acrobat, and a fanatical enthusiast of engines and motor vehicles of all kinds, especially flying machines. Educated at the Dresden Cadet School, he applied for a transfer to the reserves after obtaining his commission as a junior officer and began studies at the Dresden Technical High School with the goal of making a career as a mechanical engineer. His free time he devoted to dancing, motoring, and promoting the cause of aviation through his membership in the Air Fleet League and his participation in model-building evenings for young people. His brother Franz remembered him as an enthusiastic official darting about the old Dresden airdrome at Caditz during the flying competitions of 1913–14.[26] When war broke out, the Immelmann brothers had immediately responded to the Inspectorate of Aviation's call for technically educated volunteers interested in undergoing flight training.[27]

Also posted to the 62nd Squadron was Oswald Boelcke, a seasoned combat pilot whom Immelmann quickly came to like and admire. The two young men had much in common. Almost the same age as Immelmann, Boelcke was an accomplished sportsman who played tennis, ice-skated, ran cross-country races, swam and dived competitively, and skied and climbed mountains during his prewar vacations. Since childhood he had fought against a tendency toward asthma by disciplining his body and submitting himself to exacting physical challenges. According to his father, a practiced mountain climber, Oswald Boelcke was drawn toward the steepest cliffs. "It was when danger threatened that his young soul leaped with joy."[28]

Immelmann's first assessment of Boelcke was less heroic. He got on well with him because he did not smoke, seldom drank, and was, in Max's view, "an extraordinarily quiet level-headed fellow with intelligent views."[29]

Like Immelmann, Boelcke had been educated as an army cadet and had attended aviation meets that had made a deep impression on him and whetted his appetite for flight. Boelcke never tired of watching planes fly and stared at them "with eyes of longing." "It must be a wonderful sport – more beautiful even than riding!" the young cadet wrote to his parents in 1912 from Metz, where he was attending the War Academy.[30]

In May 1914, unknown to his parents, Boelcke obtained a transfer from his communications company to the Halberstadt Flying School where he began pilot training. By 15 August he had his pilot's certificate and in September, during the second month of the war, he began flying reconnaissance missions with his brother Wilhelm as observer in the sector of the Argonne Forest near Varennes. Boelcke soon noticed that he was capable of flying more missions and longer hours than the other pilots. Their nerves, he reported proudly to his parents, could only take two or two and a half hours of flight a day. "If only I knew what sort of things nerves are! Luckily I know nothing of them, and is all the same to me whether I fly an hour longer or not."[31] By May 1915, when he joined the 62nd at Douai, Boelcke had already been awarded the highly coveted Iron Cross, First Class. He was also considered by his commanding officer and many of his fellow pilots as a man of ruthless ambition who was set upon monopolizing for himself missions likely to result in official recognition.[32]

When he arrived in Douai, Boelcke had yet to engage an enemy airplane in combat. This was not because of any lack of skill or aggressiveness on his part – as later events were to show – but because of the mediocre performance capabilities of the aircraft he had been given to fly. During the winter and spring of 1915 German pilots on reconnaissance missions in the Champagne region and in northern France were forced to flee before the faster and more maneuverable Nieuport and Morane single-seater fighters that the French were deploying. The consequences of this situation were extremely demoralizing for German pilots and ground troops. The Germans were unable to carry out their reconnaissance missions, thus depriving their ground forces and artillery of essential information about the movements of the enemy; whereas the French could photograph German positions, direct the fire of their batteries, and carry out bombing raids almost at will behind the German lines. Though these attacks did little damage, they were a constant reminder to the Germans that their adversaries dominated the air.[33]

In an effort to remedy this situation, the German air forces were reorganized in April 1915 and put under the command of Colonel Hermann von der Lieth-Thomsen of the General Staff. One of Lieth-Thomsen's first acts was to press the German aircraft industry to develop new types of airplanes capable of standing up against the machines being flown by the French and British. The first of these to see service was the C type, a two-seated biplane with a more powerful engine (150 hp) and a machine-gun built into the seat located behind the pilot, which allowed the observer to fire sideways, backwards, upwards, but not directly into the line of flight. Boelcke was given the first of these machines allotted to the 62nd. The results were immediate. At the end of June he reported to his parents that the 62nd was now able to protect its reconnaissance flights from French attack: "if a Frenchman comes along, I pounce on him like a hawk, while our other machine goes on calmly flying and observing. Meanwhile I chase away the Frenchman by flying up to him and blazing away at him with the machine-gun.

Those guys clear out so quickly that it is really great. I have already chased away over a dozen. It was great fun."[34]

This was only the beginning. On 4 July 1915, Boelcke registered his first victory. Assigned to protect an artillery reconnaissance flight, he spotted a French Parasol with two occupants that was crossing over the German lines at a slightly higher altitude. Unnoticed by the French, he banked, put his machine into a climb, let the enemy machine pass, and then set off in pursuit as the French plane penetrated more deeply into German-held territory. After about thirty minutes the French saw Boelcke's plane but were unable to lose him despite a series of curves and zigzag turns. Faster than the French, Boelcke overtook them and positioned himself in such a way that his observer was able to fire at the enemy aircraft from a distance of a little over a hundred feet. "It was a wonderful thing," Boelcke later wrote to his parents. He could see clearly the expression of the enemy aviators; he could make out every wire of their machine. Shortly before the French machine began to dive towards the earth, the observer made a gesture with his hand as if to say, "Let us go, we are beaten and surrender." "Still who can trust an enemy in the air!" Boelcke asked rhetorically, as if to justify the gruesome details he was about to provide. Boelcke's observer fired another thirty or forty rounds, and they watched with joy as the enemy plane plunged and disappeared into a thick wood.

After landing nearby, they were delighted to discover that the French pilot had been hit by seven bullets and the observer by three. Both were dead. On the following day, the two French flyers were buried with military honors. Boelcke and his observer visited their graves. Boelcke noted in his letter to his parents that they were covered with a bouquet of blue, white, and red flowers. Sensitive to the achievements of others, Boelcke also reported proudly that his observer had placed 27 of the 380 shots he fired in the enemy aircraft and had been awarded the Iron Cross, First Class.[35]

The events of 4 July 1915, catapulted Boelcke from the status of a skilled pilot, appreciated by his commanding officer and looked up to by his comrades, to that of a national hero. On the following day, Boelcke and his observer were summoned by the Crown Prince of Bavaria to give a full report on their aerial adventure. The orders of the day, issued by the headquarters of the German Sixth Army on 4 July and signed by Crown Prince Rupprecht, congratulated "the valiant flyers" on their success and expressed the hope that their daring and skill would sweep clear the sky above the German armies from the incursions of the enemy. The following day the general in command of the Sixth Army Corps von Pritzelwitz, singled Boelcke out for commendation and praised his energy and circumspection.

Within two weeks, Boelcke was struggling with the burdens of renown. Somewhat reluctantly he authorized his father to release for publication in the newspapers the account he had written him of his victory on 4 July.

> You know that I do not think much of publicity in the press. Also I believe that my account does not contain the proper style and scope for a newspaper. Their good readers want something much more poetic and awesome, with trembling and nerve-jarring tension, with exultant glee, with heaven-high clouds that tower like the Alps or with the zephyr-blue of the heavens. Still if it gives you great pleasure to see it published, I will not object. But naturally without names.[36]

Boelcke would quickly learn to live with fame and to like it.

If such highly placed military authorities as the Crown Prince Rupprecht and the commander of the Sixth Army Corps had gone out of their way to praise Boelcke so highly, it was because they hoped that his example would inspire other German aviators. For his part, Boelcke understood that his newly gained position as the most famous German combat pilot depended on his ability to continue scoring victories. In pursuing this end, Boelcke received assistance from an unexpected quarter.

When Garros was forced down in April 1915, his plane was seized before he could destroy it. The talented Dutch aircraft designer Anthony Fokker was summoned to Berlin to adapt Garros's innovation for German use. Given free access to a prewar German design by the LVG engineer Franz Schneider, he quickly developed a mechanical interrupter gear that allowed a machine-gun attached to the fuselage to fire through the arc of the propeller blades in the direction of flight without having, as Garros had done, to arm the blades with deflectors.[37] Fokker then designed a small 80 hp single-seater fighter armed with a machine-gun – the Fokker E – that was capable of speeds of 130 kilometers per hour. Fokker came to Douai to demonstrate his machine in June 1915 and left two behind him. As the 62nd's leading pilot, Boelcke naturally was designated to fly the new machine. He was delighted because, as he explained to his parents, "I believe in the saying that 'the strong man is mightiest alone.' I have attained my ideal with this single-seater, now I can be pilot, observer and fighter all in one."[38]

Unfortunately, from Boelcke's point of view, French reconnaissance pilots were careful to avoid him after his success on 4 July.

> As soon as I arrive on the scene, they clear out as quickly as they can. Since I cannot catch any of them here, I have to look for them behind their lines, where they believe themselves to be safe when spotting for their artillery. I have to prowl about stealthily and unseen, using every wile and trick. In this fashion I have succeeded in shooting at four of them. But since they always make a dive for home, I could not bag any of them because I cannot pursue them behind the enemy's lines without exposing myself to their artillery fire.[39]

While Boelcke was seeking his second victory, his friend and squadron-mate Immelmann emerged as a potential rival. About 6.00 a.m. on an overcast Sunday

264. The Fokker E.

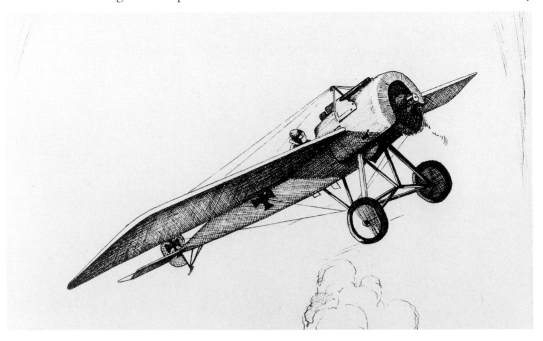

214

morning on 1 August, Boelcke was sound asleep in bed when he was awakened by an orderly who announced that a group of British bombers were attacking the 62nd's base. Boelcke jumped on his motorbike and headed for the field. Within a few minutes he had his Fokker in the air, in pursuit of the English planes. Immelmann too had made his way to the base. Unable to persuade his observer to fly because of the bad visibility, he rashly ordered the other Fokker to be removed from its shed and, despite his lack of familiarity with its handling characteristics and its machine-gun, took off hoping to find and assist Boelcke. He located him halfway between Douai and Arras, only to see Boelcke abandoning the fight, as he later discovered, because his machine-gun had jammed. Immelmann also had a problem with his gun, but not before he had hit one of the British pilots in the elbow and forced him to land in German territory.

Needless to say, Immelmann was exceedingly pleased with his success. His inspection of the British machine revealed that he had scored forty hits. "In the mess I was the hero of the day. There was no jealously in the congratulations of my comrades."[40] Boelcke may not have been jealous, but he was far from pleased. In his description of the incident to his parents, he left no doubt that he considered Immelmann's victory to have been a fluke. "Three days earlier I had given him instruction for the first time in the Fokker . . . The day before he had flown it alone for the first time and had only with great difficulty been able to land. He had never flown it against the enemy and had never fired its machine-gun – then he had the luck to catch over our base a defenseless biplane because to save weight for his bombs the Englishman had left his observer at home." Yet he quickly added that Immelmann had handled himself with style, and he insisted "with all honesty" that he did not begrudge Immelmann his success. Any fighter pilot would appreciate Boelcke's feelings: it was frustrating and annoying after four weeks of unsuccessful hunting to have an enemy plane directly before his gun sights and then to have his machine-gun jam.[41]

Immelmann's victory in the Fokker E, though perhaps lucky, was no fluke. He was a born pursuit pilot who combined aggressive instincts with a shrewd sense for where to place his machine so that the enemy could never get a clear shot at him. Every evening at six o'clock, Immelmann and Boelcke set out in their Fokkers in search of enemy reconnaissance planes cruising at an altitude of about seven thousand feet. In late August, after having signalled to each other to head for home before night fell, Immelmann saw an enemy biplane attack Boelcke from behind. "As if by agreement, we both turned around. First Boelcke had him in his sights, then I, and finally both of us did, and we came within about 80 or 50 meters of our foe. Boelcke's machine-gun appeared to have jammed. I fired three hundred rounds. Then I suddenly saw – I could hardly believe my eyes – the enemy flyer throw up both his arms. His crash helmet fell out and went down in wide circles, and a moment later his machine plunged downward from a height of seven thousand feet. A pillar of dust showed where he hit the ground."[42]

Meanwhile Boelcke too had scored his second victory when he forced an English pilot to land in his own front lines. Victory now followed victory for both men, as each vied to excel the other, while the German newspapers kept score. Though small potatoes by the double-digit figures accumulated by German and Allied aces during the last two years of the war, the victories of Immelmann and Boelcke were taken very seriously by the German High Command. This was in part because of their military value in discouraging Allied reconnaissance and artillery spotting flights over German positions, but also because of their potential impact on combatant and civilian morale. Boelcke and Immelmann's duels often took place in full view of Allied and German trench soldiers. An Allied plane plunging to the ground was an immediate and powerful symbol of the German domination of the air above the stalemated land armies. For audiences at home, accounts of Boelcke and Immelmann's victories confirmed the image of the German soldier that the General Staff was anxious to promote: an idealist, pure in soul and body, fearless and disciplined, who was prepared to sacrifice his life willingly, gladly, even lightheartedly to the cause of the *Vaterland*. For fledgling pilots, Boelcke and Immelmann set an example; their successors would outdo themselves trying to equal as surpass their exploits.[43]

Consequently, the German High Command was prepared to reward its top aces, and to reward them handsomely. One way of doing so was by citing them in despatches. To be mentioned by name in a brief communiqué that summed up the daily clash of armies involving millions of men was a singular honor, especially when it was frequently repeated, as in the case of Immelmann and Boelcke. Another form of flattery, to which men of middle-class background could hardly be indifferent, was an invitation for private conversations, lunches, and intimate dinners with members of the German royal houses and high-ranking military officers. In late December 1915 Immelmann reported to his mother that, after forcing down his seventh plane, he had been invited to dinner with the Crown Prince of Bavaria. "It was quite a small affair; we were only seven men."[44] Boelcke became a favorite of the Kaiser's son and was invited to lunch and dine with him. The King of Saxony was also moved to associate himself with aviation aces. He went so far as to commission a plate of Meissen china from the Royal Saxon Porcelain Works, portraying an aerial battle between a German Taube and an enemy biplane, which he bestowed on Immelmann after a special flying exhibition by his most famous subject. Cinematographers stood by to record the event so that it could be shown in movie theaters throughout Germany. Occasionally the Kaiser himself would write, sometimes in his own hand, to express his appreciation for the splendid achievements of his top aviators.[45] When Immelmann scored his thirteenth victory before the Kaiser could congratulate him on his twelfth, Wilhelm is supposed to have complained: "One cannot write as fast as Immelmann shoots."[46]

265.   Boelcke at the height of his fame. After Boelcke's death, Field Marshall von Mackensen wrote to his parents: "I have never gazed into a finer pair of gleaming blue eyes. I encountered the eyes of a man who was absolutely fearless, a true hero." (Quoted by Johannes Werner, *Boelcke* (Leipzig: K. F. Koehler, 1932), p. 5.)

266.   A painting of "our unforgettable Boelcke" commissioned by Crown Prince Wilhelm and given to his parents as a Christmas gift in 1916. The artist has failed to capture (or has suppressed) the deadly intensity of Boelcke's glance and has aged him by ten years.

267. Boelcke and two other winners of the Pour le mérite with Crown Prince Wilhelm (second from the right).

268. Immelmann receiving a Meissen porcelain plate from the King of Saxony.

269. A postcard showing Immelmann with his medals and his highly disciplined dog.

Probably the most effective expression of praise, though, because it could be worn on the uniform and thus prominently displayed, was the decoration. Certainly it was the type of recognition the German aces seem to have appreciated most. Both Immelmann and Boelcke recorded carefully, for the sake of their parents, every distinction they received. Indeed, in their letters home, they devote almost as much space to their honors as they do to their dogfights. One also gets the impression that celebrations of their achievements and visits to the home front in 1916 left less and less time for flying missions. By a strange turn of fate, Immelmann and Boelcke each downed his eighth enemy aircraft on 13 January 1916. Immediately thereafter, both these "dauntless officers" were awarded the Pour le mérite, the highest military decoration the Kaiser could bestow. They were showered with letters of congratulation, feted by royalty, and soon afterwards promoted. On 8 April 1916, Immelmann had the pleasure of sending his mother his full address: "The Royal Saxon Reserve-Lieutenant, Herr Max Immelmann, Pilot in Flying Section 62, Commander of the Order of St. Heinrich, Knight of the Ordre pour le Mérite, Knight of the Iron Cross, First and Second Class, Knight of the Military Order of St. Heinrich, Knight of the Albrecht Order, with Swords, Knight of the Hohenzollern Order, with Swords, Knight of the Bavarian Order of Military Merit, with Swords, Holder of the Friedrich August Silver Medal, Holder of the Hamburg Hanseatic Cross, Field Post Station 406."[47] But he added coyly that among the fifty or so letters he received every day from admirers, many were simply addressed to "Lieutenant Immelmann, Western Front," "and that is quite enough."[48]

270. Immelmann's funeral procession in Douai.

On 18 June 1916, Immelmann was killed on a combat mission when the interrupter gear governing his machine-gun misfunctioned, one of his propeller blades was hit and

shattered, the engine slipped forward, and the struts and wings of his Fokker E were subjected to loads that they could not withstand. Eyewitnesses on the ground saw the fuselage break in two and the front part, with the pilot and engine, plunge toward the ground, making a whistling sound as it fell, from a height of six thousand feet. Boelcke first heard the news at an airdrome near Verdun where he had been transferred in January. At first he refused to believe that Immelmann was dead; then, after Immelmann's death was confirmed, he flew to Douai where his rival's body had been laid out in the courtyard of a hospital. "The ceremony was very festive . . . All around him stood obelisks with torches on them. Various princes appeared, among them the Crown Princes of Bavaria and Saxony, and over twenty generals."[49] Far away, in the eastern reaches of Germany, the mother of Manfred von Richthofen recorded the event in her diary: "Crashed and dead. Inconceivable. He lived in the entire *Volk*. Everyone knew him, even if they had never seen him. He was the first great *Kampfflieger* (combat pilot) in the grand style . . . With him, one of the immortals of the war has passed away."[50]

Leaving aside his personal feelings for Immelmann, Boelcke feared the impact his death might have on German morale. In the short term, it spelled the end of the Fokker E. No German aviator would now want to trust his life to a machine that had proved uncontrollable by one of Germany's greatest pilots.[51] Even worse, Allied aviators would now feel free to venture across the German lines between Lille and Arras where Immelmann had previously "maintained order."

What Boelcke did not immediately suspect was that Immelmann's death would temporarily bring his own flying career to a halt. Ordered to present himself to the head of air force operations in Charleville, he was told that he would be transferred to a staff job, in order "to care for his nerves." Under no circumstances was he to fly any combat missions. Further inquiries by Boelcke at staff headquarters revealed that this had been a direct command of the Kaiser, coming he suspected at the suggestion of his son, the Crown Prince, who during the preceding months had taken a special interest in Boelcke's survival. Boelcke was told that Germany's leading aviator should no longer consider himself a private person; he belonged to the German people and could no longer play with his life. Yet if he had some special wish – such as perhaps to visit Turkey and the other eastern fronts – he had only to express it. Disgusted at the thought of being bottled up in Charleville in an office while the Battle of the Somme raged, Boelcke jumped at the chance to head eastwards.

Before leaving, however, he returned to his base where, in violation of his recent orders, he seized the opportunity to fly a combat mission and shoot down a French plane. Passing through Berlin on his way east he was invited to breakfast with the Kaiser,

271. Boelcke swimming near Smyrna: Boelcke is the fourth from the left, between the two women.

who greeted him by saying: "So you see, we now have you on a leash." "What a joke," he commented bitterly to his parents, "everybody takes delight in the fact that I must now sit in a glass case!"[52]

Despite his frustration at being taken out of the war at a moment when the Allied air forces had achieved unquestioned aerial superiority over the battlefields of the Somme, Boelcke gave every sign of enjoying his time in Turkey and the Balkans.[53] Treated as a national hero, he was wined, dined, and honored by Germany's Turkish and Bulgarian allies and received by Germany's highest-ranking military officials in those regions. But Boelcke's Aegean vacation was cut short when in August he received a telegram from the Chief of the Air Service ordering him to return to Germany as soon as possible. Anxieties about the morale of German infantrymen fighting at the Somme had overcome concerns about the possible loss of Boelcke's life. Trench soldiers had begun to wonder why the "flying heroes" about which they had heard so much were nowhere to be seen.[54]

Stopping at the German Army's Russian headquarters in Kovel, where his brother Wilhelm was stationed, Boelcke received the news he had been longing for: he was to return to the west with all possible haste to organize and lead a fighter squadron, Jagstaffel 2, on the Somme front. After lunching in Berlin with the newly appointed chief of the German High Command Paul von Hindenburg and his assistant Erich Ludendorff, Boelcke left for France, taking with him from Kovel two pilots recommended by his brother, Erwin Böhme and Manfred von Richthofen. The first would inadvertently and tragically be responsible for his death; the second would become his most talented disciple whose fame would eventually supersede his own.

The months that followed may have been the most satisfying of Boelcke's short life. When he arrived toward the end of August at Bertincourt, to the southwest of Cambrai, he had nineteen victories to his credit. Within a few days he had raised his score to twenty when he forced down a British pilot, who was so impressed with Boelcke's flying that he would later write that his dogfight with Boelcke had been "the greatest memory" of his life.

Boelcke's victories now came in quick succession. Once equipped with fast and sturdy Albatros D.1 biplanes, his fellow squadron members followed suit.[55] Yet the pressure showed on Boelcke's face and weighed heavily on his comrades. In the language used by Boelcke in the letters to his parents, the "fun" of 1915 now became "work." One can understand why. In October 1916 it was not uncommon for Boelcke's squadron to engage in seventeen or eighteen dogfights a day and score five or six victories in the course of making some thirty-odd sorties. Altogether they registered 87 victories during September and October and wrested air superiority from the enemy, making possible for the first time since the beginning of the battle of the Somme in July successful German reconnaissance flights and helping to bring the Allied advance to a halt.[56]

Someone who flew as much and fought as much and took as many chances as Boelcke did was at the mercy of an accident. In less than two months after returning from the east, he had forced or shot down 21 Allied machines. In the late afternoon of 28 October, just two days after scoring his fortieth victory, Boelcke led a squadron of six Albatroses against two British planes that had ventured across the German lines. The air was bumpy and visibility was bad. In the dogfight that followed, as he and Erwin Böhme sought to trap one of the British fighters between them, they suddenly found themselves heading toward a British machine whose pilot was desperately trying to escape from Richthofen. Both swerved to avoid the British plane, and in the confusion

272. The Albatros D.1 flown by Boelcke in September 1916. The D.1 had two synchronized machine guns and a bottom wing smaller than the top.

273. The last photograph taken of Boelcke before his death.

they temporarily lost sight of each other. When Boelcke came into Böhme's view again they were separated by only a few feet and on a collision course. Böhme pulled his nose up, Boelcke lowered his, then they felt a sudden jolt. Though the two machines had barely grazed each other, their velocity was such that they were both thrown out of control.

Böhme was lucky: he lost part of his undercarriage but was able to reestablish level flight. The outer tip of Boelcke's wing was torn away. Böhme watched as Boelcke's biplane descended in slow spirals in the direction of the German lines. Only when it reached a layer of low-level clouds, at about fifteen hundred feet, did it show signs of severe shaking and begin to plummet toward the ground. What Böhme could not see was that the damaged wing had been unable to withstand the low-level turbulence and had broken away from the fuselage. Boelcke died from a severe skull fracture immediately on hitting the ground. When Böhme arrived at the site of the crash, he noted ruefully that his friend was not wearing a crash helmet, nor had he bothered to attach the Albatross's shoulder harnesses. Probably Boelcke's main concern, before taking off, had not been safety.

A funeral service was held in the cathedral at Cambrai during the afternoon of 31 October. The reluctance of the local archbishop to lend his church was quickly overcome by the German military authorities. A reigning prince could not have been more splendidly commemorated. Cinematographers were on hand to record the event on film so that it could later be shown in German cinemas and thus participated in by the movie-going public. In the presence of the Crown Prince Rupprecht of Bavaria,

221

274. The funeral service for Boelcke in the cathedral at Cambrai.

275. Manfred von Richthofen (left center) carrying Boelcke's medals and decorations during his funeral.

General Below, commander of the First Army, and other military dignitaries, the pastor of the Fourth Infantry Guards Division explained the meaning of Boelcke's death:

> from a soldier's point of view, there could be for Boelcke no more beautiful way to end his life than to die flying for the Fatherland. No enemy can pride himself on having defeated him. Up to his death he was unconquered. Now he is not only someone who was great, now he will remain great forever. Now nothing can cloud the shining image of him that all we Germans bear in our hearts.[57]

The German authorities had understood that a hero of Oswald Boelcke's stature could be made to serve their country's military effort even when dead. Colonel Lieth-Thomsen, Head of the Air Service, made the point succinctly but impressively in a speech he gave at the elaborate ceremonies later held at Dessau before Boelcke's grave site. Henceforth, the flying corps would be moved by Boelcke's spirit. Their slogan would become: "We want to be a Boelcke."[58]

Walking in front of the casket in the ceremonies at Dessau and carrying Boelcke's decorations on a cushion, which he held in full view of the onlookers who had gathered to pay their honors to the dead aviator, was one of Boelcke's comrades, Manfred von Richthofen. Whoever made the decision to confer on Richthofen this honor had been moved by a brilliant intuition; for it was Richthofen who would become Boelcke's successor and who would take upon himself the glory and burden of becoming Germany's next great *Kampfflieger* in what his mother called the "grand style." His extraordinary success at assuming this role is demonstrated by the fact that today it is he, not his mentor Boelcke, who is remembered as the greatest aviator of the First World War.

Of all the pilots of the Great War, the one we think we know best is Manfred von Richthofen. The cold, hard, finely chiseled face looks out at us from dozens of photographs. A Prussian, a soldier, an aristocrat, a man who obviously enjoys his medals and decorations. But look again and you will also see a maverick whose clothes are always slightly rumpled and whose non-regulation cap has a rakish tilt – a prankster who likes to be photographed with his dog and his friends. He has a mocking glint in his eye. What did he really think of it all?

Judged by the bare facts of his military dossier, Richthofen appears to have much in common with Immelmann and Boelcke. He too was born around 1890 (1892 to be exact) in the eastern part of Germany. Like his predecessors, he was educated in military schools and then was commissioned as a lieutenant. He too was an indifferent student who excelled in athletics, especially gymnastics. He too went to war in 1914 as a young officer determined to distinguish himself and bring honor to his family. After participating in the invasion of France as a cavalry lieutenant and winning an unremarkable

276. Richthofen (center) with squadron members and his brother Lothar (second from the right). Compare with the highly idealized portraits in Pl. 339, p. 283.

277. Richthofen (right) with friends.

278. Richthofen playing with his dog Moritz, to whom he devoted a chapter in his autobiography.

decoration – the Iron Cross, Third Class – he asked to be transferred to the Flying Corps, where he served as an observer on the Russian Front in the summer of 1915.

In September 1915 Richthofen got his first taste of aerial combat. He shot down a French Farman but was not given credit for the victory because the machine went down behind the enemy lines. In October 1915 he was posted to Metz. On the train going there he met Boelcke, who had already achieved fame after downing four enemy planes. Richthofen sought Boelcke out, walked and played cards with him, and asked him for his secret. Boelcke replied that if Richthofen was really serious about scoring victories, he should become a fighter pilot and learn how to fly a Fokker. Richthofen took Boelcke at his word and persuaded a pilot friend, with whom he had flown in Russia, to teach him how to fly. After twenty-five hours of instruction he soloed, and by Christmas 1915 he had passed the three examinations required of German military pilots. He served briefly at Verdun during the great battle there in the spring of 1916, shot down another French plane (for which – again – he was not given credit because it came down on the other side of the lines), and was transferred in June with his squadron to the Russian Front.

Richthofen was at Kovel in August 1916 when Boelcke passed through on his way to create a Jagstaffel to fight on the Somme. He dared not ask "the famous man" to select him out of fear that he might appear to be bored with life in his squadron; but he did not hesitate for a moment when Boelcke appeared at his door early the next morning wearing the Pour le mérite and asked him if he would like to become one of his "pupils." "I almost hugged him when he asked me if I wanted to go with him to the Somme. Three days later I was on the train traveling across Germany to my new post. My fondest wish was fulfilled, and now began the most beautiful time of my life. I dared not hope at the time that it would turn as successful as it has. As I was about to leave, a good friend called to me: 'Don't come back without the Pour le mérite!' "[59]

Richthofen turned out to be an especially gifted student. Cruising behind Boelcke on 17 September, he caught sight of a group of seven British two-seat bombers crossing the German lines in the direction of Cambrai. After a series of maneuvers, Richthofen succeeded in getting behind one of the bombers, closed to the point that he was afraid of ramming the enemy machine, and fired a short burst at point-blank range. The British plane began to sway, the observer disappeared from sight, and the British pilot brought his plane down at a nearby German airfield. Richthofen could not contain himself with joy. He landed close to the crippled British aircraft, jumped out of his machine, and ran toward his fallen prey. A group of soldiers was already streaming toward the enemy. "Arriving there, I found that my assumption was correct. The engine was shot to pieces, and both occupants were severely wounded. The observer had died instantly, and the pilot died while being transported to the nearest field hospital. Later I placed a stone in memory of my honorably fallen enemies on their beautiful grave."[60]

Not satisfied with the goblet that the Chief of the Air Service awarded to all German airmen who downed an enemy plane, Richthofen wrote to his own jeweler in Berlin and ordered a two-inch high silver cup. On it he instructed the jeweler to engrave the type of aircraft he had brought down, the number of its occupants, and the date of the victory. He would eventually accumulate seventy such cups before Germany's shortage of silver in 1918 forced his jeweler to interrupt the production of these trophies, ten victories before Richthofen himself ran out of luck.

Richthofen was flying with Boelcke on 28 October when "the great man" collided with Erwin Böhme. Though Richthofen was deeply shaken by Boelcke's death and thereafter always kept his photograph in his bedroom, once his leader was gone he set out consciously to take his place as Germany's premier fighter pilot and greatest *Fliegerheld*. He later expressed annoyance at the fact that whereas in Boelcke's and Immelmann's time it was sufficient to have downed eight enemy planes in order to win the Pour le mérite, he had been required to accumulate twice as many victories before receiving that honor. Downing enemy aircraft in 1916–17, he insisted, was more demanding than it had been the previous year.[61]

Leaving aside the accuracy of Richthofen's perception about the relative difficulties of winning victories in 1915 and 1916, he clearly had little to complain about when it came to gaining official recognition and public fame. In November 1916 he was decorated with the Saxe-Coburg-Gotha Medal for Bravery and the Order of the House of Hohenzollern with Swords. Later that month he brought down Major Lanoe Hawker, widely believed to be Britain's finest fighter pilot. If he was good enough to beat the aviator that many called "the English Boelcke," it stood to reason that he had now taken Boelcke's place. The following January, after downing his sixteenth plane, Richthofen was awarded the Pour le mérite and given command of his own fighter group, Jasta 11. Reporters came to the front to interview him; his photograph was reproduced in newspapers and on postcards in hundreds of thousands of copies; and fan mail arrived by the bagful. Ordered on leave in April 1917 after scoring his fifty-second victory – twelve more than Boelcke – he was promoted to Rittmeister (cavalry captain), given a hero's welcome in Cologne, and invited to breakfast by the Kaiser, who presented him with a life-sized bronze bust of himself. No honor Germany had to offer seemed beyond his reach. Had not General Ludendorff himself said that Richthofen was worth two divisions?[62]

While visiting Air Service Headquarters on his way home to enjoy his leave, Richthofen was persuaded to write his memoirs. The suggestion came from one of Germany's most successful publishers, but the German High Command clearly liked the idea because it offered a means of capitalizing on Richthofen's growing celebrity and of stiffening morale at a moment when the German people's willingness to carry on the war effort was beginning to weaken. The first draft of *Der rote Kampfflieger* (The Red Combat Flyer) was dictated by Richthofen to a stenographer furnished by the publisher Ullstein in May and June 1917. It was revised and completed in October during another period of leave, edited and censored by the press office of the Air Service, and published

279. A widely diffused postcard image of Richthofen.

first in the form of magazine articles, then as a small book in late 1917. Though many have dismissed *Der rote Kampfflieger* as propaganda and though the hand of the Air Service censorship office is sometimes visible, there is no reason not to regard it as a faithful representation of the way that Richthofen wanted to appear before the German public. Written during a period when he had ample reason to reflect on his own mortality, it can also be considered as his testament to posterity. In many respects, it is a remarkable and unique document and, curiously, one that has escaped the attention of the many scholars who have studied the literature produced by the First World War.

The most extraordinary thing about this slender volume is that it was ever written. Both Immelmann and Boelcke had sent letters to their parents during the war that were collected and published after they died. Neither, however, had considered taking time from service at the front to construct a literary narrative of their life. Nor, it is safe to assume, would Richthofen have done so if he had not first been persuaded that his autobiography would be as important a part of his legacy to his country as his next ten enemy planes.

Richthofen began his memoir by distancing himself from the profession of arms. This is curious in view of the fact that his father was a retired army officer; that he was named after a great-uncle who commanded a cavalry corps; and that he himself had spent almost his entire life in the army. While he mentions these military connections, Richthofen prefers to present himself as the product of a family of gentleman farmers whose only concerns had been the cultivation of their lands, riding horses, and hunting game.[63] Hunting, in fact, is the master metaphor that runs throughout the 49 chapters of Richthofen's autobiography and unites the carefree prewar youngster with the incomparable flying ace of 1917. How otherwise are we to understand the long account of a hunting expedition on the wildlife preserve of the Prince of Pless that Richthofen dates exactly for us to 26 May 1917?

To be sure, one of Richthofen's aims in narrating this story is to place himself on the same level with "the many crowned heads" and famous generals (including Hindenburg) who had earlier traveled this "famous road." But beyond mere name dropping, Richthofen was also seeking to describe an emotion that hunting inspired in him. When a mighty bison comes into sight two hundred and fifty paces away and begins to move in his direction at high speed, he experiences "the same feeling, the same hunting fever that grips me when I sit in an airplane, see an Englishman, and must fly toward him for five or so minutes in order to overtake him." The "giant black monster" disappeared into a gathering of thick spruce before Richthofen could take a shot, and he elected not to pursue the beast because searching for it would have been a difficult task and missing it, once the hunt had been engaged, would have been a disgrace. Before long another bison, equally powerful, appeared and offered a better target. When it was at a distance of about a hundred paces, Richthofen shot, then shot again, and finally brought the animal down when it had come within fifty feet of the platform on which he was standing. Richthofen reports his satisfaction. "Five minutes later the monster was finished . . . all three bullets had lodged just above his heart. Bull's eye."[64]

The message is clear: airmen and bisons can sometimes be difficult to kill. Patience is required. Better to break off combat if the conditions are not right. Another, equally tempting prey can be counted on to appear. Then, if the hunter is skillful, he will have his game. Whether hunting men or beasts, the emotions are the same: excitement at the prospect of the kill and, afterwards, satisfaction with a job well done.

The war itself plays a strange role in Richthofen's narrative. In the style of the classic war literature, the outbreak of the conflict comes as a surprise. "We who were on the [Russian] border . . . believed least in the possibility of war."[65] From this point on, the war is treated as something natural rather than extraordinary: it was natural that French monks should be hanged if they obstructed the German advance, just as it was natural that soldiers should die in the performance of their duty.[66] The war is present as a necessary condition for the unfolding of Richthofen's destiny as a great fighter-pilot, but he shows no interest in its causes or the issues for which it is being fought. He is neither awed nor enthused by it. Nor does he comment on its progress. Richthofens serve in the war because it is their duty. But some, like Richthofen himself and his brother Lothar, who also won the Pour le mérite as a pilot in Manfred's squadron, are able to use the war to experience emotions not available to ordinary human beings. Instead of being victimized by the war, they become its beneficiaries. Hence Richthofen devotes considerable space to the experiences of his brother, who shot down twenty enemy planes within a month of passing his third examination for the military pilot's license. Had anyone in the history of aviation ever equalled this feat, he asked, full of admiration.[67]

Richthofen portrays the enemy as potential game and evaluates them not as individuals but according to the characteristics of the nation to which they belong. In this respect, he thinks exactly like the prewar writers of fiction who imagined war in the air. Richthofen describes French aviators as cowards who shrink from combat and look for opportunities to pounce on unsuspecting German planes. The British are sporting and brave – to the point of stupidity.[68] They are capable of noble gestures, but they are also perfidious and consequently not to be trusted to lay down their arms if spared from death. Richthofen illustrates his point with a story. One day he forced down a British Vickers, then crashed while trying to land beside it. The British pilot asked him why he had been so careless in descending. "I told him the reason was that I could not do otherwise." Then the "rascal" confessed to Richthofen that he had tried to shoot him during his descent. Luckily for Richthofen, the British pilot's gun had jammed. From this experience, the German ace learned a lesson he would never forget. "I had spared his life. He took my gift and subsequently repaid me with an underhanded attack. Since then I have been unable to speak with any of my opponents, for reasons you will understand."[69]

Reading *Der rote Kampfflieger* is enough to shake anyone's faith in the idea that the air war between 1914 and 1918 was a chivalric contest free of those aspects of technological mass murder that alienated and numbed a generation of men. Richthofen leaves no doubt that his job is killing. He writes with evident relish of bombing and strafing large bodies of soldiers. If he prefers one-to-one combat, it is because success in a single-seater fighter is the road to fame. He has nothing but disdain for aviators who fly for the fun of it and engage in aerobatics. Flying upside down is not necessary to bag your game. Unlike Boelcke in his letters, Richthofen is insensitive to the aesthetics of flight and aerial combat. He identifies himself as a sportsman, to be sure, but he is the type of sportsman who likes to load the deck against his quarry. When he hunts bison, he does so from an elevated platform. If you elect to play his game, you can expect to die.[70]

One indication that Richthofen's manuscript was edited by the propaganda office of the Air Service is to be found in his strange statement that the quality of the airplane does not matter as much as the pilot who sits at the controls.[71] Precisely at the time when Richthofen was dictating his memoirs, he wrote a letter to a friend complaining about the equipment with which he and his pilots were forced to fight the English.

280. The Fokker D7.

I can assure you that it is no longer any fun being leader of a fighter unit at this [Sixth] Army . . . For the last three days the English have done as they pleased. Our airplanes are inferior to the English in a downright ridiculous manner. The [Sopwith] triplane and the two-hundred-horsepower Spad, like the Sopwith single-seater [the famous Sopwith Camel], play with our D5s . . . You would not believe how low morale is among the fighter-pilots presently at the front because of their sorry machines. No one wants to be a fighter pilot any more.[72]

Nor did Richthofen confine himself to complaints. He was instrumental in persuading the Air Services Command to commission a new Fokker fighter, the D7, that many consider to be the best pursuit plane produced during the First World War.[73]

The jaunty tone Richthofen adopted in his memoirs contrasted sharply with his real feelings about the war at the moment they were published. The best of Germany's pilots and the closest of his friends had been killed, one after another. He himself was shot down and suffered a serious head wound in July 1917. Laborers in the munitions factories had begun to strike, and Richthofen was sent to try to persuade them to resume their work. In January 1918 he went home on a brief leave. The young hero had no illusions about the future. His mother found him transformed, almost beyond recognition. He lacked the gayness, the carefreeness, and the playfulness that had given him his boyish charm. "He was taciturn, distant, almost unapproachable." There was something hard and painful in his eyes. Reminded of a dental appointment, he was overheard by his mother to say: "Really, there's no point."[74] Not long afterwards he returned to the front for the last time.

281. A very grand but no long playful Richthofen whose luck was running out.

When Richthofen rejoined his squadron in February 1918, France's greatest ace had been dead for six months. Yet the presence of Georges Guynemer had never been more keenly felt in France than it was at the beginning of the war's last year. For it was at this time that a biography of Guynemer by a well-known writer appeared in the *Revue des deux mondes*, France's most prestigious political and cultural review. From France's highest scoring ace, Guynemer was suddenly catapulted into the realm of legend, where he remains firmly fixed.[75] Yet what an unlikely candidate for such an exalted fate! The many photographs, drawings, and paintings we have of him reveal a stooped young man of slight build and an unprepossessing face who seldom allows himself to be caught smiling. One cannot help wondering how he came to be a hero.

Two years younger than Richthofen, Guynemer was also the son of a retired army officer. The profits earned by his great-grandfather in the insurance business had enabled two generations of Guynemers to live a comfortable, country-squire life. Georges's father Paul brought his son up to respect his distant aristocratic ancestors who had practised the profession of arms. The Guynemers took themselves and their lineage seriously. Georges was no exception. Struck by one of his instructors at the fashionable Parisian secondary school he attended, Georges returned the slap. Noblesse oblige.

Young Guynemer was an unenthusiastic student. The only books his mentor could remember him enjoying were the adventure novels of Emile Driant, which he read and then reread. Though Georges was destined for an engineering career after further study at the exacting Ecole Polytéchnique, he had already informed his father before 1914 that

282.   Guynemer in 1916.

283. The flag of the Cigognes.

he intended to become an aviator. To say the least, Paul Guynemer was not pleased. Aviation, he replied testily, was a sport, not a profession.[76]

When war broke out, Georges was vacationing with his family at the fashionable Atlantic resort of Biarritz. His parents hoped that the sea air would strengthen his weak physique and get him in shape to prepare for the demanding entrance examinations required for admission to the Ecole Polytéchnique. With his father's enthusiastic permission, Georges rushed to the town of Bayonne to volunteer for the army, only to be rejected on the grounds of a feeble constitution. How could this girl-like adolescent who looked five years younger than his nineteen years hope to carry a soldier's pack or sit a horse for days at a time?

What happened afterwards is unclear because the witnesses remembered what they had seen and heard through the inevitable grid of Guynemer's later glory. Georges asked his father to pull strings with his former army friends, now high-ranking officers, to get him into the army. He was turned down by a medical board on at least one, and perhaps more than one, occasion. Then Georges remembered his vocation for aviation, perhaps as a result of an encounter with a pilot who had been forced to land on the beach at Biarritz. In November, armed with a letter of recommendation, he payed a visit to the military airfield at Pont-Long near Pau where, by one means or another, he convinced the base commander Captain Bernard-Thierry to take him on as a non-combatant mechanic. Two months later the captain gave in to Georges's entreaties and managed — perhaps with the aid of Paul Guynemer's Parisian contacts — to get Georges on the list of student pilots who were due to arrive in Pau at the end of January 1915. After learning the rudiments of flight, he was transferred to Avord in the valley of the Loire for further training. While there he made a sorry impression and came close to being dismissed by his commanding officer as a pilot who was likely to kill himself or — which was worse — one of his fellow cadets. Captain Bernard-Thierry intervened one more time, imploring George's chief not to wash him out.

By June, despite a series of accidents, Georges had somehow miraculously passed his examinations and become a military pilot. One of the central aspects of the Guynemer legend was already in place: the contrast between the feeble body and the iron will. Unable to pass an army physical and apparently without any aptitude for flight, Georges had forced his way into the air arm by sheer determination.[77]

Guynemer was posted to the squadron MS 3, stationed not far from his parents' home at Compiègne, directly east of Paris. By chance, he had been assigned to a unit that would become the most famous French squadron of the First World War. He had also found another mentor who would play a key role in his life and contribute importantly to his myth. The MS 3 was commanded by Captain Brocard, a demanding leader and an aggressive pursuit pilot who shot down his first German Aviatik on 3 July 1915 with a Winchester rifle and a Mauser pistol. Brocard meant to give an example to his pilots later known — when the group was expanded in 1916 to include four squadrons — as the Cigognes (the Storks).

Guynemer needed no encouraging. He quickly distinguished himself by his indifference to anti-aircraft fire while on reconnaissance missions. On 19 July he and his observer downed their own Aviatik, which went down in flames near Coucy not far from Laon. Upon landing near the wreckage of the plane, they were greeted by the officers of an artillery unit and taken to meet their colonel who offered them champagne.

"Who is he?" the colonel asked, glancing at Guynemer.
"The pilot."

284. Guynemer and his observer in front of their Parasol after Guynemer's first victory.

285. Guynemer with medals and surrounded by members of the Cigognes in March 1916; note the insignia of the Cigognes on the collars of his tunic.

"You. How old are you?"

"Twenty."

"And the observer?"

"Twenty-two."

"*Allons*! Now only children are up to making war."[78]

Contrary to what Richthofen claimed in his autobiography, victories did not come easily in 1915. Even a pilot as determined as Guynemer had to wait almost six months before bringing down his second machine. While waiting, he volunteered for special missions, in which he flew French spies behind the German lines, landing and taking off under hazardous conditions.

Finally on 5 December, now flying a Nieuport, Guynemer downed his second German plane; one can imagine his frustration when the French military authorities would not immediately credit him for it. Consumed by the desire to "get his Boche," he engaged two Fokkers on 14 December, shot one down – "thirty-five bullets at point-blank range" – and almost collided with the second. "During one moment we almost telescoped each other, I jumped over him, his head must have passed within 50 centimeters of my wheels. That disgusted him, he disappeared in the distance and let me leave."[79]

The victories and the honors now began to pile up. Guynemer had survived long enough to learn his craft.[80] The French military authorities, in turn, were now more inclined to recognize the achievements of individuals than they had been at the beginning of the war, especially if these individuals were aviators.[81] On 24 December, his twenty-first birthday, Guynemer was named knight of the Legion of Honor and proclaimed a "pilot of the highest quality, a model of dedication and courage." More victories followed in January, and Guynemer was discovered by the Parisian press. In February 1916, with seven enemy planes to his credit, the General Staff proclaimed him an "ace" and he was accorded a full-page photograph in *L'Illustration*. A "young hero of the air," another magazine proclaimed him.[82] Soon afterwards he was promoted to second lieutenant. The cross of the Legion of Honor, the military medal, the Croix de Guerre with an increasing number of palms, a commission, his photograph splashed across the pages of France's most widely read magazines – no one ever again would call Georges Guynemer, as they had in flight school, *un petit jeune homme* or a *filette*.

As with Immelmann, Boelcke, and Richthofen, success and fame only whetted Guynemer's appetite for more victories. A reckless pilot who preferred to execute his victims at close quarters, Guynemer collected trophies and recorded his mounting list of kills with the precision of a professional big-game hunter. To improve his score, he sometimes flew five sorties a day. On his best days he brought down several planes. His mechanics and comrades grew accustomed to seeing him return to base with his Nieuport and clothes riddled with bullets. On 13 March he was hit in the left arm and forced down. It was an experience he would repeat seven more times. Recovering in Paris at the Astoria, midway between the Madeleine and Montmartre, a quarter known for its pleasures, Guynemer wrote to his father commenting on his sudden renown: "I've read while in bed that the crowd gave me an ovation in Paris. It's a result of ubiquity. Modern science really does wonderful things, the journalists also."[83]

Especially the journalists. Among them, the most active in promoting Guynemer's fame was Jacques Mortane. A long-standing friend and admirer of Roland Garros, Mortane had begun his career as a sports-writer and had served as editor of the widely read magazine, *La Vie au grand air*. Just before the war, he had begun to specialize in aviation, a sport with obvious implications for France's military strength. When war

286. The ace of aces at the zenith of his glory in February 1917; as in the case of the portrait of Boelcke commissioned by Crown Prince Wilhlem, the artist has found it desirable to confer greater maturity on his young subject.

287. Guynemer photographed shortly before his death.

broke out, Mortane volunteered for service in the air arm. The military authorities evidently realized, however, that Mortane could be most useful practicing his profession as a journalist. No one was better placed than he was to celebrate the prowess of France's aviator-soldiers who were improvising new ways of fighting in the skies.

In November 1916 Mortane founded a review, *La Guerre aérienne illustrée*, in which he recounted the exploits of military pilots, while providing photographs and colorful details about their private lives. Looking for some historical reference with which to convey his admiration for the French aces (as they were now regularly being called), Mortane could think of no one more appropriate than that most French of all heroes, Cyrano de Bergerac, known to the world through Edmond Rostand's famous play. Indulging himself in a bit of poetic license he could be certain his readers would understand, Mortane pronounced the French aces similar to those "hale and hearty sons of Gascony, quick to provoke and mock but also men, like their ancestor Cyrano, who know how to die with a smile on their lips."[84] For Mortane, the slender, intense, anemic-looking Guynemer, with a face like one of El Greco's angels, was the ace of aces and his squadron, the Cigognes, the bravest group of men who had ever flown.[85] Not averse to publicity, Guynemer responded to Mortane's attention by confiding to him his logbooks and recounting to him his most spectacular dogfights.[86]

Guynemer was shot down over Flanders on 11 September 1917, the victim of shattered nerves and an approach to aerial combat that prized intimidation and sheer temerity above careful preparation and prudent positioning of his aircraft. He was in pursuit of his fifty-fourth victory. Because of heavy artillery barrages in the area where he went down, his plane and his body were not immediately found. This circumstance offered an opportunity for mythologizing that the Academician Henri Lavedan could not pass by. On 6 October, writing in *L'Illustration*, he commented on the strange disappearance of Guynemer and his aircraft. "How did he do it? Where did he go? On

which wing was he able to slip so well into immortality? At which point of the zenith was he aware of landing in heaven? We don't know. We don't know anything. His is an ascending death, a veritable flying away. Perhaps later on people will say: *The ace of aces* one day flew so high in combat that he never came back to earth."

When Guynemer's death was confirmed by the German authorities, the Chamber of Deputies voted by acclamation to perpetuate his memory by inscribing his name on the walls of the Panthéon, the final resting place of royalty, saints, and poets. He was to become a "symbol of the aspirations and enthusiasms of the Nation." The letter Major Brocard sent to justify this action, which was read to the Chamber before the vote and was later recited in schools throughout France, rose to heights of eloquence far beyond anything Driant had imagined in his novels and provided a ready-made theme and narrative line for a Guynemer biography.

> A modest soldier but one conscious of the grandeur of his role, he had the qualities native to the soil he so well defended: tenacity, perseverance in effort, indifference to danger, to which he joined the most generous heart. His short existence knew neither bitterness, nor suffering, nor disillusionment. From the lycée where he learned his history of France and which he left only to write yet one more page, he went to the war, his determined eyes fixed on the final goal, pushed by some mysterious force that I respected as one respects death or genius. Guynemer was nothing but a powerful idea in a frail body, and I lived close to him with the secret sorrow of knowing that one day the idea would kill the envelope.[87]

But who was to write this life? While Guynemer was alive, Jacques Mortane, perhaps inspired by the appearance of Immelmann's and Boelcke's letters, had suggested to Georges that they should collaborate on his biography. But Paul Guynemer had other ideas. Soon after his son's death, he contacted the well-known novelist and defender of traditionalist values, Henry Bordeaux, and proposed that he should immediately embark on a biography of the fallen aviator. Brushing aside Bordeaux's objection that he preferred to wait until the war was over, Guynemer's father produced an argument that Bordeaux was unable to resist: "In France this terrible war . . . is beginning to provoke lassitude and defeatism. He [Guynemer] will be the Standard."[88]

One can understand why Paul Guynemer was so determined to convince Bordeaux to undertake his son's biography. A captain attached to the General Staff and already a serious candidate for a seat in the French Academy, Bordeaux had recently demonstrated his narrative abilities and deeply patriotic values with a series of books on the battle at Verdun. Bordeaux had visited the Guynemers at home in June 1917, when Georges was on leave and at the height of his glory; he shared his father's belief that the son embodied the finest qualities of the French race. Bordeaux's notes of that meeting, which he later published, portray Guynemer as an ancient athlete, a "fragile god of aviation." "*He* is seduction itself, with his graceful bearing of a 'goddess of the clouds' . . . his incomparable eyes, his perpetual movement, his electric force, the combination of natural elegance and insatiable ardor, this élan with which his entire being strives toward a single goal."[89]

Here, then, was an ideal assignment for a writer who viewed himself as a conduit for the expression of eternal French values.[90] Throwing himself into the task and assisted by a sustained period of leave, Bordeaux managed in less than a month to forge a packet of Guynemer's letters, his notes on air combat, and a few scattered memories of his teachers and fellow pilots into a narrative so powerful that it was published in installments in the *Revue des deux mondes* and soon thereafter translated into dozens of foreign

288. The heroic death of Guynemer evoked by Lucien-Hector Jonas in October 1918 in a work he entitled "Les heros de l'air ne meurent pas." Guynemer's escape from ordinary human death and his ascension into heaven quickly became integral parts of his legend and iconography. As one prize-winning poet expressed it,
> To the very end Glory lifted him
> on her wing,
> And having died, this unsullied hero remains alive.
> This young god, so handsome on
> his moving throne,
> Will never dive into the eternal night.

languages, with forewords by such well-known personalities as Rudyard Kipling in England, Vicente Blasco-Ibañez in Spain, and Theodore Roosevelt in the United States.

The central idea of Bordeaux's biography was ingeniously simple, and had already been anticipated in Brocard's letter to the Chamber of Deputies, when he wrote that Guynemer had become a living example of the heroes of the past that French youth had been taught to love. As a skilled writer and a student of modern and ancient literature, however, Bordeaux knew how to develop this idea, how to embellish it, and how to embed it in a moving narrative structure derived from the genre of romance. Taking his inspiration from the essay of an eleven-year-old schoolboy, sent by his teacher to the mother of the dead aviator, Bordeaux wrote that Guynemer was the Roland of his time. Like the hero of the famous *chanson de geste*, he was brave, and like him also he had died for France. Guynemer had Roland's "gruff youth and burning flame." Why had the French loved him so much and taken so to heart his death? "France loved herself in loving Guynemer." In him France recognized "her élan, her generosity, her ardor, a blood line undiluted by the passing of centuries."[91]

289. Guynemer, the angel of death, about to take off in 1917.

Bordeaux's *Guynemer* was a long paean to the nobility of the dead aviator's blood and the selflessness of his love of France. Bordeaux invited his readers to interpret Guynemer's victories in combat as a testimony to the hardiness and valor of his race. He was, as Bordeaux emphasized throughout, "the last of the knights-errant, the first of the knights of the air."[92] The justification for singling Guynemer out from the thousands of combatants who had died unremarked deaths and were condemned to oblivion was not because he was an aviator or a hero, but because he represented "the obscure force of the anonymous crowd." By a leap of the literary imagination, a single individual could become a symbol of millions of French youth in arms. "In the name of Guynemer one must hear the battle cry of all French youth . . . just as one hears in a seashell the noise of an entire ocean with its innumerable waves."[93] Guynemer was "the inspired god of French Youth."[94] He was "the deep reservoir" from which the race would derive its strength.[95]

Reading Bordeaux's biography today, one realizes that he was both fascinated and appalled by the young man whose hagiography he had been commissioned to write. Bordeaux makes no effort to hide Guynemer's lack of culture, the monotony of his letters enumerating his victories, his dependence on his father's money and connections, the shortness of his temper, the brusqueness of his manners, the frightening look that he had glimpsed in Guynemer's eyes, or the cruel joy with which the hero displayed photographs of his victims. Instead, he cleverly distances his readers from the reality of Guynemer's persona by enveloping him in a context of myth. The spoiled *fils de papa* and cold-blooded killer is placed in the company of Achilles, Hector, Charlemagne, and El Cid, warriors who like Guynemer slayed their enemies mercilessly and took pride in the trophies their prowess earned.

Still, any aversion Bordeaux may have felt for Guynemer's character was more than counterbalanced by his admiration for Guynemer's will power and his belief that his example would live on as an inspiration for French soldiers and those too young to fight who would have to rebuild France after the war. Thus Bordeaux quoted with approval a line in which Guynemer, responding to his father, who had begged him to take a respite from aerial combat on the grounds that there was a limit to human strength, had replied: "yes, a limit that one must always go beyond. *Tant qu'on n'a tout donné, on n'a rien donné.* [As long as one has not given everything, one has given nothing.]"[96] It was this quality – Guynemer's unswerving dedication to the cause of France – that would ensure that his sacrifice would not have been in vain.

290. Guynemer with his father in front of the family home at Compiègne in 1917. Guns, medals, and glory.

To drive home his point about the meaning of Guynemer's death, Bordeaux devised a chapter organized around a reference to D'Annunzio's novel *Forse che sì forse che no*. By means of this episode, Bordeaux wanted to suggest that, just like Paolo Tarsis after the fatal accident of Giulio Combiaso during the air meeting at Brescia, Guynemer's companions – the Cigognes – had been inspired by his death to emulate his achievements. They too would feel their dead friend's presence beside them as they engaged the enemy in battle. Yet curiously, the dialogue Bordeaux reports, heard during a visit to the Cigognes's base at Saint-Pol-sur-Mer in September 1917, hardly supports his optimistic and very literary conclusion. Alluding to Guynemer's death, the new squadron leader Raymond says: "It's the fate that awaits us." Bordeaux protests: "The country needs men like you." To this the ace Albert Deuillin responds darkly: "What for? There'll be others, and when you've led the kind of life that we have . . ." The group leader, Captain d'Harcourt, ends the debate. "Let's hurry up and have dinner. The moon will soon rise. The night will be clear. We'll be bombed."

As the Cigognes finished their coffee, the bombardment began. Searchlights illuminated the sky. They felt the ground vibrate with the force of exploding bombs. Indifferent to the danger but anxious to get to sleep, one of the Cigognes said: "The weather will be good tomorrow. We'll be able to leave early."

Referring once more to D'Annunizo's novel, Bordeaux recalls the impact that Giulio Combiaso's death had exercised on Paolo Tarsis. The same would be true of Guynemer. "The fighting spirit of these young men has not been at all diminished. Guynemer is always with them. Guynemer, multiplied many times over, accompanies each of them and incites them to exceed, as he did, their limits in the service, in the cult of the *patrie*."

As Bordeaux sped in his automobile toward the safety of Dunkerque, he marvelled at the lack of tenderness with which these young pilots had spoken about Guynemer. His conclusion: "They find in his memory something that excites them to action and inspires them to emulation. It's a male and fortifying pain, the pain of these young men's hearts."[97] Thus in Bordeaux's *Guynemer* did literature triumph over life. Bordeaux was more sensitive to the values embodied in D'Annunzio's novel than he was to the grim mood of the Cigognes. Raymond and Deuillin knew better. Yes, they would fly tomorrow, but alone, without Guynemer, and for how long? If Guynemer had fallen, how long would *they* last? And if they did survive the war, what kind of life awaited them when they returned?

While Immelmann, Boelcke, Richthofen, and Guynemer were writing the book of aerial combat, Roland Garros was recording his memoirs in a series of German internment camps of various degrees of discomfort and harassment. The account Garros has left of his flying experiences during the five years before the war is precious and without equivalent.[98] Laced with self-irony, displaying a fine sense for people and places, full of closely observed details, these fragments suggest that, had Garros survived the war, he might have become the first aviator to produce a literary masterpiece based on his experiences in the air.

But as he wrote, Garros's mind was elsewhere. He had only one thought: to escape and to rejoin the air war. Time and again he was foiled, more often by chance than by German wiles. Finally, on 15 February 1918, he and another well-known French aviator escaped from the notorious Scharnhorst camp in Magdeburg disguised as German officers and by train reached the Dutch border, which they crossed by foot. They then returned to Paris by way of England. Honored at a large banquet given by the Aéro-Club de France, promoted to officer of the Legion of Honor, proclaimed a great prewar aviator and praised for his intelligence, audacity and ingenuity, Garros soon realized that he was considered a man of another era, closer to Wilbur Wright than to the reigning French aces, Charles Nungesser and René Fonck, who flanked him during his celebration.

Garros's return to France coincided with the publication of Bordeaux's biography of Guynemer. One can only wonder at Garros's thoughts as he read the epic of the aviator-hero whom Bordeaux had christened the modern Roland. Did he feel deprived of his name as well as his status as France's premier pilot? We know that during the months following his return from captivity Garros's friends found him brooding, distant, and lacking his usual zest for the good things of life. He had his reasons to feel depressed. His first flight made him wonder if he had lost his fabled feeling for an airplane's controls. The new premier of France, Georges Clemenceau, was determined to consign him to a desk job. Garros had no illusions about the changes in the equipment and techniques of aerial warfare that had occurred since his capture. If he wanted to fight again in the sky, he would have no alternative but to go back to flight school. After a brief period of much needed rest and recuperation in the south of France, this was precisely what he did.

On 20 August 1918, after training in navigation, gunnery, and the new techniques of aerial combat, Garros joined the 26th Squadron of the Cigognes, then stationed at Helmesnil near Dunkerque in northeastern France. A photograph of Guynemer hung

291. Garros (second from lower left) at the banquet of the Aéro-Club de France, surrounded by the aces Alfred Heurteaux (lower left), Charles Nungesser (lower right), and René Fonck (upper center).

on the wall of the officers's bar. Garros's first experiences in the air were not encouraging. His prewar myopia had worsened to the point where he could barely see through the windscreen of his Spad, which had an air speed double that of the Morane Parasol in which he had achieved his victories three and a half years earlier. Little by little, with the aid of his squadron leader Captain de Sevin, he began to gain confidence in his ability to fight effectively in the air. On 2 October in the area around the Argonne forest where his squadron had been transferred, he brought down a German plane by diving from an altitude of twelve thousand feet into a group of five Fokkers, as de Sevin covered his rear. The two were so elated that they finished their patrol with "a good session of aerobatics."[99] But three days later, in the chaos of a dogfight with seven Fokkers, de Sevin lost Garros from sight. Later that afternoon a French pilot reported that he had seen a Spad in their vicinity disintegrate in mid air like a "house of cards." Disgusted by the elaborate funerals being staged for aviators, Garros would have been relieved to know that, like Guynemer, he had disappeared *en plein ciel*, leaving "no human shadow among the eternal stars."[100]

By the time of Garros's death, every belligerent country had its aces. They liked to think of themselves as a brotherhood of knights; and leaving aside the dubious appropriateness of the medieval imagery for an activity so modern and technological, it is true that they had much in common. Almost without exception, they were young, usually in their early or mid twenties. They loved sport and fast machines. As a French pilot explained to an American audience in January 1918, aerial combat was a "game – an amazing game, a game of adventure, of countless thrills, of soul-stirring excitement, a game in which courage, daring, resource, determination, skill, and intelligence achieve honor in life, or if the fates so decree, glory in death."[101]

As one reads lines like these, one tends to discount them on the grounds that they were meant as propaganda, hence empty of any real content. This would be a mistake. Eddie Rickenbacker, America's leading ace and up to 1917, a man who earned his living racing cars, confessed in 1919 that he had volunteered for the air service because he wanted to pit himself against the vaunted prowess of Germany's pilots. "I loved flying. I had been familiar with motors all my life. Sports of every sort had always appealed to me. The excitement of automobile racing did not compare with what I knew must come with aeroplane fighting in France."[102] Air combat was the ultimate sport. There had never been anything like it before; there would never be anything like it again.[103]

The aces also shared a lighthearted attitude toward loss of life. Among themselves, they delighted unabashedly in their victories. Many aces regarded the day they shot down their first enemy plane as "the most beautiful" of their lives.[104] Some reported shouting with joy as they saw their opponent go out of control and spiral down toward the earth.[105] When addressing civilians, however, they sometimes went out of their way to emphasize that their job was not the taking of human life but the downing of enemy planes.[106] Rickenbacker portrayed himself as thinking before an aerial combat was about to begin: "Let the best man win!" But the British aviator Cecil Lewis was perhaps more to the point when he wrote (with the hindsight of twenty years and perhaps with thoughts of the war that was about to come): "The Angel of Death is less callous, aloof, and implacable than a fighting pilot when he dives."[107]

Yet success as an ace was won at an exorbitant price. A moment came when even the most supremely self-confident aces began to wonder when their turn would come. "You sat down to dinner faced by the empty chairs of men you had laughed and joked with at lunch. They were gone. The next day new men would laugh and joke from those chairs. Some might be lucky and stick it for a bit, some chairs would be empty very soon. And so it would go on. And always, miraculously, you were still there. Until tomorrow."[108]

Why did they continue? For love of country? Or because they had become prisoners of their own myth? For some of the most famous – and hence best documented – aces, patriotism seems to have been a precondition rather than a cause of their behavior. In this respect, Guynemer may have been something of an exception, at least among the aces flying on the Western fronts; and even in his case, the imperatives of acedom appear to have driven him on. The decorations and high honors aces were given so profusely were not only a recognition of past achievement but an incentive toward even greater deeds to come. So long as one had not given everything, one had given nothing.

Moreover, like all eminent sportsmen, aces found it difficult to retire while still winning; and in their sport, losing generally meant to die. Then there was the consideration of one's comrades: was one willing to abandon them while withdrawing to a desk or training job safely behind the lines? In any case, what is clear from the documents the aces have left us is that most of them identified more with other aviators, including their adversaries, than they did with their countrymen or fellow combatants on the ground. How could it have been otherwise? The aces inhabited a world quite unlike the one below. "The air was our element, the sky our battlefield. The majesty of the heavens, while it dwarfed us, gave us, I think, a spirit unknown to sturdier men who fought on earth. Nobility surrounded us."[109]

A noble thought, nobly put. But what form did the nobility of the air war take? Aviators sometimes allowed defenseless opponents to escape.[110] They were scrupulous about informing their adversaries of the circumstances of the death or disappearance of one of their companions, and occasionally took considerable risks in doing so. They were sensitive to the achievements and decorations of their opponents – and sometimes to their social standing. They treated a defeated rival as an equal and saw to it that he was respectfully treated, whether in life or death.

Naturally, aviators gave priority to such moments when reporting their experiences of aerial combat, thus validating the conception of the air war as a chivalric contest

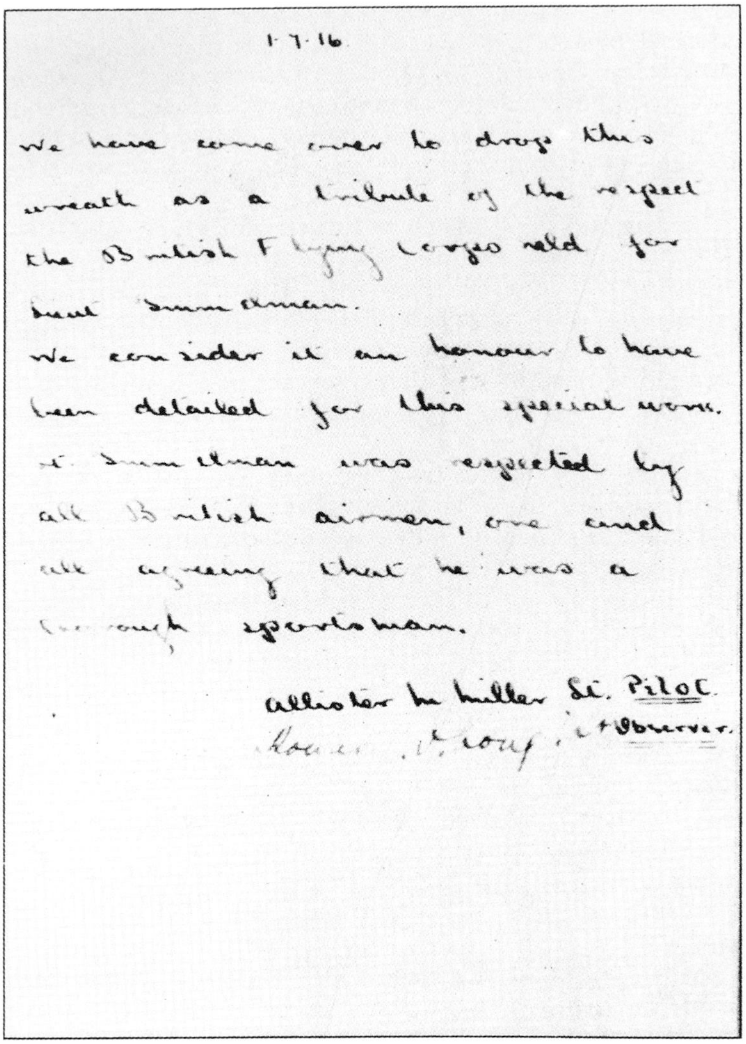

1·7·16.

We have come over to drop this
wreath as a tribute of the respect
the British Flying Corps held for
Lieut. Immelmann.
We consider it an honour to have
been detailed for this special work.
Lieut. Immelmann was respected by
all British airmen, one and
all agreeing that he was a
thorough sportsman.

Allister M. Miller 2t. Pilot.
Lewis 1st Group, 1st Observer.

292. The message
announcing Max Immelmann's
death dropped by two British
aviators over the German lines.

qualitatively different from the struggle taking place on the ground.[111] Yet they also recounted the enjoyment they experienced when bombing and strafing ground troops. Ground strafing, Rickenbacker remembered, was "probably the most exciting sport in aviation."[112] Pilots got a kick out of watching soldiers scurrying on the ground when attacked by airplanes; and many enjoyed dropping bombs.[113] Amazingly few aviators who wrote about their wartime experiences noted the ironic contrast between their image of the air war as a chivalric contest and the destruction they were prepared to wreak on the earthlings below.

This was not necessarily for lack of compassion or imagination, but because the elevated position of aviators in the sky encouraged, and perhaps even dictated, a spectatorial attitude toward the war on the ground. Foot soldiers fought and died by the thousands to advance across territory that aviators overflew at will. The perspective of the infantryman was limited to the yards that separated his trench from the enemy's; the aviator's eyes scanned the horizon and saw "objective after objective receding, fifty, sixty, seventy miles beyond."[114] The aviator could admire the tenacity of the men on the ground, but he could not thrill to their achievements. Viewed with detachment from the air, the trench soldiers appeared like players in a "grotesque comedy," whose plot and denouement they themselves would be the last to know. Witnessing artillery

293. "The patrol has fun," from Marcel Jeanjean's amusing evocation of a French military aviator's life during the First World War, *Sous les cocardes* (Paris: Hachette, 1919).

294. The battlefield of the Somme seen from the airman's perspective on 10 October 1916.

barrages and infantry attacks from "the exalted eminence" of the "endless fabric of the changing sky," it was easy for aviators to develop the feeling that the war was an "exhibition," a "scene," a "show," a vast and oddly beautiful entertainment. They came to appreciate the aesthetics of the spectacle, just as some of them liked to mock the soldiers below who fired shrapnel at them by doing aerobatic displays amidst the exploding shells.[115]

Without young men willing to risk their lives, of course, there would have been no

295. Like the Italian ace Francesco Baracca, many First World War aviators had originally been cavalrymen and conceived of their plane as a mount that responded to their commands. "Try then to tighten the grip of your fingers, nothing but your fingers, on the controls . . . and you'll tell me if your airplane isn't going to react immediately by rearing or kicking? Or just as an experiment, simply press your heel down on your rudder bar and tell me if the machine isn't going to feel it immediately and begin to turn? The rudder bar is the equivalent of a horse's flank. An airplane? It's much more alive than you think!" (René Chambe, *Hélène Boucher, pilote de France* (Paris: Baudinière, 1937), p. 220.)

aces. Yet others also participated in the fabrication of this strange phenomenon whose lifetime would by no means be limited to the period of the war. Governments and general staffs used aces to bolster their propaganda and to boost sagging morale. They singled out aviators in dispatches and awarded them their most prestigious decorations in ceremonies attended by thousands of soldiers and dignitaries. Italy's top ace, Francesco Baracca, was awarded his country's highest military medal in a ceremony at La Scala in Milan while thousands of his admirers mobbed the streets outside.[116]

Journalists and men of letters also played an indispensable role in creating the mythology of aces. Some, like the Frenchman Jacques Mortane and the American Laurence Driggs, made a virtual profession out of writing about the "heroes of the air."[117] Their task – by no means simple – was to bring to the attention of the public the extraordinary qualities of the aces while at the same time emphasizing the ways in which they incarnated the widely diffused virtues of the countries to which they happened to belong. No one carried out this task more brilliantly than Henry Bordeaux, who squared the circle of the ace phenomenon by pointing out that in loving Guynemer, the French had loved themselves. In Bordeaux's hands, the career of this wan young man was made to symbolize the triumph of Gallic spirit and élan over brute Teutonic force.

296. Baracca before his Spad. One of Baracca's admirers was Enzo Ferrari, who adopted the prancing horse painted on the side of Baracca's pursuit plane as the emblem of his famous racing cars.

297. Guynemer and the Cigognes captured for posterity by an artist.

After some hesitations and halfhearted protests, the aces themselves usually became willing collaborators in this operation. They allowed their letters to be published in newspapers and magazines. They gave interviews to journalists. They sometimes shared with them their notes and logbooks. They posed for photographs and drawings. Few, though, went so far as Richthofen who wrote his autobiography; or Rickenbacker who, at the instigation of an army cinematographer, agreed to stage a filmed dogfight between a captured German Hanover and his own Spad. Firing with real tracer bullets, the American ace of aces was supposed to frighten the German pilot (impersonated by an American) into hurling himself from the burning plane. This early experiment in the aviation film came close to being fatal when some French pursuit pilots from a nearby airfield decided to join Rickenbacker in demolishing the German adversary. The film of this incident was later shown in Paris and throughout the United States.[118]

The public towards whom this type of propaganda was directed, both civilians and combatants, appears to have responded in a generally enthusiastic way. For this there was a variety of reasons. To begin with, aces inherited the prewar mystique of aviation. Pilots were perceived as dashing, brave, foolhardy, and unlike the usual run of human beings. Women were reported to be especially receptive to their charms. According to Garros's biographer, "There was not a mail delivery that failed to bring these magnificent young men an amorous proposal."[119] The fighting in the air seemed more dramatic than fighting on land or sea. There was "something in the dizzy height, the deadly plunge into space, and the plain simplicity of plane against plane, of aerial squadron against aerial squadron" that was unique and captured the imagination.[120] Moreover, the feats of aces, like the exploits of sportsmen, lent themselves to quantification.[121] The merit of an aviator could be measured by the number of enemy airplanes and balloons he had shot down, whereas the courage of a trench soldier generally consisted in his capacity for resistance – his ability to avoid collapsing under the strains and pressures of front-line service. The first made better copy than the second and could be more neatly summarized in a citation. There seems no doubt that high decorations were more easily come by in the air forces than in the other arms.

With regard to ground troops and their attitude toward aces, the evidence is more ambiguous. Aviators were acutely conscious of the fact that trench soldiers often complained of their absence when they were most sorely needed. As an Italian soldiers' song went,

244

The aviator is that thing
Who goes up into the sky to explore.
If the enemy appears,
He hightails it away as fast as he can![122]

Aviators were generally believed to have a cushy life behind the lines, with warm beds and plentiful amounts of alcohol and women. Aces were also frequently observed on leave where they sported their decorations and drove about in flashy cars. Infantry-men requesting transfers to the air service were sometimes accused of being "shirkers" and treated with disdain.[123] This explains why those who recounted the exploits of the aces went out of their way to emphasize the close bond between the men on the ground and the heroes in the sky. Guynemer, for example, was said to be adored by the *poilus* in the trenches, who risked their lives by standing up in order to watch and applaud his air battles. A brief and anonymous biography of Guynemer, published in 1918 and prefaced by Philippe Pétain, General-in-Chief of the French Armies, emphasized that the fallen hero's influence over ground troops was "irresistible." "Upon seeing him, our soldiers were transported and carried away by a magnificent surge of enthusiasm. During great offensives, he flew at low altitude toward the enemy positions, leading the way for the waves of infantry that leapt behind him."[124] Similarly, the official biographer of Francesco Baracca tells us that whoever had known the anxieties and torments of the trenches had come to love intensely the Italian aviator's "warlike wings."[125]

One reads accounts like these with justified skepticism; but there is ample evidence that after their victories descending aviators were embraced, applauded, toasted, and "carried in triumph" by ground soldiers and their officers.[126] This inspired in some aces the perception that they were artists performing a deadly ballet before an admiring audience of thousands of onlookers below.[127] Some of the more imaginative conceived

298. Pampered French aviators relaxing in their mess.

245

BRAVO! GUYNEMER

299. Guynemer scores a victory as French trench soldiers applaud his exploit. The artist who did this illustration for a book about Guynemer's life was also the illustrator of Emile Driant's *L'Aviateur du Pacifique* and *Au-dessus du continent noir*, Georges Dutriac.

300. Baracca (center) being congratulated by infantrymen.

301. "A Boche in our lines," by Marcel Jeanjean.

247

302. An English ace downs his German adversary as search lights sweep the night sky. The artist, Howard Leigh, has attempted to convey the aesthetics of aerial combat during the later stages of the First World War.

THERE SHE GOES ! SPLENDID, OLD SON !

that it was only thus, vicariously, that trench fighters could participate visually in a war they fought most of the time from underneath the level of the ground. Gabriel Voisin, one of the pioneer French aircraft designers, conceded that there was something about the "spectacle of falling planes" in the open sky that stirred the imagination of soldiers massed in the trenches below.[128] Yet the awe, admiration, and envy these soldiers felt could also be mixed with animosity, bitterness, and the suspicion that aviators had somehow managed to escape from the degradation and daily torment of the trenches. Baracca was killed during a strafing mission after his squadron had been accused by an infantry officer of failure to support a ground attack.[129]

Trench soldiers were not the only combatants, however, who had reason to be annoyed at the fuss the civilian world made about the aces. Reading the literature on the air war, both during the war and after its end, it would be easy to forget that the most important military consequences of the new technology of aeronautics were the ability to observe the movements of the enemy, to support attacking ground troops, and to bomb military and civilian targets well behind the lines.[130] Yet it was not the pilots of reconnaissance planes, tactical aircraft, or bombers who captured the imagination of the public during and after the First World War. It was the ace who (regardless of the formation flying practiced in 1917–18) was portrayed as fighting and triumphing alone. Few were aware that the aces built up their scores by attacking inexperienced pilots, who were often flying slow and relatively defenseless reconnaissance aircraft. Aces seldom bothered to point out that the most successful combat pilots were those who avoided battle when the odds were even or against them.[131] Why not give the public what they wanted? For years after the Armistice, Rickenbacker and other aviators supplemented their income with popularizations of their adventures during the war that had little to do with what had actually happened.

Nor was this phenomenon short-lived. In 1935 the British publisher John Hamilton, advertising a book entitled *Fighting Planes and Aces* by W. E. Johns, author of the famous Biggles series, stated that "interest in war planes and the Fighting Aces of the air is

303. The funeral service for Richthofen at Bertangles on 22 April 1918; Australian troops fire a volley as some local peasants look on.

greater now than at any period since 1918. The words Camel, Spad and Fokker and such names as Ball, Fonck and Richthofen are regarded by those who took part in the great struggle, and thousands of others, with the veneration they deserve."[132]

Thirty years later the Doubleday Press launched a series of reprints of classics portraying the adventures of aces of the First World War. Among the first volumes was a new translation of Richthofen's autobiography, retitled *The Red Baron*. Translated to the realm of comic books by the creator of Snoopy, exploited by a manufacturer of frozen pizzas, drawn upon by the Led Zeppelin rock band, Richthofen's fame has proved more lasting than that of any other "hero of the air." Is it because his score was higher than that of any other ace? Because he was an aristocrat? Because he looked the part? Or is it because he embodies more fully than any other First World War pilot the multifaceted mythology of the ace?

In any case, the fascination Richthofen exercised over his adversaries was as great as that which he has come to have for later generations. In 1918 a dinner was given by his squadron for a British aviator who had just received the Distinguished Service Order, one of the highest decorations a British soldier can win. "In returning thanks, the hero of the evening, as gallant a lad as ever flew, stood up and proposed the health of von Richthofen. And the fighting pilots of the squadron arose and duly honored an enemy whom they respected." The journalist who recounted this story added that there was not a man in the Royal Flying Corps who would not have gladly killed Richthofen. "But there is not one who would not equally gladly have shaken hands with him had he been brought down without being killed or who would not so have shaken hands if brought down by him."[133] The war was not yet over; but the myth was already in place.[134]

304. "He is dead, but his spirit lives on."
W. B. Yeats captured one of the most elusive aspects of the ace's mentality when he wrote in his poem *An Irish Airman Foresees his Death*:

Nor law, nor duty bade me fight,
Nor public men, nor cheering crowds,
A lonely impulse of delight
Drove to this tumult in the clouds . . .

München, 14. Mai 1918   A. g. XIII.   Preis 50 Pfg.   23. Jahrgang Nr. 7

SIMPLICISSIMUS

Bezugspreis vierteljährlich 6 Mark
Alle Rechte vorbehalten

Begründet von Albert Langen und Th. Th. Heine

Bezugspreis vierteljährlich 6 Mark
Copyright 1918 by Simplicissimus-Verlag G.m.b.H. & Co., München

Richthofen

(Th. Th. Heine)

Er ist tot, aber sein Geist lebt weiter.

8

Towards a High Culture

> The most beautiful dream that has
> haunted the heart of men since
> Icarus is today reality.
>
> Louis Blériot[1]

WHEN explaining the significance of aviation for twentieth-century architecture and city planning, Le Corbusier liked to evoke the frenetic enthusiasm that the flights of 1909 inspired in the Parisian masses:

One night in the spring of 1909, from my student's garret on the Quai St. Michel I heard a noise which for the first time filled the entire sky of Paris. Until then men had been aware of one voice only from above – bellowing or thundering – the voice of the storm. I craned my neck out of the small window to catch sight of this unknown messenger. The Count de Lambert, having succeeded in "taking off" at Juvisy, had descended toward Paris and circled the Eiffel Tower at a height of three hundred metres. It was miraculous, it was mad! Our dreams then could become reality, however daring they might be.[2]

In Le Corbusier's memory, everything was "prodigiously accelerated" during that spring of 1909, when a series of dramatic flights convinced even the skeptical Parisians that men could now fly. Curiously, his narrative associates the passion for flight with a breakdown of public order and an explosion of anarchy. One fine spring Sunday, he recalls, a crowd of three hundred thousand people set out for the suburb of Juvisy where Latham and other aviators had announced that they would fly at 2:00 p.m. The railroad authorities were completely taken by surprise by the size of their clientele. Not even doubling the number of carriages could begin to deal with the raging sea of passengers determined to make their way to Juvisy. Le Corbusier left central Paris at midday. When he arrived at Juvisy, 15 kilometers away, it was seven o'clock and already dark. During their long journey, the frustrated passengers had smashed everything that was breakable in their own car and thrown rocks at the trains passing them on their return to Paris. When they finally arrived, they headed for the town in search of food, only to discover that the station gates had been closed and that they were guarded by soldiers with fixed bayonets. Inside the station, masses of angry people were waiting impatiently for coaches that would transport them to Paris.

There was then a beautiful manifestation of human intelligence, human solidarity and

305. Paris as seen by the Count de Lambert as he rounds the Eiffel Tower in October 1909. Georges Scott succeeds in suggesting in this striking image the majesty of the city when viewed from an aerial perspective and the fact that flying was not for the fainthearted.

306. Paris's Grand Palais as the center of the coming air age.

253

307. Le Corbusier (far left) and friends in the late 1920s. "The airplane, advance guard of the conquering armies of the New Age, the airplane arouses our energies and our faith." (Le Corbusier [pseudonym of Charles Jeanneret-Gris], *Aircraft* (New York: Universe 1985; original edn, 1935), p. 6.)

the collective spirit. The mob, one knows, generally becomes inspired when it is necessary to take action . . . As our train did not leave and other trains arrived in the night, filled with would-be spectators for the "aviation meeting," we set to work to demolish the station. The station at Juvisy was a big one. The waiting-rooms went first, then the staff offices, then the stationmaster's office. I can still see that room with its overturned furniture, its innumerable electric wires in wild strands: a gentleman carrying a cane, with a temperament of steel, played methodically at throwing his makeshift javelin at the mirrors. At eleven we returned to Paris. The restaurants were already closed. We went to bed hungry.[3]

As Le Corbusier himself warned, his account was not to be trusted in its details. The Count de Lambert's flight and the Juvisy meeting did not take place in the spring of 1909 but in October. Juvisy was 23 kilometers from Paris, not 15. The Parisian newspapers estimated the size of the crowd not at three hundred thousand but at closer to a hundred thousand. The riots he describes were not general but confined to the

308. "A day that will live in the memory of 100,000 Parisians." Anarchy erupts on the trains to Juvisy on 10 October 1909.

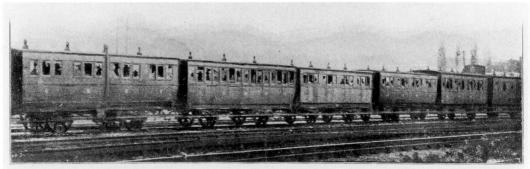

Un des trains sur lesquels s'est exercée la colère des voyageurs.

ENTRE PARIS ET PORT-AVIATION : UNE JOURNÉE QUI RESTERA DANS LE SOUVENIR DE 100.000 PARISIENS

254

Compagnie d'Orléans, whose personnel were unable to handle the number of people who appeared early in the afternoon at their Parisian stations.[4]

Nonetheless, Le Corbusier was not mistaken about the powerful emotions that the flights of 1909 inspired. Commenting on the Count de Lambert's reception at Juvisy, after the completion of his 49-kilometer flight over central Paris and its suburbs, a contemporary source reported that the half-mad enthusiasm of the masses who greeted him would be impossible to convey. From the Place de la Concorde to the working-class suburb of Montrouge, "anxious crowds" had gathered to observe Lambert's machine. The impression left throughout Paris by this unprecedented flight, *La Revue aérienne* concluded, had been extraordinarily intense.[5]

Nor were such outpourings of feelings limited to France or to the year 1909, when flight was still perceived by many as a miracle. Attempting the first flight from Munich to Berlin in June 1911, Hellmuth Hirth and his copilot landed en route in Nürnberg. They were met by a cheering throng of twenty thousand whose hurrahs could be heard clearly from a height of fifteen hundred feet. "What happened then I will never forget as long as I live," Hirth later wrote. The mob rushed forward with such force that Hirth feared that his flying machine would be destroyed by the pressing masses. Finally a detachment of two hundred infantrymen from the nearby military garrison succeeded in cordoning off the plane. "The look of the crowd was something out of this world. I could only see heads and above them floated a cloud of dust. Out of the mass loomed, like plants, bicycles, baby carriages, children, canes, umbrellas, which people had to hold above their heads so they would not be done in or broken to pieces. It was a topsy-turvy world." The colorful ring of soldiers, attempting to cordon off the plane, heaved back and forth through the mob like a rubber band. When Hirth stood up in his flying machine and begged the crowd to be reasonable, his voice was drowned out by a roaring cheer as a hundred men threw their hats in the air. Even after Hirth's plane had been towed by automobile to the apparent safety of the military garrison's inner courtyard, only the firm intervention of the camp's commandant prevented the crowd from storming the site and tearing Hirth's machine to pieces.[6] What explains such powerful emotions?

Regardless of what one might be tempted to think today, the popular passion for aviation had little to do with public transportation or thoughts of commercial utility, present or future. Though some aviators may have looked forward to a day when people would travel by airplane, there was no reason to believe that ordinary human beings would want to forsake the comfort, safety, regularity, and relative rapidity of trains for city-to-city journeys and steamships for transoceanic voyages.[7] Védrines's prize-winning flight from Paris to Madrid in 1911 took three days to complete; by train, it was an easy and – for those who could afford it – a luxurious overnight journey. Airships seemed more likely to provide an attractive and dependable means of transportation through the air, if only because of their size and their ability to stay aloft for long periods of time. Airplanes, on the other hand, were small, frail, at the mercy of the elements, and notoriously unreliable. A dangerous toy for dare-devils rather than a trustworthy vehicle for prudent travelers.[8]

For the handful of those who flew before 1914, of course, the danger of flying machines and their fragility were part of their charm. The risk of death was the price that had to be paid for heightened emotions – what one prewar French woman aviator called the "intoxication of flight."[9] Indeed, some argued that the possibility of death was ultimately what gave meaning to flight, which was nothing but a metaphor for our longing for higher forms of being. As one aviator put it, if we value things according to

309. To ease the transportation problem, a cartoonist imagines commuting between Juvisy and Paris by plane.

310. "Before a hundred years have passed, monsieur, the sky will be inhabited. There will be no one left on earth."
"I believe you. But we'll be six feet under."

255

311. The airliner of the future as imagined by J. Xaudaró. "Thanks to the air express, New York will be only one and a half hours away from Paris. Price of the trip: 1000 dollars (including the catastrophe)."

the stake we have in them, what greater stake was there than life itself, what greater source of value thus than flight in which we constantly risk death?[10]

Moreover, so long as he or she survived, what incomparable experiences the aviator could look forward to. If the bargain was Faustian, how much richer the rewards than those that Faust had ever known![11] First of all, the elation of mastering a machine in an era when people marvelled at the unending triumphs of technology.[12] The sensation of escape from the limitations and pettiness of the earth.[13] The surprise of discovering panoramas and visual mysteries that earthbound beings would never know. Then, the "wild joy" that came from successfully resisting the perils caused by turbulence, wind, rain, ice, and fog.[14] How exhilarating to feel the lash of the wind on your face and to feel at one with the world as you flew above it! Could there be any experience more intense than pitting your flying skills against the fickle moods of the "wayward air"?[15]

All this culminated in an extraordinary sense of power, enhanced by the inevitable awareness that the aviator was doing something that men had dreamed of doing for centuries. Claude Grahame-White, though not ordinarily given to lyricism, let himself go when attempting to communicate to an American audience the fascination of flight. "To be in the air! To feel your motor speeding you on! To hold the lever and feel the machine while in flight answer to your slightest move! To look below and see the country unfolding itself to your gaze, and to know that you and you alone are the master of the situation – the man who is doing this wonderful thing!" The result, he said, was a "feeling of awe."[16]

To which other prewar aviators would have added: and also a remarkable sense of freedom: "freedom, this leap that detaches you from the ground and opens to you the sky. Freedom, this road without limit that can cross all roads at any altitude and in any direction. Freedom, this infinite conquest of trees, of towns, of plains and mountains."[17]

Condemned to remain on the ground, spectators could only guess at the emotions of aviators, who seemed to belong to a different race of beings. Yet those below who watched were also deeply moved by the experience of aviation and played essential roles in the public spectacle that flight became during the years before 1914. Convoked by impresarios to attend exhibitions and aerial meets, they dug their heels impatiently in the ground as the pilots prepared for flight; peered admiringly at their machines from a distance and wondered impatiently when their "greasy hearts" would spring to life; thrilled to their ascent as they left the earthly world for a domain of mysteries which only *they* would know; sighed as they disappeared like delicate birds of prey into the sun's rays or the descending dusk; gasped as they glided silently and ominously toward the earth only to reverse direction at the last moment and climb once more at full throttle toward the sky; felt their hearts enlarged by the aviators' heroic deeds; communed happily with the other members of the crowd forgetting their differences of class, station, and party; and then, after the aviators had returned to earth, they left the field in a mixture of exhilaration and depression, hoping against hope that they would miraculously retain within themselves something of the music of those "dynamic symphonies" that had given them for a brief moment the vicarious sensation of being a god.[18]

Aviators who performed professionally knew that the crowds came to see them flirt with death. They compared themselves to circus performers or the gladiators of ancient Rome.[19] Though the comparison is not unjustified, they might have done better to relate the masses's enthusiasm for flight to the increasing popularity of spectator sports. Combining speed, the competition of clearly identified individuals and magical machinery that opened up a new dimension of movement, flying was the ultimate spectacle, an aphrodisiac for people who longed after faster music and stronger wine and enjoyed the collective emotions of excited crowds.[20]

But the feelings aviation aroused went far beyond the realm of public amusement and cheap thrills. People marvelled at the new invention and took immense pride in the "conquest of the air." This phrase has been so overused that it no longer has the powerful resonance it had during the years before 1914. Let us see if by digging down into the buried debris of past emotions we can salvage some of its original meanings.

Coming as it did on the heels of an apparently never-ending series of technological innovations, the flying machine was interpreted as confirmation that the Western peoples had subjugated Nature to their will and intelligence, and hence a promise, even a guarantee, of greater victories to come.[21] To a civilization that had recently extended its dominion throughout the world by means of imperialist expansion and annexation, it seemed natural to turn its energies and its attention to the mastery of the sky.[22] Now that Western man had successfully escaped from the earth and invaded the heavens – a realm formerly reserved for birds, angels, and God – who could say with any certitude where his limitations lay? Time, space, even death might be overcome.

The external sign of the flying machine's deepest meaning was the rapidity with which it moved through the air. Born of the "Spirit of Speed," as one pre-1914 poet

LA CONQUÊTE DE L'AIR

312. A French postcard depicting "The Conquest of the Air."

put it, the airplane was "the youngest child of motion" – the younger brother and successor to the locomotive, the bicycle, and the automobile. As a symbol of modernity and technological progress, it promised to shrink the world, collapsing days of travel into hours and by doing so enriching and extending life. What did it matter how many years one lived, if one could pack more experience into the existing life span?[23]

Powered flight, then, was both a realization of an age-old human fantasy and a portent of a "great new future of the world."[24] The sky was no longer a limit; it was instead a new frontier. The aviator was the messenger of another, "vaster" life; flight, the metaphor for a bright and shining future. "The music of new times stood above us in the heavens; the song of the future roared confidently. A new world had been born of a different kind and a different form."[25] Those who truly believed in aviation knew that life would never be the same again. Freed of all shackles, humanity would now be able to dash without hindrance along the "highway of the air."[26]

Yet there is one more element we must add if we want to understand fully the feelings that aviation inspired before 1914. By the date of the first powered flights, nationalist antagonisms, imperialist rivalries, and mutual suspicion and anxiety had brought Europe dangerously close to the brink of war. Few Europeans could think about airplanes without wondering what implications they would have for the survival

258

of their nation and the prospects for continued peace. This meant that during the years before 1914 attitudes toward aviation were almost always filtered through the lens of patriotic feelings. To see an aviator in the sky was to receive a powerful political message.

Not that most informed people believed that airplanes would prove to be a decisive weapon in the coming war. They were much too slow, too fragile, and too unreliable. Wars would be won or lost by armies in the field and, to a lesser extent perhaps, by gigantic dreadnoughts at sea. But in the meantime, the readiness to take to the air was a sign of national vitality and a reassuring indication that young people were willing to subject themselves to a demanding discipline and to give up their lives for the sake of higher values.[27] By contrast, not to do so – to yield the air to one's adversaries – would be to demonstrate a dismaying lack of moral fiber and national determination. To excel in aeronautics, then, was to put to rest nagging doubts about those national virtues needed to survive in a Darwinian world where the weak were doomed to fall prey to the strong. Hence the pride Europeans felt at the exploits of their nation's aviators; hence the eagerness with which they grasped at any evidence that seemed to indicate that their countrymen had been born to fly.

Nowhere was this truer than in France. As Alfred Leblanc, the victor of the patriotically-inspired race toward the Franco-German frontier in 1910 explained, "All the French have aviation in their blood . . . Foreigners may one day equal our machines, but never our aviators. In order to know how to fly, it's necessary to possess the qualities that constitute our national patrimony."[28] A comforting thought, perhaps, but wishful

313. By June 1912, when the Circuit d'Anjou was held, the French General Staff had begun to manifest a serious interest in the future of aviation.

314. In this painting, executed shortly after the conclusion of the First World War, Adolphe Ananie captured in a striking visual image the patriotic emotions that aviation had aroused in prewar France and that had been expressed in René Fauchois's prize-winning poem *La Victoire ailée*, published on the front page of *Le Matin* on 17 August 1910:
Once more we feel our souls thirsty
The need for laurels, songs, and tropheys!
The hunger for nobler successes
Tears us from the languor of despicable dreams!
Like you, we want to fill with our victories
The majesty of the French sky!

thinking. The French would soon learn that they were not the only Western people capable of taking to the air.

Flight thus evoked intense feelings throughout the Western world during the years between 1908 and 1914. It created a sense of power and pride and endless possibility – and in the minds of some less given to optimism about the increasing mechanization of life, it gave rise to anxiety and a sense of encroaching doom. It was understandable, therefore, that intellectuals and artists with an ear to the new music of their time would attempt to appropriate flight as a theme and draw on it as a source of inspiration. How they did so gives us an interesting glimpse into the culture and mentalities of the period.

The great majority of writers brought up in late nineteenth-century Europe and America shared an education in the Greek and Roman classics, a pride in the achievements of their civilization, an ambivalent attitude toward industrial society and the technologies it had spawned,[29] and a belief, supported by long tradition, that important events deserved to be celebrated poetically in verse. It was taken for granted that the poet's task was to give voice, in aesthetically pleasing language, to collective feelings. Poetry, in other words, possessed a public as well as a private function. It was above all in poetry that the Western peoples defined themselves and indicated their relationship to the past, the present, and the future. The poet, as the airminded Rostand put it, was thus a "lengthener of wings," someone who made it possible by means of his poetic gifts for the ordinary person's imagination to soar.[30]

In air poetry as in aeronautics itself, the French were determined to be leaders. On 17 June, 1909 – just a month before Blériot succeeded in flying across the English Channel – the Académie Française announced a poetic competition on the theme of "the conquest of the air." In view of recent French aeronautical achievements, the Academy considered it fitting to commemorate poetically the "daring discovery" of heavier-than-air flight and the "astonishing flowering of heroism" it had aroused.[31] Prize money amounting to 4,000 francs ($800) was to be distributed to the winner or winners who would be announced in 1911; and no poem was to exceed three hundred verses in length.

One hundred and fifty-four persons submitted poems. Their verses, now lying unread in a musty box in the Academy's archives, were only a fraction of the "air poetry" produced throughout the West during the years before the First World War, much of it published in daily newspapers or widely read weeklies, some of it the work of prominent writers.[32] These poems celebrate Western man's ingenuity and talent for making machines; they sing the praise of the heroes, both living and dead, who have risked their lives to extend humanity's dominion to include the skies; they oscillate between national self-congratulation and an affirmation that aviation will unify humanity and bring about an end to war; and they strive for metaphors with which to express the new reality.

These metaphors tend to be organic. It is as if the taste of the period felt ill at ease with machines and required them to be translated into living beings before they could be used for poetic purposes. A flying machine becomes transformed by one poet into a "bird" that takes off with his cage, an immense "dragonfly," an "eaglet," a "flying fish," a "white bat" with a long angular body, a prehistoric bird "such as one saw in the infancy of the world when the pterodactyl frightened the blue lakes."[33] Another poet, imagining Chavez in flight over the Alps, compared his Blériot to a "fragile bird, without feathers nor claws, without hunger nor beak, without heart nor life."[34] Yet a third depicts an airplane as a "fiery serpent" that slithers through its propeller wash like a "monster from the deep."[35]

One understands the poets' problem: prewar flying machines seemed more the creation of an artist or an artisan than a product of advanced industrial technology. Made of wood, cloth, and piano wire, they had little to do with the fiery furnaces that produced steel or the huge turbines that generated electrical power.[36] Yet the roar of their propellers sounded like the music of a new postindustrial age. But how could one evoke these new realities without abandoning the lexicon consecrated by the official culture[37] – that is, without ceasing to be a poet? Poets struggled with this dilemma and complained about the limitations of the poetic language with which they had to work.[38]

Aviators presented less of a problem to the period's imagination because, in their attempt to give "the conquerors of the air" poetic stature, writers could draw on a rich array of imagery, ranging from classical mythology and Teutonic folklore to Christian tradition, especially as it had been filtered through the minds of nineteenth-century Romantics like Shelley, Victor Hugo, and Richard Wagner.[39] Aviators were identified by poets with a host of flying figures who had haunted (and delighted) the Western imagination for hundreds of years: with angels and archangels; with the Arabian prince of *A Thousand and One Nights*; with the Greek hero Perseus and his winged horse Pegasus; with Wagner's flying female warriors the Valkyries; with the Athenian inventor Daedalus and his son Icarus; and with Zeus's cousin Prometheus, as in the final lines of Rostand's 1911 poem, which embodied all the classical virtues the French Academy had hoped to find in the poems it had solicited for the competition of 1909–1910:

315. Ernest Montau's poster for the 1909 Exposition Internationale de Locomotion Aérienne.

261

316. A defiant Icarus spreads his wings to protect his twentieth-century heirs.

Plus haut! toujours plus haut, pilote! et gloire aux hommes
    De grande volonté!
Gloire à ces dérobeurs de flamme que nous sommes!
    Gloire à l'Humanité!
Gloire au vieil Enchainé qui, supputant la joie
    De planer à son tour,
Etudia, pendant qu'il lui rongeait la foie,
    Les ailes du Vautour![40]

Higher! always higher, pilot! and glory to men
    of great will!
Glory to these stealers of flame that we are!
    Glory to Humanity!
Glory to the old Enchained One who, guessing the joy
    of soaring when his turn came,
Studied the wings of the Vulture,
    While it gnawed away at his innards!

The effect of poems like Rostand's – and I am using *Le Cantique de l'aile* as an example of the official culture's response to aviation – was to insert flying machines and aviators

262

into a tradition that reached back at least as far as the Ancient Greeks, their heroes, and their gods.[41] Viewed in this way, aviation was not something new and potentially disruptive or destructive but rather the shining fulfillment of one of humanity's oldest dreams.

This poetic interpretation of aviation could easily be combined, as it was by D'Annunzio's German translator Karl Vollmoeller, with a contrast between the "tyrannical" machines of the previous century – the furnaces, cranes, and hammers that blackened Western society with smoke and steam – and the new *Fabeltier* (mythical animal) whose wings were made of "light linen, thin wood, and bamboo" and whose taut wires sang like a harp. As was the case with most prewar poets, Vollmoeller could not resist the temptation to refer to the debacle of Icarus's flight when he sought to escape from King Minos of Crete with wings of eagle's feathers made by his father; but in his 1911 poem "Lob der Zeit" (In Praise of Our Time), it is the propeller of a twentieth-century flying machine that roars forth the song

> Vom finstern Konig und faschem Schmied,
> Das Leid vom hohen Flug und lahnen Neide,
> . . . Vom Götterliebling und vom Sonnenross. . . .
>
> Of the dark king and false smithy,
> The song of the high flight and lame envy,
> . . . Of the gods' darling and the sun-steed . . .[42]

In Vollmoeller's imagination, the flying machine brought the promise of liberation from a tawdry time of industrial drudgery and constricted space; aviators were like Eric the Viking who, along with his companions, had the courage to venture forth on the open sea and discover a new land; every flight they made brought us closer to the "highways of the future;" those who died were the price that had to be paid for salvation; the victims of aviation, the "many silent dead," would, like Oedipus, find welcome, refreshment, and happy repose in the realm of the shadows; and the living should be willing to follow in their footsteps and sacrifice themselves "in the light of the sun's eternal rays." "Fly away!" Vollmoeller's poem admonished. Emulate Lilienthal, the first victim of flight; Ferber, the Frankish captain with the German name; and Chavez, who had stared the ghost of the Alpine passes in the eye before crashing into the abyss. "VOLARE NECESSE EST – VIVERE NON NECESSE!" (To fly is necessary – to live is not necessary).[43]

With its denunciation of the "servile" nineteenth century, its proclamation of a new and shining era in which machines would realize ancient myth and reality would become dream, its call for heroism and its scorn for danger, its association of the roar of the propeller with the bright blast of the huntsman's horn and the ringing of warlike steel, and its Latin declaration that flying was more important than life itself, Vollmoeller's poem was a partial poetic transcription of D'Annunzio's *Forse che sì forse che no*. What it lacked was the unambiguous nationalism of the novel, its feverish exaltation of war, and its contrast between the heroes of the sky and the turbid earthly mob. D'Annunzio's aviators were not to be confused with ancient mariners; they were the precursors of a new race of modern men whose Luciferian ambition it was to raise themselves above the poisonous emotions of women and the mediocrity of the common crowd in order to become gods. To win this elevated status, to leave behind for ever the turpitude of earth, they had to learn to live with Death, their omnipresent companion in the conquest of the skies.

It was this D'Annunzian interpretation of aviation that attracted those poets who identified themselves with the prewar avant-garde. Following in the footsteps of Baudelaire, Mallarmé, Rimbaud, and above all Nietzsche, for whom metaphors of ascension signified artistic creation, the triumph of spirit over matter, and personal transfiguration, avant-garde poets celebrated the fusion of man and machine, the rupture with the past, and the victory over space, time, and mortality.[44] Among them, no one went further than Marinetti in seeking to spell out the implications of aviation for literature and art. To circulate his ideas to the largest possible audience, he had recourse to, and perfected as no one had before him, the literary manifesto. In Marinetti's manifestoes, the experience of flight became a source of inspiration for the renewal of poetry and other forms of culture and a metaphor for the coming liberation from the chains of reason and scientific intelligence. Take, for example, the opening lines of his 1912 "Technical Manifesto of Futurist Literature":

> In an airplane, seated on a cylinder of gasoline, my belly warmed by the aviator's head, I felt the ridiculous absurdity of the old syntax inherited from Homer. A furious need to liberate words, liberating them from the prison of the Latin sentence! . . . This is what the propeller told me as I flew at two hundred meters over the powerful smoke stacks of Milan.[45]

Marinetti first attempted to implement this radical program in his 1914 poem *Zang tumb tumb*. A work meant to be declaimed rather than read, *Zang tumb tumb* contained a "symphonic map" that sought to convey the "sounds, noises, colors, images, odors, hopes, wills, energies, nostalgias" of war as they had been observed by an aviator during the battle for the Turkish city of Adrianople (Edirne) in 1912. In the middle of this aerial map of bursting shrapnel and sputtering machine gun fire, a Bulgarian biplane plummets toward the ground from a height of 860 meters. The poem's text suggests in telegraphic spurts of violent verbal imagery the emotions of an aviator as he "penetrates" and "drills" through the sky:

> lente spirali di un aviatore verso Adrianopoli
> penetrazione d'un soffitto di nuvole
> sforzo d'un trivello verso l'azzurro invisibile
> vRRR FINALEMENTE
> essere solo padroni del sOLE
> avere il proprio azzurro ricino agilità monopolio
> del cielo avere sotto i piedi pianure pianure
> pianure pianure di nuvole nuvole nuvole nuvole
> VRRRRRRRR morbidezze di pelliccie gasose
> NAVIGAZIONE DI
> MONTAGNE MALLEABILI

> slow spirals of an aviator toward Adrianople
> penetration of a ceiling of clouds
> the effort of a drill toward the invisible azure
> vRRR FINALLY
> to be alone masters of the sUN
> to process the azure itself oil agility monopoly
> over the sky to have beneath one's feet flatlands flatlands
> flatlands flatlands of clouds clouds clouds clouds
> VRRRRRRRR smoothness of gaseous furs
> NAVIGATION OF
> MALLEABLE MOUNTAINS[46]

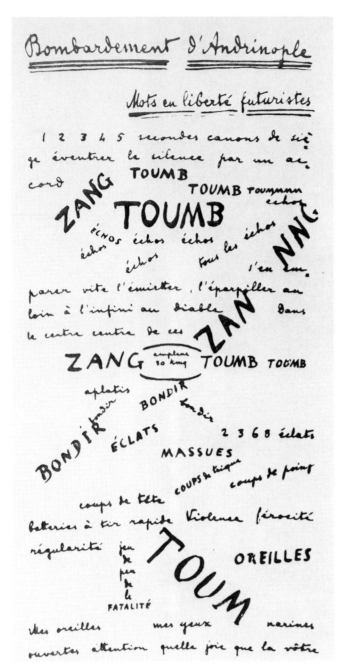

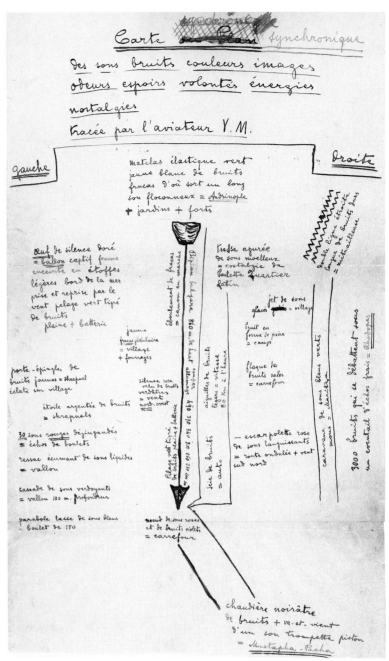

Marinetti's Italian disciples responded to his summons and his example by writing "winged verses" that evoked, through analogy and juxtaposition, the emancipating effects of aviation and the outlets for aggression that it offered. Establishing a connection between the daring of aerobatic pilots and the innovations of Futurist poets who broke with dead conventions and flew off toward "an intangible goal," Mario Bètuda artfully used variations in typography to suggest the shuddering take-off, death-defying loop, thundering recovery, and intoxicating descent of an airplane that ended in a

> giro di costole allo scheletro della morte in un precipitare
> di audacia

> turn of the back to the skeleton of death in a crashing
> of audacity

317 "The bombardment of Adrianople. Futurist words in liberty." In a page of *Zang tumb tumb* designed to evoke the simultaenity of impressions created by an artillery barrage, Marinetti revels in "violence," "ferocity," and "fate."

318. "Symphonic Map." from *Zang tumb tumb*.

qu'il allait dire : « Celui-là est heureux, il a le temps rêvé pour se livrer à ses orgies de couleurs ! »

Cézanne se plaisait à ces amusements de rapin. Ainsi, à l'époque lointaine où l'on avait mis à la mode le cri « Ohé Lambert ! » il aperçoit, un jour de promenade aux environs de Paris, le sympathique peintre de chats du même nom, qu'il connaissait un peu. Voulant « faire une petite blague », il crie : « Ohé Lambert ! » en mettant, ou plutôt en croyant mettre une sourdine à sa voix. L'autre se retourne, et, naturellement, vient vers lui. Alors Cézanne, tout saisi, et pensant qu'il aurait une lutte à soutenir, ramassa une pierre, s'apprêtant à défendre chèrement sa vie. Mais Lambert s'avançait la main tendue, en souriant, heureux d'avoir rencontré quelqu'un de connaissance. « Excusez les sons gutturaux qui sortent de ma gorge ! » lui dit Cézanne. Lambert, qui ne comprenait rien à ces excuses, lui donna une bonne poignée de main, on se promena ensemble, mais Cézanne resta sur ses gardes : « Quand on est faible dans la vie ...! »

VOLLARD.

BÈTUDA.

LOOPING THE LOOP

PAROLE IN LIBERTÀ

Alzata di mano   sciamento rapido
fremito lungo ansare del motore vortice dell'elica
specchio di raggi turbinosi nel sole
azzurro di viola ingoia l'ali e il rumore
l'areoplano è nel cielo   alto immobile
quasi   piccolo punto sull'I dell'antenna
s'impenna   poi
un urlo della folla brividire di freddo di voluttà per le reni gli occhi immobili pieni d'un baluginore di morte di sangue diaccio un morirr di sogno

PRECIPITA A PICCO

un pezzo di MACIGNO il sospiro sospeso come una spada sul cuore un abisso di silenzio freddo e vivo come serpe rapido e pur lento come un supplizio l'acrobatico esercizio di morte si esplica nel suo giro di ritorno e il funambolo pipistrello di fuoco

RICOMPIE ... VIA ... OROLO ... spola

che riattacca nel telaio del cielo il suo aereo filo di audacia e di sfida
un ansito nella folla   un levarsi di grida
    un gioire di spasimo soffocato   un vibrare di nervi tesi come corda di minugia spezzati d'un sol colpo e sibilanti al vento avviticchiati
e
la magica macchina di

FORZA AUDACIA PENSIERO

segna
un suo sentiero ideale
nel campo dell'infinito
come splendida idea di poeta
verso una meta intangibile

SCIVOLA SALE FUULMIINAA in avanti DISCENDE

sogna le parole di una nuova vitale fulgenza nel gran libro del cielo   è fermo a un tratto

SCENDE SPIRALE D'EBBREZZA SCENDE

giro di costole allo scheletro della morte in un precipitare di audacia   ha più voce il motore   in un lento volo ecco alfine che l'uomo

319. Mario Bètuda's free-word poem "Looping the Loop." Source: *Lacerba*, 1 April 1914.

The "man butterfly" lands on the "petal of the flower-Universe-land" only to be met by the

> applauso straziante del passato
> che vede il suo cielo straziato
> e spezzato e sfioccato e violato
> dal gesto fermo e sicuro
> di audacia di forza di impero
> dal filibustiero del cielo
> dal pioniero del futuro

> heart-rending applause of the past
> that sees its sky wripped apart
> and shattered and unravelled and violated
> by the firm and steady act
> of daring of force of dominion
> of the adventurer of the sky
> of the pioneer of the future[47]

Other Futurist poets, like Paolo Buzzi, sought to capture in their rhymes the speed and weightlessness of flight:

> Si corre
> Si sale.
> Bisogno un canto di corsa,
> Bisogno un cato d'ascesa.
> Presto avremo pulmoni di spugno di spazio
> ed ali di piuma di nube.
> O uomini d'ieri
> piantatevi un'asta nel seno!
> Nata è la razza che vi sorpassa
> d'un salto di cielo, la razza
> che come formiche vi schiaccerà!

> They run along the ground
> They take off
> We need a song for take off,
> We need a song of ascent.
> Soon we will have lungs made out of sponges of space
> And wings made out of plumes of clouds.
> Oh, men of yesterday
> Put a lance in your breasts!
> Born is the race that will leave you behind
> With a leap into the sky, the race
> That will squash you like ants.[48]

Marinetti and his disciples were unsurpassed in the violence with which they combined images of flight, anticipations of war, and disdain for the "human anthill' of the masses. Yet they were by no means alone among the avant-garde in their longing for liberation from the earth and their admiration for the new race of men who had invaded God's realm. Though far from being a nationalist, the Austrian writer Stefan Zweig was no less excited by the purifying effects of flight. In the poem he dedicated to the aviation theme, entitled "The Flier," the protagonist leaves behind the "stinking" tombs and decay of the ground and challenges the elements to do battle with him, as he ascends defiantly towards the heavens crying:

> Frei!
> Allein!
> O weites unendliches Einsamsein!
> Mein Blick zerstösst sich nicht mehr an den Dingen,
> Die Luft ist von Atem und Worten rein.
> Leben ist Schweben,
> Seliges Ruhn auf wandernden Schwingen!
> Doch ich fühle
> Noch uber dem Schweigen sphärisches Klingen,
> Ich will durch die Kühle
> In den feurigen Kern aller Himmel eindringen,
> Ich will steigen und steigen
> Bis auf zu den Höhn,
> Wo selbst die Engel geblendet sich neigen
> Und Gott ins ewige Auge sehn.

Free!
Alone!
Oh vast unending loneliness!
My glance no longer batters itself against things,
The air is pure of breath and words.
To live is to soar,
Blessed glory on wandering wings!
Still I feel
Over the silence the sound of heavenly sounds,
I want to penetrate through the cold
Into the fiery center of heaven,
I want to rise and rise
Up to the heights,
Where even the angels bow down dazzled
And see God with eternal eyes.[49]

The quickness with which avant-garde poets adopted the aviation theme and the aspirations they identified with it suggest that they were driven by a deep, almost irrational hatred for the bourgeois society into which they had been born.[50] They seized on the flying machine as proof that the old narrow world of the nineteenth century was doomed to extinction and that another world of iron and steel was about to take its place. Any means that hastened the day of apocalypse was to be embraced. Celebrating his first flight, the German Expressionist Walter Hasenclever proclaimed his liberation from the earth:

Noch einmal erfülle mich brausendes Spiel!
Vom Gedärm der Erde ackre dich bloss;
Stampfe, bäume dich, schwanke los,
Steige – sei ohne Grenze und Ziel!

One more time fulfill me you roaring plaything!
Work yourself free from the bowels of the earth;
Tample, prance, soar,
Climb – be without limit or goal!

Filled with a longing for wings, Hasenclever felt far away from the "crippled men" he watched on the ground.

Höre den Strom! Er fliegt vor dir her.
Hinter dir schreit der Motor. Lass ihn morden.
Mensch aus Fleisch – Du bist Stahl geworden!

Hear the flow of air! It flies toward you.
Behind you strides the motor. Let it bite.
Man born of flesh – you have become steel!

It was time to break out of the narrowness of the past, to complete the revolution begun in the nineteenth century, and to assume the form of the machine. But not just any machine – the one that had made it possible to fly away from earth.

Hinaus denn, Zeit nach der ich dränge!
Sei Eisen! Sei Höhensteuer! Sei Flug!

Come forth then, the age toward which I rush!
Be iron! Be an airplane's elevator! Be flight![51]

It was aggressive voices like Hasenclever's that were dominant in the air poetry of the prewar avant-garde. They celebrated the coming airborne civilization and, like Vasily Kamensky, they imagined aviators spitting on the sorry mob below after performing heroic aerial feats.[52] Or as Kamensky put it in another poem, now that "clean" and "sublime" technological achievements had surpassed nature's beauty and rendered the wisdom of the ancients obsolete, true human history could begin. Electric lights and billboards would shine brighter than the sun or moon. Radiotelegraphy would transmit news simultaneously from the furthest corners of the world. Record-breaking aviators would take possession of the earth and decipher for the first time the planet's true course.[53] Hubris has seldom gone further.

To be sure, there were some poets who expressed uneasiness about the fusion of human pilots with the "steel passionless birds" they flew. None was more eloquent than the great Russian Symbolist Aleksandr Blok. Blok ended his 1912 poem "The Aviator" with the terrifying vision of a nocturnal flier hurling dynamite at the earth.[54] He wondered where the twentieth century's "incessant gnashing of machines" was leading: was it only toward "cold fog – and emptiness"?[55] Yet even Blok was moved by the sublimity of flight and believed that the propeller had given a new music to the world. There was "something ancient," he wrote, in the spiralling turns of dead wings, bending downwards toward the earth.[56] And, like so many other pre-1914 poets and artists, Blok was drawn irresistibly to the airdromes where aviators risked and sometimes lost their lives. He came to see in flight a metaphor for art. What, after all, was art, if not "a winged dream, a mysterious airplane with which to escape the earth?"[57]

With the exception of D'Annunzio and Marinetti, who were equally at home in prose and poetry, the first novelists who took up the aviation theme marched in the footsteps of Jules Verne and the now forgotten but then widely read Albert Robida. They were interested in anticipations of the future and cast their narratives in the form of the adventure tale, as Verne and Robida had done.[58] Where they differed from the poets was in the detail with which they evoked the new technology and the specific uses they foresaw for it, especially in warfare. They were not so much interested in the emotions that flight produced as in its social, military, and geopolitical consequences. Whereas the poets groped for images that would convey the deeper significance of the flying machine, the novelists described the machines themselves and showed them in action. They presented them not as the fulfillment of myth and dream, but as the result of a century of technological progress and Western will to power.

The Vernian adventure novel could be given an imperialist twist, as it was by Emile Driant in *L'Aviateur du Pacifique* and *Au-dessus du continent noir*, to show how flying machines could be used to maintain Western domination over non-Western peoples and their lands; or it could be used to speculate about the impact of aviation on the coming war. Both H. G. Wells and Rudolf Martin described in detail the bombing of Western capitals. They left no doubt that the destruction and human suffering would be terrible. Their intentions in writing these prophetic novels, however, were quite different. Wells foresaw that future wars would be fought on a worldwide scale. Westerners could not assume that they would retain a monopoly over aeronautical technology. More Eurocentric in his vision, Martin wished to serve notice on the British and the French that their traditional means of defense could no longer be counted upon; German Zeppelins could now reach their heartlands in a matter of hours. Whereas in *The War in the Air* Wells spared the emotions of his British readers by displacing the scene of slaughter from London to New York and writing in a comic vein, Martin conjured up the image of a German attack on central Paris. There was nothing lighthearted in the resulting scene. "As the German airships, at an altitude of 1,200 meters, took up an eastward course, the whole of the inner city of Paris was in flames. Not a single house was standing from the Magasin du Louvre to the Opéra and from the Opéra to the Palais de l'Elysée . . . Even at the high altitudes, I heard the sound of hundreds of people crying for help."[59]

Though the attitude of the visionary novelists toward aviation differed markedly according to their nationality, they all agreed that the flying machine would transform warfare and create a new military elite. Soldiers would watch with awe and admiration the flying men who soared above them. Aviators, in turn, would feel detached from those earthlings they saw below. Viewed from high altitudes, human beings lost their humanity and appeared like ants. This was even truer if the people on the ground were not Westerners, as in the case of the 1911 French fictional hero who felt exalted with pride as he flew at a height of fourteen hundred meters above the African mountains. "Slumped forward between wings of white cloth and surrounded by the explosive reverberations of my engine, I feel like a sort of avenging angel who dives, with the anger of the heavens, on the peoples of damned villages."[60] None of these pre-1914 novelists yet foresaw the moment, however, when human beings would be replaced by bleeps on a radar screen.

Novelistic visions of aerial warfare, encapsulated within the traditional dimensions of the adventure tale, would have a long life.[61] Fictional wars in the air would eventually give way to fictional wars in space. In the aftermath of Blériot's exploits, however, as heavier-than-air flight became a reality and as aviation began to claim its first victims, novelists and short story writers turned their attention away from anticipations of the future toward the experience and motivations of aviators. Like the poets, they were fascinated by the struggle of pilots with nature and the symbiotic relationship they established with their machines, and they wondered what drove them to risk their lives in the search for ephemeral records that would be broken tomorrow, the day after, or the following month. Was it a trivial quest for fame and fortune, a dark drive toward self-destruction, or an uncontrollable aspiration toward the heights? They also asked what heroism would come to mean in an increasingly technological age. Was there not a danger that the artists and poets who had realized the dream of flight would be replaced by cool and unimaginative technicians?

The first aviation writers were not themselves aviators, though some, like D'Annunzio and Marinetti, had been taken up in the air as passengers for brief flights. Beginning in 1911, however, some writers began to pilot planes. The logic seemed inescapable. If flight offered a new perspective on the world, then writers should not simply insert aviators into their narratives; they should themselves experience what it meant to fly a plane. That experience could be terrifying, especially when a fragile flying machine was caught in the eye of a storm. "A blast of wind sent the wing into a perpendicular bank and pushed us downward on our starboard side. We plunged downwards through the whirlwind with heavy limbs and thoughts. My brain was hammering, my skin burned, I heard roaring in my ear. Was it my heart and pulse that were racing madly, or was it the motor and propeller?"[62] After such battles with the elements, aviators knew how sweet it was to find themselves once more on the ground, alive, safe if not completely sound, and in the company of other human beings.[63] How far removed this was from the sensibility of those more popular earthbound writers, like the Russian Leonid Andreyev, whose fictional pilot defied nature with "harsh and courageous serenity" and yearned to escape from his body and ascend into the skies![64]

Just as writers had begun to fly before 1914, so had fliers begun to write. When Jean Conneau published *My Three Big Flights* in 1911, he could hardly have suspected that he

was launching a literary genre that would prove to have remarkable staying power. As Conneau discovered, a mass public awaited those aviators capable of narrating their adventures in the air.[65] The problem was that, whereas flying generated intense feelings because of its potential dangers, merely describing what a pilot did while airborne was repetitive and boring. Famous aviators who aspired to write thus discovered that they had to combine carefully selected moments of high drama, when they suddenly encountered life-threatening perils, with autobiographical flashbacks that created a context for the flight and reflections about the land and people they overflew, the spectrum of emotions through which they passed while in the air, and the reception they received upon returning to earth. Anticipated by Blériot in his accounts of his Channel flight but first fully realized by Conneau, it was a formula that would be exploited profitably by generations of airmen and women, including Charles and Anne Morrow Lindbergh, Italo Balbo, Jean Mermoz, and Amelia Earhart, and one that in the hands of a talented writer like Antoine de Saint-Exupéry was capable of attaining a level of great literary distinction. Flying and literature, it turned out, were more compatible than anyone could have imagined when Wilbur Wright arrived in France to demonstrate his flying machine and discovered, to his great amusement, that people were proclaiming him a poet.[66]

Almost all writers who ventured into the sky in flying machines were struck by the fact that the earth looked different when viewed from great heights. Objects that were perceived on the earth as distinct and different blended together into strange configurations with unexpected textures; land or cityscapes that had appeared ugly or without

271

interest became beautiful when looked at from above; bodies of water refracted a kaleidoscope of colors; people and animals were reduced to tiny spots in a panorama far grander than the ordinary person was used to see; clouds, in the past remote from human life and action, became part of the magic realm through which the aviator moved and provided a never-ending spectacle to delight his or her eye. Small wonder that aviators often had the sensation of having escaped from the petty cares and discord that prevailed on earth and come closer to eternal truths.[67]

Aviation thus offered a new way of seeing the world and the objects in it; moreover, it did so precisely at the moment when visual artists were aggressively exploring new techniques for the representation of space. Between 1908 and 1914, avant-garde painters and sculptors throughout the West abandoned traditional laws of perspective. They distorted the objects they portrayed, refused to view them from a single point of view, and experimented with the depiction of pure form and color.

We know that many avant-garde painters shared the popular enthusiasm for aviation. The Futurist Gino Severini considered pursuing a career as a professional aviator and spent a month at the Farman flight school before deciding that he was not cut out to be a "chauffeur of the air."[68] The Cubists Georges Braque and Pablo Picasso often made their way to Issy-les-Moulineaux to watch the planes take off and land and reportedly even tried their hand at making model aircraft. The scaffoldings of Braque's paper sculptures reminded Picasso of Wilbur Wright's Flyer, and he sometimes referred to his fellow Cubist as "Vilbour," a nickname Braque had been given by the aviators he had met at Issy. About the same time, in 1912, Picasso executed a painting entitled *Nature morte: "Notre avenir est dans l'air"*, which through its use of letters and the red, white, and blue of the tricolor indicates Picasso's awareness of the extent to which French national security had become identified in the public mind with primacy in aviation.[69]

Few pre-1914 avant-garde painters, however, attempted to explore the new perspective on the world that aviation offered. When painters did portray flying machines in the air, they almost always did so from the point of view of someone watching from below.

322. Picasso's 1912 painting *Nature morte: "Notre Avenir est dans l'Air"* (Still Life: Our Future is in the Air). Private collection.

323. Spectators applaud Santos-Dumont's prize-winning dirigible flight of September 1901.

With a handful of exceptions, such as Robert Delaunay, Roger de la Fresnaye and Carlo Carrà, the artistic avant-garde remained resolutely earthbound.[70]

Why was this so? Was it because avant-garde painters lacked a firsthand knowledge of flight? Was it because they were more interested in expressing states of mind and reconceptualizing the more familiar objects that surrounded them in the countryside and in the recently modernized cities? Or was it because the first years of powered flight coincided with a tendency in the avant-garde toward the suppression of easily recognizable objects from their works of art?[71]

The case of Robert Delaunay is instructive in this regard. Delaunay was a member of the first generation of Parisians to grow up in the electrically lit city that Baron Haussmann had expanded and redesigned. The symbol of Delaunay's Paris – the emblem of its cultural and technological dominance – was the Eiffel Tower, a three-hundred-meter-high iron structure that was capable of transmitting invisible but powerful radio waves throughout the world. By 1909, when the 24-year-old Delaunay set out to paint it, the Tower had become inextricably associated with aeronautical achievement; it was to the Tower that first Santos-Dumont and then the Count de Lambert had flown before the astounded eyes of hundreds of thousands of Parisians. It is not surprising, then, that some of Delaunay's most important prewar paintings juxtapose the Tower with images of aircraft. Yet, as an avant-garde painter what

273

fascinated Delaunay was not so much the airplane as an object or the new view it offered of the world but the inspiration it provided to experiment with form, color, and light: not the machine as such but the symbol of modernity.

What held for Delaunay was even truer of other prewar avant-garde artists. In so far as the impact of aviation made itself felt on their work, it did so primarily by validating the idea of a cultural break and confirming their intuition that new modes of perception were at hand.[72] Airplanes and aviators served as metaphors for liberation from the world of the nineteenth century, a flying up and away from the past; but few avant-garde artists felt the compulsion that Malevich did to paint them. It was not until the 1920s and 1930s that a new generation of Italian Futurists would attempt to create an aviation art that explored the world as it looked from an airplane hurtling through the sky at high velocities; and they did so within the context of a fascist regime whose dictatorial leader gave a high priority to aviators and flight.

In any case, artists who worked in the new media that exploited the recently invented technologies of mechanical reproduction showed no such hesitations. Flying machines were used to advertise alcoholic drinks and above all to attract the public to flying meets. The poster for the April 1910 meet in Nice, for example, shows the city, the coastline, and the surrounding mountains from the perspective of an aviator peacefully soaring

324. Gerardo Dottori, *A 300 km sulla città* (300 kilometers an hour above the city), 1934. Private collection.

through the air, suggesting in a powerfully poetic image the exhilaration of flight and the majestic, almost godlike panoramas it offered. Aerial calendars portrayed cities as they appeared from an aviator's perspective. Millions of postcards depicting dirigibles and airplanes circulated through Europe and the United States during these years.[73] People delighted in having themselves photographed with friends in mock airplanes, thus associating themselves vicariously with the excitement and prestige of flight.

The editors of illustrated newspapers and magazines, such as *Colliers* in the United States or *L'Illustration* in France, also quickly realized that aviation imagery helped maintain circulation. They understood that photographs of airplanes in flight or even at

325, 327. The connection between flying and drinking seemed irresistible, as these advertisements for apertifs suggest.

326. The romantic poster for the April 1910 meet in Nice in which the poetry of flight is combined with the spring-like fragance of the Côte d'Azur.

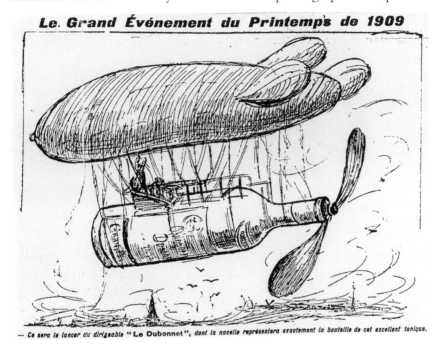

Le Grand Événement du Printemps de 1909

— Ce sera le lancer du dirigeable " Le Dubonnet ", dont la nacelle représentera exactement la bouteille de cet excellent tonique.

MEETING D'AVIATION NICE
10-25 AVRIL 1910

AU BON MARCHE

AU DESSUS DE TOUT ET PARTOUT
CINZANO
ASTI-VERMOUTH
DÉLICIEUX   TONIQUE   APÉRITIF

328. An aviator in the sky reveals the wonders of the Bon Marché department store in late 1910.

275

329. A 1911 calendar portrays Paris from the perspective of a flying machine.

330. Franz Kafka (on the extreme left) and friends have themselves photographed in a mock airplane.

331. Film frames showing the crash at Issy-les-Moulinaux in May 1911 that killed the French Minister of War.

rest on the ground could galvanize the fantasies of their readers and bestow on their magazines an unmistakable cachet of modernity. One of France's most distinguished photographers, Jacques Lartigue, launched his career by selling shots of airplanes in flight to Parisian sporting magazines.[74] Lartigue's enthusiasm for aviation was such that when he attended the *Rite of Spring* in June 1913, what he liked about Stravinsky's music was that its throbbing rhythms – *vroum, vroum, vroum* – reminded him of the roar of airplane engines taking off at Issy-les-Moulineaux.[75]

Yet of all the new cultural forms that lent themselves to mechanical reproduction, the one with the greatest natural affinity for aviation was the cinema; only a movie camera could convey the way the world looked when viewed from a speeding airplane. Always a step ahead of the competition, Wilbur Wright grasped the compatibility between these two turn-of-the-century inventions, which had in common their ability to offer new means of seeing, new modes of perception.[76] Already in April 1909, while giving flying lessons at the Centocelle airdrome, he took aloft a cinematographer who captured the Roman campagna as it appeared from Wright's Flyer as he skimmed at low altitude through the sky. Still spellbinding to watch today, one can only imagine the effect these pictures had on the spectators who saw them over eighty years ago.

Eager to turn a profit, the creators of cine-magazines, the predecessor of the newsreel, soon discovered that images of flight had the power to delight and mesmerize their growing audiences, especially in cases where danger or death was involved. Few thrills could match the sight of an aircraft falling helplessly toward the ground. When a flying machine plunged into a group of dignitaries assembled to watch the beginning of the Paris-Madrid race in May 1911 and killed the French Minister of War, moving picture shots of the accident were on view in Paris's cinemas the same afternoon. Lartigue was so struck by these images that he recorded the experience in his diary. "One sees [the aviator] Train . . . make a very steep turn, hit the ground and enter a small crowd (8 or 10 people) . . . The rest of the show is very entertaining: a close-up film about ants (they look as big as cats) and Védrines, the great winner of [the race] Paris-Madrid . . . who capsizes while landing."[77]

What worked so well in newsreels was bound to attract the makers of feature films. In 1912 the Neapolitan director Elvira Notari made a movie entitled *The Heroism of an Aviator in Tripoli*, which was aimed at exploiting the Italian public's enthusiasm for Captain Piazza and the winged warriors of the Libyan war. The story of a passionate

332. Photograph by Jacques Lartigue of Issy-les-Moulineaux in December 1911. A bleak industrial setting for such a moving sight.

love affair between a rich and dashing aviator of the upper classes and a humble florist was interwoven with a patriotic chronicle of the Italian "aerial fleet" fighting heroically in Libya to wrest that colony from Ottoman control. A contemporary fictionalization of the film explained, with exuberant exaggeration of the actual events, that "the rain of bombs" had "confused and destroyed the enemy." "Strange spectacle! Powerful means of destruction." Wounded while fighting in Libya, the hero returns home to die – but not before giving a long kiss to the heroine and another to the Italian flag.[78] The aviation film was launched. The formula combined romance, danger, and airplanes. Women were a reward for valor in the sky. Hollywood would follow in Notari's footsteps and make hundreds of such movies.[79]

Early writers on aviation assumed that flying machines would change the shape of cities. The roofs of buildings, they predicted, would be flattened so that their inhabitants could land and take off from their private residences; the terraces of hotels would be provided with landing strips and hangars for air taxis that spared their guests the inconvenience of having to traverse the city's crowded streets; the value of the upper stories of buildings would increase as people changed their orientation away from the ground toward the heavens; and richer city dwellers would want to spend as much time in the air as possible because it was clearer, healthier, and less congested.[80]

The first airdromes bore little relationship to these fantasies about the future. Located in suburbs outside major cities, they consisted of bumpy fields without clearly demar-

278

cated landing strips, isolated hangars and repair shops, parking places for automobiles, and sometimes a factory or two for the construction of flying machines.[81] It would take decades for the air*field* to give way to the air*port*, now a city in itself and usually far removed from the people it serves. But already in 1914 a young Italian architect connected with the Futurist movement, Antonio Sant'Elia, had begun to sketch gigantic multi-level terminals, designed for cable cars, trains, and airplanes, from which elegantly slim rectangular towers rose above the upper landing strip – a cathedral for the coming air age, but one which bears little resemblance to the crowded terminals through which frazzled and over-burdened air travelers trudge today.

If one thinks of the dominant images of the aviator produced within aviation culture before 1914 – the ingenious inventor, the daring sportsman, the Nietzschean superman, the courageous soldier and imperialist, the merciless man machine – one cannot help but be struck by the absence of women as protagonists of flight. In the male imagination's visions of the sky, there was no place for women. Yet in the real world of prewar aviation, there existed a small but remarkable group of female pilots who shared with their male counterparts the passion for flying machines. One found women aviators in almost all the larger Western countries – in the United States, in France, in Britain, in Germany, in Italy, in Belgium, in Sweden, and in the Russian Empire. They competed with men for records, carried them as passengers, thrilled them with their exploits, and sometimes taught them how to fly.[82]

The achievement of these women aviators is all the more impressive in view of the obstacles they had to overcome. Most male pilots believed, like Claude Grahame-White, that women had no business in the sky. They were temperamentally unfitted to

333. Antonio Sant'Elia, *Airplane and railroad station with cable cars and elevators on three street levels*, 1914.

279

334. Harriet Quimby in a flying outfit of her own design.

335. Helene Dutrieu modelling her flying costume.

336. Princess Eugenie Shakhovskaya (Princess Shakhovskaya was ordered into active service in November 1914 and given the rank of Enseign of Engineers. She was probably the first female military pilot. Shakhovskaya was later shot by the Communist Secret Police, not however before she had killed two of her lovers, themselves members of the Cheka.)

337. An early caricature of famous aviators, including a hobble-skirted Raymonde de Laroche in otherwise exclusively male company.

338. A precariously perched woman is consigned to the ground as aviators soar through the sky in this poster for the 1909 Vichy air show.

fly because they were prone to panic and lacked the physical strength to deal with emergencies.[83] Besides, flying was dangerous, and women had no right to risk their lives. This was a male prerogative, like fighting wars and killing. Consequently, many male aviators were reluctant to give women flight training or to sell them airplanes.[84] When they did, they sometimes confessed that they regretted it.[85]

Women who persevered in their pursuit of flying careers, like the French aviatrix Raymonde de Laroche, the beautiful American journalist Harriet Quimby, and the free-spirited Russian princess Eugenie Shakovskaya, won notoriety. Their photographs often appeared in illustrated magazines, showing them modelling the flying outfits they designed. But they were viewed as curiosities, aberrations from the feminine norm whose independent life styles and accidents confirmed those who believed that a woman's place was not in the air but at home.

One might suppose that such women would inspire the literary imagination. But this was not the case. When women appeared in aviation literature, they did so as the admirers of pilots, their prize for having accomplished a daring exploit, or an obstacle that stood between them and the fulfillment of their destiny in the sky. Whatever their role, women were usually portrayed on the ground, gazing upward toward the hero in his machine. In this aspect of aviation culture, as in so many others, Gabriele D'Annunzio turned out to be a precursor. For his fictional hero Paolo Tarsis, flight was above all a means of escape from the sordid and demeaning world of women. Later practitioners of the genre would find this equation irresistible. Henceforth in aviation

literature, and later in aviation film, women would be a greater threat to the heroic aviator than wind, fog, sleet, or snow.

Did this interpretation of women in aviation culture reflect an abysmal ignorance of their capabilities and true desires, the existence of a middle-class social code based on the segregation of the sexes that was so ingrained that few men *or* women thought to question it, or a hidden fear that the "new woman" was determined to invade the cloistered worlds that early twentieth-century males considered their own? My suspicion is that all these factors were at play, though by far the most important was the belief – shared by even such a celebrated student of the human psyche as Freud – that women were profoundly different from (and inferior to) men. Comradeship among males was often represented as a deeper bond than the more sensual and superficial motivations that united men and women; and comradeship thrived in situations of life-threatening danger. Most men of the period found it difficult to believe that "real" women wanted anything beyond home, hearth, and children.[86] Sexism, like colonialism, could easily be rationalized on the grounds that those whose lives were being constrained benefited from their subordination. Jean Conneau is typical of the attitudes I am describing. While appreciative of the brightness, gaiety, and graceful bravery of those "few bold aviatresses" who frequented the airdromes, he concluded that "aviation is for adults, alert, vigorous, of robust health, and capable of resisting fatigue. Such organic qualities are rarely found in women, and it's really a pity."[87] In the real world as in fiction, men were determined to keep the air for themselves.[88]

The Great War only reinforced the image of the sky as a privileged male space. Though many women aviators volunteered for wartime duty, only a handful were allowed to serve, almost exclusively in reconnaissance missions.[89] Flying in combat was too important a task to entrust to a woman. Moreover, the image of the ace, which combined the daring of the acrobat, the sporting code of the amateur athlete, the courage of the soldier, the gallantry of the medieval knight, the killer instinct of the hunter, and the male bonding of an all boy's school, left little room for women. Aces exemplified more purely than any other figure of their time what it meant to be a man.

In retrospect, it is astonishing how deeply this image of the aviator became embedded in the popular culture of the Western countries. Scores of books and films were devoted to this theme.[90] Among other things, they testify to the longing for a different kind of war than the one that most combatants knew during the years between 1914 and 1918. The vision of helmeted knights wrapped in white scarves and jousting in the air with blazing machine-guns would capture many a young imagination. Charles Lindbergh was only one of thousands of young boys who decided to become an aviator after reading an account of the adventures of a First World War ace.[91] How ironic that he, more than any other postwar aviator, would be responsible for replacing the image of the hot-blooded and reckless ace with that of the cool, sober, and dependable aerial technician, the taciturn and unflappable captain who flies your commercial jet today.[92]

The ace was a translation into reality of Marinetti's prewar fantasies: the aviator fused with his machine and transformed into an engine of death. Yet another pre-1914 vision that was realized during the war was H. G. Wells and Rudolf Martin's scenes of airmen hurling bombs at civilians from the sky. Both London and Paris were bombed by Zeppelins in 1914. When Zeppelin attacks proved too costly in lost airships and men, they were replaced in 1917 by bombing sorties carried out by giant Gotha airplanes. The Allies retaliated by bombing German and Austrian cities. Though these attacks had no impact on the outcome of the war, they demonstrated that Wells and Martin had been

right in asserting that civilian populations were no longer beyond the reach of enemy fire; and they encouraged some military specialists to assert that airpower would have a revolutionary impact on warfare.[93]

Among those people who believed that the airplane had forever changed the nature of war, one of the most vociferous was the Italian Giulio Douhet. A professional soldier who had been court-martialed and imprisoned during the First World War for his insistence on pressing his views against the unyielding opposition of his army superiors, Douhet argued that large armies and heavily armed ships would no longer be able to guarantee a nation's security because airplanes could easily overfly them. Defense against air attack would require a deployment of men and materiel that no nation could afford. Furthermore, military forces on the ground or sea would be vulnerable to attack from above. The only sure means of defense in future wars therefore would be the ability to attack the enemy within his own territory. Nations unable to mount such raids would be doomed to defeat. This meant that victory in war would henceforth depend upon the command of the air. Douhet optimistically concluded that the decisive role played by airpower would make future wars shorter and less bloody. No government, he thought, would be able to carry on the struggle when faced with the prospect of the continued bombardment of its cities. "And even if a semblance of order could be maintained and some work done, would not the sight of a single enemy airplane be

339. The death of Giulio Combiaso from D'Annunzio's novel, *Forse che sì forse che no*: Paolo Tarsis looks on as the doctor examines his dead friend.

340. Manfred von Richthofen's Squadron. After attending a dinner given in honor of a German squadron commander to celebrate his twentieth victory, the young footsoldier Ernst Jünger described in his diary the aviators he had met. "They come from the mighty army that lies forward in the trenches under unending fire, and they constitute an elite that the drive towards ever more daring forms of battle has brought together." (Ernst Jünger, *Das Wäldchenizs* in *Werke* (Stuttgart: Ernst Kett Verlag, n.d.; original edn 1915), I. p. 367.

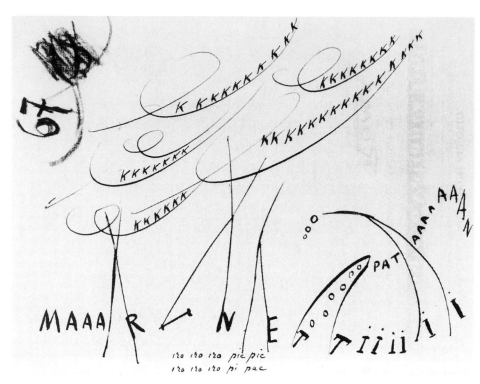

341. A German postcard showing hysterical Londoners fleeing, as Zeppelins bomb the city.

342. During the course of the First World War, even the author of *Le Monoplan du Pape* gained a new appreciation of what it meant to be bombarded. Here projectiles fall on the letters of Marinetti's name while the airplanes in the sky celebrate by performing delicate loops.

enough to induce a formidable panic? Normal life would be unable to continue under the constant threat of death and imminent destruction."[94] Thus was launched a debate about the uses of strategic bombing that continues up to our own day.

Writers who witnessed the first air attacks against London and Paris from the ground could not conceal the terrible beauty of the spectacle they had seen and searched for cultural references capable of giving meaning to their experience. For Marcel Proust the squadrons of aviators that darted into the night to repulse the Zeppelins were like "human shooting stars" and Wagnerian Valkyries that flew to the "heart-breaking" music of sirens, as searchlights ceaselessly crossed the sky, tracking the enemy and suddenly filling the abyss of the black night with light.[95] Enthralled by the sight of the bombing attacks, Proust could not bring himself to find anything tragic in these nocturnal visits by enemy aircraft – until one night "the gesture of a bomb dropped on us" brought home to him the "murderous" mission of the enemy aircraft that was partially hidden in the stormy clouds above. Suddenly he realized that the city he loved so much might disappear in a fiery blast of bombs.[96]

D. H. Lawrence was also dazzled by what Proust called "apocalypse" in the sky. Watching a Zeppelin bombing London, seeing "the splashes of fire" as the antiaircraft shells burst in the sky, and hearing the "shaking noise" as the bombs exploded, Lawrence could not help but think of Milton's *Paradise Lost*.

> then there was war in heaven. But it was not angels. It was that small golden zeppelin, like a long oval world, high up. It seemed as if the cosmic order were gone, as if there had come a new order, a new heavens above us: and as if the world in anger were trying to revoke it . . . So it seems our cosmos is burst, burst at last, the stars and moon blown away, the envelope of the sky burst out, and a new cosmos appeared, with a long-ovate, gleaming central luminary, calm and drifting in a glow of light, like a new moon, with its light bursting in flashes on the earth, to burst away the earth also. So it is the end – our world is gone, and we are like dust in the air.[97]

A scene that to spectators on the ground appeared like the end of the world had a different significance for those who looked at the war from above. The passion for aces and their exploits – which far outlasted the realities of aerial warfare in 1918 when formation flying became dominant – concealed the fact that airplanes were used primarily during the First World War to observe movement on the surface of the earth. Again the technologies of aviation and cinema turned out to be fatefully intertwined. In October 1915, Oskar Messter, a German film technician, invented a device that automatically took a sequence of photographs from an airplane, creating the effect of a motion picture of the ground. With Messter's machine, it was possible in the course of a single reconnaissance flight to film a surface 60 kilometers long and 2.4 kilometers wide. The result was a flattened and cubistic map of the earth that had little in common with the three-dimensional perspective on the world that human beings were accustomed to have. Only trained interpreters could decipher such aerial maps. As airplanes had to fly higher to escape ever more accurate antiaircraft fire, aviators increasingly yielded the task of reconnaissance to their cameras.[98] Famous for his hawk-like vision and himself an observer before becoming a pilot, Manfred von Richthofen came to doubt whether an aviator flying at an altitude of 15,000 feet could discern with any degree of certainty objects moving on the ground.[99] War thus brought with it a new way of seeing in which machines replaced eyes and the earth became a target as far removed from the personal experience of the observer or the bombadier as a distant planet.

Where Proust and Lawrence associated aircraft in the sky with the end of their world and theorists of air power like Douhet thought that bombers would revolutionize warfare by eliminating the importance of frontiers and the distinction between civilians and soldiers, others glimpsed a commercial opportunity. If airplanes could transport bombs, they could also be used to carry goods and people. Irregular passenger and airmail service had already been launched in the United States and Europe during the war. When the Armistice was signed, the surfeit of unneeded military planes, the greater range and dependability of aircraft engines, the presence of large numbers of experienced military pilots who wished to continue flying, and the sorry state of surface transportation systems in some European countries encouraged the organization of more ambitious air transport companies operating regularly across long distances.[100] Out of these would grow many of the airlines that carry us today.

Among those who grasped that the technological advances made in aeronautics during the war had rendered the transportation of goods, mail, and people a real possibility, none thought bigger or more boldly than the French industrialist and

343. Oskar Messter's camera for taking sequential aerial photographs. The camera is situated directly behind the pilot's seat in this Albatros biplane.

344. An example of the type of composite aerial photographs that Messter's invention made possible. The importance the German High Command assigned to these missions is shown by the fact that two reconnaissance pilots received the coveted Pour le mérite medal, usually reserved for aces, and a third was awarded the Knight's Cross of the House of Hohenzollern for his successful reconnaissance flight over Paris in the summer of 1918.

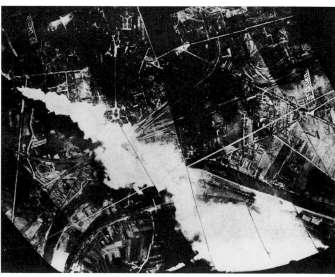

345. The cover of a brochure depicting the Latécoère Line's routes from its base at Toulouse to Casablanca: Africans welcome the French air service with open arms.

engineer, Pierre-Georges Latécoère. Where his European counterparts set out to link Europe's administrative and commercial capitals by air, he envisaged an aerial network emanating southward from his industrial base at Toulouse that would connect the cities along Spain's eastern coast with France, reach across the Mediterranean to Algeria and Morocco, continue down the African coast to the French colony of Sénégal, and then, at the narrowest point between Africa and Latin America, overfly the Atlantic, making it possible to unite by air the cities of Europe with faraway Rio de Janeiro, Buenos Aires, and Santiago de Chile. To accomplish this goal, Latécoère assembled a nucleus of First World War pilots, including several aces. What even he could not have imagined was that the realization of his vision by these men would leave a lasting imprint on French literature. It would create a new image of the aviator as a disciplined member of a team who subordinated his sense of individual freedom in the sky to the interests of the airline for which he worked and the goals of commerce and international communication. From Latécoère's wartime fantasy would come the astonishing enterprise that inspired the exploits of Jean Mermoz and his fellow Aéropostale pilots and the books of Joseph Kessel and Antoine Saint-Exupéry. A *chanson de geste* for the twentieth century.[101]

Another dreamer who glimpsed the possibilities that aviation offered was Benito Mussolini. Mussolini's passion for flight and his intuition into the wider significance of aviation went back to the years before 1914. On the eve of Latham's unsuccessful attempt to fly the Channel in July 1909, Mussolini wrote an article for a regional Italian newspaper in which he expounded on the meaning of the Channel flights. Exploits like these, the young Mussolini insisted, could not be understood simply in terms of sport. They were an expression of the deepest tendencies of the new century. Our age was heroic, perhaps even more so than the Ancient World. The word that summed up the new century was movement. "Movement toward the icy solitudes of the poles and toward the virgin peaks of the mountains, movement toward the stars and toward the depths of the seas . . . Movement everywhere and acceleration in the rhythm of our lives."[102] And when Blériot succeeded in flying the Channel, Mussolini saluted him as one of the first champions of a new race of Nietzschean *dominatori*, one of those restless figures who give meaning to life through the pursuit of an ideal.[103]

The war, which Mussolini experienced from the immobility of the trenches, only increased his reverence for aviators. What a difference between his inglorious earth-bound war and the glamorous aerial exploits of D'Annunzio, who had organized and led several daring raids against Austrian cities and military installations, including one against Vienna! Even before the war ended, Mussolini had begun to seek out the

347. The text of the message that D'Annunzio and his fellow aviators dropped over Vienna on 9 August 1918. It begins: 'On the wind of victory that is rising from the rivers of liberty, we only came for the joy of the exploit and in order to demonstrate what we can dare and do when we want, at the time that we choose." (Signed: Gabriele D'Annunzio "in the sky of Vienna.")

company of military pilots and aces. Several would be at his side when he came to power in Ocotber, 1922.

Mussolini understood that the full mystique of aviation would only adhere to those who learned how to pilot a plane. The ace Mario Stoppiani, who took Mussolini up for one of his first flights, remembered him as being in a state of "enthusiastic delirium." Mussolini himself later wrote that when they reached 1700 meters he urged Stoppani to continue climbing. "*Ancora, ancora, più in alto*" (Go on, go on, higher), he urged with excited gestures. As the plane nosed up, Mussolini had the exhilarating sensation, shared by so many early aviators, of the earth receding into the distance. "What diaphanous serenity in the twilight sky!"[104] Driving away from the airfield with a group of aviators, it occurred to Mussolini that these men represented "the new Italian race of producers, builders, and creators." They were the Italians of the future who would conquer the land, the sea, and the sky.[105]

I end with Mussolini because he illustrates so many of the themes I have sought to develop in this history. Only twenty years old when the Wrights first flew, Mussolini had experienced in all of its initial intensity the passion for wings. Moreover, as a professional journalist, he understood the power of aviation imagery on the imagination of the masses. He realized that aviation had symbolic implications that went far beyond its technological or utilitarian significance; an airplane was more than a machine. Flight was a metaphor for the new Nietzschean age that was dawning. The deeds of the technological heroes of the twentieth century would equal, and perhaps exceed, those of the mythical figures of the Ancient World. The conquest of the air followed naturally from the conquest of colonial peoples, the exploration of the earth, and the penetration of the seas by submarines. The urge to dominate, to master, to conquer, was the motivation that drove men to fly. Speed was the divinity of the new century, to be worshipped at any cost. The cult of movement required victims. In its service, no sacrifice was too great. Aviators were the new aristocracy. Power and primacy would come to those peoples who dominated the air. No admirer of Marinetti, Mussolini had nonetheless grasped intuitively the central message of his work. Death was the price that men would have to pay in order to live like gods in a world of fast machines.[106]

348. Gerardo Dottori, *Ritratto del Duce*, 1933. Galleria d'Arte Moderna, Milano. "Not every Italian can or should fly. But all Italians should envy those who do and should follow with profound feeling the development of Italian wings." (From a speech given to the Aero Club of Italy on 5 November 1923, reproduced by Guido Mattioli in *Mussolini aviatore* (Rome: L'Aviazione, 1938, 3rd edn), p. 153.)

Notes

Introduction

1 "Many wonderful inventions have surprised us during the course of the last century and the beginning of this one. But most were completely unexpected and were not part of the old baggage of dreams that humanity carries with it. Who had ever dreamed of steamships, railroads, or electric light? We welcomed all these improvements with astonished pleasure; but they did not correspond to an expectation of our spirit or a hope as old as we are: to overcome gravity, to tear ourselves away from the earth, to become lighter, to fly away, to take possession of the immense aerial kingdom; to enter the universe of the Gods, to become Gods ourselves." (Jérôme Tharaud, "Dans le ciel des dieux," in *Les Grandes Conférences de l'aviation: Récits et souvenirs* (Paris: Editions du Comité des Oeuvres Sociales du Ministère de l'Air, 1934), p. 5). For studies of two other important early twentieth-century technologies and their impact on culture and society, see David E. Nye, *Electrifying America: Social Meanings of a New Technology* (Cambridge, Mass.: MIT Press, 1992) and Wolfgang Sachs, *For Love of the Automobile: Looking Back into the History of Our Desires* (Berkeley: University of California Press, 1992).

2 Robert Wohl, *The Generation of 1914* (Cambridge, Mass.: Harvard University Press, 1979), p. 119. Only recently did I discover (or rediscover) that one of the protagonists of *The Generation of 1914*, the poet Wilfred Owen, had written to his mother in 1916 declaring his intention to become a pilot. "By Hermes, I will fly. Though I have sat alone, twittering, like even as it were a sparrow upon the housetop, I will yet swoop over Wrekin with the strength of a thousand Eagles, and all you shall see me light upon the Racecourse, and marvelling behold the pinion of Hermes, who is called Mercury, upon my cap . . . If I fall, I shall fall mightily. I shall be with Perseus and Icarus, whom I loved; and not with Fritz, whom I did not hate. To battle with the Super-Zeppelin, when he comes, this would be chivalry more than Arthur dreamed of. Zeppelin, the giant-dragon, the child-slayer, I would happily die in any adventure against him . . ." (From *Wilfred Owen: Collected Letters*, ed. Harold Owen & John Bell (London, New York, & Toronto: Oxford University Press 1967), p. 408).

3 By Theodore Zeldin in the *Sunday Times* (London), 16 March 1980.

4 Since I conceived the idea for a book on "Aviation and the Western Imagination," many other historians have published works that seek to integrate aviation into the central narrative of Western history. I will be citing their books and articles in the pages of this and forthcoming volumes.

5 For early visions of flight and flying machines, see The *Poetry of Flight*, ed. Stella Wolfe Murray (London: Heath Cranton, 1925), pp. 21–39, and Clive Hart, *The Prehistory of Flight* (Berkeley: University of California Press, 1985). In the nineteenth century the balloon and later the dirigible had been especially important in preparing the ground for aviation culture. Note, for example, these verses from Victor Hugo:

> Loin dans les profondeurs, hors des nuits, hors du flot,
> Dans un écartement de nuages qui laisse
> Voir, au-dessus des mers, la céleste allégresse,
> Un point vague et confus apparaît, dans le vent.
> Dans l'espace ce point se meut, il est vivant,
> Il va, descend, remonte, il fait ce qu'il veut faire;
> Il approche, il prend forme, il vient: c'est une sphère,
> C'est un inexprimable et surprenant vaisseau,
> Globe comme le monde, et comme l'aigle, oiseau.
> C'est un navire en marche. Où? Dans l'éther sublime!

> Faraway in the depths, beyond the nights, beyond the waves,
> In a series of clouds that
> Lets one see, above the seas, the celestial joy,
> A vague and obscure point appears, in the wind.
> The point moves in space, it's living,
> It goes, descends, climbs, it does what it wishes;
> It approaches, it takes on form, it comes: it's a sphere,
> It's an inexpressible and surprising vessel,
> A globe like the earth, and like the eagle, a bird.
> It's a ship under way. Whither? In the sublime ether!

Quoted in *Le Livre d'or de la conquête de l'air* (Paris: Kapp, 1909), pp. v–vi.

6 F. T. Marinetti, *Poupées électriques* (Paris: E. Sansot, 1909), p. 36.

7 Le Corbusier [Charles Edouard Jeanneret-Gris], *Aircraft* (New York: Universe, 1985; original edn 1935), p. 6.

8 *Ibid.*, p. 6. See also Le Corbusier's slightly later *Sur les 4 routes* (Paris: Gallimard, 1941, 4th edn), p. 125, where he writes: "On the cutting edge of technological progress, [the airplane] opens the way toward the new times; it hurtles toward them *à coup d'ailes* (by beating its wings)." By "modernism," I refer to the adversary culture that arose in late nineteenth-century Europe and flourished during the years between 1890 and 1933. See my essays "The Generation of 1914 and Modernism" in *Modernism, Challenges and Perspectives*, ed. Monique Chefdor, Ricardo Quinones and Albert Wachtel (Urbana: Univeristy of Illinois Press, 1986), pp. 66–78 and my introduction and conclusion to *The Lost Voices of World War I* (London: Bloomsbury, 1988), especially pp. 2–4 and 385–6.

9 Vasily Kamensky, *Put' entusiasta* (The Path of an Enthusiast) (New York: Orpheus, 1986; original edn 1931), p. 110.

10 Friederich Nietzsche, *Werke in drei Bänden*, ed. Karl Schlechta (Munich: Carl Hanser Verlag, 1966), vol. II, p. 456. For the forms that agression took in nineteenth-century Europe, see Peter Gay, *The Cultivation of Hatred* (New York: Norton, 1993). Curiously, Gay has little to say about the relationship between the European will to power and technology.

1. The Fanatic of Flight

1 For the noise of the Wright Flyer, as remembered by the *Daily Mail*'s aviation correspondent, see Graham Wallace, *Flying Witness* (London: Putnam, 1958), p. 84.

2 François Peyrey, *Les Premiers Hommes-Oiseaux* (Paris: Guiton, 1908), p. 40. See also Wallace, *Flying Witness*, p. 81.

3 René Gasnier, quoted by Fred Howard in *Wilbur and Orville* (New York: Knopf, 1987), p. 258.

4 Frantz Reichel in *Le Figaro*, 11 August 1908. Reichel later killed himself by jumping off the Eiffel Tower in a hang glider of his own design.

5 Peyrey, *Les Premiers Hommes-Oiseaux*, p. 40.

6 The following biographical sketch is based on *Miracle at Kitty Hawk: The Letters of Wilbur and Orville Wright*, Fred C. Kelly, ed., (New York: Farrar, Straus and Young, 1951); Marvin W. McFarland, ed., *The Papers of Wilbur and Orville Wright* (New York: McGraw-Hill, 1953), 2 vols.; Howard, *Wilbur and Orville*; and Tom D. Crouch, *The Bishop's Boys* (New York: Norton, 1989).

7 Crouch, *The Bishop's Boys*, p. 97.

8 For invention in late nineteenth-century America, see the suggestive study by Thomas P. Hughes, *American Genesis* (New York: Viking, 1989), especially pp. 1–137.

9 The connection between bicycle technology and the Wright's breakthroughs in aeronautics is convincingly argued by Crouch in

The Bishop's Boys, pp. 114–5, 168–70, 243–4.

10 Kelly, *Miracle at Kitty Hawk*, p. 27.

11 *L'Illustration*, 5 August 1908.

12 Wilbur Wright to his father, 23 September 1900, *The Papers of Wilbur and Orville Wright*, I, p. 26.

13 *Ibid.*, II, pp. 731–2.

14 For the nature and significance of these breakthroughs, see the fascinating volume edited by Howard S. Wolko, *The Wright Flyer: An Engineering Perspective* (Washington, D.C.: National Air and Space Museum, 1987).

15 See Wilbur Wright's Notebook A for 1900–1 in *The Papers of Wilbur and Orville Wright*, I, pp. 34–6, 44.

16 Louis Blériot & Edouard Ramond, *Les Ailes de la gloire* (Paris: Les Editions de France, n.d. (1928?)), p. 50.

17 Howard, *Wilbur and Orville*, p. 67.

18 Orville Wright, "How We Made the First Flight," *Flying* (December 1913), quoted by Crouch in *The Bishop's Boys*, p. 242.

19 Amelia Earhart, *The Fun of It* (New York: Harcourt Brace, 1932). In a letter to Chanute on 13 May 1900, Wilbur wrote: "I make no secret of my plans for the reason that I believe no financial profit will accrue to the inventor of the first flying machine, and that only those who are willing to give as well as to receive suggestions can hope to link their names with the honor of its discovery. The problem is too great for one man alone and unaided to solve in secret." (*The Papers of Wilbur and Orville Wright*, I, p. 17). But by 26 November 1900, after his first season at Kitty Hawk, Wright had become more guarded about sharing his discoveries with the outside world. "It is not our intention to make a close secret of our machine, but at the same time, inasmuch as we have not yet had opportunity to test the full possibilities of our methods, we wish to be the first to give them such test. We will gladly give you for you own information anything you may wish to know, but for the present would not wish any publication in detail of the methods of operation or construction of the machine." (*Papers*, I, p. 45). One of the attractions of Kitty Hawk for the Wrights, aside from the predictable winds, was its distance from the prying eyes of the press and other competitors.

20 See their letter to Captain Ferdinand Ferber of 4 November 1905, in which they express the opinion that, once it becomes known that the French are experimenting with motorized flying machines, other nations will be compelled to have recourse to the Wright's "science and practice." "With Russia and Austria in a truculent mood, a general conflagration could break out at any moment. No government will want to delay in the perfection of a flying machine. In order to be ready one year before the others, they will find modest the sum [one million francs] that we are asking for our invention." (Quoted in Peyrey, *Les Premiers Hommes-Oiseaux*, p. 63). The Wrights were incensed when Ferber published this letter in the French aeronautical monthly, *L'Aérophile*. The letter was not included in McFarland's edition of *The Papers of Wilbur and Orville Wright*, although he refers to it on p. 524, n. 1.

21 Kelly, *Miracle at Kitty Hawk*, pp. 136–7 and 142–3.

22 *L'Aérophile*, April 1903, p. 82. Indeed the Wrights' 1901 glider, with Orville standing to the left of it, was identified in *L'Aérophile* as "the Chanute machine" (p. 82).

23 *L'Aérophile*, February 1904. Two Frenchmen, Joseph and Etienne Montgolfier, were the first to make a successful balloon ascension in 1783. Throughout the nineteenth century the French were active in the development of balloon and later dirigible technology. The French also claimed primacy in powered flight on the basis of Clement Ader's frequently repeated assertion that he had left the ground on 9 October 1890 in his steam-driven *Eole*. Unfortunately for Ader, his exploit could not be verified because of the absence of official witnesses; and his attempts to repeat the experiment with later versions of the bat-like *Eole* met with ignominious failure, despite generous subventions from the Ministry of War. Accused of being a charlatan, abandoned by the French military, in 1903 Ader destroyed the *Eole* and all his aeronautical records, sparing only his last machine, *Avion III*, which was deposited in the Conservatoire des Arts et Métiers as a symbol of France's leadership in aeronautics. To this day, experts debate whether Ader, rather than the Wrights, deserves recognition for the first powered flight. If nothing else, Ader gave the French their word for airplane, *avion*. For Ader's career and differing assessments of his achievement, see Pierre Lissarrague, *Clément Ader, inventeur d'avions* (Paris: Editions Privat, 1990) and Claude Carlier, *L'Affaire Clément Ader: la vérité rétablie* (Paris: Perrin, 1990).

24 Andrée Ferber & Robert Ferber, *Les Débuts véritables de l'aviation française* (Paris: Fayard, 1970), pp. 44–6. This important collection of materials from Ferber's personal archive gives some interesting insights into the activities of Chanute who in August 1902 wrote Ferber giving the impression that he and the Wrights were working together in the development of a flying machine. "The exploit that tempts us is to do a little gliding. We think we know how the vultures do it, but it's quite difficult" (p. 51). In a letter written on 1 January 1904 to Ferber, Chanute informed him that the Wrights had succeeded in achieving powered flight but urged him to continue his own experiments. "For it's very possible that the Wrights will have an accident and that it will be you who are destined to perfect a flying machine" (p. 81).

25 *Ibid.*, p. 73.

26 *Ibid.*, p. 134.

27 Charles H. Gibbs-Smith, *The Rebirth of European Aviation* (London: Her Majesty's Stationery Office, 1974), p. 192.

28 On 10 January 1906, Wilbur Wright wrote Chanute that Robert Coquelle's articles – picturesquely entitled "The Conquest of the Air by Two Bicycle Salesmen" – were 95 per cent pure fantasy, but he acknowledged that it would have been harmful to their cause if Coquelle had disputed their claims. (*The Papers of Wilbur and Orville Wright*, II, p. 680).

29 Crouch, *The Bishop's Boys*, p. 309.

30 As Wilbur explained to Chanute on 13 April, "The time was too short for any preliminary practice, and almost too short for what we had already agreed to perform." (*Miracle at Kitty Hawk*, pp. 174–5).

31 *Ibid.*, pp. 181, 179.

32 Alfred Gollin, *No Longer an Island* (London: Heinemann, 1984), p. 183.

33 *Ibid.*, p. 199.

34 Russia had recently signed a peace treaty with Japan after having suffered a humiliating defeat at the hands of the Japanese.

35 *Miracle at Kitty Hawk*, pp. 209–10, 212, 217, 233.

36 Remarks made at the monthly dinner of the Aéro-Club de France and reported in *L'Aérophile*, November 1908, pp. 307–8.

37 *The Papers of Wilbur and Orville Wright*, II, p. 841.

38 *Ibid.*, I, p. 267.

39 *L'Illustration*, 6 June 1908.

40 According to Frederick J. Hooven in *The Wright Flyer*, ed. Wolko, p. 53. Previous to their brief test flights of May 1908 at Kitty Hawk, the Wrights had last flown in October 1905. They had then dismantled the Flyer and put it in storage while attempting to sell it in order to ensure that no one could plagiarize their design.

41 Kelly, *Miracle at Kitty Hawk*, p. 292.

42 Gabriel Voisin in an interview published in *Le Matin* on 19 September 1908. Orville was flying at Fort Myers in order to meet the conditions posed by the United States Army Signal Corps for purchase of the Wright machine.

43 As exemplified by a British visitor to Auvours, Archibald Marshall, whose impressions of Wilbur Wright the *Daily Mail* published on 21 December 1908. Wright, he wrote, was a "working mechanic" with a thin face and long neck who looked like a bird. "He is the sort of man who we are accustomed, perhaps, to think is to be found more often in England than in America – a man who does things and does not talk about them . . . He is a quiet man of few words, but sometimes his face lights up with a smile which makes up for his taciturnity." His airplane "looked like the work of an amateur. It was rough, almost makeshift. The two tiny seats on the lower plane [wing] seemed to be made out of biscuit boxes. There were people on the ground who could have improved it, and said as much. But they could not fly, and Wright could, and was getting ready to do so." After watching and cheering several flights by Wright, Marshall returned to Le Mans by automobile to have dinner. "The room was crowded with people who had come to this little-visited French town to see what we had also come to see.

And six miles away, among the pines and heather, under the lonely stars, the man whose name will go down through the rest of the world's history was perhaps cooking his modest supper in a corner of his shed, in the shadows of which his great machine was stretching its ghostly wings."

44 The comment about parrots was made on 12 September 1908 during a banquet given by the Aéro-Club de la Sarthe in his honor. Wright then went on, however, to make a gracious speech in which he praised the hospitality of the French and especially of his friends in the region around Le Mans. "A few months ago, when I arrived among you, I knew no one, and today I can say that I count my warmest friends here. This feeling extends to your entire country, to France. The population of this country has treated me like a fellow citizen; I thank it from the depth of my heart . . ." (Quoted by François Peyrey in *Les Oiseaux artificiels* (Paris: Dunod & Pinot, 1909), p. 199, n. 2).

45 Wright bathed himself with water from a hose sixty feet away from the shed in which he lived while at Auvours.

46 *L'Illustration*, 5 August 1908.

47 Peyrey, *Les Premiers Hommes-Oiseaux*, p. 46.

48 *Ibid.*, p. 47.

49 *Ibid.*, p. 48.

50 Describing Wright for the readers of *Le Figaro* after his first flights at Hanaudières, Franz Reichel had singled out his eyes for special comment. They are ". . . superb, blue-grey with reflections of gold . . . courageous, gentle, determined, intelligent: the reflections of gold ignite an ardent flame, for Wilbur is a fanatic" (17 August 1908). The aviation correspondent of the *Daily Mail*, Harry Harper, who witnessed Wilbur Wright's first flights at Hanaudières, also remembered his "extraordinary keen, observant, hawk-eyes" (*My Fifty Years in Flying*, pp. 110–11).

51 Many journalists commented on Wright's apparent unflappability during moments of danger. One described with evident astonishment and admiration the American aviator's reaction during a flight on 18 November 1908 when the chain driving the right propeller of his Flyer broke while he was at a height of 75 feet: "Always on the alert, Wright understood the danger; he stopped his motor and went into a gliding descent. There was no trace of emotion on his phlegmatic face when his friends, only just recovered from their fright, congratulated him" (*L'Auto*, 19 November 1908).

52 Peyrey, *Les Oiseaux artificiels*, p. 180.

53 Peyrey was not alone in this period in identifying technological achievement with poetry and cultural creativity. According to Cecilia Tichi, American popular novels published between 1897 and 1911 often portray the engineer as an artist: ". . . the engineer's vision is both prophetic, in that it foresees the future, and poetic, since it originates within the imagination" *Shifting Gears: Technology, Literature, Culture in Modernist America* (Chapel Hill and London: University of North Carolina Press, 1987), p. 119. Tichi cites a writer for the *Atlantic Monthly* in 1913 who extolled "the engineers whose poetry is too deep to look poetic" and whose gifts "have swung their souls free . . . like gods." "Machinery," this writer concluded, "is our new art form" (p. 184). For a further inquiry into the relationship between aviation and French literature, see my essay "Par la voie des airs: l'entrée de l'aviation dans le monde des lettres françaises 1909–1933," *Le Mouvement social*, no. 145 (December 1988), pp. 41–64; later published in a slightly different form as "The Bards of Aviation: Flight and French Culture, 1909–1939," *Michigan Quarterly Review*, Summer 1990, pp. 302–27.

54 Peyrey, *Les Oiseaux artificiels*, pp. 199–202.

55 *The Papers of Wilbur and Orville Wright*, I, p. 306.

56 Peyrey, *Les Oiseaux artificiels*, p. 200.

57 The quoted lines are from an anonymous poem published by the *Daily Mail* on the occasion of Wright's death (31 May 1912).

58 According to Kelly in *Miracle at Kitty Hawk*, p. 333.

59 *Ibid.*, pp. 293, 297, 300. The italics are Wilbur's.

60 "Once above the treetops, the narrow roads no longer arbitrarily fix the course. The earth is spread out before the eye with a richness of color and beauty of pattern never imagined by those who have gazed at the landscape edgewise only. The rich brown of freshly turned earth, the lighter shades of dry ground, the still lighter browns and yellows of ripening crops, the almost innumerable shades of green produced by grasses and forests together present a sight whose beauty has been confined to balloonists in the past." ("Flying as a Sport," *Scientific American*, 29 February airminded 1908, p. 139).

61 The obituary in the airminded Parisian daily *Le Matin* was especially critical of Wright for having wished to make a fortune in return for his services to humanity. "American, original, mysterious, and very well backed up [presumably by Charles Flint's European agent, Hart O. Berg], Wilbur Wright enjoyed an extraordinary success on the airfields near Le Mans . . . Once the moment of enthusiasm had passed, people began to think. They criticized the idea of the two propellers, the absence of longitudinal stability, the defective system for taking off by means of a rail and a pylon. And since then, the Wright machine has been completely forgotten, completely abandoned." (31 May 1912).

2. French Wings over Dover

1 Writing in *Le Matin*, 25 July 1909.

2 On 11 April 1908 Delagrange had set a "world record" by flying 3925 meters (less than two and a half miles) in six minutes. The Wrights, of course, had been capable of remaining in the air for forty minutes or more since September 1906. This gap between what the French regarded as the latest in aeronautical progress and what the Wrights were capable of doing helps to explain the shock experienced by the French when Wilbur Wright first flew in France in August–September 1908.

3 Peyrey, *Les Oiseaux artificiels* (cited ch. 1), p. 180.

4 *Les Sports*, 1 January 1909.

5 Frantz Reichel quoted in the *Daily Mail*, 5 October 1908.

6 The contract that Hart Berg negotiated with Lazare Weiller and his associates in La Compagnie Générale de Navigation Aérienne required the Wrights to make a series of demonstration flights and to train three French pilots. After satisfactory completion of the terms of the contract, they were to receive 500,000 francs upon delivery of the first Flyer, fifty per cent of the company's shares, and 20,000 francs for each of the four additional Flyers that were to be delivered to the company. According to *Le Matin*, Weiller had already offered to give Wright his check for 500,000 francs in mid-October of 1908.

7 Ferdinand Ferber, *L'Aviation* (Paris & Nancy: Berger-Levrault, 1909), p. 144.

8 Ferber thought that in order to escape from the limitations of airplanes and to fly higher, men would have recourse to "a controllable missile (fusée)." Threatened by a decrease of heat from the sun, humanity would have to choose between returning to nothingness "by means of the slow decrepitude of regression" or escaping from earth in a new machine. Such an escape would certainly be desired and carried out by ". . . a group of the supermen of the future, a thousand times stronger and more intelligent than we are, who nonetheless obscurely conceive of them in spirit and know them to be contained in the most profound parts of our being. They will certainly abandon this inhospitable planet, and this is the ultimate aim of the heavier-than-air [flying machine], which has just been born before our astonished and delighted eyes." (Ferber, *L'Aviation*, p. 161).

9 Among other things, the conditions for the Ruinart prize required contestants to make their flights on a Saturday or a Sunday and stipulated that they must announce their intention to enter the competition in writing at least sixty days before the attempted flight. By contrast, the *Daily Mail* required notification only forty-eight hours before an attempted flight. For a full list of the conditions imposed by Ruinart and the *Daily Mail*, see Michel Lhospice, *Match pour la Manche* (Paris: Denoël, 1964), pp. 34–5, 320–1.

10 For Alfred Harmsworth's rise to prominence and his later role in promoting British aviation, see Gollin, *No Longer an Island* (cited ch. 1), pp. 186–97 and *passim*.

11 Wallace, *Flying Witness* (cited ch. 1), p. 24.

12 Quoted by Peter Wykeham, *Santos-Dumont* (London: Putnam,

1962), p. 21. The engineer protagonist of *Robur-le-Conquérant* (originally published in 1886 and translated into English as *Captain of the Clouds*) is the designer of an electrically powered heavier-than-air flying machine made out of reinforced paper with 76 propellers, called the *Albatros*, with which he becomes the master of a realm greater than Australia, Oceania, Asia, America, and Europe, "this aerial *Icarie* that millions of *icariens* will one day populate." After having kidnapped two American balloonists who scoffed at his lecture on the conquest of the air, Robur takes them on a flight around the world. Through his conversations with these two Americans, Uncle Prudent and Phil Evans, Robur comes to understand that late nineteenth-century mentalities are not yet ready to grasp the importance of the revolution that the conquest of the air will one day bring. At the novel's end, he disappears in the *Albatros*, promising that the secret of heavier-than-air flight will not be lost to humanity. "Will Robur-le-Conquérant reappear one day, as he announced? Yes! He will return to hand over the secret of an invention that can modify the social and political conditions of the world." But only when humanity will be "sufficiently educated to take advantage of it and sufficiently wise never to abuse it." Jules Verne, *Robur-le-Conquérant* (Paris: Hachette, 1935 edn), pp. 75, 249–50. For a perceptive analysis of Verne's conception of the machine, see Andrew Martin, *The Mask of the Prophet* (Oxford: Clarendon Press, 1990), especially, pp. 152–76.

13 Wykeham, *Santos-Dumont*, p. 45.

14 Santos-Dumont, *Dans l'air* (Paris: Charpentier & Fasquelle, 1904), p. 42.

15 Raymond Saladin, *Les Temps héroïques de l'aviation* (Paris: Editions Arcadiennes, n.d.), pp. 55–6.

16 Santos-Dumont tells the story in *Dans l'air*, pp. 179–80.

17 *Ibid.*, p. 22.

18 Ferber, *L'Aviation*, p. 98.

19 Santos-Dumont's method of operating these ailerons was "a trifle bizarre for, since his other control arrangements left him with no hand to spare, he had the wires led to a metal T-piece sewn into the back of a special coat. Thus by movements, strongly suggesting the action of a rumba dancer, he could sway the aeroplane one way or the other." (Wykeham, *Santos-Dumont*, p. 215).

20 Wallace, *Flying Witness*, p. 52.

21 *Ibid.*, p. 52.

22 Gollin, *No Longer an Island*, p. 194.

23 *Ibid.*, p. 52.

24 Wallace, *Flying Witness*, p. 53.

25 German enthusiasm for the Zeppelins only increased when Count Zeppelin's LZ4 went up in flames near the village of Echterdingen on 5 August 1908. A national subscription raised 5 million marks in weeks. By the end of the summer of 1909 two more giant airships had been built, and twenty more would be constructed before the outbreak of war in August 1914. For the "Zeppelin fever" of 1908–1909 and their performance in the First World War, see Peter Fritzsche, *A Nation of Fliers* (Cambridge, Mass.: Harvard University Press, 1992), pp. 9–58.

26 Gollin, *No Longer an Island*, p. 339.

27 Quoted in *ibid.*, p. 364.

28 Wilbur to Orville Wright, 18 October 1908, in *The Papers of Wilbur and Orville Wright* (cited ch. 1), II, p. 932. The *Daily Mail* prize of £500 for a Channel crossing by airplane and the conditions of the competition were announced on 5 October 1908 while Wilbur Wright was making demonstration flights at Auvours.

29 Kelly, *Miracle at Kitty Hawk* (cited ch. 1), p. 327.

30 Gollin, *No Longer an Island*, p. 365. Still, as late as 12 January 1909, Orville gave an interview to the *Daily Mail* in which he stated that he had come to Europe "to discuss future plans with my brother Wilbur, particularly in connection with a possible attempt to fly the Channel. There does not seem to be anything insuperable in such a feat."

31 Wilbur Wright to Bishop Milton Wright, 1 January 1909, *The Papers of Wilbur and Orville Wright*, II, p. 948.

32 For the meanings and role of the bicycle in late nineteenth-century France, see Eugen Weber, *France, Fin de Siècle* (Cambridge, Mass.: Harvard University Press, 1986), pp. 195–212.

33 In a generalization typical of the period before 1914, Captain Ferber ascribed Farman's "tenacity" and his "methodical patience" to his Anglo-Saxon origins; see *L'Aviation*, p. 124.

34 For Henry Farman's career, see Jacques Sahel, *Henry Farman et l'aviation* (Paris: Grasset, 1936), an account that must be used with great caution. For the significance of Farman's 1908 flights, see Henry de la Vaulx, *Le Triomphe de la navigation aérienne* (Paris: Jules Tallandrier, 1911), pp. 304–6, 325–6. The technical section of the German General Staff took special note of Farman's cross-country flight. "With this flight of 30 km. a new epoch in aviation has dawned. Farman is the first aviator to leave the maneuver field and undertake a flight to a distant destination – admittedly over flat but nonetheless built-up terrain." (Quoted by John H. Morrow, Jr., in *The Great War in the Air: Military Aviation from 1909 to 1921* (Washington, D.C.: Smithsonian Institution Press, 1993), p. 7).

35 Harper, *My Fifty Years in Flying* (cited ch. 1), p. 121.

36 For Latham, see Jacques Mortane, *Louis Blériot* (Paris: Baudinière, 1940), pp. 52–4 and Tom D. Crouch, *Blériot XI: The Story of a Classic Aircraft* (Washington, D.C.: Smithsonian Institution Press, 1982), pp. 33–4.

37 *Daily Mail*, 13 July 1909.

38 Quoted by Lhospice in *Match pour la Manche*, p. 101.

39 Wallace, *Flying Witness*, pp. 110–11.

40 In a period when a clerk working in a Parisian ministry made 1,800 francs. The Wrights, by contrast, had a combined income equivalent to between 10,000 and 15,000 francs a year.

41 Beyond the evident allure of *gloire*, Blériot's eagerness to compete for the *Daily Mail* prize may have been heightened by his realization that his capital, severely eaten into by almost a decade of aeronautical experiments, sorely needed replenishing. By 1909 he had invested nearly 800,000 francs of his own money in aviation. In January 1909 the *Daily Mail* had doubled the amount of the prize it was offering for the first Channel crossing from £500 to £1,000 (25,000 francs), thus making the exploit considerably more attractive from a sheerly financial point of view.

42 Wilbur Wright's student, Count Charles de Lambert, had also announced his intention to try for the *Daily Mail* prize and had set up a camp near Calais. But Lambert was several days behind Latham and Blériot in terms of his preparations and could only hope to win the prize if they failed. He withdrew from the competition on 27 July after badly damaging his Wright airplane in a training flight.

43 Mortane, *Louis Blériot*, p. 58.

44 Two days later Latham tried again but went down into the sea in sight of Dover when his engine stalled. Henceforth in his aviation career he was dogged by bad luck, though much appreciated by the audiences who flocked to see him fly. Latham was killed in 1912 by an enraged buffalo while big-game hunting in Africa.

45 Quoted by Crouch in *Blériot XI*, p. 39. The pioneer aviator Claude Grahame-White, who learned how to fly in a later version of the Blériot XI, presented an even more harrowing account of Blériot's descent in a book he published not long after the flight. "The few people who were privileged to see the arrival of the aeroplane on English soil were terrified when they observed its violent movements as it was caught by wind gusts. Choosing a smooth piece of grass for his descending point, M. Blériot came planing down. As he did so, however, three or four especially violent gusts of wind caught his machine. It was actually spun around three times, like a top, before it touched earth." (*The Story of the Aeroplane* (Boston: Small, Maynard, 1911), pp. 51–2).

46 "In the middle of the Channel a terrible wind began to rise. I maintained an altitude of 80 meters. Most of the time during the next ten minutes I saw neither the coast nor a ship but only the sky and sea; it seemed to me that I was motionless." From an interview given to the *Daily Telegraph* and republished in *L'Echo de Paris* on 26 July 1909. For a longer, more literary account of the flight by Blériot, see *Le Matin*, 26 July 1909. Here he remembers the ten minutes spent lost in the mist with no horizon to orient him as a period of calm. "This calm, broken only by the roaring of the engine, was a dangerous lure of which I was fully conscious."

47 Blériot's airplane was evidently equipped with a compass, but if we can believe his accounts of the flight, he at no time relied on it, preferring instead to maintain (or attempt to maintain) the direction

he had taken when leaving the French coast. See Lhospice, *Match pour la Manche*, pp. 132–3, 176–7.

48 Writing in 1932, the French aeronautical expert Charles Dollfus insisted that "no pilot of today, no matter how great, could repeat this exploit in such an aircraft, with such an engine." (Quoted by Crouch, *Blériot XI*, p. 42). Though it is admittedly ambiguous, I take this statement to mean that Blériot was lucky to have succeeded where Latham had failed. A more recent student of the period also refers to the Anziani engine as "notoriously unreliable." (See Graham Wallace, *Claude Grahame-White* (London: Putnam, 1960), p. 49). For the flying characteristics of the Blériot XI, see the exceptionally lucid discussion by Tom Crouch in *Blériot XI*, pp. 113–16. Crouch's book is, in general, a model for the history of classic aircraft.

49 For the reaction of French and British newspapers, see Charles Fontaine, *Comment Blériot a traversé la Manche* (Paris: Librairie Aéronautique, 1909), pp. 132–46.

50 *Le Matin*, quoted in Fontaine, *Comment Blériot a traversé la Manche*, p. 134. For *L'Echo de Paris*, Blériot's flight was also a victory for the "imperishable genius" of the French race and "the most magnificent enterprise a century had ever seen" (see "Blériot le Voyageur," 29 July 1909).

51 The *Daily News*, quoted in Wallace, *Flying Witness*, p. 123.

52 Quoted by Fontaine in *Comment Blériot a traversé la Manche*, p. 137.

53 Wallace, *Flying Witness*, pp. 100–1.

54 As related by Fontaine in *Comment Blériot a traversé la Manche*, p. 54. See also his account in *Le Matin*, 27 July 1909, where Northcliffe is said to have made allusion to all the great inventions that had come from France: the bicycle, the automobile, photography, radium, and *aviation*.

55 Harold Penrose, *British Aviation: The Pioneer Years 1903–1914* (London: Putnam, 1967), p. 179.

56 According to Pierre Funeste, writing in *L'Auto* on 29 July 1909, "No sovereign, no head of state, no man in the history of the world had ever had such a reception." The correspondent of *L'Auto*, of course, can be suspected of hyperbole; but writing in 1912, the generally conservative Count de la Vaulx, who had followed the course of French aviation both as a participant and observer ever since the beginning of the century, claimed that Parisians would remember Blériot's arrival at the Gare du Nord and the passage through the streets of the Blériots and their entourage as "the most glorious and spontaneous manifestation of popular enthusiasm that I have ever witnessed." (De la Vaulx, *Le Triomphe de la navigation aérienne*, p. 337).

57 *Le Petit Parisien*, 29 July 1909.

58 *L'Auto*, 29 July 1909.

59 *Daily Mail*, 26–27 July 1909.

60 Alfred Gollin, *The Impact of Air Power on the British People and their Government, 1909–1914* (London: Macmillan, 1989), pp. 76–88.

61 Fontaine, *Comment Blériot a traversé la Manche*, p. 58.

62 De Jouvenel was so determined to underline the patriotic nature of Blériot's flight that, acting through Fontaine, he persuaded Blériot to disavow a story in which he had acknowledged the presence of a British coastguardsman on the meadow where he landed. (According to Lhospice, *Match pour la Manche*, pp. 228–9.)

63 *Le Matin*, 31 July 1909. De Jouvenel went on to say that the French are sometimes considered *plus légers* than other peoples. Blériot had now clarified the real meaning of this widespread idea. "It signifies no doubt that of all peoples the French people is the one that progress bears fastest and most easily, and farthest."

64 For the preoccupation with decline and decadence in late nineteenth and early twentieth-century France, see Eugen Weber, *France Fin de Siècle*, pp. 9–26.

65 *L'Aérophile*, quoted in Fontaine, *Comment Blériot a traversé la Manche*, p. 132.

66 G. de Lafrète in *L'Echo de Paris*, quoted in Fontaine, *Comment Blériot a traversé la Manche*, p. 138.

67 *Le Temps*, quoted in Fontaine, *Comment Blériot a traversé la Manche*, p. 135.

68 Maxime Vuillaume in *L'Aurore*, quoted in Fontaine, *Comment Blériot a traversé la Manche*, p. 140.

69 Fontaine, *Comment Blériot a traversé la Manche*, p. 54.

70 Quoted in Fontaine, *Comment Blériot a traversé la Manche*, p. 67.

71 It is ironic that the term *raid*, which originally referred to an expedition by horse or a forced march across long distances and which by extension was used to apply to long-distance automobile races or flights, eventually came to mean a bombing attack in enemy territory. For the evolution of the term's meaning, see Edouard Bonnaffé, *Dictionnaire étymologique et historique des anglicismes* (Paris: Delagrave, 1920), p. 114, and the *Grand Larousse de la langue française* (Paris: 1977), p. 4849.

72 Lhospice, *Match pour la Manche*, p. 249.

3. War in the Air

1 H. G. Wells, *The War in the Air* (London: George Bell and Sons, 1908), p. 240.

2 According to Etienne Taris in *La Revue aérienne* (1908–9), p. 454.

3 Marieluise Christadler, *Kriegserziehung im Jugendbuch* (Frankfurt/Main: Haag Herchen, 1978), p. 193.

4 Quoted by Fred Culick in the introduction to his unpublished translation of Ferber's *L'Aviation*, pp. 73–4, n. 7.

5 As late as March 1913, Ferdinand Foch, future Allied commander-in-chief, is reported to have said that "aviation is fine as sport. I even wish officers would practice the sport, as it accustoms them to risk. But, as an instrument of war, it is worthless." (Quoted by Morrow, *The Great War in the Air*, p. 35. (cited in ch. 2)). For a judicious account of pre-1914 European military attitudes and policies with regard to the airplane, see Morrow, pp. 1–29. He concludes that "the military response [to aviation] was certainly less conservative than that of other European institutions" (p. 10). One wonders what other European institutions Morrow has in mind.

6 Wells quoted by David C. Smith in *H. G. Wells. Desperately Mortal* (New Haven and London: Yale University Press, 1986), pp. 85–6.

7 Quoted by David C. Smith from an 1893 essay titled "The Literature of the Future" in *ibid.*, p. 85.

8 In a recent survey of the period, Eric Hobsbawm includes Wells, along with Arnold Bennett, Romain Rolland, Roger Martin du Gard, Theodore Dreiser, and Selma Lagerlöf, in a list of highly regarded prose writers of the years between 1870 and 1914 whose literary reputations have not held up as well as those of Thomas Hardy, Marcel Proust, and Thomas Mann. (*The Age of Empire* (New York: Pantheon Books, 1987), p. 221).

9 Ferber, *L'Aviation*, p. 146, n. 1.

10 H. G. Wells, "The Advent of the Flying Man – an Inevitable Occurrence," *Pall Mall Gazette*, 8 December 1893.

11 Wells, "The Argonauts of the Air," in *The Complete Stories of H. G. Wells* (London: Ernest Benn, 1927), pp. 354, 358.

12 Wells himself acknowledged the deficiencies of fiction as a means for anticipating the technologies of the future. "Of [such] fiction, of course, there is abundance . . . But from its very nature, and I am writing with the intimacy of one who has tried, fiction can never be satisfactory in this application. Fiction is necessarily concrete and definite; it permits of no open alternatives; its aim of illusion prevents a proper amplitude of demonstration, and modern prophecy should be, one submits, a branch of speculation, and should follow with all decorum the scientific method. The very form of fiction carries with it something of disapproval; indeed, very much of the fiction of the future pretty frankly abandons the prophetic altogether, and becomes polemical, cautionary, or idealistic, and a mere footnote and commentary to our present discussion." (*Anticipations* (London: Chapman & Hall, 1902, 8th edn, original edn 1901), p. 2. n. 2).

13 *Ibid.*, p. 191.

14 *Ibid.*, p. 191.

15 Douglas Botting, *The Giant Airships* (Alexandria, Virginia: Time-Life Books, 1981), pp. 34–8.

16 For Edwardian novels that expressed fears of a German invasion of the British Isles, see Samuel Hynes, *The Edwardian Turn of Mind* (Princeton: Princeton University Press, 1968), pp. 15–53. Hynes points out that *The War in the Air* differs from most other invasion literature in that it was not written from a Tory perspective; but it

is also noteworthy that in Wells's novel German aggressiveness is directed not against Great Britain but rather against the United States. As Hynes observes, Wells had understood that the coming war would be global in nature (p. 43).

17 Wells, *The War in the Air*, p. 67.
18 *Ibid.*, pp. 162–3.
19 *Ibid.*, pp. 165–6.
20 *Ibid.*, p. 168.
21 *Ibid.*, p. 207.
22 *Ibid.*, p. 208.
23 *Ibid.*, pp. 205–6.
24 *Ibid.*, pp. 245–6.
25 *Ibid.*, p. 249.
26 *Daily Mail*, 27 July 1909.
27 Wells, *The War in the Air*, p. 107.
28 In 1906 Martin predicted the collapse of the Russian Empire and advised all those owning Russian securities to unload them as soon as possible. The Russian Revolution, he said, would open a "great epoch" for the German people. Berlin would become the capital of continental Europe. And the stronger Germany was on the continent of Europe, the more its friendship would be prized by Great Britain and Japan (*Die Zukunft Russlands* (Leipzig: Theodor Weicher, 1906), pp. 175–6). Martin was dismissed from his post in the Imperial Statistical Bureau in 1908 by a disciplinary commission. Subsequently, he devoted himself to writing, producing, in addition to his many books on aviation, several exposés of *Machthaber* (the powerful) and millionaires in Wilhelmine Germany.
29 Rudolf Martin, *Der Zeitalter der Motorluftschiffahrt* (Leipzig: Theodor Thomas, 1907), p. 1.
30 Martin, *Berlin-Bagdad* (Stuttgart & Leipzig: Deutsche Verlags-Anstalt, 1907), pp. 6–7.
31 *Ibid.*, p. 19.
32 *Ibid.*, pp. 120–31.
33 Albert Robida, *Le Vingtième Siècle*, (Paris: Georges Decaux, 1883).
34 Martin, *Das Zeitalter der Motorluftschiffahrt*, pp. 44, 49, 70, 72.
35 *Ibid.*, p. 77.
36 *Ibid.*, pp. 80–5.
37 *Daily Mail*, 11 July 1908. Yet a little less than three months later, Wile reported on a meeting in Berlin at which Martin had "fired the imagination of his hearers . . . with a plan for the conquest of England by airships. He asserted that the principal duty of aerial navigators was to induce the combined Continental Powers to construct a fleet of 10,000 Zeppelins, each to carry twenty soldiers, which should land and capture the sleeping Britons before they could realize what was taking place." (*Daily Mail*, 9 October 1908; quoted by Gollin, *No Longer an Island* (cited ch. 1), p. 395).
38 Martin, *Der Zeitalter der Motorluftschiffahrt*, p. 82.
39 *Daily Mail*, 25 September 1908.
40 *L'Illustration*, 26 December 1908.
41 *Souvenir de la fête du centenaire de la naissance du colonel Driant* (Neufchâtel-sur-Aisne, 1955), no pagination.
42 Gaston Jollivet, *Le Colonel Driant* (Paris: Delagrave, 1918), p. 112.
43 Emile Driant, *L'Aviateur du Pacifique* (Paris: Flammarion, 1909), p. 61.
44 *Ibid.*, p. 1.
45 *Ibid.*, p. 54.
46 *Ibid.*, p. 221.
47 *Ibid.*, p. 222.
48 *Ibid.*, p. 231.
49 *Ibid.*, p. 240.
50 *Ibid.*, p. 509.
51 Emile Driant, *Alerte!* (Paris: Flammarion, 1912; original edn 1910), p. 245.
52 Emile Driant, *Au-dessus du continent noir* (Paris: Flammarion, 1911), p. 106.
53 *Ibid.*, p. 448.
54 *Ibid.*, p. 65.
55 *Ibid.*, p. 62.
56 *Ibid.*, p. 63.
57 *Daily Mail*, 27 July 1909.
58 Wells, *The War in the Air*, p. 102–3.
59 See, for example, R. P. Hearne, who argued that, if developed by all the major European powers, the airship could be an important factor in temporarily preserving peace: "war will be deemed more uncertain, more costly, more terrible; and the enterprise will be too rash to commend itself to any business nation until something more definite is known about aerial navigation. Therefore the general adoption of airships will defer war, until the new arm can be given its correct value." (*Aerial Warfare* (London: John Lane, The Bodley Head, 1909), pp. xxvii, xxxii).
60 Paul d'Estournelles de Constant, *Pour l'aviation* (Paris: Librairie Aéronautique, 1909) and his introduction to Jacques Mortane, ed., *L'Aéronautique* (Paris: Pierre Lafitte, 1914), p. xi.
61 In his introduction to *Aerial Warfare*, Hearne concluded that "When England takes her right place among the rulers of the air, when her army and navy have been equipped with the best airships extant, and when her inventors, designers, and aeronauts have full scope for their talents we may expect that the peace of the world will be more secure than ever; and then we may look forward with some hope to that glorious day when the great nations will strive to end those internal disorders and inhuman practices which predispose to war; whilst aerial locomotion, by leaping over many old barriers, will open the way to international amity, and perhaps to universal and uninterrupted peace" (p. xxxii). For a detailed exploration of the paradoxes of deterrence with special emphasis on the American case, see H. Bruce Franklin, *War Stars: The Superweapon and the American Imagination* (New York: Oxford University Press, 1988).
62 Driant, *Alerte!*, p. 243.
63 Driant, *L'Aviateur du Pacifique*, p. 256.
64 Edmond Petit, *La Vie quotidienne dans l'aviation en France au début du xxe siècle 1900–1935* (Paris: Hachette, 1977), p. 95.
65 Martin, *Das Zeitalter der Motorluftschiffahrt*, p. 88.
66 Martin, *Berlin-Bagdad*, p. 6.
67 Rudolf Martin & Gustav Schalt, *Von Ikarus bis Zeppelin: Ein Luftschifferbuch für die Jugend* (Leipzig, 1908), pp. 110–20.
68 See, for example, the note the Kaiser made on a telegram he received from his ambassador in St. Petersburg on 30 July 1914, notifying him that the Tsar had made the decision to mobilize his army against Germany. "For I have no doubt about it: England, Russia and France have *agreed* among themselves – after laying the foundation of the *causus foederis* for us through Austria – to take the Austro-Serbian conflict for an *excuse* for waging a *war of extermination* against us . . . So the famous 'encirclement' of Germany has finally become a complete fact, despite every effort of our politicians and diplomats to prevent it. The net has been suddenly thrown over our head, and England sneeringly reaps the most brilliant success of her persistently prosecuted purely *anti-German-world-policy*, against which we have proved ourselves helpless, while she twists the noose of our political and economic destruction out of our fidelity to Austria, as we squirm *isolated* in the net." (Quoted by Stephen Kern in *The Culture of Time and Space* (Cambridge, Mass.: Harvard University Press, 1983), p. 251). The underlinings are the Kaiser's.
69 Wells, *The War in the Air*, pp. 242–3.
70 *Ibid.*, p. 272.
71 Wells, *Tono-Bungay* (London: Heron Books edn, 1968, original edn 1909), p. 520. Nonetheless, the protagonist of *Tono-Bungay* devotes himself to aeronautical experiments and ends the novel testing a new destroyer he has designed.
72 Wells, *The War in the Air*, p. 349.
73 Fritzsche, *A Nation of Fliers* (cited in ch. 2), p. 190.
74 For the circumstances of Driant's heroic death, see Alistair Horne, *The Price of Glory*, pp. 83–90. According to Horne, "Driant's gallant stand had held up the [German] Crown Prince's offensive for one vital day; XVIII Corps could no longer attain its objectives set for the 22nd [of February 1916]. On his death, Driant deservedly became one of France's legendary heroes of the First World War, and his defence of the Bois des Caures was acclaimed even on the other side of the Rhine" (p. 90).
75 Horne writes that had the Germans not misused their numerical superiority in the air and had the French flyers not responded with such elan and skill, the outcome of the Battle of Verdun might well have been different. *The Price of Glory*, p. 207.

4. Poets of Space

1 In an interview with *Le Matin*, quoted by Ricciotto Canudo, "Gabriele D'Annunzio et la vie moderne," *Mercure de France*, 1 July 1910, p. 53.

2 For European military aviation on the eve of the First World War, see Morrow, *The Great War in the Air* (cited ch. 2), pp. 29–57.

3 Ferber, *L'Aviation* (cited ch. 2), pp. 143–4.

4 Reported by Martin in *Der Zeitalter der Motorluftschiffahrt* (cited ch. 3), p. 32.

5 Ferber, *L'Aviation*, p. 145.

6 *Ibid.*, 144–5.

7 According to the prices listed in the Salon International de la Locomotion Aéronautique, an exhibition of flying machines held annually in Paris, it cost at least 50,000 francs a year to acquire, maintain, and use an airplane and its motors. This made airplanes an extraordinary extravagance, twice as expensive as a luxury car. At the beginning of 1913 the Aéro-Club de France could list only six members who owned airplanes, all of them wealthy. See Emmanuel Chadeau, *L'Industrie aéronautique en France 1900–1995* (Paris: Fayard, 1987), p. 36. Graham Wallace reaches the same conclusion in *Claude Grahame-White* (cited ch. 2), p. 77, but he also points out that the monetary rewards for well-known aviators were far greater than the investment in equipment and maintenance they were required to make. In 1910 the secretary of the Harvard Aeronautical Society offered the British aviator Grahame-White a $50,000 guarantee and all expenses, if he would agree to participate in the forthcoming Boston-Harvard Aviation Meeting. During a period of three months in the United States, Grahame-White grossed $250,000 in prize money and exhibition fees, a very large sum of money in that period when a Blériot XI with a Gnôme engine could be bought for under $5,000.

8 *L'Auto*, 3 July 1909.

9 For a discussion of Ader and the controversies stemming from his aeronautical experiments in the 1890s, see Carlier, *L'Affaire Clément Ader* (cited ch. 1); for Langley, his achievements, and his ultimate failure just nine days before the Wrights' first powered flight, see John D. Anderson, Jr., "The Wright Brothers: The First True Aeronautical Engineers," in *The Wright Flyer*, ed. Wolko (cited ch. 1) pp. 7–15. Ader received 250,000 francs in subsidies from the French Ministry of War; Langley was awarded a contract for $50,000 from the United States War Department and spent another $23,000 from the funds of the Smithsonian Institution, which he headed.

10 Ferber, *L'Aviation*, p. 144.

11 This point is convincingly argued by Chadeau in *L'Industrie aéronautique en France,* pp. 67–72.

12 According to François Peyrey, "L'Aéro-Club de France literally galvanized aviation; it illuminated its night," (*L'Oeuvre de l'Aéro-Club de France* (Paris: Dunod and Pinot, 1909), p. 12. As of 20 May 1909, the Aéro-Club alone was offering 476,800 francs in prize money to aviators (p. 87).

13 De la Vaulx, *Le Triomphe de la navigation aérienne* (cited ch. 2), p. 331.

14 According to *Le Matin* (16 February 1909), some potential competitors may have been put off by the conditions set by the organizing committee, which required a flight of nine and a half kilometers over water.

15 Chadeau, *L'Industrie aéronautique en France,* p. 34.

16 In addition to representatives from the Aéro-Club de France, the organizing committee invited members of the Automobile-Club and the Ligue Aérienne to participate in the planning and overseeing of the meet. Together they formed a group known as the Commission Aérienne Mixte or C.A.M. Nonetheless, responsibility for the organizing and judging of the various competitions was eventually given to three *commissaires* from the Aéro-Club: the Count de Castillon de Saint-Victor, Paul Rousseau, and Edouard Surcouf. Eventually, the C.A.M. created a small Executive Committee or General Secretariat of five persons, presided over by the Marquis de Polignac. For the details of the meet's organization, see the account by Henri-Georges Laignier in his history, *Livre d'or de la grande semaine d'aviation de la Champagne* (Paris: Dunod & Pinot:

n.d. (1909?)), pp. 4, 8. A member of the organizing committee's General Secretariat, Laignier was understandably often vague about questions that historians would like answered, such as: who was responsible for what, how the necessary money was raised, and who benefited from the event's success? His tendency is to present the Rheims meet as a result of the generosity of the people of Rheims and Epernay, especially of course the generosity of the champagne manufacturers.

17 Pommery, Ruinart, Moët et Chandon, Mercier, Mumm, Veuve Cliquot, and Heidsieck-Monopole were all represented on the organizing committee. Laignier claims that his original intention had been to publish the names of all the donors and their contributions at the end of his book, but he goes on to explain that the committee decided not to include details about individual donors because they believed that "often a modest gift demonstrated as much sacrifice and generosity as the thousands of francs contributed by a few people favored by good fortune." (Laignier, *Livre d'or de la grande semaine d'aviation de la Champagne*, p. 13).

18 Etienne Taris in *La Revue aérienne*, 23 August 1909, p. 488. Taris emphasized that the organizers of the Rheims meeting had done everything possible to give it "a national character." There was no industry more French than wine, and no wine more French than champagne: "its qualities are precisely the same as those of our race."

19 The weather on the day of Fallières's visit was so bad, with heavy and chilly winds, that it appeared he might leave Bétheny without seeing a single flying machine in the air. Finally, just before he was scheduled to depart, Etienne Bunau-Varilla, followed by Louis Paulhan, took to the air. (Laignier, *Livre d'or de la grande semaine d'aviation de la Champagne*, pp. 54–5.)

20 Penrose, *British Aviation* (cited ch. 2), p. 184.

21 Quoted by Wallace, *Flying Witness* (cited ch. 1), p. 135. Of the many good accounts of Rheims, Wallace's is the best and the most reliable.

22 Crouch, *The Bishop's Boys*, pp. 402–6; Howard, *Wilbur and Orville*, pp. 319–21 (both cited ch. 1). Wilbur Wright himself put the point somewhat differently in an essay he wrote for a French book on aviation. "To invent is one thing; to establish records is another." (*Livre d'or de la conquête de l'air* (Paris: Pierre Lafitte, 1909), p. 278.)

23 Max Avery in *Le Petit Parisien*, 22–3 August 1909.

24 *L'Intransigeant*, 22 August 1909.

25 The 10,000-franc prize offered by the Parisian daily, *Le Petit Journal*, was awarded to Latham "for his style and the beauty of his flights" (Laignier, *Livre d'or de la grande semaine d'aviation de la Champagne*, p. 86).

26 Quoted by Penrose in *British Aviation* (cited ch. 2) p. 185.

27 Quoted by Felix Philipp Ingold, *Literatur und Aviatik* (Basel & Stuttgart: Birkhäuser Verlag, 1978), p. 107.

28 Chadeau, *L'Industrie aéronautique en France*, pp. 34–5. By contrast, in his official history Laignier claimed that, taking into account the 225,000 francs raised through donations in early 1909, the organizing committee had actually lost 160,000 francs (Laignier, *Livre d'or de la grande semaine d'aviation de la Champagne*, p. 129).

29 Reported by Howard in *Wilbur and Orville* (cited ch. 1), p. 318. Laignier scoffed at this rumor, which was evidently widespread at the time, pointing out that only 3,500 bottles of champagne had been consumed in the grandstands, whereas Rheims and Epernay shipped an average of 100,000 bottles of champagne every day (Laignier, *Livre d'or de la grande semaine d'aviation de la Champagne*, p. 130). Nonetheless, the correspondent of the *Echo de Paris* noted that the road that led to Bétheny was lined with cafés and stands erected by the champagne manufacturers. "Let's hope that the public does not engage in an exaggerated consumption. This could pose a danger in the case that unpleasant incidents occurred." (21 August 1909).

30 *Le Livre d'or de la conquête de l'air*, p. 325.

31 Crouch, *The Bishop's Boys* (cited ch. 1), p. 404.

32 *Le Petit Parisien*, 24 August 1909.

33 H. Desgrange in *L'Auto*, 30 August 1909.

34 *Le Petit Parisien*, 8 September 1909.

35 Quoted in *Le Petit Parisien*, 23 September 1909.

36 Max Brod, *Franz Kafka* (New York: Schocken Books, 1960 edn),

p. 102.

37 In a letter of 19 July 1909 quoted by Frederick R. Karl, *Franz Kafka: Representative Man* (New York: Ticknor & Fields, 1991), p. 236.

38 Ronald Hayman, *Kafka* (New York: Oxford University Press, 1982), p. 77. Brod's account of the same events, "Flugwoche in Brescia," was published in *März* 3 (October–December 1909), pp. 219–26.

39 Franz Kafka, "Die Aeroplane in Brescia," first published in a shorter version in the Prague review *Bohemia* at the end of 1909. I quote from the full text published by Max Brod in *Über Kafka* (Frankfurt am Main: Fischer Taschenbuch Verlag, 1983), p. 359. An English translation by Willa and Edwin Muir is available in Kafka, *The Penal Colony: Stories & Short Pieces* (New York: Schocken Books, 1948). To judge by the story filed by the correspondent of *L'Echo de Paris*, Kafka and his friends had reason to fear the methods of the organizers of the Brescia meeting. The return from the airdrome after the first day of the competition, wrote Georges de Lafrète on 9 September 1909, had been "terrible." Because of insufficient tramway service, twenty thousand people had been forced to make the fifteen-kilometer trip by foot amidst thick dust caused by automobiles. "I met elegant women walking while clinging on to their husband's arm, on the verge of exhaustion. Peasant carts, requisitioned at sky high prices, transported as many as fifty people. Clearly, the masses had been carried away by aviation."

40 Brod, *Kafka*, p. 103.

41 Brod, *Über Kafka*, p. 361.

42 *Ibid.*, p. 362.

43 *Ibid.*, p. 363.

44 *Ibid.*, p. 363.

45 *Ibid.*, p. 365.

46 *Ibid.*, p. 365.

47 Blériot, whose fastest machines had been destroyed at Rheims, was satisfied to make a few flights of "short duration," presumably to satisfy those spectators who had come to see the famous Frenchman fly.

48 Brod, *Über Kafka*, p. 366. Calderara had not yet flown because his Wright Flyer was damaged.

49 *Ibid.*, p. 366–7. Rougier set a new altitude record by reaching 189.50 meters; but two months later Latham left him far behind when he flew to 410 meters.

50 When Kafka went to Brescia, he had published eight prose-poems, some no longer than a paragraph; see Karl, *Franz Kafka*, p. 214.

51 Brod, *Über Kafka*, p. 364.

52 *Ibid.*, p. 364. Brod's impression of D'Annunzio was quite different. He noted that the organizing committee treated him like "a second king of Italy"; he praised the "very beautiful verses" about Icarus that the poet recited before the assembled journalists and photographers; and he was by no means indifferent to his "feminine" charm. Indeed, concluded Brod, there were moments when D'Annunzio appeared "marvelous through and through." "Flugwoche in Brescia," *März* 3 (October–December 1909), p. 222.

53 Gabriele D'Annunzio, *Le Livre secret de Gabriele D'Annunzio et de Donatella Cross*, ed. Pierre Pascal (Padua: Edizioni Letterarie "Il Pelicano', 1947), vol. I, p. 54.

54 Quoted by Angelo Lodi, *Il volo a Roma* (Rome: Editrice Press Italia, 1981), p. 205.

55 Quoted by Antonio Foschini in *Baracca* (Rome: Editoriale Aeronautica, 1939 edn), p. 105.

56 Gabriele D'Annunzio, *Forse che sì forse che no* (Milan: Treves, 1910), pp. 71–2.

57 A French ornithologist not unlike Louis-Pierre Mouillard, whose book *L'Empire de l'air* had inspired Wilbur Wright to attempt to resolve the problem of flight. See Howard, *Wilbur and Orville*, pp. 28–9. Wilbur had read excerpts of Mouillard's book in the *Annual Report* of the Smithsonian Institution.

58 D'Annunzio, *Forse che sì*, p. 81.

59 *Ibid.*, p. 85.

60 *Ibid.*, p. 89.

61 *Ibid.*, p. 88.

62 *Ibid.*, p. 83.

63 D'Annunzio, *Le Livre secret*, I, pp. 113-15. Commenting on the weather the day D'Annunzio arrived in Brescia, the correspondent of the *Corriere della Sera* wrote: "No flying today. Looking at the sky, we have an exact idea of the spectacle that will be offered to us on that future day when the first general strike by aviators breaks out, and we will vainly wait for the aerial tramway that takes us home." (Luigi Barzini, "D'Annunzio fra gli aeroplani," *Corriere della Sera*, 11 September 1909).

64 D'Annunzio, *Forse che sì*, pp. 68–9.

65 *Ibid.*, pp. 99–100.

66 *Ibid.*, p. 99.

67 *Ibid.*, pp. 109–10.

68 *Ibid.*, p. 110.

69 *Ibid.*, p. 113.

70 *Ibid.*, p. 115.

71 *Ibid.*, p. 117.

72 *Ibid.*, p. 159.

73 *Ibid.*, p. 125.

74 *Ibid.*, p. 506.

75 *Ibid.*, p. 517.

76 *Ibid.*, p. 520.

77 *Ibid.*, p. 523.

78 Paolo Alatri, *D'Annunzio* (Turin: UTET, 1983), p. 298. Already in 1910, the Futurist Paolo Buzzi had complained that Paolo Tarsis was a failure as a fictional characterization. He conveyed "not a glimmer of a real contemporary living man." (Quoted by Ingold in *Literatur und Aviatik*, p. 47, n. 53). Buzzi's article appeared in the Russian journal *Apollon*, V, p. 1.

79 D'Annunzio, *Forse che sì*, p. 67.

80 Henry Bordeaux, *Histoire d'une vie: La Douceur de vivre menacée 1909–1914* (Paris: Plon, 1956), pp. 37–8.

81 D'Annunzio, *Le Livre secret*, I, 294.

82 *Mercure de France*, 1 July 1910, p. 60, 56–7.

83 D'Annunzio, *Forse che sì*, p. 97.

84 Alatri, *D'Annunzio*, p. 297. For a spirited defense of the political radicalism and literary innovations of D'Annunzio's novels that mentions but does not emphasize *Forse che sì forse che no*, see Paolo Valesio, "The Lion and the Ass: The Case for D'Annunzio's Novels," *Yale Italian Studies*, I, no. I (Winter 1977), pp. 67–82.

85 D'Annunzio, *Forse che sì*, p. 108–9.

86 *Ibid.*, p. 101.

87 *Ibid.*, p. 106.

88 *Ibid.*, p. 68.

89 *Ibid.*, p. 230.

90 *Ibid.*, p. 78–9.

5. A Rendezvous with Death

1 Romain Rolland, *Jean-Christophe* (Paris: Albin Michel, 1931), III, p. 433.

2 When the Russian Tsar and his wife came to France in 1901, the French government chose Rostand to commemorate the occasion. See Emile Ripert, *La Vie et l'oeuvre d'Edmond Rostand* (Paris: Hachette, 1968), p. 135.

3 In September 1910 after seeing a flying machine over his house in the French Pyrenees, Rostand wrote a poem that ended:

> Mais j'ai crié d'orgueil et j'ai pleuré de joie
> Lorsque j'ai vu mon ciel devenir un chemin!

> But I shouted with pride and I cried with joy
> When I saw my sky become a road!

Rostand, *Le Cantique de l'aile* (Paris: Eugène Faquelle, 1922), p. 18.

4 In Paris *Le Figaro* commented: "[It is] prodigious and at the same time very sweet for our French *amour-propre* for us to be able to confirm once again that it is always our compatriots who arrive first every time that daring, energy, and courage are required." (Quoted by Wallace in *Claude Grahame-White* (cited ch. 2), p. 75).

5 Petit, *La Vie quotidienne dans l'aviation en France* (cited ch. 3), pp. 80–1.

6 After the completion of his flight, Védrines gave the following

interview to *Excelsior*: "I was over the basin of Pancorbo when suddenly I caught sight of an immense bird with outstretched wings. Who was this competitor in the Paris-Madrid [race] who came to challenge me? It was an eagle, and I assure you that if I could have convinced him to come with me, I would have been happy to donate him to the zoo. Offended to see me cross his domain so calmly, he began to show me that he could fly faster than I could. Then, having done this, he seemed to be a bit annoyed to see me at his side. He threw himself furiously at my propeller. I played the role of an aerial toreador: I dived and avoided him. I went underneath him. He came at me three times; three times I repeated my first maneuver. And humiliated by his defeat, the splendid creature who measured between two and three meters in breadth, fled confessing his defeat." (Quoted in Jean-Pierre Lefèvre-Garros, *Roland Garros* (Paris: Carrière, 1988), pp. 253–4).

7 *L'Illustration*, 23 March 1912.

8 Rostand, *Le Cantique de l'aile*, p. 19.

9 André Beaumont [pseudonym of Jean Conneau], *Mes Trois Grandes Courses* (Paris: Hachette, 1912), p. 129.

10 *Ibid.*, pp. 143–4. Conneau's book was quickly translated into English and published under the title *My Three Big Flights* (London: Everleigh Nash, 1912).

11 Alphonse Berget, *La Route de l'air* (Paris: Hachette, 1909), p. xii.

12 Charles Rolls was co-founder of the firm Rolls-Royce. When he died, he was on the verge of registering a Rolls-Royce aircraft company. Today, of course, Rolls-Royce is one of the principal manufacturers of airplane engines as well as the maker of the expensive automobiles that bear Rolls's name.

13 Harper, *My Fifty Years in Flying* (cited ch. 1), p. 153. See also Penrose, *British Aviation* (cited ch. 2), pp. 299–30. According to Penrose, "A test flight [shortly before the accident] proved the previously unrealised consequence that the increased longitudinal stability [provided by the new rear elevator] seriously diminished the nose-elevator response. Under the spur of competition, Rolls's habitual caution was overcome, and he decided to increase control power by pivoting the new tail to work in conjunction with the forward elevators" (p. 229).

14 On hearing of Rolls's exploit, Blériot is reported to have remarked, perhaps with unintended condescension: "What is after all interesting in Mr. Rolls's fine performance is the fact that he is an Englishman. It means that we shall have to reckon with that great friendly nation in the domain of the air." (Quoted by Terry Gwynn-Jones in *Farther and Faster: Aviation's Adventuring Years, 1909–1939* (Washington, D.C.: Smithsonian Institution Press, 1991), p. 20.)

15 Luigi Barzini, "L'Ala che valicò le alpi" in Saverio Laredo de Mendoza & Alfredo Russo, *Ali e Squadriglie* (Milan: Impresa Editoriale Italiana, 1933), p. 198.

16 Grahame-White, *The Story of the Aeroplane* (cited ch. 2), p. 176.

17 Terry Gwynn-Jones, *The Air Racers* (London: Pelham Books, 1984), p. 75. By July 1911, 24 Frenchmen had died in flying accidents; another 84 would die during the next two years. Roland Garros et al., *L'Aéronautique* (Paris: Pierre Lafitte, 1914), pp. 216, 338.

18 Cited by Pierre Moutin, *L'Aviation civile et commerciale à Marseille, 1900–1935* (doctorat de 3e cycle, University of Provence, 1980), I, p. 60.

19 Rostand, *Le Cantique de l'aile*, p. 5.

20 *Ibid.*, pp. 4–5.

21 *Ibid.*, p. 5.

22 *Ibid.*, p. 7.

23 *Ibid.*, pp. 14–15.

24 Beaumont, *Mes Trois Grandes Courses*, p. 13.

25 Rostand, *Le Cantique de l'aile*, p. 9.

26 *Ibid.*, p. 10.

27 *Ibid.*, pp. 1–2.

28 *Ibid.*, p. 2.

29 *Ibid.*, p. 12.

30 *Ibid.*, pp. 10–11.

31 *Ibid.*, p. 16.

32 *Ibid.*, p. 10.

33 *Ibid.*, p. 5.

34 *Ibid.*, p. 9.

35 Alfred Leblanc in his preface to Garros, *Guide de l'aviateur* (cited ch. 3), p. 11.

36 René Bazin quoted by Petit, *La Vie quotidienne dans l'aviation*, p. 95.

37 F. T. Marinetti, *La Conquête des étoiles* (Paris: E. Sansot, 1909 edn), p. 4. Marinetti's 1905 celebration of the automobile "A Mon Pégase" ended similarly:

Hurrah! Plus de contact avec la terre immonde!
Enfin, je me détache et je vole en souplesse sur la grisante plénitude des Astres ruisselants dans le grand lit du ciel!

Hurrah! No more contact with this filthy earth!
Finally, I break away and fly smoothly on the intoxicating plenitude of streaming Stars in the great bed that is the sky!

F. T. Marinetti, *La Ville charnelle* (Paris: E. Sansot, 1908), p. 172. In my reading of Marinetti texts, I am especially indebted to Ingold, *Literatur und Aviatik* (cited ch. 4); Fanette Roche-Pézard, *L'Aventure futuriste 1909–1916* (Rome: Ecole Française de Rome, 1983); and Luciano De Maria, "Marinetti poeta e ideologo," in F. T. Marinetti, *Teoria e invenzione futurista* ed. L. De Maria (Milan: Mondadori, 1968). pp. xxix–c.

38 See, for example, the prose poem "La Mort tient le volant" (Death Holds the Steering Wheel), composed in September 1907 and inspired by the automobile races at Brescia. Originally called "Le Circuit de la Jungle," this poem served as an epilogue to the collection *La Ville charnelle*, pp. 221–9. Celebrating the death-defying speed of the race drivers, Marinetti cried: "Il s'agit de vouloir! Se détache qui veut! Monte au ciel qui désire! Triomphe qui croit! Il faut croire et vouloir! O désir, ô désir, éternelle magnéto! Et toi, ma volonté torride, grand carburateur de rêves! Transmission de mes nerfs, embrayant les orbites planétaires! Instinct divinateur, ô boîte des vitesses! O mon coeur explosif et détonnant, qui t'empêche de terrasser la Mort? Qui te défend de commander à l'Impossible? Et rends-toi immortel, d'un coup de volonté!" (It's all a matter of willing! Let him who wishes break away! Let him who desires it ascend into the sky! We must believe and will! Oh desire, oh desire, eternal magneto! And you, my torrid will, great carburetor of dreams! Transmission of my nerves, throwing into gear the planetary orbits! Divining instinct, oh gear box! O my explosive and detonating heart, what prevents you from flooring Death? Who prohibits you from ordering the Impossible? And making yourself immortal with an act of will!) (p. 229).

39 Giovanni Lista, *Futurisme* (Lausanne: L'Age d'Homme, 1973), p. 87.

40 *Ibid.*, p. 85.

41 *Ibid.*, p. 87.

42 *Ibid.*, p. 87.

43 Indeed, Marinetti was a close observer of D'Annunzio, to whom he had dedicated two cleverly ironic books before 1909. The second of these, *Les Dieux s'en vont, D'Annunzio reste* (The Gods Depart, D'Annunzio Remains) (Paris: E. Sansot, 1908) situated the famous man of letters as a figure of the past, not yet dead but as buried in cultural terms as the recently deceased giants, the composer Giuseppe Verdi and the poet Giosè Carducci whose disciple D'Annunzio had been. For D'Annunzio's relationship to Carducci, see Alatri, *D'Annunzio* (cited ch. 4), pp. 10–14.

44 Lista, *Futurisme*, pp. 105–12. This manifesto was published in an Italian version as the introduction to Paolo Buzzi's collection of poems, *Aeroplani* (Milan: Edizioni di "Poesia", 1909).

45 F. T. Marinetti, *Mafarka le futuriste* (Paris: E. Sansot, 1910), p. ix.

46 *Ibid.*, p. 217. For an analysis of *Mafarka* that emphasizes its highly self-conscious primitivism, see John J. White, *Literary Futurism: Aspects of the First Avant-Garde* (Oxford: Clarendon Press, 1990), pp. 316–21.

47 Marinetti, *Teoria e invenzione futurista*, p. 136.

48 *Ibid.*, p. 46.

49 F. T. Marinetti, *Le Monoplan du pape* (Paris: E. Sansot, 1912).

50 For the political and literary context of *Le Monoplan du pape*, see the informative article by Giovanni Lista, "Sur un vol de Beaumont ou 'Le Monoplan du pape,'" *Europe*, January–March 1975, pp. 53–64.

51 F. T. Marinetti, *La Bataille de Tripoli* (Milan: Edizioni Futuriste di "Poesia", 1912), pp. 43–4.

52 *Ibid.*, p. 53.

53 *Ibid.*, p. 55.

54 *Ibid.*, p. 45.

55 Marinetti, *Le Monoplan du pape*, pp. 7–8.

56 *Ibid.*, p. 57.

57 *Ibid.*, p. 85.

58 *Ibid.*, p. 102.

59 *Ibid.*, p. 346.

60 Quoted by Jeffrey Schnapp in his essay "Propeller Talk," forthcoming in *Modernism/Modernity*.

61 Marinetti, *Le Monoplan du pape*, p. 319.

62 *Ibid.*, p. 267.

63 Marinetti, *Teoria e invenzione futurista*, p. 309.

64 Quoted by Renzo De Felice in his essay "L'avanguardia futurista" in Marinetti, *Taccuini 1915–1922* (Bologna: Il Mulino, 1987), ed. Alberto Bertoni, p. xiii. For the replacement of literature by technology, see Lista, "Sur un vol de Beaumont ou 'Le Monoplan du pape'," p. 60. Jeffrey Schnapp offers some fascinating speculations about the meaning motors and propellers held for Marinetti in his "Propeller Talk." (cited n. 60).

65 Marinetti, *Le Monoplan du pape*, 251. For a penetrating analysis of the complexities and contradictions in Marinetti's view of technology, see Roberto Tessari, *Il mito della macchina* (Milan: Mursia, 1973), pp. 209–28. Marinetti, he argues, is not a fanatical worshipper of technology, but a man of letters who believes that he can exploit a mythical celebration of the machine in order to transform bourgeois consciousness (p. 222). One should not, however, underestimate the depth of Marinetti's conviction that the new twentieth-century technologies offered possibilities for radical transformations in culture and styles of life. For him, the machine was more than a myth and a metaphor. See, for example, his manifesto "Geometrical and Mechanical Splendor and the Numerical Sensibility" of March 1914, where he defined his program as "the instinct of man multiplied by the motor" and "the enthusiastic imitation of electricity and the machine." A dreadnought, he said, had a hundred thousand times more interest for Futurists than "the psychology of man with its limited combinations" (reproduced in Lista, *Futurisme*, p. 148).

66 *Ibid.*, p. 254.

67 Lista, *Futurisme*, p. 88.

68 Marinetti, *Poupées électriques* (cited Intro.), p. 33. The Swedish aeronaut Salomon August Andrée had disappeared in 1897 while trying to reach the North Pole in a balloon. The remains of Andrée and his two companions were not discovered until 1930.

69 Kamensky, *Put' entusiasta* (cited Intro.), pp. 106–7. Another factor in Kamensky's choice may have been his disappointment with the reception of his novel and problems with his first wife that led to their divorce. See Vladimir Markov, *Russian Futurism: A History* (Berkeley and Los Angeles: University of California Press, 1968), p. 31. In addition to Kamensky's 1931 memoir *Put' entusiasta* and Markov's study of Russian Futurism, I have based my account of Kamensky's life and flying career on his 1918 autobiography *Ego-Moya: Biografia velikogo futurista* (Moscow: Knigoizd-vokitovras, 1918) and Vladimir Burlin's 1982 doctoral dissertation at the University of Toronto, "Mud Huts and Airplanes: The Futurism of Vasily Kamensky."

70 According to Von Hardesty in "Aeronautics Comes to Russia: The Early Years, 1908–1918," in *National Air and Space Museum: Research Report* 1985 (Washington, D.C.: Smithsonian Institution Press, 1985), pp. 23–44. But even earlier Russian interest in aviation is suggested by the fact that two Russian officers on official mission from the imperial government were present during Wilbur Wright's first flights at Hanaudières. One of them, when asked by a French journalist for his reaction, replied that "we think that such a machine could be used in the army. To be sure, there are certain details that need to be modified, but such as it is, this airplane is capable of making a contribution to reconnaissance." (*Le Matin*, 9 August 1908).

71 I am grateful to Louise McReynolds for pointing out to me the prominence that aviators had achieved in Russian newspapers by 1911. For the role of the Russian press in this period, see her informative book *The News under Russia's Old Regime: The Development of a Mass-Circulation Press* (Princeton: Princeton University Press, 1991), ch. 10.

72 Kamensky, *Put' entusiasta*, p. 107.

73 B. Roustam-Vek, *Aerial Russia* (London: John Lane the Bodley Head, 1916), pp. 34–5.

74 Kamensky, *Put' entusiasta*, p. 112.

75 It seems strange that Blériot did not send Kamensky to his flight school in Pau where purchasers of Blériot machines were given free instruction. Perhaps he doubted Kamensky's aeronautical abilities or the solidity of his financial means.

76 Kamensky, *Put' entusiasta*, p. 122.

77 *Ibid.*, p. 124.

78 *Ibid.*, p. 127.

79 *Ibid.*, pp. 126–7.

80 *Ibid.*, p. 128.

81 *Ibid.*, pp. 131–2.

82 *Ibid.*, pp. 132.

83 Savvaty Gints, *Vasily Kamensky* (Perm: Permskoe Knizhnoe Isdatel'stvo, 1974), p. 90.

84 Markov, *Russian Futurism*, pp. 117–18. By the use of this term, Burlyuk and Mayakovsky did not mean to identify themselves with Marinetti's movement; instead, their intention appears to have been to indicate that they represented the most advanced wing of the Russian avant-garde. Since the term "Futurist" was now being used indiscriminately to refer to any avant-garde art and literature, Burlyuk and Mayakovsky appear to have believed that the adoption of the Futurist label would help them to achieve hegemony over their avant-garde rivals. In his letter summoning Kamensky to Moscow, Burlyuk was careful to emphasize the connection between Futurism and aviation. "My dear friend and bold aviator Vasya! Come quickly to Moscow to proclaim with new force [the Stenka Razin cry] 'Riffraff to the bows!' It's time. New warriors have signed up — Volodya Mayakovsky and A. Kruchenykh . . . Mayakovsky is longing to meet you and to talk to you about aviation, poetry and other such Futurism . . . Bring your 'Razin' [the novel Kamensky was working on at the time]. Hurry! We eagerly await you. Fly express!" (Quoted by Burlin, "Mud Huts and Airplanes," pp. 15–16).

85 Kamensky, *Put' entusiasta*, p. 139.

86 Kamensky, *Zhizn s Maykovskym* (Moscow: "Khudozhestvennaya Literatura," 1940), p. 36. This poem, *Vyzov* (The Summons), was later published in a slightly different form in Kamensky's collection of "ferro-concrete" poems, *Tango s korovami* (A Tango with Cows) (Moscow: Isdatelya Igo Zhurnala Russkikh Futuristov, 1914), no pagination.

87 Kamensky, *Put' entusiasta*, p. 143.

88 From a contemporary newspaper account of the recital, quoted by Kamensky, *Ibid.*, pp. 150–1. See also the summary by N. Khardzhiev, "Turne Kubo-Futuristov 1913–1914 gg." in *Mayakovsky: materialy i issledovaniya*, ed. V. O. Pertsova & M. I. Serebryanskogo (Moscow: Gosudarstvennoe Isdatel'stvo "Khudozhestvennaya Literatura," 1940), especially p. 405.

89 Kamensky, *Put' entusiasta*, p. 153. Nonetheless, Kamensky was booed in Odessa for suggesting that Leonid Andreyev, the city's most famous writer, should be thrown off "the steamer of modernity" (Reported by Burlin in "Mud Huts and Airplanes," p. 18).

90 For an appreciation of the qualities of this poem, see Gerald Janecek, *The Look of Russian Literature: Avant-Garde Visual Experiments, 1900–1930* (Princeton: Princeton University Press, 1984), pp. 158–9. It was published in Kamensky's collection *Tango s korovami* (Moscow: 1914).

91 See Markov, *Russian Futurism*, pp. 326–34.

92 Quoted by Ingold, *Literatur und Aviatik*, p. 130, from Karl Kraus, *Beim Wort genommen* (Munich: Koesel, 1955), p. 402 (vol. III of *Werke*).

93 In a letter to the *Times* of London, 7 April 1911.

94 Romain Rolland, *Jean-Christophe* (Paris: Albin Michel, 1931), III, p. 429.

95 *Ibid.*, p. 426.

96 *Ibid.*, p. 433.

97 *Ibid.*, p. 427.

98 *Ibid.*, p. 439.

99 In my thinking about the relationship between Marinetti and aviation, I have learned much from Laurence Goldstein, *The Flying Machine & Modern Literature* (Bloomington: Indiana University Press, 1986), especially, pp. 14–33; and Jeffrey Schnapp's essay "Propeller Talk," which he kindly made available to me before its publication in *Modernism/Modernity*.

6. Painters Take Flight

1 K. S. Malevich, *Essays on Art 1915–1928*, I, ed. Troels Andersen (Copenhagen: Borgen, 1968), p. 122. I have slightly modified the translation by Xenia Glowacki-Prus and Arnold McMillin.

2 "A Slap in the Face of Public Taste" was the title of a manifesto published by Alexei Kruchenykh, David Burlyuk, Vladimir Maya-kovsky, and Viktor Khlebnikov in 1912. It is available in English translation in *Russian Futurism through its Manifestoes 1912–1928* (Ithaca & London: Cornell University Press, 1988), ed. and trans. Anna Lawton & Herbert Eagle, pp. 51–2. In this manifesto, the authors demanded the right as poets:

　1. To enlarge the *scope* of the poetry's vocabulary with arbitrary and derivative words (Word-novelty).

　2. To feel an insurmountable hatred for the language existing before their time.

　3. To push with horror off their proud brow the Wreath of cheap fame that You have made from bathhouse switches.

　4. To stand on the rock of the word "we" amidst the sea of boos and outrage.

Victory over the Sun was conceived and written with the purpose of carrying out this program.

3 *La Victoire sur le soleil* (Lausanne: L'Age d'Homme, 1976), p. 30. This French translation of *Pobeda nad solntsem* by J.-C. and V. Marcadé contains the original Russian text on facing pages.

4 *Ibid.*, p. 52.

5 Reviewing three recent publications devoted to Malevich, Igor Golomstock writes: "Today, few doubt that Kazimir Malevich is one of the greatest innovative artists of the twentieth century and one of the founders of abstract art" (*Times Literary Supplement*, 3 April 1992, p. 25).

6 According to Camilla Gray, *The Russian Experiment in Art 1863–1922* (London: Thames & Hudson, 1982 edn), p. 145. Remarkably little is known about Malevich's early years. Biographical notes made by the artist in the 1920s emphasize his love of nature and determination to escape from his job as a draftsman for the imperial railroad and move to Moscow to study art. In the 1930s Malevich wrote an autobiographical sketch in which he evoked his early years in the Ukraine and his first experiences in Moscow, now available in Russian in *K istorii ruskogo avangardia/The Russian Avant-Garde* (Stockholm: Hylaea Prints, 1976), pp. 103–27, and in French translation in *Malevitch 1878–1978* (Lausanne: L'Age d'Homme, 1979), ed. Jean-Claude Marcadé, pp. 153–68. Fragments of these "Chapters from an Artist's Autobiography" have been translated into English and reproduced in *Kazimir Malevich* (Los Angeles: Armand Hammer Museum, 1990), pp. 173–5. For a recent reassessment of Malevich's artistic training, see Irina Vakar, "Malevich's Student Years in Moscow: Facts and Fiction," in *Malevich: Artist and Theoretician*, trans. Sharon McKee (Moscow: Krasnyi Proletarii, 1991), pp. 28–30.

7 *K istorii russkogo avangardia/The Russian Avant-Garde*, p. 122.

8 It may be, as several scholars have suggested, that in mechanizing his art, Malevich was influenced by Fernand Léger, whose work he knew and prized highly. But it is interesting that in 1919 Malevich singled out Cézanne as the artist who had "recognized the reason for geometricisation and, with full awareness of what he was doing, showed us the cone, cube and sphere as characteristic shapes on the basis of which one should build nature, i.e. reduce the object to simple geometrical expressions." (Malevich, *Essays on Art 1915–1928* I, p. 94). It was not until 1929 that Malevich addressed Léger's work directly and then he emphasized the distinctive quality of Léger's painting and the differences between him and the other Cubists and Futurists, especially Picasso and Braque (*Essays on Art*

1928–1933, ed. Troels Andersen (Copenhagen: Borgen, 1968), pp. 62–7).

9 Khlebnikov wrote a poem between 1908 and 1910 about the devastating impact of a giant crane on the inhabitants of St. Petersburg, who worshipped the creature – part bird, part flying machine – as a god. For an English translation of *Zhuravl'* (The Crane), see Velimir Khlebnikov, *Snake Train: Poetry and Prose* (Ann Arbor: Ardis, 1976), pp. 83–8.

10 I first became aware of this aspect of Malevich's art when I read John Golding's article "Supreme Suprematist," *New York Review*, 17 January 1991, p. 18. John E. Bowlt has shown in his fascinating and suggestive essay, "Beyond the Horizon," how frequently metaphors of flight were used in Russia in the early twentieth century by avant-garde poets and painters (in *Kasimir Malewitsch zum 100. Geburtstag* (Cologne: Galerie Gmurzynska, 1978), pp. 232–52). One of the best-known examples was Aleksandr Blok's conclusion to a 1908 lecture in which he used an aviation meta-phor to describe the situation of the Russian intelligentsia vis-à-vis the peasantry. "Already we see ourselves, as if against the back-ground of a glow, flying in a light, rickety aeroplane, high above the earth; but beneath us is a rumbling and fire-spitting mountain and down its sides, behind clouds of ashes, roll streams of red-hot lava." (Quoted by W. Sherwin Simmons, *Kasimir Malevich's Black Square and the Genesis of Suprematism 1907–1915* (New York & London: Garland, 1981), p. 39).

11 In his unpublished memoirs, Matyushin wrote: "At the beginning of our century great interest was shown in the fourth dimension. It was talked about, written about and a whole literature arose. What interested us painters in terms of measurement was the question of space. The former method of visual representation did not satisfy us. We grasped how little our spatial imagination had developed as yet, how narrowly our eye perceived." (Quoted by Larissa A. Zhadova, *Malevich: Suprematism and Revolution in Russia 1910–1930*, p. 32). For the impact of Ouspensky on Matuyshin and Malevich, see Linda D. Henderson, *The Fourth Dimension and Non-Euclidean Geometry in Modern Art* (Princeton: Princeton University Press, 1983), pp. 265–94.

12 P. D. Ouspensky, *Tertium Organum: The Third Canon of Thought: A Key to the Enigmas of the World* (London: Routledge & Kegan Paul, 1957, first published in Russian in 1911), p. 231.

13 Ouspensky, *Tertium Organum*, p. 301. For a detailed discussion of Ouspensky's interpretation of the fourth dimension and its impli-cations for culture, see Henderson, *The Fourth Dimension and Non-Euclidean Geometry in Modern Art*, pp. 245–55.

14 Henderson, *The Fourth Dimension and Non-Euclidean Geometry in Modern Art*, p. 375. Matyushin's interpretation of Cubism and its objectives reflected the theoretical formulations of artists like Jean Metzinger and Albert Gleize and critics like Guillaume Apollinaire and Maurice Raynal rather than the practice of Pablo Picasso and Georges Braque, the two most original and influential Cubist painters. See Matyushin's article "O knige Gleza i Metsanzhe *Du Cubisme*" ("About Gleize and Metzinger's book *Du Cubisme*") first published in *Soyuz moldezhdi*, 3 (March 1913), reproduced and translated by Henderson in *The Fourth Dimension and Non-Euclidean Geometry in Modern Art*, p. 368. Matyushin's emphasis in this essay on the need for artists to break with accepted canons and common forms is reminiscent of Vasily Kandinsky's definition of the artist as a "seer" on whom had been bestowed "the secret gift of 'seeing.'" In seeing in new ways, Kandinsky argued, the artist also "re-vealed." Artists might try to refuse "this noble gift," but they did not have the power to do so. "Surrounded by malice and derision, he [the artist] drags behind him the heavy burden of mankind, ever forwards, ever upwards." (From Vasily Kandinsky, *On the Spiri-tual in Art*, a paper read by N. I. Kulbin at the Second All-Russian Congress of Artists in St. Petersburg in December 1911 and trans-lated by John E. Bowlt in *The Life of Vasilii Kandinsky in Russian Art: A Study of On the Spiritual in Art* (Newtonville: Oriental Research Partners, 1980) ed. John E. Bowlt & Rose-Carol Washton Long, p. 65). For the relationship between Kandinsky and the Russian avant-garde, see John E. Bowlt's informative essay "Vasilii Kandinsky: The Russian Connection," *ibid.*, pp. 1–41.

15 *Russian Futurism through its Manifestoes*, p. 72. I have slightly altered

16 *Ibid.*, pp. 72–73.

17 *Ibid.*, p. 77.

18 Quoted by Charlotte Douglas in *Swans of Other Worlds: Kazimir Malevich and the Origins of Abstraction in Russia* (Ann Arbor: UMI Research Press, 1980), p. 34.

19 *Ibid.*, pp. 35–6. I have modified the translation slightly.

20 *Russian Futurism through its Manifestoes*, p. 70. Kruchenykh identified Ouspensky explicitly as the source for his conception of the coming revolution in perception. In his unsigned introduction, Matyushin drove home the point: "And perhaps the day is not far off when the vanquished phantoms of three-dimensional space, of seemingly drop-like time, of melancholy causality and many other things will prove to be for all of us exactly what they are: the annoying bars of a cage in which the human spirit is imprisoned – and that's all." (Quoted by Susan P. Compton in *The World Backwards: Russian Futurist Books 1912–1916* (London: The British Library, 1978), p. 102).

21 Quoted by Douglas in *Swans of Other Worlds* from a letter written by Malevich to Matyushin in June 1913, p. 51. Xenia Hoffmann translates this letter quite differently in Malevich, *The Artist, Infinity, Suprematism: Unpublished Writings 1913–1933*, ed. Troels Andersen (Copenhagen: Borgen, 1978): "I think that first of all art is that not everyone can understand a thing in depths, this is left only to the black sheep of time" (p. 203).

22 From "Glavi iz avtobiografii khudozhnika," in *K istorii russkogo avangardia/The Russian Avant-Garde*, p. 123.

23 For a thought-provoking, if not altogether convincing, attempt to interpret this lithograph in terms of Einstein's Special Theory of Relativity, see Rainer Crone & David Moss, *Kazimir Malevich: The Climax of Disclosure* (Chicago: University of Chicago, 1991), pp. 145–53. "In this unassuming lithograph, Malevich articulated a concept of universal importance: the recognition of subjectivity in an object-oriented world" (p. 152).

24 This was also true of another drawing done in 1913, *Universal Space*, in which Malevich sought to portray the sensation of flight. For an analysis of this drawing and speculation about the possible influence of Fernand Léger on Malevich at this time, see Simmons, *Kasimir Malevich's Black Square*, pp. 83–4.

25 Quoted by Compton, *The World Backwards*, p. 109.

26 *Russian Futurism through its Manifestoes*, p. 77. The italics are Kruchenykh's.

27 "Hand-controlled spotlights had been used for some time in the theatre, but it was not until 1913 that the modern system of console-controlled lighting became available. Instead of each spot having to be controlled by a different technician, making the effects unreliable – they could be changed from a single central source; the long-desired effect of lighting orchestration could be properly realised for the first time." (Compton, *The World Backwards*, p. 55).

28 Benedikt Livshits, *The One and a Half-Eyed Archer*, transl. John E. Bowlt (Newtonville: Oriental Research Partners, 1977), p. 164.

29 Translated by John E. Bowlt in *Russian Art of the Avant Garde* (New York: Thames & Hudson, 1988), p. 131. Under a lithograph of 1913, in which the image of a cow is superimposed on that of a violin, Malevich wrote: "Logic has already constituted an obstacle to new subconscious movements; the movement of alogicism has been created to liberate us from conventional assumptions." (Quoted by Marc Le Bot, *Peinture et machinisme* (Paris: Klincksieck, 1973), p. 224).

30 For a detailed interpretation of *Aviator*, see W. Sherwin Simmons, "Kasimir Malevich's 'Black Square': The Transformed Self: Part Two: the New Laws of Transrationalism," in *Arts Magazine*, vol. 53, no. 3 (1978), pp. 130–6. I am indebted to Simmons's pioneering research for my understanding of the role played by the objects that appear in Malevich's painting.

31 Douglas, *Swans of Other Worlds*, p. 33.

32 Malevich, *Essays on Art 1915–1928*, I, p. 41.

33 Livshits, *The One and a Half-Eyed Archer*, p. 214.

34 Quoted by Simmons in "Kasimir Malevich's 'Black Square'," p. 132, from Viktor Skhlovsky, *Mayakovsky and his Circle* (New York: Dodd, Mead, 1972), p. 94. The poem is in Mayakovsky,

Sobranie sochineniy, 6 vols. (Moscow: Pravda, 1973), I, p. 180.

35 Simmons, "Kasimir Malevich's 'Black Square'," p. 132.

36 *Ibid.*, p. 133.

37 Quoted by Simmons, *ibid.*, p. 133.

38 *Ibid.*, pp. 133–4. Malevich and his friends were fascinated by cards and their occult meanings. They often used the metaphor of the card game to suggest a process by which people can escape from fate and create a new reality. In *Ka*, whose composition Khlebnikov dated to those days "when people first flew regularly over the capital of the north," the poet wrote: "Needless to say, many of you are on good terms with a deck of cards . . . But did you ever happen to play not with a concrete personage . . . but with a collective personage – say, the Universal Will? . . . Ka was a confidant in this pastime." (Khlebnikov, *Snake Train*, pp. 164–5).

39 In "From Cubism to Suprematism in Art, To the New Realism in Painting, To Absolute Creation," trans. Douglas in *Swans of Other Worlds*, p. 110.

40 Quoted by Robert C. Williams, *Artists in Revolution: Portraits of the Russian Avant-Garde, 1905–1925* (Bloomington and London: Indiana University Press, 1977), p. 121.

41 Quoted by Douglas in *Swans of Other Worlds*, p. 53.

42 Quoted by Douglas, *ibid.*, p. 54.

43 Commenting on this painting, Dmitri Sarabianov observes that while its peasant topic is fully in keeping with the official Soviet iconography of the period, Malevich creates the tragic impression of a rural world that is beginning to fall apart because of the intrusion of mechanical civilization symbolized by the airplane. See his essay "Malevich at the Time of the 'Great Break'" in *Malevich: Artist and Theoretician*, p. 144.

44 Bowlt, *Russian Art of the Avant Garde*, p. 126. I have slightly modified the translation.

45 Malevich, *The Non-Objective World* (Chicago: Paul Theobald, 1959), p. 68.

46 Malevich, *Essays on Art 1915–1928*, I, p. 124.

47 Note, for example, this passage from an unpublished essay written in 1916–17. "We must prepare ourselves by prayer to embrace the sky. And those who will prepare themselves will be led out from the ashes of earthly sin towards the sky and will be resurrected. All those who will not have prepared themselves will die on earth in the kingdom of ashes . . ." (Malevich, *The Artist, Infinity, Suprematism: Unpublished Writings 1913–1933*, ed. Troels Andersen p. 151). I agree with Margaret Betz (in "From Cézanne to Picasso to Suprematism: The Russian Criticism," *Artforum*, April 1978, p. 34) that Malevich's interpretation of contemporary art and culture was deeply influenced by an atmosphere permeated with eschatological, even apocalyptic, portents of impending change.

48 Malevich, *The Non-Objective World*, pp. 74–5. Malevich believed that people created machines to express sensations that they had felt but had not been capable of formulating. "The aeroplane has appeared, not on account of the socio-economic conditions being an expedient cause, but only because the sensation of speed and movement looked for an outlet and in the end took the form of an aeroplane." The same, he thought, was true of works of art. "Works are sensations, not linen in which one can wrap a picture." (From an unpublished manuscript entitled "Suprematism" that Troels Andersen dates to April–May 1927; Malevich, *The Artist, Infinity, Suprematism*, p. 145).

49 Malevich, *The World as Non-Objectivity: Unpublished Writings 1922–1925*, ed. Troels Andersen (Copenhagen: Borgen, 1976), p. 112.

50 Malevich, *Essays on Art 1915–1928*, I, p. 107.

51 *Ibid.*, I, p. 116.

52 Malevich, *The World as Non-Objectivity*, p. 287. In *Kazimir Malevich: The Climax of Disclosure*, Crone and Moos argue that Malevich broke with one of the most important conventions of Western art by hanging his Suprematist paintings in different spatial orientations, thus undermining the notion of a fixed horizon placed within a picture-frame against which objects can be read. "In Malevich's work, for the first time in the history of Western art, the elements that constitute a picture are dealt with autonomously and individually within the same painting" (p. 157). The effect of this method, Crone and Moos conclude, is to enable us "as observers to become participants in realizing the subtleties of

signification in the everyday world. With the breakdown and substitution of representational thought and narrative, we are free" (p. 160).

53 Sonia Delaunay carried on an active correspondence with many Russian intellectuals and artists, including Georgy Yakulov, Vasily Kandinsky, Vladimir Mayakovsky, and Alesandr Smirnov. According to Jean-Claude Marcadé, Smirnov became "the intelligent propagator of the Delaunays' 'simultaneity'" in December 1913 when he gave a lecture on their art in St. Petersburg at the well-known artists' cabaret Brodyachaya Sobaka (The Stray Dog) ("La Correspondance d'A. A. Smirnov avec S. I. Terk (Delaunay) 16 septembre-8 avril 1905," *Cahiers du Monde Russe et Soviétique*, XXIV, no. 3 (July–September 1983), p. 291). About the same time, Georgy Yakulov tried to arrange a trip for the Delaunays to Moscow to show their work, but in a letter of 27 November 1913 he confessed to Sonia Delaunay that her husband's name would mean nothing to the group of art collectors he represented. Yakulov thought that Sonia Delaunay would have a better chance of selling in Russia than Robert because her (more decorative?) work might appeal to the imperial family and their court. (Bibliothèque Nationale, Fonds Robert et Sonia Delaunay, Dossier Artistes Russes). John Milner, in *Vladimir Tatlin and the Russian Avant-Garde* (New Haven & London: Yale University Press, 1983), p. 176, suggests that Tatlin's famous monument to the Third International may have been influenced by Delaunay's paintings of the Eiffel Tower, especially *L'Equipe de Cardiff. Troisième Représentation*.

54 Malevich would also have discovered that he and Delaunay shared an interest in light and color. One of Delaunay's first essays, translated into German by Paul Klee and published in *Der Sturm* in January 1913, was entitled "La Lumière" (Light). Malevich wrote at length on the same theme during the early 1920s in an unpublished manuscript, available in English in *The World as Non-Objectivity*, pp. 34–146.

55 Sherry A. Buckberrough, *Robert Delaunay: The Discovery of Simultaneity* (Ann Arbor: UMI Research Press, 1982), pp. 2–3.

56 Robert Delaunay, *Du Cubisme à l'art abstrait,* ed. Pierre Francastel (Paris: S.E.V.P.E.N., 1957), p. 194.

57 Buckberrough, *Robert Delaunay*, p. 31.

58 Sonia Delaunay, *Nous irons jusqu'au soleil* (Paris: Laffont, 1978), p. 37.

59 *Ibid.*, pp. 38–9. "He [Robert] painted on the canvas a dedication that sealed our intimate pact of alliance: 'Movement depth France-Russia 1909.' A code between us. Let he who can, understand its meaning. Two unknown young lovers can to do more to bring together the souls of peoples than the great strategists of politics."

60 For an analysis of this painting, which emphasizes Delaunay's attempt to integrate technology and nature by means of elliptical forms, see Buckberrough, *Delaunay*, pp. 32–6.

61 Gustav Vriesen & Max Imdahl, *Robert Delaunay: Light and Color* (New York: Henry N. Abrams, 1967), pp. 29–30.

62 Roger Allard in *La Revue de France*, March 1912, p. 70, quoted by Michel Hoog in *Robert Delaunay* (Paris: Editions des Musées Nationaux, 1976), p. 61.

63 Guillaume Apollinaire, *Chroniques d'art (1902–1918)*, ed. L.-C. Breunig (Paris: Gallimard, 1960), pp. 224–5.

64 Delaunay, *Du Cubisme à l'art abstrait*, p. 98.

65 Delaunay's italics. (From notes made by him in October 1913 in *Du Cubisme à l'art abstrait*, p. 110).

66 See Pierre Francastel in his introduction to Delaunay, *Du Cubisme à l'art abstrait*, p. 32.

67 *Ibid.*, p. 146. Delaunay's italics.

68 *Ibid.*, p. 186. From a letter to August Macke, dated 1912.

69 *Ibid.*, p. 147. Delaunay's italics.

70 *Ibid.*, p. 160. From "Note sur la construction de la réalité de la peinture pure," published in *Der Sturm* in February 1913.

71 In 1927 in an article on Apollinaire written for the *Mercure de France*, Sylvain Bonmariage wrote: "*Le Matin* had announced a competition for poets. It involved composing a poem about aviation. Apollinaire had sent two hundred verses in good alexandrines and alternating rhymes that he read to us one evening at his house on the rue Gros in Auteil. It was a masterpiece. But it was René

Fauchois who won the prize. Three years later, when his volume *Alcools* appeared, I rediscovered our friend's poem in a quite altered state. I commented on it to him. "What do you expect," Apollinaire replied. "For the sake of principle, I ruined my poem!" (Quoted by Giovanni Lista in "Apollinaire et la conquête de l'air," *Guillaume Apollinaire* 12, ed. Michel Décaudin (Paris: *Lettres Modernes Minard*, 1974), pp. 116–17).

72 Guillaume Apollinaire, *Oeuvres poétiques*, ed. Marcel Adema & Michel Décaudin (Paris: Gallimard, 1965), p. 39.

73 *Ibid.*, p. 40.

74 *Ibid.*, pp. 40–1.

75 For an enlightening discussion by Kirk Varnedoe of the relationship between this painting and contemporary French advertising, see Kirk Varnedoe & Adam Gopnik, *High and Low: Modern Art Popular Culture* (New York: Museum of Modern Art, 1990), pp. 246–9.

76 Apollinaire in *Montjoie!*, 18 March 1913, p. 4.

77 Franz Marc to Delaunay, 14 April 1913, quoted by Vriesen in *Robert Delaunay*, p. 57.

78 Delaunay to Marc, April 1913, quoted by Vriesen, *ibid.*, p. 57.

79 Notes made by Delaunay on his own paintings around 1924 in Delaunay, *Du Cubisme à l'art abstrait*, p. 63.

80 Dorival, *Robert Delaunay*, p. 56; Peter-Klaus Schuster, ed., *Delaunay und Deutschland* (Cologne: DuMont Buchverlag, 1985), p. 283.

81 Delaunay, *Du Cubisme à l'art abstrait*, p. 75.

82 For Delaunay's "intellectual weakness," see Virginia Spate, *Orphism* (Oxford: Clarendon Press, 1979), p. 163; for the influence his literary friends exerted over him see *ibid.*, p. 225; and Buckberrough, *Robert Delaunay*, pp. 205–6. It is just as possible to argue that Delaunay and his paintings influenced the writers who moved in his circle of friends. Sonia Delaunay later wrote that "No painter has inspired so many poets. Among the great ones who sought his friendship were: Apollinaire, Cendrars, Aragon, Breton, Crevel, Tzara, Joseph Delteil, Soupault, etc." (*Nous irons jusqu'au soleil*, p. 39).

83 Delaunay, *Du Cubisme à l'art abstrait*, p. 63. Without mentioning Delaunay's name, Apollinaire also alluded to the similarity. "In Roger de La Fresnaye's *Conquête de l'air* there is a great effort toward pure color, we are almost in [the world of] simultaneous contrasts . . ." (In *L'Intransigeant*, 14 November 1913, reproduced in *Chroniques d'art*, p. 337). Germaine Seligman writes that "La Fresnaye had been fascinated by the experiments in pure color which Robert Delaunay was already making in 1912 – simultaneous colour-contrasts, Delaunay termed them – and there is no doubt that La Fresnaye's palette was influenced by the Orphist painter." (*Roger de la Fresnaye* (New York: New York Graphic Society, 1969), p. 48).

84 Though later in his life, Delaunay acknowledged the problems he had encountered in trying to combine figurative and non-objective painting: "And, nonetheless, these reminiscences of objects, these residues of objects in my pictures, appeared to me to be harmful elements. To be sure, I intended to merge these objective images with colored rhythms, but the images were of a different nature. The integrity of these concrete forms was not of the same nature, hence there was a lack of harmony (*dissociation*)." (*Du Cubisme à l'art abstrait*, p. 82). Many art historians would agree.

85 Sonia Delaunay, *Nous irons jusqu'au soleil*, pp. 37–8.

86 Quoted by Buckberrough in *Robert Delaunay*, pp. 227–8, and reproduced in the original French in note 75, pp. 367–8. I have slightly altered Buckberrough's translation.

87 Delaunay, *Du Cubisme à l'art abstrait*, p. 126.

88 I am indebted to Sherry Buckberrough for this and many other insights about this complex painting. See *Robert Delaunay*, p. 231.

89 Franz Meyer, "Robert Delaunay, Hommage à Blériot: 1914," *Jahresbericht der Öffentlichen Kunstsammlung Basel*, 1962, p. 74. Franz Meyer's masterly essay remains the most comprehensive and reliable analysis of *L'Hommage à Blériot*. Meyer concludes that it represents a high point in Delaunay's artistic production. "Never before nor afterwards was the harmony so great between the will to the presentation of non-objective (*ungegenständlichen*) light and the artist who [sought] to make it possible to experience the

impetus of the modern world through the 'representation of absolutely new spectacles.' The non-objective forms with which he represents light emerge strongly, but they are nonetheless held in tension with the objective forms, and it seems as if this relationship is the precondition for the astonishing freedom of movement, which manifests itself in the picture" (pp. 76–7).

90 Delaunay, *Du Cubisme à l'art abstrait*, pp. 63–4.

91 While working on *L'Equipe de Cardiff*, Delaunay stated his artistic credo in a letter to Franz Marc: "Yes, I think that art is dramatic, that its perfect expression is found in the Life that leads toward light!" (Delaunay to Marc, 11 January 1913, in *Du Cubisme à l'art abstrait*, p. 188). See also p. 121, where Delaunay writes: "The new Art tends toward the formal representation of a space that is continually in movement – of real volumes. And the colors, in their simultaneous contrasts, are the marvelous means of expression for constructing movement . . ."

92 Delaunay himself later used the musical analogy in describing his paintings of 1912–13. "I played with colors as one could express oneself in music by the fugue of colored phrases . . ." (*Du Cubisme à l'art abstrait*, p. 81).

93 Edouard Helsey, *Le Journal*, 2 March 1914, quoted by Bernard Dorival, *Robert Delaunay* (Brussels: Jacques Damase, 1985), p. 53.

94 Apollinaire, *Chroniques d'art*, p. 352.

95 *Ibid.*, pp. 348, 353–8.

96 *Ibid.*, p. 474.

97 *Ibid.*, p. 475.

98 If Delaunay reacted so ferociously to this letter, it was because this was not the first time he had been forced to defend himself against charges by the Italian Futurist painters that he had imitated their experiments in simultaneous art; nor was it the first time that Apollinaire had been involved in the dispute. In his review of the First German Autumn Salon of October 1913, Apollinaire had mentioned in passing that Delaunay had borrowed the term "simultaneous" from the Futurists' vocabulary. (*Les Soirées de Paris*, 15 November 1913, p. 2). Annoyed at the condescending reviews his works had received in France – especially by Apollinaire who took every opportunity to point out that Italian Futurist painting derived from French precedents – Boccioni had seized the opportunity in order to write a letter to *Der Sturm* reminding its readers that he, not Delaunay, had been the founder of simultaneous art. Quoting Apollinaire's article as substantiation of his claim, Boccioni concluded: "We watch with pleasure as our powerful DISCOVERIES are propagated everywhere, above all in France and in the work of M. Delaunay who, obsessed with simultaneity, specializes in it, as if it were his own discovery." (*Der Sturm*, 15 December 1913). Affecting the tolerant manner of a *grand seigneur* forced to deal with a feckless inferior, Delaunay was satisfied to publish a letter in *Der Sturm* in which he cited Apollinaire to the effect that the Italian Futurists had found no followers in France: "this painting of rapid movement [Apollinaire wrote and Delaunay quoted] has stood still and remains in the place where it was born." (*Der Sturm*, 15 January 1914, p. 167).

99 Apollinaire, *Chroniques d'art*, p. 476.

100 *Ibid.*, p. 475.

101 Pierre Francastel claims that Apollinaire was jealous because Delaunay had given Cendrars credit for writing the first simultaneous poem, *Les Pâques à New York* (Delaunay, *Du Cubisme à l'art abstrait*, p. 135). Delaunay, in turn, may have been displeased by Apollinaire's flirtation with Marinetti, which resulted in a pro-Futurist manifesto the French poet published in *Lacerba* in the summer of 1913. See Francis Steegmuller, *Apollinaire: Poet among the Painters* (New York: Farrar, Straus, 1963), pp. 262–6. In this manifesto, Apollinaire had associated his name closely with those of Marinetti and Boccioni and, ironically, had coupled the name of Delaunay with that of Carlo Carrà.

102 Apollinaire, *Chroniques d'art*, p. 476.

103 Note, for example, Blaise Cendrars's letter of 28 June 1914 to Robert Delaunay in which he urges the painter to write "without delay" to the *Paris-Journal*, denouncing Henri-Martin Barzun (editor of the avant-garde review *Poème & Drame*) and supporting his claim to have written "the first simultaneous book." (Bibliothèque Nationale, Fonds Robert et Sonia Delaunay, Carton Blaise

Cendrars). For the controversies in the Parisian avant-garde in 1912–14 regarding primacy in artistic and literary innovations, see Pär Bergman, *"Modernolatria" et "Simultaneità": Recherches sur deux tendances dans l'avant-garde littéraire en Italie et en France à la veille de la première guerre mondiale* (Uppsala: Svenska Bokförlaget, 1962), especially pp. 291–411.

104 For Delaunay's influence on Apollinaire's conception of Cubism and Apollinaire's intention to write a book on the Orphic painters in which Delaunay would have the leading role, see the introduction by Leroy C. Breunig & Jean-Claude Chevalier to Apollinaire, *Les Peintres cubistes* (Paris: Hermann, 1980), pp. 23–30, especially p. 25, n. 24.

105 See Delaunay, *Du Cubisme à l'art abstrait*, which consists largely of notes dedicated to this task.

106 On 11 July 1914, Carrà wrote to Severini about this collage, telling him that he had recently "done a work that I have called "patriotic festival – painterly poem" and that has many points in common with yours [Severini's drawing *Serpentine Dance* that had appeared in *Lacerba* on 1 July 1914]. I abolished any representation of the human figure because I wanted to produce an abstraction of urban tumult." (In Maria Drudi Gambillo & Teresa Fiori, eds., *Archivi del futurismo* (Rome: De Luca, 1958), I, p. 341).

107 A sequential view of the world spinning in the form of a propeller's arc would later become a widely used technique in Hollywood newsreels and films. See, for example, Dorothy Arzner's 1933 film *Christopher Strong* in which the heroine, a daring aviatrix played by Katherine Hepburn, sees her life unfold before her eyes on a spinning altimeter as she plunges deliberately to her death after learning that she is pregnant.

108 For conflicting interpretations of this collage, see White, *Literary Futurism* (cited ch. 5), pp. 87–99. I agree with White that it is quite misleading to argue, (as Willard Bohn does in "Circular Poem-Paintings by Apollinaire and Carrà," *Comparative Literature*, 31 (1979), pp. 246–71) that Carrà's work is apolitical because it predates the outbreak of the war and the interventionist campaign in Italy. Judicious and generally persuasive as White's analysis is, however, he sometimes loses from sight the crucial distinction between Carrà's *intentions* in creating this collage and the *impact* it had on viewers, both at the time it was first published and afterwards when it was given an explicitly political content under the title *Manifestazione interventista*. Christine Poggi concludes that "With *Festa Patriottica* the Futurist effort to synthesize the resources of poetry and the visual arts reached its apogee. Poets and artists continued to experiment with collage techniques and with combining verbal and visual elements, but their works rarely achieved the unity and sense of explosive power that characterizes *Festa Patriottica*." (*In Defiance of Painting: Cubism, Futurism, and the Invention of Collage* (New Haven & London: Yale University Press, 1992), p. 225).

109 Carrà later sought to explain the attitude that lay behind his interventionism and exaltation of war. "I considered therefore the love of the *patria* as a glorification of individual life, as a fundamental liberty and stimulus to any type of action at that time." (Carlo Carrà, *La mia vita* (Milan: Rizzoli, 1943), p. 217).

110 When first published, *Festa Patriottica* appeared in black-and-white, thus inevitably losing some of its aesthetic appeal but heightening, if anything, its political impact because of the prominence in black-and-white of its intensely patriotic language.

111 Gambillo & Fiori, *Archivi del futurismo*, I, pp. 341–2.

112 On Marinetti's express instructions, the title of the collage was changed from *Festa patriottica – poema pittorico* to DIPINTO PAROLIBERO (FESTA PATRIOTTICA). "We have all agreed, including Severini, henceforth to always call this fusion of Futurist painting and words in liberty in this way so as to avoid confusion and determine the direction [of avant-garde art]." (*Archivi del futurismo*, I, p. 342). By this change in title, Marinetti intended to associate Carrà's collage with the program for avant-garde poetry – "words in liberty" – that he had announced in May 1912 in his "Technical Manifesto of Futurist Literature." Marinetti's manifesto is reproduced in *Teoria e invenzione futurista* (Milan: Mondadori, 1968), ed. Luciano De Maria, pp. 40–8. Ironically, it was precisely at this time that Carrà began to express his dissatisfaction with Futurist theories

of art. See Vittorio Fagone's introduction to Carlo Carrà, *La mia vita*, p. xxxix.

7. Aces

1 H. G. Wells, *The World Set Free* (London: Macmillan, 1914), p. 116.

2 According to Daniel Porret, author of an exhaustive study of French aces, up to 1917 French pilots were awarded the title of "ace" after five victories witnessed by combatants who did not belong to the unit of the pilot in question. In 1917 the number of victories was raised to ten; and when the war ended in 1918, the number required was about to be raised once more to twenty. (*Les "As" français de la grande guerre* (Vincennes: Service Historique de l'Armée de l'Air, 1983), I, pp. xi–xii). There seems to be no consensus about the origins of the term. Gino Bastogi claims that it originated in France and came from the *s* ending of the plural *A* that was used to designate pilots (*aviateurs*). From this, he says, the transition was easy to the identification of high-scoring aviators with the dominating figure used in many card games. (Gino Bastogi, *Baracca* (Rome: no publisher, no date), p. 35). The authors of *Legend, Memory and the Great War in the Air* (Seattle and London: University of Washington Press, 1992), Dominick A. Pisano, Thomas J. Dietz, Joanne M. Gernstein, & Karl S. Schneide, maintain that "the designation 'ace' originated in 1915, when a Paris newspaper eulogized Adolphe Pégoud as *l'as de notre aviation* (the ace of our aviation), after he had achieved his fourth victory" (p. 35).

3 Marinetti, *La Bataille de Tripoli* (cited ch. 5), p. 43.

4 Marinetti, *Mafarka le futuriste* (cited ch. 5), p. 217. Marinetti's imagined aviators, of course, were anything but chivalrous. In 1913, Basil Liddell Hart, later to become a noted military historian, wrote an unpublished story in which he imagined an air war between England and Germany that was conducted like a medieval tournament. The story's protagonist, British flyer Denis Harcourt, saves a German pilot by supporting the damaged tail of his machine with his wing. Though Liddell Hart (like Edmond Rostand before him) had anticipated an important aspect of the aces myth by emphasizing the chivalrous spirit of aviators, Marinetti was closer to understanding what would become the reality of air combat: kill or be killed. Liddell Hart's story is in the Liddell Hart Papers in the Liddell Hart Centre for Military Archives, King's College, University of London, and is discussed by Michael C. C. Adams in *The Great Adventure: Male Desire and the Coming of World War I* (Bloomington: Indiana University Press, 1990), p. 69. For the cult of chivalry in Edwardian England, see Mark Girouard, *The Return to Camelot: Chivalry and the English Gentleman* (New Haven & London: Yale University Press, 1981).

5 Saladin, *Les Temps héroïques de l'aviation* (cited ch. 2), p. 175.

6 Jacques Mortane writing in *La Vie au grand air*, reproduced in Garros, *Guide de l'aviateur* (cited ch. 3), p. 14.

7 The most thorough account of Garros's career is Lefèvre-Garros, *Roland Garros* (cited ch. 5), but Jean Ajalbert's *La Passion de Roland Garros* (Paris: 1926), 2 vols., remains indispensable for its evocation of the man and his values. There is also much useful information and a magnificent photographic record of Garros's life in *Icare*, 1988, n. 4. Lefèvre-Garros claims that Garros identified with the hero of Rimsky-Korsakov's opera *Antar*, a man in whom love inspired high moral virtue and magnificent courage, a warrior-poet whose sword protected the weak and whose song consoled the unfortunate (p. 49).

8 I discuss these writings in *The Generation of 1914* (Cambridge, Mass.: Harvard University Press, 1979), pp. 5–18. There is an uncanny resemblance between Garros and Romain Rolland's fictional character Georges Jeannin, introduced in the final volume of *Jean-Christophe*. Like Jeannin, Garros was a talented but unschooled musician who was drawn toward the arts. Rolland was writing his portrait of Georges Jeannin precisely at the moment when Garros achieved European fame.

9 Garros spent part of the summer of 1904 in England and was so taken by the experience that he decided that he wanted to take up residence in that country. See Lefèvre-Garros, *Roland Garros*, p. 31.

10 Roland Garros, *Mémoires* (Paris: Hachette, 1966), p. 11.

11 *Ibid.*, p. 12.

12 *Ibid.*, p. 220.

13 *Ibid.*, p. 245.

14 On the problems of early airplane engines, see the informative discussion by Grahame-White in *The Story of the Aeroplane* (cited ch. 2), pp. 59–73.

15 Garros, *Mémoires*, p. 251.

16 *Ibid.*, pp. 253–4.

17 *Ibid.*, pp. 254–7. Jean Cocteau's version of Garros's invention is more poetic, if unsubstantiated by other witnesses. It was in his room on the rue d'Anjou, Cocteau wrote, that Garros got the intuition for his device while looking at a photograph of [the poet] Verlaine through the blades of a fan. According to Cocteau, Garros had said to him: "there are some glances that don't pass [through the blades of the fan] and some glances that do pass." (Quoted in *Icare*, 1988, no. 124, pp. 3–4). Cocteau was so taken by Garros that he wrote several poems about him, now collected in *Le Cap de Bonne-Espérance*, in *Poésie 1916–1923* (Paris: Gallimard, 1925). In the initial poem, dedicated to Garros, Cocteau identifies himself as an "aviator of ink" and presents his verses as "my loopings and my altitude records" (p. 14).

18 Garros, *Mémoires*, p. 264.

19 For an account of Garros's first victory in the context of aerial combat during the first phase of the war, see René Chambe, *Au temps des carabines* (Paris: Flammarion, 1955), pp. 159–75.

20 Garros, *Mémoires*, p. 260.

21 *Ibid.*, pp. 261–2.

22 Garros to Frédéric Quellennec, 16 April 1915, quoted by Chambe in *Au temps des carabines*, pp. 173–4. Garros had written a similar letter to Cocteau on 3 April 1915: "I went to see the debris [left by the downed German aircraft] – some bits and pieces and two naked bodies, not incinerated. But grilled and bleeding all over their stiff and twisted flesh. What an awful nightmare!" (In Pierre Chanel, *Album Cocteau* (Paris: Henri Veyrier-Tchou, 1979), p. 23).

23 Garros, *Mémoires*, p. 262.

24 *L'Illustration*, 17 August 1915.

25 Though ironically, Garros is not included in Porret's compendium, *Les "As" français de la grande guerre*, because he scored only four victories: the three in April 1915 and one more when he returned to air combat in 1918.

26 In March 1912 France had over four times as many aviators as Germany – 800 versus 175. Concerned that the Germans had fallen dangerously behind the French in heavier-than-air flight, Prince Heinrich of Prussia suggested the creation of a Reichskomitee for the promotion of aviation in Germany. Over a period of six months 7,250,000 marks were raised through a public subscription to strengthen the nation's heavier-than-air fleet. Max Immelmann was one of many young Germans who responded enthusiastically to the call for greater support of aviation during the years immediately preceding the war by participating in the Air Fleet League and attending flying meets. Authorities differ over the relative strength of French and German military aviation in 1914. For an assessment, see Morrow, *The Great War in the Air* (cited ch. 2), p. 57, who concludes that it is difficult to accept Peter Supf's statement (in *Das Buch der deutschen Fluggeschichte* (Berlin-Grunewald: Verlaganstalt Hermann Klemm, 1935), see especially pp. 323, 374, 382–3) that France was two years ahead of Germany. Such claims, as Morrow points out, had a political function in Germany during the 1930s because they enhanced retrospectively the heroism of German aviators during the war and constituted a warning to readers in the Third Reich that Germany must never again fall behind its adversaries in military airpower, as it presumably had done during the years before 1914.

27 For Immelmann's early life and flight training, see Franz Immelmann, *Immelmann* (London: John Hamilton, 1935), pp. 15–42, and the abridged version of his wartime letters, Max Immelmann, *Meine Kampfflüge* (Berlin: August Scherl Verlag, 1916).

28 In his introduction to *Hauptmann Boelckes Feldberichte* (Gotha: Verlag Friedrich Andreas Perthes, 1916), p. 11.

29 Immelmann, *Meine Kampfflüge*, p. 43.

30 Johannes Werner, *Boelcke* (Leipzig: K. F. Koehler, 1932), p. 24.

31 *Ibid.*, p. 67.

32 *Ibid.*, pp. 79, 83.

33 Werner, *Boelcke*, p. 87. For French bombing raids in 1915, see Morrow, *The Great War in the Air*, pp. 93–5. According to Morrow, "French aerial ascendancy [over Germany] lasted through the summer of 1915" (p. 102).

34 Werner, *Boelcke*, p. 101, and *Hauptmann Boelckes Feldberichte*, p. 36. Carried away by his own enthusiasm, Boelcke neglected to point out that it was the observer, not he, who was firing the machine gun. *Hauptmann Boelckes Feldberichte* omits the last sentence.

35 *Hauptmann Boelckes Feldberichte*, p. 40.

36 Werner, *Boelcke*, p. 106.

37 John H. Morrow, Jr., *German Air Power in World War I* (Lincoln & London: University of Nebraska Press, 1982), pp. 40–1. Fokker's account is in Anthony H. G. Fokker & Bruce Gould, *Flying Dutchman: The Life of Anthony Fokker* (New York: Henry Holt, 1931), pp. 122–39.

38 Werner, *Boelcke*, pp. 106–7.

39 *Ibid.*, p. 107.

40 Immelmann, *Immelmann*, p. 120.

41 Werner, *Boelcke*, pp. 109–10.

42 Immelmann, *Immelmann*, p. 130.

43 Ernst von Hoeppner, *Deutschlands Krieg in der Luft* (Leipzig: K. J. Koehler Verlag, 1921), p. 78.

44 Immelmann, *Meine Kampfflüge*, p. 89.

45 Immelmann, *Immelmann*, p. 188; Werner, *Boelcke*, p. 143.

46 Quoted by Kunigunde Freifrau von Richthofen, *Mein Kriegstagebuch* (Berlin: Ullstein, 1937), p. 75.

47 Immelmann, *Meine Kampfflüge*, pp. 118–19.

48 Immelmann, *Immelmann*, p. 156. This passage was omitted from the 1916 collection of Immelmann's letters.

49 Werner, *Boelcke*, p. 163.

50 Kunigunde Freifrau von Richthofen, *Mein Kriegstagebuch*, p. 75.

51 Fokker, who examined the wreckage of Immelmann's plane, insisted his plane had gone down because its control wires had been shot through by enemy machine-gun fire. Whatever its cause, concludes Morrow, the death of Immelmann "damaged Fokker's position and spelled the monoplane's demise." (*The Great War in the Air*, p. 150).

52 Werner, *Boelcke*, p. 167.

53 By July 1916, when the Battle of the Somme began, the French and British possessed new Sopwith and Nieuport biplanes equipped with synchronized machine-guns, both faster and more maneuverable than the sluggish Fokker E. Moreover, because of continuing German commitment to triumph at Verdun, the German High Command was slow to counter the challenge posed by the allied aerial forces at the Somme. (Charles Dollfus & Henri Bouché, *Histoire de l'aéronautique* (Paris: L'Illustration, 1932), 300–3; and Fritzsche, *A Nation of Fliers* (cited ch. 2), p. 69.)

54 For the decline in German morale and the hostility of German infantrymen toward German aviators, see Fritzsche, *A Nation of Fliers*, pp. 69–70, and Morrow, *The Great War in the Air*, p. 151. Henri Bouché writes of the "moral and profound divorce" between the German air force at the Somme and exhausted ground troops, who were struck by the absence of their aviators in the skies above the battlefields (Dollfus & Bouché, *Histoire de l'aéronautique*, pp. 300–1).

55 According to Morrow, the plywood construction of the Albatros was crucial to its success. "The British and the French used primarily fuselages of longerons trussed with wooden and wire struts and ties and covered with linen. When they used plywood, it was to cover flat or slightly curved areas. In crashes, a wrecked truss body became 'a crumpled mass of kindling wood,' while the Albatroses often held together well after crashes even when riddled with holes. On the Albatros, the plywood skin, molded and united as an integral part of the structure, added strength and stiffness to the frame and minimized wind resistance. The Mercedes [engine] thus drove the Albatros 20 per cent faster than had been practicable with earlier forms of fuselage construction." (*The Great War in the Air*, pp. 162–3).

56 Werner, *Boelcke*, pp. 196–7. During the month of September 1916, the British and French lost 123 aircraft over the battlefields of the Somme, whereas the Germans lost only 27 – despite the fact that the Allied air forces outnumbered the Germans by two to one. See Fritzsche, *A Nation of Fliers*, p. 73.

57 Werner, *Boelcke*, pp. 210–11.

58 It took a man of letters, however, to find an aesthetic form in which German youth – the source of the Boelckes of the future could respond more fully and emotionally to Lieth-Thomsen's laconic and soldierly formulation. In October 1917, on the occasion of the commemoration of the first anniversary of Boelcke's death, Rudolf Flex, father of the famous author of *The Wanderer between Two Worlds*, put Lieth-Thomsen's words and thought into lyrics that were sung by the Boys Choir of the Dessau Gymnasium:

> Ich will ein Boelcke werden,
> Ein Boelcke so wie er!
> Und stürzt' ich ab zur Erden
> Jählings von ungefähr
> Ich wollte gerne sterben!
> Was hätt' es denn für Not?
>
> I want to be a Boelcke
> A Boelcke just like him
> And should I crash to earth
> Suddenly and by chance,
> I should gladly die!
> What else could I want?
>
> (Werner, *Boelcke*, p. 218)

59 Manfred Freiherr von Richthofen, *Der rote Kampfflieger* (Berlin: Ullstein, 1917), p. 89.

60 *Ibid.*, p. 93.

61 *Ibid.*, p. 99.

62 After his seventy-fifth victory, Richthofen was awarded the Order of the Red Eagle, Third class, with Crown and Swords. According to William E. Burrows, this decoration had never before been given to someone other than a general, a high noble, or a member of the royal family (*Richthofen* (New York: Harcourt, Brace & World, 1969), p. 192).

63 The initial chapter of Richthofen's memoirs was omitted from the new edition published by Ullstein in 1933. This was the version used for the American translation by Peter Kilduff in 1969 under the title *The Red Baron* (Garden City, N.Y.: Doubleday).

64 Richthofen, *Der rote Kampfflieger*, p. 179.

65 *Ibid.*, p. 19.

66 *Ibid.*, p. 38.

67 *Ibid.*, pp. 170–1.

68 For the contrast in style between British and German aviators during the Battle of the Somme in the summer and fall of 1916, see Morrow, *The Great War in the Air*, pp. 170–5. Morrow concludes that "the strategy of unrelenting offensive patrols [espoused by the commander of the Royal Flying Corps Hugh Trenchard] thrust British pilots deep into enemy territory in inferior craft, and they flew determined to give combat regardless of the grim circumstances" (p. 172). By Morrow's calculations, the Royal Flying Corps lost more planes and pilots during the Battle of the Somme than it possessed at the beginning (p. 173).

69 Richthofen, *Der rote Kampfflieger*, p. 109.

70 Elliott White Springs, the author of the diary published under the title *War Birds* (London: John Hamilton, n.d. (1927?)), recorded on 6 June 1918: "The new flight commander for A flight arrived. His name is Randall and he is known as Randy. He was badly wounded at Gallipoli and got trench fever when he was with the infantry. Then he was transferred to the flying corps and was out on D. H. Twos. He was shot down by Richthofen. He says that Richthofen may have the reputation of being a good sport but that he showed him no mercy, – shot his engine up and then followed him down while he was trying to land and shot him three times. He got one bullet in his rear and they had to cut off a slice. He sits down and leans like the tower of Pisa" (p. 172).

71 Richthofen, *Der rote Kampfflieger*, p. 151.

72 Quoted by Morrow, *The Great War in the Air*, p. 217.

73 *Ibid.*, p. 301. For Richthofen's role in the development of German fighters, see *ibid.*, pp. 230–1, 300. Morrow concludes that

Richthofen was a worthy successor to Boelcke. "For him the responsibilities of command went beyond frontline service; they encompassed securing the best materiel possible for German fighter pilots" (p. 231).

74 Kunigunde Freifrau von Richthofen, *Mein Kriegstagebuch*, pp. 150–1.

75 René Fonck would later accumulate more victories than Guynemer, but he could never take the place that Guynemer occupied in his countrymen's hearts.

76 My account of Guynemer's early life is based on Jules Roy, *Guynemer* (Paris: Albin Michel, 1987), pp. 15–62, and Henry Bordeaux, *Vie héroïque de Guynemer: Le Chevalier de l'Air* (Paris: Plon-Nourrit, 1918), pp. 21–64. All biographies of Guynemer, including Roy's, draw heavily on Bordeaux, since he had access to the archives of the Guynemer family, which disappeared during the German Occupation.

77 Roy, *Guynemer*, pp. 65–91; Bordeaux, *Vie héroïque de Guynemer*, pp. 65–89.

78 Bordeaux, *Vie héroïque de Guynemer*, pp. 109–10.

79 Roy, *Guynemer*, pp. 145–6.

80 Cecil Lewis once flew against Guynemer in a mock combat. "I knew our machines were fairly evenly matched and judged that my own flying skill would give me the edge over the Frenchman. But soon I found it otherwise. Guynemer's little Spad was smaller and more maneuverable than an SE5a. He had the better climb and could turn in a smaller circle. The result was that as I sat in a vertical turn with the stick right back, circling as tightly as an SE5a could go, Guynemer just sat right on my tail in a slightly smaller circle so that he always kept his sights on me. Had I been an enemy I should have been dead five times in the first minute. Do what I would – spin, half roll, drive, climb – there he sat just as if I had been towing him behind me." (Quoted by Denis Winter in *The First of the Few: Fighter Pilots of the First World War* (Athens, Georgia: University of Georgia Press, 1983), p. 135.)

81 The original censorship ordinances issued by the French High Command in September 1914 prohibited stories and photographs which identified units, individuals, or locations. On 23 January 1915, however, *L'Illustration* published a photograph of two French aviators standing beside a German plane they had shot down; and subsequently exceptions to the censorship rules were increasingly made for aviators. I am indebted to Donald English for this information.

82 Roy, *Guynemer*, p. 153.

83 *Ibid.*, p. 165.

84 *La Guerre aérienne*, no. 43 (1917), p. 2.

85 Mortane was not alone to think so. Laurence Driggs, who appears to have been an attentive reader of *La Guerre aérienne*, later wrote of the Cigognes: "Always sent where trouble was thickest, always found facing the most dangerous fliers of the enemy, always a step or two in advance of the styles in war aviation, this incomparable squadron of Flying Storks will go down in history as the most celebrated band of comrades that ever died for France. Rivalling in romance and in affectionate comradeship D'Artagnan and the Three Musketeers, Guynemer and his Aces who led this band at the zenith of its fame set a new notch on the heights of human achievement for the youth of the world to attain." (*Heroes of Aviation* (Boston: Little, Brown, 1918), p. 79). These lines were written when the war was still under way. The more recent assessment of the Cigognes by Morrow in *The Great War in the Air*, pp. 201–3, emphasizes their relutance in 1917 to give up individual combat even when the Germans began to concentrate their fighters in ever larger formations.

86 Roy, *Guynemer*, p. 169.

87 *Un Héros de France: Guynemer* (Paris: Jean Cussac, n.d.), no pagination.

88 Henry Bordeaux, *Vie et mort des héros* (Paris: Plon, 1937), p. ii.

89 Bordeaux, *Vie héroïque de Guynemer*, pp. 223–4. Bordeaux's italics.

90 A best-selling novelist before the war, Bordeaux had taken up the aviation theme in the direct aftermath of the Rheims meeting of August 1909. *La Robe de laine* (Paris: Plon, 1910) echoes, if it does not borrow directly from, D'Annunzio's *Forse che sì forse che no*. "I have to climb," thinks Bordeaux's protagonist Raymond Cernay,

a millionaire sportsman. "It's an irresistible attraction, a need. Above my two wings, I possess the vastness of the horizon. The wind surrounds me, bathes me, caresses me just as water caresses a boat. I forget the noise of the motor, the buzzing of the propeller. My strength reverberates in me. My wings warp like outstretched arms to maintain my course. No rider is more united to his mount than I am to my machine. I experience a new calm, a religious peace" (p. 45). But as a traditionalist and a Catholic, Bordeaux connected the enthusiasm for aviation with other aspects of modernity that were corrupting French youth; and before dying by climbing ever higher and disappearing into a cloud, Raymond Cernay recognizes that he went astray and caused the death of his unspoiled and beautiful wife by his obsession with fast women and Parisian sophistication.

91 Bordeaux, *Vie héroïque de Guynemer*, pp. 15–16 (first published in the *Revue des deux mondes* between 15 January and 1 March 1918).

92 *Ibid.*, p. 12.

93 *Ibid.*, p. 316.

94 *Ibid.*, p. 200.

95 *Ibid.*, p. 307.

96 *Ibid.*, p. 259.

97 *Ibid.*, p. 282.

98 With the possible exception of the memoir by Garros's German friend Hellmuth Hirth, *Meine Flugerlebnisse* (Berlin: Ferd Duemmlers Verlags-buchhandlung, 1915, 2nd edn). But Hirth's flying experiences were not nearly so varied or gripping as those of Garros.

99 Ajalbert, *La Passion de Roland Garros* (Paris: Les Editions de France, 1926), II, p. 370.

100 *Ibid.*, II, p. 383. In June 1918 Garros had made a new will and sent it to his friend Audemars, who had shared with him the adventure of flying for John Moissant's International Aviators in 1910: "I don't give a damn about what they will do after my death," Garros wrote, "but as long as I live I can't bear the prospect of one of those disgusting comedies that we've seen." In the case of his death, there were to be no ceremony, no flowers, no wreaths, and above all no speeches. "Let no one make himself into a spectacle that contributes to the sadism of the crowd." (*Ibid.*, II, pp. 325–6).

101 Jacques de Sieyès, "Aces of the Air", *National Geographic*, XXXIII (January 1918), p. 5.

102 Edward V. Rickenbacker, *Fighting the Flying Circus* (New York: Frederick A. Stokes, 1919), p. 7.

103 For the connection between aerial combat and sport, see Irene Guerrini & Marco Pluviano, "Dandismo e cavalleria nelle lettere di Francesco Baracca," in *La grande guerra*, ed. Diego Leoni & Camillo Zadra (Bologna: Il Mulino, 1986), p. 153. Morrow finds the attitude toward aerial combat as a "wonderful game" and a "gloriously exhilarating sport" to have been particularly pronounced in the Royal Flying Corps (*The Great War in the Air*, p. 239).

104 See Pietro Caproilli, ed., *Baracca: memorie di guerra* (Rome: Edizioni Ardita, 1934, third edn), p. 68; and Rickenbacker, *Fighting the Flying Circus*, pp. 105–6, for examples of the reactions of Francesco Baracca and Eddie Rickenbacker to their first victories.

105 Caproilli, *Baracca*, p. 76.

106 The British ace James McCudden was quite typical in this regard. Shortly before dying in 1918, he wrote: "It seems all very strange to me, but whilst fighting Germans I have always looked upon a German aeroplane as a machine that has got to be destroyed, and at times when I have passed quite close to a Hun machine and have had a good look at the occupant, the thought has often struck me: 'By Jove! there is a man in it.' This may sound queer, but it is quite true, for at times I have fought a Hun and, on passing at close range, have seen the pilot in it, and I have been quite surprised." (*Flying Fury* (London: John Hamilton, 1930, originally published in 1918), p. 173). See also Rickenbacker, *Fighting the Flying Circus*, p. 106 and Boelcke's letter to his mother, 17 September 1916, quoted by Werner, *Boelcke*, p. 192.

107 Cecil Lewis, *Saggitarius Rising* (London: Penguin, 1977 edn, first published in 1936), p. 141.

108 *Ibid.*, pp. 56–7.

109 *Ibid.*, p. 81.

110 As for example when Guynemer allowed the German ace Ernst

Udet to escape unharmed after Udet's gun jammed. Udet went on to shoot down 52 more Allied aircraft and became Germany's second highest-scoring ace. On 10 March 1918 Eddie Rickenbacker wrote in his diary: "Resolved that thereafter I will never shoot at a Hun who is at a disadvantage, regardless of what he would do if he were in my position." (*Fighting the Flying Circus*, pp. 338–9).

111 And needless to say, non-aviators who wrote about the war also gave chivalrous incidents a prominent place in their narratives. See, for example, Edgar Wallace's *Tam o' the Scoots* (New York & Chicago: A. L. Burt, 1919), in which the novel's protagonist is chosen by the squadron-leader to drop a wreath on the airdrome of a dead adversary. "Soon he [Tam] was above the lines and was heading for Ludezeel. Archies blazed and banged at him, leaving a trail of puff balls to mark his course; an enemy scout came out of the clouds to engage him and was avoided, for the corps made it a point of honor not to fight when engaged on such a mission as was Tam's. Evidently the enemy scout realized the business of this lone British flyer and must have signaled his views to the earth, for the anti-aircraft batteries suddenly ceased fire, and when, approaching Ludezeel, Tam sighted an enemy squadron engaged in a practise flight, they opened out and made way for him, offering no molestation. Tam began to plane down. He spotted the big white-speckled cemetery and saw a little procession making its way to the grounds. He came down to a thousand feet and dropped his parachute. He saw it open and sail earthward and then someone on the ground waved a white handkerchief. 'Guid,' said Tam, and began to climb homeward" (pp. 29–30). Charles Lindbergh later remembered this novel as having inspired his decision to become an aviator. See p. 282 below.

In a later episode in Wallace's novel, the British aviators discover that the Germans are bombing British hospitals and collecting stations for the wounded. "It's positively ghastly that a decent lot of fellows like German airmen can do such diabolical things," remarks Tam's captain. To which the wing commander responds: "Fritz's material is deteriorating . . . there's not enough gentlemen to go round. Everybody who knows Germany expected this to happen. You don't suppose fellows like Boltke [sic] or Immelmann or Richthove [sic] would have done such a swinish thing?" (p. 207).

112 Rickenbacker, *Fighting the Flying Circus*, p. 30.
113 Caproilli, *Baracca*, p. 152; and Lewis, *Saggitarius Rising*, pp. 92–3.
114 Lewis, *Saggitarius Rising*, p. 82.
115 Rickenbacker, *Fighting the Flying Circus*, p. 57; Caproilli, *Baracca*, pp. 83, 106, 130, 126; Guerrini & Pluviano in *La grande guerra*, pp. 150–1. Writing to a friend on 26 March 1916, Erwin Böhme commented on the way flight transformed one's perspective on the war. "The view of the extended battleground from high up in the sky is peculiarly interesting. Since one doesn't see the effect on individuals from great heights, the sight of burning villages and firing artillery batteries almost completely loses its horror – one is all the more struck by the interconnection of individual events and the grandiose overall picture of the giant battle." (*Briefe eines deutschen Kampffliegers an ein junges Mädchen,* ed. Johannes Werner (Leipzig: K. F. Keohler, 1930), p. 19).
116 Among the Great Powers, however, there were significant differences in the way fighter-pilots were treated. The Germans had elevated Boelcke and Immelmann to the status of national heroes already by the fall of 1915. The French had followed suit with Guynemer by January 1916. To the end of the war the British High Command refused to name aviators responsible for bringing down enemy planes. The Italian government followed the British precedent until May 1917. For the opposition of the Chief of the Royal Flying Corps Hugh Trenchard to publishing the names of outstanding pilots, see Morrow, *The Great War in the Air*, p. 242. According to Winter, the R.F.C.'s highest-scoring ace, Edward Mannock, was hardly known by the British public at the end of the war. He was awarded the most prestigious British military decoration, the Victoria Cross, posthumously, largely through the efforts of Winston Churchill. (*The First of the Few*, pp. 133, 210).
117 Jacques Mortane in *La guerre aérienne illustrée* and numerous books; Laurence Driggs in *Heroes of Aviation* (Boston: Little, Brown:

1918), articles for widely read magazines, and his series of Anthony Adair novels.
118 Rickenbacker, *Fighting the Flying Circus*, pp. 321–8.
119 Ajalbert, *La Passion de Roland Garros*, II, p. 359.
120 Lowell Thomas, *European Skyways* (Boston & New York: Houghton Mifflin, 1927), p. 132.
121 In January 1918, Laurence Driggs printed a table consisting of the victories scored by aviators during the war. These figures, he commented, were "as familiar to the citizens of France as are the batting averages of the New York's famous Giants to our populace. America's participation in the war will eventually make them of even more interest to us." (Laurence Driggs, "Aces of Aviation," *Outlook*, 30 January 1918, p. 184).
122 Quoted by Guerrini & Pluviano in *La grande guerra*, p. 139, n. 7.
123 For French examples, see Marcel Jullian, "Ces 'as' qui traînaient tous les coeurs après eux," in Gilbert Guilleminault, La *France de la Madelon 1914–1918* (Paris: Denoel, 1966), p. 118; and Gaston Vedel, *Le Pilote oublié* (Paris: Gallimard, 1976), p. 8.
124 *Un Héros de France: Guynemer.* The citation naming Guynemer officer of the Legion of Honor, the youngest soldier to receive that distinction in the French army, was careful to emphasize that his exploits had helped "to exalt the courage and enthusiasm of those in the trenches who are the witnesses of his victories." (*Ibid.*, no pagination).
125 Caproilli, *Baracca*, p. 9. An early biographer of Eddie Rickenbacker presented a more American view of the bond between the ace and the men in the trenches. Writing in *Motor Age* in 1918, David Beercroft claimed that whenever Rickenbacker "got his wind up he had one remedy that always worked. After returning to the squadron headquarters he got in a motor-car and drove over to one part of our front where he had some friends in the front line trenches. Leaving his car well back he made his way into the trenches and spent the night there. That was sufficient. If those dough boys could live in those trenches, with all the hell that went with it, as well as mud and all the discomforts to which life in a fighting squadron was heaven, then the fighting scout with his Spad should never complain." Thus reinforced, Rickenbacker "returned to squadron headquarters ready to carry on." (David Beercroft, "America's Ace of Aces," *Motor Age*, 13 February 1919, p. 9). Rickenbacker himself did not mention this practice in his memoirs of the war published the same year.
126 Ground troops were usually present when aviators went to inspect the enemy airplanes they had downed. For the reaction to Guynemer's first victory, see pp. 230–231 above. Baracca reports similar incidents in Caproilli, *Baracca*, pp. 77, 95.
127 Caproilli, *Baracca*, pp. 58, 78, 93, 163.
128 Gabriel Voisin, *Mes 10,000 cerfs volants* (Paris: La Table Ronde, 1960), p. 232.
129 See Gino Bastogi, *Baracca* (Rome: no publisher, n.d.), p. 58.
130 See Lee Kennett, *The First Air War* (New York: The Free Press, 1991). According to Morrow, "The airplane established its real significance in support of the army on the battlefield. Aircraft reconnaissance made it difficult for armies to achieve surprise and forced the movement of men and materiel behind the lines at night. Then, in 1917 and 1918, in its increasingly aggressive strikes against troops and supplies on and behind the battlefield, it became even more effective. Politicians and generals such as Churchill, Ludendorff, and Pétain recognized the importance of air power. Control of the skies over the battlefield had become essential to victory in World War I, just as it would be 20 years later" (*The Great War in the Air*, p. 365).
131 For a discussion of the prudence displayed by First World War aces, see Winter, *The First of the Few*, pp. 139–43. Boelcke's famous *Dicta* for German fighter pilots emphasized the necessity of seeking the advantage before attacking and never forgetting the line of retreat while over enemy territory (see Morrow, *The Great War in the Air*, pp. 150–1). The British ace James McCudden said that his system "was always to attack the Hun at disadvantage if possible and if I were attacked at disadvantage, I usually broke off the engagement for in my opinion the Hun in the air must be beaten at his own game which is cunning. I think the correct way to wage war is to down as many as possible of the enemy at the least risk,

expense and casualties to one's own side." (Quoted by Winter in *The First of the Few*, p. 143). Rickenbacker wrote that "all pilots, German and Allied alike, strove to gain an advantage over the adversary. The advantage could have been in superior flying ability and marksmanship, in equipment, in numbers. When the sides were even and neither could gain the advantage, there was no battle" (Edward V. Rickenbacker, *Rickenbacker* (Englewood Cliffs: Prentice-Hall, 1967), p. 106). Boelcke was killed in a freak collision during a dogfight in which his squadron outnumbered the enemy six to two.

132 Advertising supplement to Immelmann, *Immelmann*, p. 13.

133 Laurence Driggs, "Aces among Aces," *National Geographic*, XXXIII (June 1918), p. 574.

134 In 1991, when announcing the publication of a new series entitled "Wings of War," Time-Life Books chose to begin its letter of solicitation with a confrontation between Eddie Rickenbacker and the "Richthofen crowd." "That was all in a day's work for Eddie Rickenbacker. And it was one of his many aerial confrontations with Baron Manfred von Richthofen's crack squadron that led him to title his memoirs, *Fighting the Flying Circus*." No other reference in the history of military aviation could be more relied upon to capture the imagination of the mass public and lead to a subscription. The Red Baron still sells.

8. Towards a High Culture

1 Quoted by Louise Faure-Favrier in *Les Chevaliers de l'air* (Paris: Renaissance de l'Air, 1923), p. 164.

2 Le Corbusier, *Aircraft* (cited intro), p. 6. I have slightly altered the translation to correspond to the account Le Corbusier gives of the same incident in *Sur les 4 routes* (Paris: Gallimard, 1941, fourth edn), pp. 109–10, a work he wrote in the autumn of 1939.

3 Le Corbusier, *Aircraft*, p. 7. I have slightly altered the translation. There is a longer version in *Sur les 4 routes*, which ends: "Great things must have been in the air to have upset to such a point a quiet Sunday morning" (p. 12).

4 For a detailed account of these events, see *Le Matin*, 11–12 October 1909.

5 According to the correspondent of *La Revue aérienne*, 25 October 1909, p. 630.

6 Hellmuth Hirth, *Meine Flugerlebnisse* (Berlin: Duemmlers Verlagsbuchhandlung, 1915), 2nd edn, pp. 95–7.

7 Among those aviators who did believe that airplanes had a future as a means of transportation, the well-known French pilot Brindejonc des Moulinais was one of the most specific. Writing in 1914, he predicted that enormous multi-engined airplanes would be used to transport passengers across long distances. They would be like miniature steamships and would land in prearranged airports. Several pilots, teaming together, would take turns at the controls. They would be as unknown to their passengers as the engineer of a locomotive or the mechanic of a ship. Eventually, such planes would be able to fly non-stop from Paris to Russia. Passengers would have no fear of mechanical failure because each plane would be provided with several engines, which could be alternated while mechanics made the necessary repairs in mid-air: "thus we will possess the real airship with which people like [Albert] Robida amused us when we were children. We will experience directly the fantastic conceptions of this artist, of Jules Verne, and of Wells." (In Mortane, *L'Aéronautique* (cited ch. 3), pp. 198–9).

8 As late as August 1912, a respected German newspaper, the *Vossische Zeitung*, concluded that in view of the unreliability and danger of the flying machine, no responsible aeronautical specialist could affirm with any degree of assurance that airplanes would overcome their limitations and become a common mode of transportation, capable of supporting an "extended and large-scale industry." (Quoted by Peter Supf in *Das Buch der deutschen Fluggeschichte* (Berlin-Grunewald: Verlaganstalt Hermann Klemm, 1935), I, p. 388).

9 Marie Marvingt in *Colliers*, 30 September 1911, p. 15. "This new sport is comparable to no other. It is, in my opinion, one of the most intoxicating forms of sport, and will, I am sure, become one of the most popular. Many of us will perish before then, but that prospect will not dismay the braver spirits. In devoting themselves to the new cause, those who have the true aviator's soul will find in their struggle with the atmosphere a rich compensation for the risks they run. It is so delicious to fly like a bird!" In 1912 Matilde Moisant used the same language when she explained to an interviewer that, though retired from public exhibitions after a series of nearly fatal accidents, she was considering flying again for her own amusement. "I have the air intoxication . . . and only a flier knows what that means." (Elizabeth Hiatt Gregory, "Woman's Record in Aviation," *Good Housekeeping*, LV (September, 1912), no. 3, p. 319. I am indebted to Christine White for bringing this article to my attention.)

10 See Leonhard Adelt's introduction to his anthology of aviation fiction *Der Herr der Luft* (Munich & Leipzig: Georg Mueller, 1914), pp. vii–viii, in which he summons in unmistakably Nietzschean terms all those who love danger to take up flight: "my friends, do you love danger? . . . cast your light life in the air and learn how to fly!" See also Adelt's novel *Der Flieger* (Frankfurt: Ruetten & Leoning, 1913), especially pp. 178–82, in which a group of professional aviators discuss the feelings that motivate them and other pilots to risk their lives.

11 Indeed in his poem "Le Printemps de l'Aile" Rostand evoked the image of a Faust who would have preferred flight to the charms of Marguerite.

> Avant de soupirer: "Ma belle demoiselle",
> Faust avait rêvé d'être ou Latham ou Beaumont . . .
> Car l'amour n'est jamais que le regret d'une aile!

> Before sighing: "My beautiful young lady,"
> Faust had dreamed of being Latham or Beaumont . . .
> For love is never anything but the longing for wings!

In *Le Cantique de l'aile* (cited ch. 5), p. 25.

12 One of the most common themes of accounts by aviators in this period is their feeling of fusion with their machines. Henry C. McComas put it in the following way. "Instead of thinking of the plane as a person, think of the pilot as a machine! . . . He is a machine. The system of levers which runs from the ailerons does not stop until it reaches his shoulder socket. The cords which swing the rudder continue until they terminate in the pilot's thighs. Both machines suffer from cold, from the changes in the air densities, from prolonged flying and a number of other ills. They are not two machines, they are one. The success of the flight depends upon the combined action of the pair." (*The Aviator* (New York: Dutton, 1922), pp. 1–2).

13 William Randolf Hearst, who was taken up for his first flight by Jean Paulhan during the Dominguez Hills air meet of January 1910 in Los Angeles, described his sensations in the following way: "We left the commonplaces of this worn-out world behind us, beneath us, and lifted into a new life, a new era . . . The little people below, growing littler, too, every moment, seemed to belong to the past – to a period when man walked miserably upon the face of the earth or rolled uncomfortably in primitive automobiles over the rough surface. We, M. Paulhan and I, were of the new era; we were soaring gloriously through space; we were flying." (Quoted by D. D. Hatfield, *Dominguez Air Meet* (Inglewood: Northrop University Press, 1976), p. 129).

14 For the "wild joy" that comes from risking one's life in struggle with nature, see Adelt, *Der Flieger*, p. 230.

15 For the role of the wind in prewar aviation, see Grahame-White, *The Story of the Aeroplane* (cited ch. 2). The well-known Russian writer Aleksandr Ivanovich Kuprin was nearly killed during his first flight when a gusting tail wind blew the machine, piloted by the circus performer Ivan Mikhailovich Zaikin, out of control. He never flew again. See his gripping account of the incident in "Moi Polet," *Sobranie sochineniy* (Moscow & Leningrad: Gosudarstvennoe Isdatelstvo Khudozhestvennoy Literaturi, 1958), VI, pp. 624–7.

16 *Ibid.*, p. 101.

17 Francy Lacroix, *En plein ciel* (Paris: Plon, 1918), p. 63. Ralph Johnston, an American exhibition pilot, put the same point more prosaically. "When you get into the air, the easy motion, the sense

of freedom, the birdlike facility of flight – these qualities lead a man into a calmness that is almost hypnotic." (Quoted by Curtis Prendergast in *The First Aviators* (Alexandria, Virginia: Time-Life Books, 1981), p. 163). For a sensitive, and in many ways unique, discussion of the sensations and motivations of flight from the perspective of the postwar period, which applies also to the years before 1914, see Peter Supf, *Airman's World*, trans. Cyrus Brooks (London: Routledge, 1933), pp. 27–30.

18 The preceding paragraph and its imagery are inspired by Pierre-Jean Jouve's poem *Les Aéroplanes* (Paris: Eugène Figuière, 1911). See also, of course, Franz Kafka's reaction to the air meet at Brescia, discussed on pp. 111–114 above. Marcel Proust described his first sight of an airplane in flight in the following way: "suddenly my horse reared; it had heard some strange noise, it was all I could do to control it and not be thrown to the ground, then I looked up, my eyes brimming with tears, in the direction from which the sound seemed to come, and some fifty yards above me, against the sunlight, borne between two great glistening wings of steel, I saw the indistinct shape of what looked like a man. I was as moved as a Greek might have been upon seeing a demigod for the first time." Of course, the wings Proust saw were not made of steel. (Quoted by Pascal Ory, *The Legend of the Skies* (Paris: Hoëbeke, 1991), p. 27).

19 See Adelt, *Der Flieger*, p. 178–9. Professional aviators often felt like prisoners of the crowd's emotions. "We believed that we were free and kings of a realm that we had conquered, whereas our fate was actually subservient to the applause and envy of the crowd. For their intense pleasure and longing grabbed hold of us: we belonged to them and were the mirror of their vanity." (*Der Flieger*, p. 156).

20 Pierre-Jean Jouve's poem about exhibition flights he witnessed in June 1911 emphasizes the erotic sensations that he imagines the spectators feeling.

> Un drapeau se déroule dans le vent,
> Les talons mordent à la terre,
> Les ombrelles crues gonflent l'air
> Et dans l'étui poli des robes
> Les cuisses transpirantes jouent.

> A flag unfurls in the wind,
> Heels bite the ground,
> Raw umbrellas inflate the air
> And in the sleek sheath of dresses
> Sweaty thighs play.

Then he imagines the motivations of the aviators who are about to fly:

> Dans chaque homme il y a un faune
> Qui voudrait ouvrir au plein ciel
> Les membres de ces femmes gaies
> Réservés pour de larges lits;
> Et dans leur chair creuse descende
> La pente sans retour de la belle journée.

> In every man there is faun
> Who would like to open to the skies
> The members of these lively women
> Destined for large beds.
> And in their hollow flesh descend
> The slope without return of the beautiful day.

Later in the poem Jouve compares the feelings he experienced after witnessing these flights to those a woman feels after sex:

> Comme après l'ivresse du vin, je rentre en moi,
> Et moi qui porte mes bras et pousse mon corps,
> Dont la mémoire se renferme dans la joie,
> Comme le sexe d'une femme après l'amour.

> Just as after the intoxication of wine, I return to myself,
> And I who carry my arms and extend my body,
> Whose memory confines itself within its joy,
> Like the sex of a woman after making love.

Les Aéroplanes (Paris: Eugène Figuière, 1911), pp. 11, 38.

21 Note, for example, *La Revue aérienne*, which seized the occasion of the Count de Lambert's flight in October 1909 to make this point: "It is events of this type [such as the flights of Blériot and Lambert], which powerfully impress the mind of crowds and are capable of convincing the most incredulous or the timidest, and whose role it is to make people see in aviation something other than an amusement, namely, the beautiful triumph of human intelligence over the inexorable laws that govern the physical world in which it is a prisoner." (25 October 1909, p. 631).

22 How appropriate, therefore, for the organizers of the luncheon at the Savoy Hotel in honor of Blériot to have placed the French "conqueror of the Channel" next to Shackleton, the British "conqueror of the South Pole."

23 Alphonse Berget, *La Route de l'air* (cited ch. 5), p. 272.

24 Describing the emotions experienced by the people who saw the first plane fly above the city of Chicago, Mary M. Parker wrote: "Not a man but felt that this was the beginning of such a mighty era that no tongue could tell its impact, and those who gasped felt awestruck, as though they had torn aside the veil of the future and looked into the very Holy of Holies. . . . We bowed our heads before the mystery of it and then lifted our eyes with a new feeling in our souls that seemed to link us all, and hope sprang eternal for the great new future of the world." ("When the Biplane Flew as a Woman Saw It," *Advance*, LX (6 October 1910), p. 36. Quoted by Joseph Corn in *The Winged Gospel* (New York: Oxford University Press, 1983), p. 30).

25 Adelt, *Der Flieger*, p. 113.

26 "Isn't it wonderful to think that man, so insignificant in Nature, so feeble in comparison with the forces of the universe, even so weak in comparison to many of the living species, has been able, thanks to the sustained effort of his brain, to tame the elements, to conquer them, and to become their master? That domain of the air, which seemed prohibited to him, he has penetrated and soon he will reign over it as he reigns over the earth, as he reigns above and below the seas! Certainly the history of all his conquests is to be admired, but I think that undoubtedly the most moving is that which we have just described; it is that by which man has at last freed himself from the servitude of contact with terrestial soil; by the speed of his machines, he has broken the chains that the laws of balanced weight imposed upon him, and now, henceforth free of all shackles, he will be able to dash without hindrance along the 'Highway of the Air.'" Berget, *La Route de l'air*. pp. 290–291.

27 See, for example, the interpretation given in Germany of a cross-country flight in 1911. "For us, fliers have become the symbol of our *Volkskraft*." (Quoted by Peter Supf from an unnamed German newspaper in *Das Buch der deutschen Fluggeschichte*, I, p. 355).

28 In his preface to Garros, *Guide de l'aviateur* (cited ch. 3), pp. 10–11.

29 The ambivalence of attitudes toward technology in the late nineteenth century has been particularly well documented in the case of the United States. See John F. Kasson, *Civilizing the Machine: Technology and Republican Values in America 1776–1900* (New York: Grossman, 1976), especially pp. 139–80. In *Bodies and Machines* (New York & London: Routledge, 1992), Mark Seltzer argues that "nothing typifies the American sense of identity more than the love of nature (nature's nation) except perhaps its love of technology (made in America)" (p. 152).

30 Identifying himself with El Greco, who according to Maurice Barrès had been accused in a court of canon law of having wanted to distort the wings of angels in his paintings by making them too long, Rostand wrote:

> Je ne peins qu'avec des accents et des diphtongues.
> Mais puissé-je être un jour condamné pour avoir
> Aux hommes d'aujourd'hui fait les ailes plus longues!

> I only paint with accents and dipthongs.
> But could I be condemned one day for having
> Given the men of today longer wings!

These are the concluding lines of Rostand's poem "Le Printemps de l'aile," in *Le Cantique de l'aile*, p. 26.

31 See Thureau-Dangin's "Rapport sur les concours de l'année 1911" in *Recueil des discours de l'Académie Française* (Paris: 1917), I, p. 550,

quoted by Giovanni Lista in "Apollinaire et la conquête de l'air," in *La Revue des lettres modernes*, vol. 10 (1974), p. 120.

32 Guillaume Apollinaire may have entered a poem in the French Academy's competition. For the circumstances of the competition and Apollinaire's possible involvement in it, see Lista, "Apollinaire et la conquête de l'air," pp. 115–29.

33 All these images appear in Lucien Jeny's poem *L'Aviation* (Bourges: Sire, 1912).

34 E. A. Buti in his 1910 poem "L'elegia del volo mortale," reproduced in Mario Cobianchi, *Pionieri dell'aviazione in Italia* (Rome: Editoriale Aeronautico, 1943), p. 101.

35 Aleksandr Blok in his 1912 poem "The Aviator," in *Sobranie sochineniy*, (Moscow and Leningrad: Gosudarstvennoe Isdatel'stvo Khudozhestvenoiy Literatury; 1960) III, p. 34.

36 In this respect, pre-1914 flying machines do not seem to have fitted into the "gear-and-girder world" described by Cecilia Tichi in her study of the impact of industrial technology on early-twentieth-century American writers, *Shifting Gears* (Chapel Hill: North Carolina Press, 1987). But her central point – namely, that writers can embody the values and aesthetics of the machine age even if they never mention a machine or attempt to represent one – is clearly relevant to pre-1914 European culture and, by extension, applicable to the reaction of avant-garde painters to flight.

37 By "official culture," I mean the culture that was consecrated by academies, taught in schools, and performed in state theaters, concert halls, and opera houses. For a fuller discussion of this culture as it existed before 1914, see my introduction to *Lost Voices of World War I*, ed. Tim Cross (London: Bloomsbury, 1988), pp. 2–4.

38 Or as the French poet Lucien Jeny put it in 1912:

> Quels termes inconnus jusqu'ici, quel language
> Inventer pour décrire un spectacle inouï?

> What terms unknown up to now, what language
> Should one invent in order to describe this
> unprecedented spectacle?

L'Aviation, p. 5. For the relationship between poetic language and aviation vocabulary in France and Russia, see Ingold, *Literatur und Aviatik* (cited ch. 4), pp. 191–213.

39 For an analysis of the role flight has played in Western literature, see the essay by Walter Muschg, "Der fliegende Mensch in der Dichtung," *Neue Schweizer Rundschau*, VIII (1939–40), pp. 311–20, 384–92, 446–53. For the iconography of flight in Western art, see Clive Hart, *Images of Flight* (Berkeley: University of California Press, 1988).

40 Rostand, *Le Cantique de l'aile*, pp. 16–17.

41 For a vivid example of the mythological images that flight evoked in the mind of a British poet, see Wilfred Owen's 1916 letter to his mother in which he confesses his intention to become a pilot, quoted above on p. 290, note 2.

42 Karl Vollmoeller, "Lob der Zeit," in Ingold, *Literatur und Aviatik*, pp. 384–5.

43 Ingold, *Literatur und Aviatik*, pp. 385–6.

44 For motifs of flight in the poetry of Baudelaire, Malarmé, Rimbaud, and Nietzsche, see Ingold, *Literatur und Aviatik*, pp. 337–42. In his poem *Elévation*, Baudelaire formulated the theme that would run throughout the air poetry of the prewar avant-garde. Addressing his *esprit*, Baudelaire wrote:

> Envole-toi bien loin de ces miasmes morbides;
> Va te purifier dans l'air supérieur,
> Et bois, comme une pure et divine liqueur,
> Le feu clair qui remplit les espaces limpides.
> Derrière les ennuis et les vastes chagrins
> Qui chargent de leur poids l'existence brumeuse,
> Heureux celui qui peut d'une aile vigoureuse
> S'élancer vers les champs lumineux et sereins.

> Fly away, far away from these morbid swamps;
> Go purify yourself in the higher air,
> And drink like a pure and divine potion,
> The bright fire that fills the clear spaces.
> Behind the anxieties and the vast grief
> That extend with their weight our misty existence
> Happy is he who can with a vigorous wing
> Launch himself toward luminous and serene fields!

In Charles Baudelaire, *Oeuvres complètes* (Paris: Gallimard, 1975), p. 10.

45 Reproduced in Marinetti, *Teoria e invenzione futurista* (cited ch. 5), p. 46.

46 F. T. Marinetti, *Zang tumb tumb* (Milan: Edizioni Futuriste di "Poesia", 1914), pp. 75–6.

47 *Lacerba*, 1 April 1914, pp. 104–5.

48 Paolo Buzzi, "Inno alla poesia nuova" (1912), reproduced in Ingold, *Literatur und Aviatik*, p. 346.

49 Stefan Zweig, "Der Flieger," reproduced in Ingold, *Literatur und Aviatik*, p. 390.

50 Though Zweig would later write about that world with great nostalgia in his memoir, *The World of Yesterday* (New York: Viking, 1943).

51 Walter Hasenclever, "Erster Flug," reproduced in Ingold, *Literatur und Aviatik*, p. 383.

52 "Uletan" [They Fly Away] from *Rvkayushchiy Parnas* (St. Petersburg, 1914) quoted by Burlin in "Mud Huts and Airplanes: The Futurism of Vasily Kamensky" (cited ch. 5), p. 84.

53 "Ot ieroglifov do A" (From Hieroglyphics to A) in *Perviy Zhurnal Russkikh Futuristov* (1913), quoted by Burlin in "Mud Huts and Airplanes" p. 87. This poem was later republished in Kamensky, *Dokhlaya Luna* (Moscow, 1914, 2nd edn).

54 Blok, *Sobranie sochineniy*, III, p. 34.

55 *Ibid.*, III, pp. 305–6.

56 In his 1910 poem "Aeroplan" (Airplane), *ibid.*, III, p. 197. See also his letter to his mother on 24 April 1910 quoted *ibid.*, pp. 506–7. There is a detailed discussion of Blok's attitudes toward aviation in Ingold, *Literatur und Aviatik*, pp. 176–81.

57 "Ever more, human culture is being made of iron, ever more machine-like, ever more resembling a vast laboratory where revenge on the forces of nature is preparing: science grows in order to subjugate the earth; art grows, a winged dream, a mysterious airplane for escape from the earth; industry grows so that people can leave the earth behind them." (Aleksandr Blok quoted by Larissa A. Zhadova, *Malevich: Suprematism and Revolution in Russian Art 1910–1930* (London: Thames & Hudson, 1982), p. 11).

58 A good example is Valentin Mandelstamm's novella, *L'Aviateur* (Paris: Eugène Fasquelle, 1908; republished by Pierre Lafitte in 1911), which predicts the eventual replacement of the airplane by the helicopter.

59 Quoted from Rudolf Martin, *Die Weltkrieg in den Lüften* (1909), by Fritzsche in *A Nation of Fliers* (cited ch. 2), p. 40. I have not been able to locate a copy of this work by Martin in Germany or the United States. Wells imagined even more gruesome scenes in his 1914 novel *The World Set Free* (cited ch. 7). In Wells's vision, Paris was reduced by a German nuclear bombardment to "a crimson-purple glare and a deafening, all-embracing, continuing sound" (p. 88). All that remained of the French commander was "a piece of a man, the head and shoulders of a man that trailed down into a ragged darkness and a pool of shining black" (p. 92).

60 Paul Adam, *La Ville inconnue* (Paris: Flammarion, 1911), p. 160.

61 Following in the footsteps of Wells and Martin, Robert Knauss would later imagine a British air attack against Paris in July 1936. "For only a few minutes did the wings of Death hover over the great city. Wraithlike the apocalyptic spectre flitted across the July sky, raining down fire and blood from his fearsome clouds. Writhing wormlike in their agony of fear, the millions of the great city saw nothing of this spectre, for the drone of his engines was drowned in the roar of mighty explosions." (Major Helders [pseudonym of Robert Knauss], *The War in the Air 1936*, trans. Claud W. Sykes (London: John Hamilton, n.d. (1932?)), p. 84). Knauss emphasized the break-down of public order in Paris as a result of the bombing of civilians. Those who survived turned their anger against their own government and the air force that had failed to protect them. Gangs of plundering thugs prowled through

the smoking ruins, and Communist agitators incited the population to revolution in the working-class quarters of the city: "the last vestiges of law and order vanished. Man fought against man, driven by the sheer urge of self-preservation" (p. 171).

62 Adelt, *Der Flieger*, p. 187.

63 *Ibid.*, p. 189.

64 See Leonid Andreyev's 1913 story "Polet" ("The Flight"), originally titled "Nadsmertnoe" ("Above Death"), which reconstructs the thoughts of a famous aviator, Yuri Mikhailovich Pushkarev, during a fatal attempt to set a new altitude record. Like Adelt, Andreyev emphasizes the fusion between the aviator and his machine. "His hands had become as firm and almost as bodiless as the wood of his steering wheel, on which they lay and together with which they had been welded by means of an iron union into one direction-giving will. And if living blood circulated in the hot veins of his hands, so did it also in the wood and iron: on the ends of the wings were his nerves, they reached to the utmost points, and on the ends of his wings he felt the sweet freshness of the air and the flickering of the sun's rays." Unlike Adelt, however, who had experienced the fear of flight in pre-1914 planes, Andreyev portrays the pilot as serene and in total control of his machine. "And in this triumph of his desiring will was that severe and manly joy – the joy which viewed from without seems sad and which makes the face of the warrior and victor mysterious." As he ascends toward ever higher altitudes, Pushkarev shouts above the noise of his engine that he no longer desires to return to earth. "My soul is overflowing, it yearns for escape from its body, it yearns for heaven and the furthest flight – I ascend higher and endlessly." And when Pushkarev's plane plunges toward the earth and crashes, the aviator is nowhere to be found in the wreckage. He had decided not to return to earth. (Leonid Andreyev, *Povesti i Rasskazy v Dvukh Tomakh* (Moscow: Isdatel'stvo 'Khudizhestvennaya Literatura', 1971), II, pp. 230, 232–3.)

65 As the success of Gunther Pluschow's *Die Abenteuer des Fliegers von Tsingtau* (Berlin: Ullstein, 1916) was to show. Pluschow's book described the exploits of a navy aviator who flew reconnaissance missions during the siege of Tsingtau by the Japanese, escaped by air to China, and then made his way back to Germany after being captured in Gibraltar and interned in England. My edition, published in 1934, indicates a combined printing of 653,000 copies.

66 By 1915 the vogue for aviation literature was so great that the American writer Sinclair Lewis complained that "In English and American fiction there are now nearly as many aeroplanes as rapiers or roses. The fictional aviators are society amateurs, wearers of evening clothes, frequenters of The Club, journalists and civil engineers, and lordlings and international agents and gentlemen detectives, who drawl, 'Oh, yes, I fly a bit – new sensation y'know – tired of polo'; and immediately thereafter use the aeroplane to raid arsenals, rescue a maiden from robbers or a large ruby from its lawful but heathenish possessors, or prevent a Zeppelin from raiding the coast. But they never by any chance fly these machines before gum-chewing thousands for hire." See *The Trail of the Hawk* (New York: Harcourt, Brace, 1915), p. 169. Lewis knew what he was talking about. He had tried his hand at aviation adventure fiction on two occasions and had even written an airminded musical comedy in 1911. In 1915 he published a heavily autobiographical aviation novel, *The Trail of the Hawk*, whose protagonist he later came to see as an anticipation of the young Charles Lindbergh. The novel was not a popular success. See Mark Schorer, *Sinclair Lewis* (New York: McGraw-Hill, 1961), pp. 201–3, 221–5.

67 Take, for example, the French poet Saint-Pol-Roux, who was flown over the countryside near Brest in 1914 and marvelled at the extraordinary panorama he saw, one in which his flying machine the *Victoire* was the summit of a cone. "All these townships dispersed in the distance and divided into innumerable squares, moors, grain, vegetables, squares, crossroads – from above how they appear to be united, shreds of a single standard. Inequality, you disappear. Neither rich nor poor, to be sure. Those fields, those woods, those river banks, those sheds, those mansions belong equally to everyone, isn't it true? Several bodies, but a single soul, one would wager. Better yet, a single family. Ah! how one must

adore one another in those fields and those towns in which I discern neither their manure nor their mud and hear neither the insults nor the blows, for ugliness does not reach as far as the heights: of the earth and its creatures, one perceives only their beauty." ("Sur les ailes de la 'Victoire'," *Vie des Lettres*, January 1914, p. 537). Jean Conneau expressed similar sentiments in *My Three Big Flights* (cited ch. 5). "As he [the aviator] sails further away from our planet, the latter assumes a flat appearance. The turmoil of the earth ceases to reach his ears and life down below seems extinct. All at once, afraid of his loneliness, he levels out, stops his ascent, and hovers over hills and plains, unable to distinguish either roads, rivers, or fences. Woods, marshes, and lakes are all alike to him, the soil is discernible only as an undulating and deserted expanse. Entirely free, the airman meets with no obstacle along his track, and he can ascend, descend, perform as many evolutions as he pleases. Has he not won true freedom by mastering space as he mastered the waves?" (pp. 143–4).

68 Gino Severini, *Tutta la vita di un pittore* (Cernusco sul Naviglio: Garzanti, 1946), I, pp. 74–6.

69 For Bracque's and Picasso's enthusiasm for aviation, see Pierre Cabanne, *Pablo Picasso* (New York: William Morrow, 1977), p. 142, and Christine Poggi, *In Defiance of Painting: Cubism, Futurism, and the Invention of Collage* (New Haven & London: Yale University Press, 1992), p. 258, n. 3. Cabanne claims that Braque and Picasso applied to their Cubist works what they had learned about aerodynamics. In a book on Picasso, written in 1914, the Russian critic Ivan Aksenov suggested that the Spanish painter may have been influenced by aerial photographs "which introduce the most unexpected combinations of surface with axes, and which created unprecedented visual sensations." (Quoted by Margaret Betz, "From Cezanne to Picasso to Suprematism: the Russian Criticism," *Artforum*, April 1978, p. 37). Robert Hughes also perceives a connection between aerial views and the flatness of modernist painting in *The Shock of the New* (New York: Alfred A. Knopf, 1991 edn), p. 14.

70 Delaunay explored aerial views of Paris in some of his most successful paintings of the 1909–11 period, such as *La Flèche de Notre Dame*, *Tour Eiffel*, *Champ de Mars*, *La Ville No. 2*, and *La Ville de Paris*. Beginning with the *Fenêtres* series, however, he shifted his point of view from the sky to the ground. One can only imagine what the scene of *L'Hommage à Bleriot* would have looked like seen from a pilot's perspective.

71 Malevich was critical of the Italian Futurists for having portrayed machines in their paintings on the grounds that the true painting of the future would be non-objective: "in pursuing the forms of aeroplanes or automobiles, we shall always be anticipating new cast-off forms of technical life". (Malevich, *Essays on Art 1915–1928* (cited ch. 6), I, p. 28). Paul Klee agreed. The purpose of art, he wrote, was not to reproduce what was visible, but to make visible what most people did not see. (Klee, *Théorie de l'art moderne* (Paris: Gonthier, 1964), p. 34). For a stimulating, if unnecessarily obscure, discussion of the relationship between avant-garde painting and technology, see Marc Le Bot, *Peinture et machinisme* (Paris: Klincksieck, 1973), especially pp. 183–201. Le Bot argues that the term "abstraction" fails to capture the novelty of the works of art produced by the European avant-garde during the years between 1912 and 1914. It would be better, he suggests, to call these paintings "formalist" because the artistic techniques deployed in them emphasize the logic of their composition rather than the nature and aesthetic qualities of the optical phenomena which originally inspired them (p. 198).

72 For some stimulating suggestions about the impact of the new technologies, including aviation, on conceptions of space and time, see Stephen Kern, *The Culture of Time and Space 1880–1918* (Cambridge, Mass.: Harvard University Press, 1983). I have expressed my reservations about Kern's book and its method in the *Journal of Social History*, XVIII, no. 4 (1985), pp. 635–41.

73 French production of picture postcards in 1905–6 may have reached six hundred million; Germany, Great Britain, and the United States each exceeded this figure. See Aline Ripert & Claude Frere, *La Carte postale: son histoire, sa fonction sociale* (Lyon: Presses Universitaires de Lyon, 1983), pp. 42–3. During the 1909

air meet at Rheims, thirty thousand postcards a day were sent through the post office at Bétheny; most of these bore the images of airplanes or aviators. See Laignier, *Le Livre d'or de la grande semaine d'aviation de la Champagne* (cited ch. 4), p. 115.

74 Lartigue was not alone among photographers to be taken by aviation as a theme. On 9 February 1911 he wrote in his diary: "Today at Issy-les-Moulineaux there was a cinematographer and several photographers (at least 8 or 10), for: Labouchère tried to win the 'Almond Prize' by flying 50 kilometers! I took 12 photos. The little 'Thomann' once more turned about! And what fun I had photographing him. (What an imbecile I am: I wasn't prepared for the one when he crashed!)" (*Mémoires sans mémoire* (Paris: Editions Robert Laffont), p. 94).

75 Lartigue, *Mémoires sans mémoire*, p. 150.

76 For some stimulating speculations about the relationship between aviation and cinema in the pre-1914 period, see the essay by Daniel Gethmann, "Daten und Fahrten," in the forthcoming volume on D'Annunzio and Fiume, edited by Hans Ulrich Gumbrecht. I wish to thank Professor Gumbrecht for his generosity in providing me with copies of these unpublished papers, several of which are relevant to my theme.

77 Lartigue, *Mémoires sans mémoire*, p. 103.

78 Giuliana Bruno, *Streetwalking on a Ruined Map. Cultural Theory and the City Films of Elvira Notari* (Princeton: Princeton University Press, 1993), p. 199.

79 For a survey of the aviation film, see Stephen Pendo, *Aviation in the Cinema* (Metuchen & London: The Scarecrow Press, 1985).

80 See Berget, *La Route de l'air*, p. 320; and Andrée & Robert Ferber, *Les Débuts véritables de l'aviation française* (cited ch. 1). After seeing Wilbur Wright in August 1908 at Auvours, S. Drewiecki exclaimed: "My word . . . I can already see the moment in the near future when every town will possess a port for flying machines. These ports will be squares erected in the form of cones and surrounded by hangars." (Quoted by Peyrey in *Les Premiers Hommes-Oiseaux* (cited ch. 1), p. 46).

81 On 7 January 1911 Lartigue described the airfield outside Paris where Garros and other famous aviators learned how to fly. Issy-les-Moulineaux, he wrote, was a field formerly used by the army for maneuvers. It resembled a piece of churned-up ground, "immense and deserted . . . On one side, a few small houses; on the other, the fortifications with trees and the railway track of the little commuter train by which I arrive." (*Mémoires sans mémoire*, p. 86. See also Petit, *La Vie quotidienne dans l'aviation* (cited ch. 3), pp. 86–90).

82 In mid 1913 there were forty women of eight nationalities who had qualified for the pilot's certificate (*Flying*, July 1913, p. 23). Many more, of course, were flying without a license. For the achievements of women aviators before 1914, see Valerie Moolman, *Women Aloft* (Alexandria, Virginia: Time-Life Books, 1981), pp. 7–29; for women aviators in the Russian Empire, see Christine A. White, "Gossamer Wings: Women in Early Russian Aviation, 1910–1920," an unpublished paper.

83 Moolman, *Women Aloft*, p. 9.

84 According to Gregory, "Woman's Record in Aviation," *Good Housekeeping*, LV (September, 1912), n. 3, p. 316.

85 As was the case with Claude Grahame-White. See Moolman, *Women Aloft*, p. 9. Matilde Moissant's instructor, André Houpert, later convinced her to retire. "After he had watched this daring little woman cheat death by a shave time and again he swung back to his original opinion that woman's place was not in the air. He thought she was better suited to almost any other occupation." According to Gregory, "Woman's Record in Aviation," p. 317.

86 Take, for example, this exchange which occurs in Adelt's novel *Der Flieger*. After the protagonist suffers a serious accident while competing in a flying meet, his wife Maria confesses how difficult it is for a woman to share her husband, the source of her happiness and her goal in life, with danger – danger that may rob her of everything she holds dearest. To which the flier patiently explains that it is not with danger that she shares him but with an idea that lives in all of us, the desire to conquer the air.

"Darling," Maria replies, "does a woman want ideas? She wants the man."

"Sure enough," her husband agrees, "our life gravitates outwards – in the case of a man toward his profession, in the case of a woman toward her child."

"You're right," Maria replies, "our being is not as narrow as our selfishness would lead us to believe. During these difficult hours I've had to think a lot, and I've understood how little all the danger means when compared to the need to fulfill one's mission in life. Even childbirth brings danger and pain – however, what woman flees maternity because of this!" (pp. 195–6).

In other words, the only way a woman could grasp the idealistic dedication of an aviator to flight was through the down-to-earth analogy of childbirth.

87 André Beaumont [Jean Conneau], *Mes Trois Grandes Courses* (cited ch. 5), pp. 135–6. The English translator of Conneau's book emphasized still further the essentially *masculine* nature of the qualities required of an aviator. He wrote: "it is evident that aviation is for *grown men* . . . Such qualities are not often to be found in women, and it is a pity for the few bold 'aviatresses' who are regular visitors to the aerodromes bring with them a charm and brightness not to be despised; and we men are always ready to applaud their *womanly* bravery, for though we may be man-birds we remain nonetheless men." (*My Three Big Flights* (cited ch. 5), p. 136). My italics.

88 Not surprisingly, one of the few famous aviators of the prewar period who spoke with respect of women pilots was Roland Garros. See *Mémoires* (cited ch. 7), pp. 19, 164.

89 More, it seems, in Russia than in any other country, according to White in "Gossamer Wings: Women in Early Russian Aviation, 1910–1920," pp. 9–10.

90 W. E. Johns alone wrote almost a hundred novels about his fictional flying ace James Bigglesworth and his chums Algy, Bertie, and Ginger. For other examples of this genre, which seems to have flourished above all in Britain and the United States, see Laurence Driggs, *Arnold Adair with the English Aces* (London: John Hamilton, n.d.) and *Arnold Adair with the French Aces* (London: John Hamilton, n.d.); and Covington Clark, *Aces Up* (Chicago & New York: Reilly & Lee, 1929).

91 In 1969, in a letter written to Russell Fridley, director of the Minnesota Historical Society, Lindbergh remembered reading on his family's farm in Little Falls, Minnesota, by the light of a kerosene lamp. "The story I remember best, although I do not now recall any of the details, related to one 'Tam o' the Scoots,' a magazine serial about a mythical World War I fighter pilot who soon, of course, became an ace. I think this story had considerable effect on my decision to enlist in the army when I was old enough and to become a fighter pilot myself." (Charles A. Lindbergh, *Boyhood on the Upper Mississippi* (St. Paul: Minnesota Historical Society, 1972), pp. 39–40).

Wallace never uses the term "ace," but there are several passages in the stories (first published in *Everybody's Magazine* between November 1917 and June 1919, later published as a book in 1919) that might have caught the young Lindbergh's eye aside from the crude evocations of aerial combat. For example, Wallace writes: "It must never be forgotten that Tam [the protagonist] was a born mechanician [sic]. To him the machine had a body, a soul, a voice, and a temperament. Noises which engines made had a peculiar significance to Tam. He not only could tell you how they were behaving, but how they would be likely to behave after two hours' running. He knew all the symptoms of their mysterious diseases and he was versed in their dietary. He 'fed' his own engines, explored his own tanks, greased and cleaned with his own hands every delicate part of the frail machinery. There was neither strut nor stay, bolt nor screw, that he did not know or had not studied, tested or replaced. He cleaned his own gun and examined, leather duster in hand, every round of ammunition he took up. He left little to chance and never went out to attack but with a 'plan, an altairnitive [sic] plan an' – an open mind.'" (Edgar Wallace, *Tam o' the Scoots* (New York & Chicago: A. L. Burt, 1919), p. 67).

92 Beyond Lindbergh, of course, the prototype for this figure was Wilbur Wright himself.

93 For an assessment of the effects of bombing attacks during the First

World War, see Lee Kennett, *The First Air War 1914–1918* (New York: The Free Press, 1991), pp. 41–62, 220–1.

94 Giulio Douhet, *Il dominio dell'aria* (Rome: Stabilimento Poligrafo per l'Amministrazione della Guerra, 1921), p. 59).

95 Marcel Proust, *A la recherche du temps perdu* (Paris: Gallimard, 1954), III, pp. 800, 758–9.

96 *Ibid.*, III, pp. 802–3.

97 In a letter to Ottoline Morrell, dated 9 September 1915, from D. H. Lawrence, *Letters*, (Cambridge: Cambridge University Press, 1981), II (ed. G. J. Zytaruk & J. T. Boulton), pp. 389–90.

98 For Messter's invention and the development of aerial photography during the First World War, see Oskar Messter, *Mein Weg mit dem Film* (Berlin-Schöneberg: Max Hesses Verlag, 1936), pp. 83–87, and Bernhard Siegert, "L'Ombra della macchina alata. Gabriele d'Annunzios Projekt eines Mare Nostrum im Licht der Luftkriegsgeschichte 1909–1940," in the forthcoming volume of essays on D'Annunzio and the Fiume expedition, edited by Hans Ulrich Gumbrecht.

99 Manfred von Richthofen, *Der rote Kampfflieger* (cited ch. 7), p. 181.

100 For a detailed and reliable survey of the first airlines, see R. E. G. Davies, *A History of the World's Airlines* (London: Oxford University Press, 1964), pp. 3–90.

101 For the literary reponse to Latécoère's airline, see my essay "Par la voie des airs: l'entrée de l'aviation dans le monde des lettres françaises 1909–1939)," *Le Mouvement Social*, no. 145 (December 1988), pp. 50–60. For Latécoère, see Emmanuel Chadeau's biography based largely on unpublished archival sources, *Latécoère* (Paris: Olivier Orban, 1990).

102 Republished by Guido Mattioli in *Mussolini aviatore* (Rome: L'Aviazione, 1938, third edn), pp. 20–1.

103 *Ibid.*, p. 23.

104 *L'Ala d'Italia*, January–February 1923, p. 4.

105 *L'Ala d'Italia*, January–February 1923, p. 4. This article originally appeared in *Il Popolo d'Italia* in July 1918.

106 Indeed, Mussolini's son Bruno died at the controls of an airplane in August 1941. See Mussolini's memoir *Parlo con Bruno* (Milan: Ulrico Hoepli, 1942).

Photographic Acknowledgements

Heinrich Adams, *Der Flug* (1909), courtesy of the Smithsonian Institution: 30, 59, 337. Heinrich Adams, *Unser Flieger von Wilbur und Orville Wright* (1909): 44, 45. Leonhard Adelt, *Der Herr der Luft* (1914): 339. Albright-Knox Art Gallery, Buffalo, New York. A. Conger Goodyear Fund, 1964: 247. Archives Nakov, Paris: 193, 194, 212. Association des Amis de Jacques-Henri Lartigue: 33, 332. Art Institute of Chicago. Joseph Winterbotham Collection, 1959. Photograph © 1992 The Art Institute of Chicago. All Rights Reserved: 237. Author's collection: 16, 312. Bibliotèque Forney, Paris: 306. Bibliothèque Nationale: 228, 229. Bibliothèque des arts décoratifs: 329, 335. Henry Bordeaux, *Vie héroïque de Guynemer* (n.d.): 299. Jos Bosman, *Le Corbusier und die Schweiz*, (1987): 307. British Library: 203, 205, 204. Bundesarchiv: 292. *Carrà. Mostra antologica* (1987): 249. Pietro Caporilli, *Baracca. Memorie de guerra aerea* (1934): 296. *Collier's*: 26. Mario Cobianchi, *I pioneri dell'aviazione italiana* (1943): 142, 143. Gabriele D'Annunzio, *Forse che sì forse che no* (1910): 145, 146. Charles Dollfus and Henri Bouché, *Histoire de l'aéronautique* (1932): 10, 70, 164, 165, 259, 286, 294, 303. Emile Driant, *L'Aviateur du Pacifique* (1909): 101, 102, 103, 104, 105. Emile Driant, *Au-dessus du continent noir* (1911): 106, 107, 108, 109, 110, 111. Laurence Driggs, *Arnold Adair with the English Aces* (d.d.): 302. E.C.P. des Armées, Fort d'Ivry, France: 284, 285, 290. *Flight*: 163. *Flight* (1953): 152. Charles Fontaine, *Comment Blériot a traversé la Manche* (1909): 71, 72, 76, 79, 81, 82. Antonio Foschini, *Baracca* (1939): 295, 300. *Futuristy. Perviy Zhurnal Russkikh Futuristov* (1914): 184. Hamilton Fyfe, *Northcliffe* (1930): 48. Galleria d'Arte Moderna, Milano: 348. *Gazeta-Kopeika*: 176. Charles H. Gibbs-Smith, *The Rebirth of European Aviation* (1974): 27, 129. Savvaty Gints, *Vasily Kamensky* (1984): 178, 181, 188. Hamburger Kunsthalle: 241. René Hervouin, *Guynemer. Héros légendaire* (1944): 283. Alistar Horne, *The Price of Glory. Verdun 1916* (1963): 114. Fred Howard, *Wilbur and Orville* (1987): 12, 17. Hulton Deutsch Library: 87, 154, 159. *Icare*: 291, 298. *The Illustrated London News*: 25. *L'Illustration*: 1, 36, 55, 60, 61, 65, 67, 68, 73, 74, 75, 77, 78, 83, 85, 84, 88, 89, 100, 115, 119, 120, 123, 124, 128, 133, 147, 150, 156, 158, 162, 166, 190, 252, 256, 287, 305, 308, 320, 331. *L'Illustrazione Italiana*: 346, 347. *Imagerie d'Epinal*: 260. Franz Immelmann, *Immelmann. 'The Eagle of Lille'* (1935): 268, 270. Marcel Jeanjean, *Sous les cocardes* (1919): 293, 301. Vasily Kamensky, *Put' entusiasta* (1931): 213. Vasily Kamensky, *Tango s korovami* (1914): 187. Fred C. Kelly, *Miracle at Kitty Hawk* (1951): 28. *Lacerba*, courtesy of the Getty Center, Resource Collections: 317, 318, 319, 333. Howard Leigh, *Planes of the Great War* (n.d.): 264, 272, 280. Library of Congress: 8, 15, 29, 251. Giovanni Lista, *Marinetti et le futurisme* (1977): 168, 174. *Livre d'or de la conquête de l'air* (1909): 2, 9, 22, 23, 39, 40, 49, 51, 52, 54, 90, 121, 127, 130, 131, 135. Angelo Lodi, *Storia delle origini dell'aeronautica militare* (1976): 171, 172, 173. Kazimir Malevich, *The Non-Objective World* (1959): 223, 224, 225, 226. *Le Matin*: 11, 63, 309, 310, 325, 328.

F. T. Marinetti, *Mafarka le futuriste* (1910): 169, 170. Mattioli Collection, Milan. Photograph © DACS 1994: 250. Oskar Messter, *Mein Weg mit dem Film* (1936): 343, 344. Marvin W. McFarland, *The Papers of Wilbur and Orville Wright* (1953): 21. Minneapolis Institute of Arts: 326. *Les Mots*: 261. Musée de l'affiche, Paris: 315. Musée de l'Air et de l'Espace, Le Bourget: 80, 122, 132, 136, 137, 148, 157, 160, 161, 254, 255, 257, 313, 338, 345. Musee d'Art Moderne de la Ville de Paris: 245. Musée des Deux Guerres Mondiales, Paris: 282, 288, 297. Musée National d'Art Moderne, Centre Georges Pompidou, Paris: 230, 239, 240. Musée Nationaux, Paris: 231. Museum of Modern Art, New York: 219, 220, 246. National Air and Space Museum, Smithsonian Institution: 3, 13, 14, 18, 19, 20, 38, 42, 43, 46, 47, 66, 69, 269. Öffentliche Kunstsammlung, Basel: 191, 248/Kupferstichkabinett: 216, 217, 218, 227. Private Collections: 214, 232, 235, 100, 322, 324. By courtesy of Edmond Petit: 126, 258, 289. *Le Petit Journal*: 56. François Peyrey, *Les Oiseaux artificiels* (1909): 7, 24, 41. François Peyrey, *Les Premiers Hommes-Oiseaux* (1908): 32, 34, 35. *Ranee Utro*: 192. *La Revue aérienne*: 31, 37, 117, 118, 134, 139, 141. Manfred Freiherr von Richthofen, *Der rote Kampffliger* (1917): 275, 340. Kunigunde Freifrau von Richthofen, *Mein Kriegstagebuch* (1937): 276, 277, 278, 281. Albert Robida, *Le Vingtiéme Siecle* (1883): 50, 96, 97, 98. Russian State Archives of Literature and Art: 177, 179, 180, 182, 185, 186. Raymond Saladin, *Les Temps heroïques de l'aviation* (n.d.): 52. Sammlung Museum Ludwig, Cologne: 221. Science Museum, London: 326. *Simplicissimus*: 304. Solomon R. Guggenheim Foundation, New York. Photograph © The Solomon R. Guggenheim Foundation, New York: 200. St. Petersburg State Museum of Theatrical and Musical Arts: 206, 207, 208, 209, 210. State Russian Museum, Moscow: 196, 211, 215, 222. State Tretiakov Gallery, Moscow: 195. Stedelijk van Abbemuseum, Eindhoven: 244. Stedelijk Museum, Amsterdam: 197, 198, 199. Steegmuller, Francis, *Apollinaire* (1963): 242. By courtesy of Tonie and Valmai Holt: 341. Vaulx, Henry de la, *Le Triomphe de la navigation aérienne* (1911): 4, 5, 6, 62, 323. Henry de la Vaulx, *Les Vainqueurs de l'air* (1921): 58, 64, 48, 91, 149. *La Vie au grand air.* 253. Gustav Vriesen and Max Imdahl, *Robert Delaunay: Light and Color*, (n.d.): 233, 234, 243. Klaus Wagenbach, *Franz Kafka: Pictures of a Life* (1984): 140, 330. Graham Wallace, *Claude Grahame-White* (1960): 151. Graham Wallace, *Flying Witness* (1948): 153. H. G. Wells, *The War in the Air* (1908): 86, 92, 93, 94, 95, 99, 112, 113. Johannes Werner, *Boelcke* (1932): 262, 263, 265, 266, 267, 271, 273, 274. By courtesy of Christine White: 202, 336. Wiktor Woroszylski, *The Life of Mayakovsky* (1970): 183. Wright State University: 12. Peter Wykeham, *Santos-Dumont* (1962): 57. J. Xaudaró, *Les Péripéties de l'aviation* (1911): 116, 155, 167, 311. Yale Art Gallery, New Haven. Gift of Collection Societé Anonyme, October 11, 1941: 201.

Index